THE PETROV affair

POLITICS AND ESPIONAGE

PERGAMON TITLES OF RELATED INTEREST

THE PETROV affair

POLITICS AND ESPIONAGE

ROBERT MANNE

Pergamon
Sydney • Oxford • New York
Beijing • Frankfurt • São Paulo • Tokyo • Toronto

AUSTRALIA	Pergamon Press Australia, 19a Boundary Street, Rushcutters Bay, N.S.W. 2011, Australia
U.K.	Pergamon Books Limited, Headington Hill Hall, Oxford OX3 0BW, England
U.S.A.	Pergamon Books Inc., Maxwell House, Fairview Park, Elmsford, New York 10523, U.S.A.
PEOPLE'S REPUBLIC OF CHINA	Pergamon Press, Quianmen Hotel, Beijing, People's Republic of China
FEDERAL REPUBLIC OF GERMANY	Pergamon Press, Hammerweg 6, D-6242 Kronberg, Federal Republic of Germany
BRAZIL	Pergamon Editora, Rua Eça de Queiros, 346, CEP 04011, São Paulo, Brazil
JAPAN	Pergamon Press, 8th Floor, Matsuoka Central Building 1-7-1 Nishishinjuku, Shinjuku-ku, Tokyo 160, Japan
CANADA	Pergamon Press Canada, Suite 104, 150 Consumers Road, Willowdale, Ontario M2J IP9, Canada

First Published 1987

Copyright © 1987 Robert Manne

Cover design by Adrian Young

Typeset in Australia by Rochester Communications Group
Printed in Australia by Macarthur Press

National Library of Australia Cataloguing in
Publication Data

Manne, Robert.
   The Petrov affair.

   Includes index.
   ISBN 0 08 034424 0.
   ISBN 0 08 034425 9 (pbk.)

   1. Petrov, Vladimir Mikhailovich, 1907-   . 2. Petrov,
   Evdokia, 1914-   . 3. Espionage, Russian — Australia.
   4. Australia — Politics and government — 1945-1965.
   5. Australian Security Intelligence Organization.
   I. Title.

994.05

To Anne and Kate

CONTENTS

PART IV: RESOLUTION

ABBREVIATIONS

ACT	Australian Capital Territory
AJA	Australian Journalists Association
ALP	Australian Labor Party
ASIO	Australian Security Intelligence Organization
ASIS	Australian Security Intelligence Service
BMA	British Medical Association
CIA	(United States) Central Intelligence Agency
CIS	Commonwealth Investigation Service
CPA	Communist Party of Australia
'EM'	Soviet intelligence jargon for 'emigre' operations
FBI	(United States) Federal Bureau of Investigation
GRU	'Glavnoe Razvedyavatelnoe Upravlenie' — Chief Intelligence Directorate of the Armed Forces
KGB	'Komitet Gosudarstvennoi Bezopasnosti' — Committee of State Security
KI	'Komitet Informatsyi' — Committee of Information
MGB	'Ministerstvo Gosudarstvennoi Bezopasnosti' — Ministry of State Security
MI5	British Security Service — Domestic Branch
MI6	British Security Service — International Branch
MVD	'Ministerstvo Vnutrennik Del' — Ministry of Internal Affairs

NKGB	'Narodnyi Komissariat Gosudarstvennoi Bezopasnosti' — People's Commissariat of State Security
NKVD	'Narodnyi Komissariat Vnutrennik Del' — People's Commissariat of Internal Affairs
NSW	New South Wales
OGPU	'Obyedinennoe Gosudarstvennoe Politicheskoe Upravlenie' — United State Political Directorate
RAAF	Royal Australian Air Force
'SK'	Soviet intelligence jargon for 'Soviet Colony' operations
UNRRA	United Nations Relief and Rehabilitation Administration

PREFACE

There is, in the taxonomy of political life, a rare and peculiar form known as the Affair. Affairs emerge — usually quite unexpectedly -— when a nation's political realm comes to be dominated by bitter disputes over the meaning of a particular sequence of events. Affairs grow from those cases which seem to touch the most sensitive nerve-ends of a society — the fundamental issues of value and allegiance. They have a far deeper ideological resonance and a much longer life expectancy than what might be called mere cases. In modern history the classical example of the form occurred in late nineteenth century Europe, when the French nation tore itself apart over the fate of Captain Dreyfus. In Australia there has been only one genuine example — the Petrov Affair.

The story began with the defection in Sydney on April 3 1954 of Vladimir Petrov, a Colonel in the Soviet intelligence service, and its announcement in the Australian Parliament by the Prime Minister, Mr Menzies, ten days later. On April 20 it became for a moment a matter of world interest — and entered Australian folklore — with the highly dramatic defection at Darwin of Petrov's wife (also an intelligence officer) while she was being flown home under guard. It was transformed into a political Affair when the Leader of the Opposition in Australia, Dr Evatt, became convinced that the defections had been part of a conspiracy mounted against himself and the Labor Party he led by the Menzies Government and the Australian security service — ASIO.

From the broadest perspective the Petrov Affair might be seen as the last in a series of major Soviet spy dramas which shook the Western democracies during the period of the Cold War (1945-1954). From the strictly intelligence point of view it was most closely reminiscent of the Gouzenko defection which had occurred nine years earlier in Canada. As with Gouzenko, the Petrov defections were, as we shall see, of extreme value to Western counter-intelligence in its unending war against the Soviet espionage system. Their information was, like his, of vital significance to the West. Gouzenko, however, did not divide Canada. From the sociological point of view the Petrov

Affair was far more closely reminiscent of the Alger Hiss-Whittaker Chambers confrontation in the United States. It became for the left-liberal intelligentsia in Australia precisely what the Hiss-Chambers trial of strength had already become for the parallel social stratum in America — the symbolic case of anti-communist perfidy. From the political point of view, however, the Petrov Affair was *sui generis*. Of all the great espionage cases it alone was responsible for altering fundamentally the political alignment within a Western nation. As we shall see, it was the Petrov Affair which precipitated a split in the Australian Labor Party, which in turn kept it from government for the best part of a generation.

A number of useful memoirs concerning the Petrov Affair have been published — from the ASIO agent chiefly responsible for Petrov's defection; from the Petrovs themselves; from the Prime Minister, Mr Menzies; and from the director of ASIO counter-espionage, Michael Thwaites. However no even remotely satisfactory history of the Affair has yet been written. The best known account, *Nest of Traitors* by Nicholas Whitlam and John Stubbs, is little more than a spirited piece of partisan journalism. When in 1984 the Australian Government agreed to the public release of the vast official Petrov archive, which included the administrative records of the Royal Commission on Espionage and the hundreds of Petrov files held by ASIO, a genuine history of the Affair became possible for the first time. I have been rash enough to attempt in this book to write such a history.

Participants in a political Affair cannot hope to escape from the bitterness it breeds unscathed. Nor can its historians. To embark upon a history of the Petrov Affair is to step out voluntarily onto a minefield. The fact that this is still the case, thirty years after the events, is a reminder of the potency of the Petrov Affair in Australian political mythology and sufficient justification in itself for embarking upon such a hazardous journey.

No one could write a book such as this without incurring many debts. My first is to Sam Lipski who suggested I might help with the research for a television drama series on Petrov he had dreamt of. My second is to one of the writers of the eventual script of that series, Cliff Green, with whom I spent many profitable hours chewing over Petrov. It was during the research for the television series that I visited the Australian Archives in Canberra to peruse the newly opened Petrov files. So arresting was this new material that within hours of arriving at the Archives I became convinced that there was a book on the Affair waiting to be written. Happily, soon after, I was able to convince Jerry Mayer of Pergamon Press on this point. Our association since then has been for me a most pleasant and productive one.

Throughout the extended periods of research at the Archives I received the kind of expert and courteous assistance from the staff there to which visitors become accustomed. In particular I should like to thank most sincerely Marian Corrigan, Bette O'Brien, Gillian Redmond and Jimmy Stewart, all of whom helped me at different stages of the book. Staff at the Manuscript Room of the Australian National Library and at the Evatt collection at Flinders University were also generous with their assistance. I am much obliged to the office of the Prime Minister, Mr Hawke, for granting me access to the Caucus minutes of the Federal Parliamentary Labor Party, and to Peter Coleman for lending me his personal copy of the transcript of the proceedings of the Royal Commission on Espionage.

At various points in my research university colleagues have assisted me on points of detail. Thanks are due to Professors David Kemp and Tony Blackshield and to Drs Ferenc Feher and Michael Lawriwsky. As to the use I made of their advice they are entirely innocent. In early 1986, while working on the Evatt papers, I stayed at the home in Adelaide of the finest history teacher I have ever had, Dr Denis Grundy. I was reminded once again of how much I owe to him. In both 1985 and 1986 I received valuable financial assistance from the research fund of the School of Social Sciences at La Trobe University. I have also benefitted from the support of the Chairman of the Department of Politics, Talis Polis, and the splendid secretarial staff there. In particular I should like to express to Mary Zaccari my sincerest appreciation for the great care and diligence of her work on the manuscript.

In May 1985 Sir Charles Spry agreed to take a risk and speak to me in detail about the Petrov Affair. The several conversations which followed are among the most enjoyable of my life. Much of the drama and the humour of the Affair now came alive to me. Moreover the entire book, and in particular its Espionage section, would have been much thinner without them. For his generosity and his trust I am deeply indebted to Sir Charles.

Throughout the planning and writing of this book my wife, Anne, has taken upon herself the worst of its burdens and has shared in all of its occasional pleasures. Anne has been my truest friend and my shrewdest critic. What I owe to her is beyond words. It is to her and our daughter Kate that this book is dedicated in gratitude and love.

Cottlesbridge,
October 1986.

PART I
The Defection

I

AN NKVD COUPLE

On February 5 1951 a party of five, destined for the Soviet Embassy in Canberra, disembarked in Sydney from the liner *Orcades*. Amongst the group were Vladimir and Evdokia Petrov. An ASIO field officer noted Petrov as a round-faced, solidly built man of thirty-five or forty and (somewhat unkindly for she was an extremely attractive woman) his wife as a thirty-five year old of 'medium to stout build'. Although Petrov's official position was merely Embassy 'Referent' or clerk, Detective Longbottom of the New South Wales Special Branch, who had an informant on board the *Orcades*, let ASIO know that Petrov gave the impression of 'being the "boss" of the Soviet group'. The new arrivals were greeted on the wharf by the Soviet Embassy Second Secretary, Sadovnikov, and the 'Tass' correspondent, Pakhomov.[1] Unbeknown to ASIO at this time the group chatting on the Sydney dock that day included four full-time officers of the Soviet intelligence service, two of whom were to influence, not negligibly, the future course of Australian political history.

By the time they had arrived in Australia the Petrovs had in fact both spent almost two decades within the world of Soviet intelligence, having risen steadily if unspectacularly through its ranks and, perhaps more remarkably, having survived the purges which haemorraged all Soviet institutions, including State Security, in the late 1930s. By 1951 Petrov was a Lieutenant-Colonel and Petrova a Captain in the Soviet intelligence service. As both were of peasant origin their recruitment and advancement through the ranks represented significant but not uncharacteristic instances of post-1930 peasant upward social mobility under Stalin.[2]

The stories of the Petrovs' separate social journeys from their villages to intelligence desks in Moscow have been told in considerable detail in their post-defection book, ghosted by ASIO's director of counter-espionage Michael Thwaites. Petrov, who was born Anafasy Mikhailovich Shorokhov in a relatively prosperous Siberian village, began his working life as apprentice to the blacksmith. In 1923 at the age of sixteen he responded to the promptings of a visiting Bolshevik agitator by helping to establish a Komsomol cell

3

in his village. By 1927 Petrov had graduated to full Communist Party membership (at a time when Party members of peasant origin were, relatively speaking, thin on the ground) and had received through the Party's good offices an education of sorts at a college at Sverdlovsk. Party membership meant for him, above all else, the possibility of self-improvement through education and escape from the idiocy of rural life. His early Party work (on the eve of collectivisation) involved pressing government levies out of the sullen and resistant peasantry of his own region. Petrov later recalled how at the time he regarded this work as 'unpleasant but necessary', an attitude revealing how far the separation from his roots had already progressed. In 1929 Petrov, who now gave himself the revolutionary name of Proletarskiy, acted as youth organiser amongst factory workers at Nadezhdinsk (Serov) in northern Siberia and in the early 1930s served for some three years in the Red Navy Baltic fleet where he was trained in cyphers. By 1933 Petrov was prepared, both technically and psychologically, for his recruitment into the State Security service at Moscow.[3]

While Petrov's passage from his village to a post in the OGPU was more protracted than that of his future wife, Evdokia Kartseva, her origins were even harsher than his. During the terrible year of famine, 1919, when Evdokia was five years old, her family deserted their native village (Lipky in Ryazan province, near Moscow) in search of food.

> Vividly I recall the long train journey, our arrival at the city of Semipalatinsk, foraging through the countryside, sleeping under wagons in the open fields, Mother begging food from house to house, the prosperous looking homestead where they set their dogs on us.[4]

Only two of her mother's seven children born before 1930 survived beyond infancy. Evdokia was a survivor.

In 1924 the Kartsev family managed to get to Moscow where her father found a job as a tram driver and the family a part of a room where ten slept. Evdokia used her natural quick-wittedness and good looks, and her father's humble links with the OGPU (where he came to work as a driver in the Transport Section) to make her way into State Security. At first, as a young girl, she became a member of an elite 'Pioneers' group attached to the OGPU and in fact at the age of twelve represented it at the funeral of the legendary founder of the Soviet secret police, Felix Dzerzhinsky. At the age of nineteen, after two years of English studies at the Foreign Language Technical College in Moscow, Kartseva was encouraged by an admirer to join the OGPU. At the time the decision seemed to her 'the most normal and obvious thing in the world to do'.[5]

Entry into the OGPU, even at its most junior level, represented for both Vladimir Proletarskiy and Evdokia Kartseva a passage into a world of once undreamt of privilege. Within the OGPU salaries were high; access was opened to a reasonable level of accommodation (the possibility even of a room of one's own); food at the OGPU canteen was abundant by Moscow, let alone Soviet, standards. Moreover the work was of the highest prestige. By 1933, the year of their entry to its service, the OGPU had drawn to itself much of the most important work of the Soviet state. OGPU guarded Soviet borders. It had its own troop formations to deal with politically sensitive military campaigns at home and abroad. It administered the ever-expanding labour camp system — the 'Gulag Archipelago'. It was responsible for rooting out 'counter-revolutionary' plots and punishing the plotters — that is to say for terror and surveillance. Finally it controlled non-military aspects of foreign intelligence work — espionage and counter-espionage.

In order to fulfil its many and varied tasks the OGPU or NKVD (as it was renamed in 1934) had inevitably acquired over time an extremely complex administrative structure with specialist directorates, themselves divided into departments and sections. Within this formidable bureaucracy both Vladimir Proletarskiy and Evdokia Kartseva were placed in Moscow in the 'Spets-Otdel', the Special Cypher department which serviced the entire structure.

After a brief time in a military unit of the 'Spets-Otdel' Evdokia Kartseva moved in 1934 into its Fourth section, the section concerned with the technical work of cryptanalysis or code-breaking. Under NKVD direction she undertook courses of study in both cryptanalysis and the Japanese language. Throughout the period of 1934-1942, when she remained in the Fourth section of the 'Spets-Otdel' and was promoted through the ranks from junior-sergeant to lieutenant, her work concerned the Soviet attempt to break Japanese codes, especially those of the wireless and cable traffic transmitted to Tokyo by the Japanese diplomatic establishment in Moscow. From the point of view of Western counter-intelligence, Evdokia's cryptanalytic background gave her defection in 1954 a special significance.[6]

Vladimir Proletarskiy's work in the 'Spets-Otdel' was far less specialised than that of his future wife and far more representative of the range (and horror) of NKVD responsibilities in the 1930s and early 1940s. From 1933 to 1937 he worked in the Fifth (foreign) section, enciphering and deciphering the cables passing between Moscow Centre and the NKVD's 'legal' agents abroad, that is to say, those agents who operated under Soviet diplomatic or quasi-diplomatic cover. Between September 1937 and February 1938 he served for a time in the field as cypher clerk to the detachment of NKVD troops responsible for quelling, in characteristically brutal fashion, an anti-Soviet rebellion in the Urumchi district of Sinkiang, a dependent territory in north-western China. At the height of the 'Yezhovshchina' — the 'great terror' — Proletarskiy returned to Moscow and to the Sixth section of the 'Spets-Otdel', the section directing the cypher traffic between Moscow and NKVD stations inside the Soviet Union, a considerable part of which involved dealing with messages from Moscow to provincial outposts regarding the allotted quotas for arrests and executions, and from the provincial outposts to Moscow with the lists of the dead. While in this post he was an invited and convinced witness to the third of the Moscow show trials of former Bolshevik 'counter-revolutionary' traitors. By the early 1940s, by which time he had been promoted to the rank of NKVD Major, Proletarskiy had become chief of the 'Spets-Otdel' section responsible for maintaining links between Moscow and the swollen concentration camp system, the Gulag. By now he had risen to the position of a middle ranking communications functionary in the NKVD world of terror, slave labour and mass murder.[7] What numbness of spirit unspeakable work of this kind had visited upon this rootless young cadre, in the atmosphere of total fear which extended even to the Security organs, can only be guessed at.

The 'Yezhovshchina', through which Proletarskiy's career advanced, almost ended Evdokia Kartseva's life inside the NKVD. In 1936 she had entered a de facto married relationship with a senior member of the cryptanalytic section of the 'Spets-Otdel', Roman Krivosh. The following year, shortly after a daughter was born to them, Krivosh — whose noble and Balkan origins made him an all too obvious target of secret police suspicions — was arrested. Like his father before him (who had served in both Czarist and Soviet cryptanalysis) Krivosh was despatched to labour camp. Kartseva's NKVD Komsomol branch now moved against her. She pleaded ignorance concerning the admittedly anti-Soviet activities of her husband. Only through the intervention of someone in the higher reaches of the NKVD was she saved.[8] The all-NKVD Komsomol committee overturned the verdict of her branch and satisfied itself with a reprimand to her. Although she fought like a tiger ('shaking with rage and fear') she was also at this time compelled by the intrigues of a fellow NKVD cadre to swap Krivosh's rather splendid room for one scarcely one third its size. Of Krivosh she retained only his furniture and their daughter. The daughter of this marriage died in 1940.[9]

Shortly before this death, which shook her deeply, Kartseva married her 'Spets-Otdel' colleague, Vladimir Proletarskiy, who in 1938 had extracted himself from an inconsequential sailor's marriage. His lack of concern for the serious blemish on her record and above all his eminent NKVD respectability weighed most heavily with her.

> He was of peasant stock; he was on the Committee of the Communist Party unit in our Department, and led a study circle on the history of the Communist Party. Here, if anywhere, was surely a man with his foot set firmly on the stairway of solid progress and safe orthodoxy within the framework of the Soviet Service.

It was, *par excellence*, a marriage of convenience, NKVD style.[10]

At the height of the German invasion of the Soviet Union and after service on the skeletal NKVD cypher staff of besieged Moscow, Proletarskiy was rewarded with his first overseas posting (to neutral Sweden) and a new name — Petrov. An NKVD superior, Dekanozov (later to perish in the Beria purge) thought the revolutionary name unsuited to 'diplomatic' service. With the Baltic closed to most Allied shipping Petrov and his wife travelled from

Moscow to Stockholm via the Cape of Good Hope, and even then almost lost their lives when the ship carrying them was torpedoed off the Bay of Mozambique.[11]

The Stockholm posting gave new direction to the intelligence careers of both the Petrovs. Here Petrov combined control of cyphers for State Security with what was known in Soviet intelligence jargon as 'SK' (Soviet Colony) work, the surveillance of Soviet citizens abroad. In Sweden this work included surveillance of both Embassy personnel and a group of Soviet sailors held prisoner there. He was also involved in a special investigation into the loyalty of the Soviet Ambassador to Sweden — the grand old lady of the October Revolution — Alexandra Kollontai.[12] For her part Evdokia Petrova, freed from her specialist cryptanalytic work, blossomed in Stockholm into an all-purpose intelligence officer, working as State Security typist, accountant, cypher clerk and photographer, and even running two female Swedish agents in the field.[13]

When the couple returned to Moscow in October 1947 their career paths reflected the new directions taken in Stockholm. Both now took desks in the 'SK' section of the newly formed KI ('Komitet Informatsyi' or Committee of Information), Petrov in the section concerned with surveillance of Soviet sailors on the Lower Danube, Petrova in the section watching the Soviet work force in the Spitzbergen coal mines. As it turned out the KI represented an ill-fated attempt in the history of Soviet intelligence to combine the hitherto separated foreign political and military intelligence branches in a single bureau and to sever the traditional administrative union of the foreign and domestic branches of State Security. By 1948 this experiment had already begun to come apart. In that year military intelligence — the GRU — was restored by Marshall Bulganin to Army control, while the MGB (the Ministry of State Security) recaptured to itself the 'SK' and 'EM' fields it had in 1947 relinquished to the KI. (The 'EM' branch was concerned with operations amongst Russian émigrés and Soviet refugees.)

The transfer of 'SK' and 'EM' work from the KI to the MGB temporarily separated the intelligence careers of the Petrovs. Petrov now moved back with his 'SK' desk into the MGB in central Moscow, eventually moving his area of responsibility in the Maritime Section of the 'SK' department from the Lower Danube to the 'Anglo-American bloc'. Petrova remained within the KI, which was housed in old Comintern quarters in outer Moscow and transferred from 'SK' work to the Swedish desk at the KI. When in early 1951 the couple received their second foreign posting — to Australia — this division of their lines of work was for a time maintained. Petrov was assigned control of MGB responsibilities in Australia, that is to say control of both 'SK' and 'EM' work, the latter a task which had recently assumed great importance in Soviet eyes because of the large number of refugees Australia had received from areas of post-war Soviet control and in particular from the formerly independent Baltic States. Petrova's work in Australia continued under KI control. Her task was to give clerical, cypher and operational assistance to the KI establishment in Australia, headed at the time by Sadovnikov, the 'legal' Resident and ostensible Second Secretary at the Embassy, and assisted in Sydney by the 'Tass' representative, Pakhomov. It was these two who greeted the Petrov couple on the Sydney dock on February 5 1951.[14]

As it turned out, the Sadovnikov Residency came unstuck shortly after the Petrovs arrived in Australia. Petrova heard the full and utterly typical story of intrigue and muddle from the extremely well-informed cypher clerk at the Embassy, Prudnikov, who was one of seven Embassy staff members 'co-opted' at the time into 'SK' work, that is to say employed part-time to spy on his fellows. A young Embassy typist, who had also worked part-time for the KI, Griazanova, had fallen in love with Sadovnikov, a married man, and become pregnant to him. A case had been built against her (she had been observed outside the British Embassy), but a case had also been built against Sadovnikov who, on a visit to Sydney, had spent all night drinking at the home of an Australian resident. Such behaviour was strictly against the rules governing Soviet behaviour abroad. A coopted 'SK' worker, Galanin, had reported Sadovnikov to the Soviet Ambassador, Lifanov, who in turn reported him to Moscow. Moscow ordered Sadovnikov home. Once there he was — according to what Petrova was later to discover (she evidently retained a keen interest in the case) — charged with 'misconduct in Australia relating to Miss Griazanova, staying a night at the home of B. . . . and embezzling MVD funds'. Sadovnikov was reprimanded, demoted and, in line with his reduced rank, compelled to work as Australian desk officer for the KI.[15]

Sadovnikov's recall in April 1951, which also involved the return to Moscow of Griazanova and Sadovnikova, both of whom had given him clerical assistance in Canberra, necessitated the reorganisation of the reduced KI team in Australia. The 'Tass' man, Pakhomov, was made temporary 'legal' Resident, while Petrova, in the absence of any senior KI man in Canberra, was obliged to hold the fort there with cyphering, typing and bookkeeping. As she was also giving clerical assistance to the Ambassador and looking after the Embassy accounts, very little time remained for operational duties.

For some months after Sadovnikov's recall Petrov's intelligence responsibilities remained exclusively with the MGB, as controller of 'SK' and 'EM' activities. But soon after the KI experiment was finally abandoned, in December 1951, and the traditional supremacy of the MGB over all non-military foreign intelligence restored, Petrov was appointed as temporary head of Soviet intelligence operations in Australia with Pakhomov (before his recall to Moscow in July 1952) and Petrova working under his authority. Soon after his appointment as temporary Resident to Australia Petrov was promoted from Lieutenant-Colonel to full Colonel in the MGB. He retained this post and rank until his defection in April 1954.[16] Petrov's intelligence achievement in Australia will be considered in detail later in this book. In the succeeding chapters we are concerned solely with his road to defection.

2

DIABOLO

As cover for his intelligence duties by April 1951 Petrov had been promoted from Embassy 'Referent' to Third Secretary and given special responsibility for cultural (VOKS) and consular tasks, tasks which provided justification for the frequent travel to Sydney and Melbourne required of an intelligence officer. As VOKS representative he became a frequent visitor to the offices of the Australian-Soviet Friendship Societies in both cities and as Soviet Consul an habitué at the meeting places of pro-Soviet émigrés and sympathisers. Already by mid-1951 he was a regular visitor, usually in the company of Pakhomov, at the most important of these, the Russian Social Club in George Street, Sydney.[1] His relatively open work there amongst the disgruntled émigrés who, in line with the current Soviet repatriation drive, he encouraged to return to the Socialist Fatherland, soon came to the notice of ASIO.

A 'Q' source report states that on the 8th September, 1951, Petrov . . . visited the Russian Social Club, and was overheard talking to New Australians about going to Russia. Several of the New Australians said they would go to Russia if they could get a visa. A young man . . . said that he had applied for a visa, and was waiting for word to go. He said: 'I can help Russia when I go back. I know the aerodromes in Melbourne and in Tasmania also. When I go back to Russia, I want to join the Red Army and go to Korea and kill Yanks and bloody Australians'. Petrov, who was present, patted him on the back and said: 'That is good. You are a good Soviet citizen already'.[2]

In his visits to the Russian Social Club Petrov was, however, also on the look out for local residents who might assist him in his work on the 'EM' line, that is to say in penetrating the organisations of anti-Soviet Russians and Balts. According to Petrov, he was the first senior Soviet intelligence officer ever assigned to work in the largely undeveloped 'EM' field in Australia. During his briefing in Moscow, prior to coming to Australia, the officers of the 'EM' Department of the MGB were able to supply him with the name of only one potentially useful 'EM' agent, a Latvian whose real name was Fridenbergs and code name 'Sigma'.[3] No doubt, then, when Petrov discovered that a young pro-Soviet Polish doctor, Dr Michael Bialoguski, to whom

9

he was introduced in the Russian Social Club, had a medical practice with a clientele amongst refugees from the Soviet Union and Eastern Europe, his intelligence ears pricked.[4] Petrov began cultivating Bialoguski with the intention of bringing him into action as an agent in the 'EM' field. Before the end of 1951, on Petrov's recommendation, Bialoguski had been allocated an MGB code name — 'Grigorii'.[5]

At the time Petrov encountered him, Bialoguski had in fact been working as a part-time, undercover agent of Australian intelligence organisations for more than six years.[6] Beginning with the Commonwealth Investigation Service in 1945, Bialoguski had transferred into ASIO soon after its establishment in 1949. The interviewing officer at ASIO noted his past attainments in furnishing material of value on 'persons of particular interest to this organisation, both in the Russian and Polish community'. In the light of the later deterioration of relations between ASIO and Bialoguski it is worth noting that the ASIO officer judged him to be a man whose interest in security was 'guided more by loyalty than mercenary reasons . . . who can be trusted as far as any agent can be'. He recommended that Bialoguski start work for ASIO on a trial basis and on a fixed weekly retainer (in fact £4 per week) which might be increased or lowered according to the quality of Bialoguski's work.

> He has in the past had contact with 'THE NARK' [presumably ASIO code for the Communist Party] and various associates and as penetration into this group is most desirable at present, he would be worth a trial.[7]

Bialoguski commenced work in the branch of ASIO concerned with monitoring the activities of subversive organisations.

When he entered ASIO service Michael Bialoguski (a wartime refugee from Vilna) was already a qualified medical practitioner with a Macquarie Street surgery and a specialty in the highly illegal line of abortion.[8] He was also a violinist of sufficient quality to have been invited by Sir Eugene Goossens to play for the Sydney Symphony Orchestra and, to judge by the unpublished memoirs of an Australian wife (Patricia) and lover (Lydia Mokras), a charming and brutally cold womaniser for whom conquests of the present felt grand passion and of the past bitterness, confusion and murderous hatred.[9] His attainments as an agent for ASIO were to prove no less substantial. By the early 1950s Bialoguski had become an informant on a large number of Communist Party front organisations, a leading executive member of the New South Wales Peace Council (in 1952 selected as an Australian delegate to the Peking Peace Conference) and a prominent committee member of the Russian Social Club, where he supported the 'progressive' wing.[10] His role, moreover, in the Petrov defection was decisive. Without this extraordinary character there would have been no Petrov defection.

Bialoguski was introduced to Petrov at the Russian Social Club on July 7, 1951, according to his account, by a beautiful and exceedingly strange young Russian woman, Lydia Mokras, who was already a companion of

Dr Bialoguski (courtesy of John Fairfax and Sons)

Petrov's.*[11] Mokras talked openly at the Club of a father in Moscow well connected in Communist circles and dropped for the benefit of all and sundry none too subtle hints that there was more to her than met the eye. For some months Bialoguski's social meetings with Petrov in Sydney were in the company of Lydia Mokras, and Bialoguski and she became lovers or, in the more

---

* Lydia Mokras had been attached to the Soviet Army during the Second World War as a nurse and taken prisoner by the Germans. In order to avoid repatriation after the war she had married a Czech, Victor Mokras, whom she had met in the Displaced Persons' Camp at Aachen. The couple had lived in Czechoslovakia for some time before fleeing and migrating to Australia. Soon after, Lydia left Victor. She met Petrov and Dr Bialoguski and befriended them both. During this time she invented for herself an intelligence past and present. Her motives here are far from clear.

After the Petrov defection ASIO spoke to Lydia on a number of occasions. She admitted her intelligence stories were concocted and spent most of her time with ASIO describing her relations with Dr Bialoguski. She told ASIO he was mad, had beaten her mercilessly; that he doped horses, performed abortions and sold liquor illegally. She claimed Bialoguski would not let her out of his clutches. After the Petrov defection she wrote a novel *Cloak and Beggar* dominated by sexual-political fantasies about the diabolical Dr Bialoguski.

delicate ASIO language of the 1950s, 'intimate'. More importantly, from the point of view of our story, Lydia Mokras became for a time Bialoguski's chief source of intelligence on Petrov. In the stories she fed Bialoguski there were one or two grains of useful information — she confirmed Bialoguski's opinion that Petrov was a 'big shot' in the Embassy and that he 'liked the girls'[12] — and a considerable amount of self-consciously mysterious nonsense which Bialoguski enthusiastically reported to ASIO. On July 31 Bialoguski reported to his contact that Lydia 'spoke to [Petrov] of jobs she had done' and that 'Petrov's reaction to her talk was quite matter of fact, indicating a prior knowledge of her activities (espionage inferred)'. On August 8 he reported:

> In regard to Petrov she said he knew of her activities but is not in her ring. He had written a note stating 'Hit the enemy whenever you can BOD 3'. Source [i.e. Lydia] stated that BOD in official circles may be followed by any number from 1-75 and denoted the organisation.[13]

Eventually Lydia Mokras's stories came to irritate both Petrov and ASIO. Petrov, who had checked with Moscow Centre on Lydia's supposed father, had found the story false and believed her to be an *agent provocateur* of an anti-Soviet youth group in Sydney. He asked Bialoguski to spy on her. For its part ASIO also discounted her stories of Soviet espionage. Bialoguski's ASIO contact eventually advised him to drop her.[14]

From the point of view of the Petrov story the most important aspect of the Mokras episode was the suspicion it raised in the mind of ASIO's counter-espionage directorate (the poet Michael Thwaites and the policeman Ray Whitrod) in the capacity or bona fides of Bialoguski. At best, in the Mokras episode Bialoguski, who appeared to have been taken in by Lydia, had shown himself an agent of poor judgement. ASIO's counter-espionage branch now wondered whether Petrov had knowledge of Bialoguski's ASIO connection and was using Lydia as a 'decoy' to draw them into some embarrassing indiscretion.[15] Even worse they now wondered whether Bialoguski himself might not be playing the game not of an ASIO double agent but of a Soviet triple. A passage from ASIO's internal history of the Petrov Affair, written shortly after the defection, is most revealing on the impact Lydia Mokras had on the ASIO-Bialoguski relationship. In it *Nina* is Mokras' code-name and, revealingly enough, *Diabolo* Bialoguski's.

> Diabolo met Petrov in the Russian Social Club, to which Petrov was a regular visitor, and he was frequently in touch with him on his visits to Sydney. *The exact nature of this early relationship is by no means entirely clear as yet.* According to Diabolo, Petrov and another member of the Club encouraged his interest in Nina, a Russian girl who had recently arrived in Australia as a migrant, with whom Diabolo soon became intimately associated. For a period of months Diabolo reported sensational statements and conspirational behaviour by Nina, who claimed that she was a member of a spy ring, produced an N.K.V.D. camera, ostentatiously photographed Sydney Harbour and Mascot aerodrome and generally played the part of the would-be Mata Hari....

In general his attitude to his case officer was that Nina was mysterious and unreliable; but he expressed strong disbelief in her espionage role only when it was clear
that his case officer disbelieved it. . . .
Questioned after Petrov's defection, Nina has denied any participation in real espionage and has admitted fabricating her espionage role, but claims that this was with
the purely personal objective of interesting Diabolo. *Whether Diabolo himself was
a victim or a conscious participant in the scheme has yet to be resolved.*[16]

Over-estimation of the cunning of one's enemies and the duplicity of one's
friends are the occupational hazards of counter-espionage. During 1952 and
1953 ASIO feared that Petrov and Bialoguski might be setting them up. As
the italicised passages from the ASIO internal history reveal, the clouds of
suspicion surrounding Dr Bialoguski, which had blown up during the Mokras
episode, had not entirely cleared even after Petrov had defected. ASIO's
Petrov operation was never to be entirely free from the negative effects of
its broodings on Petrov's cunning and Bialoguski's duplicity.

During the course of 1952 and early 1953, freed from the diversion of Lydia
Mokras, the Petrov-Bialoguski relationship blossomed. They remained companions at the Russian Social Club, although after Petrov openly voiced his
suspicions to Bialoguski about the Club's penetration by counter-
intelligence, increasingly less so. (On July 14 1952, for example, Petrov
warned Bialoguski that the walls at the Club had ears and that its leading
members, the Klodnitsky couple, were 'spies and swine'.)[17] Bialoguski drove
Petrov about Sydney and was frequently invited by him to official Soviet
Embassy functions, including the Revolution Day celebrations in November
1951 and 1952. Together they attended the parties given in Sydney at the
Czech Consulate by Kafka and Zizka. Most importantly Bialoguski became
Petrov's almost constant companion in his expeditions into Sydney night life.

The dividing line between business and pleasure and between the covert and
overt dimensions in the Bialoguski-Petrov relationship became increasingly
difficult to discern. No doubt at first Petrov saw in his social relationship with
Bialoguski a cover for the intelligence relationship that was developing. By
early 1953 Petrov had begun to assign to his agent 'Grigorii' a number of
minor espionage tasks:

[Petrov] asked me to use the contacts that I have with the Immigration Department
(Bialoguski reported to his ASIO contact in March 1953) to obtain any forms relative to entry or departure from Australia,
also blank passports,
then he said he was keen to get some blank driving license forms,
blank cheques on the Rural Bank or any other bank.[18]

On the other hand the covert agent relationship with Bialoguski became
itself a cover, *vis-à-vis* his Soviet colleagues, for their vivid social life together,
which had become an inevitable feature of Petrov's trips to Sydney. Increas-

ingly when in Sydney Bialoguski noticed that Petrov would try and shake off his Soviet companions, frequently voicing to Bialoguski, when alcohol had loosened his tongue, his hostility to their presence.[19] In May 1952 Petrov complained bitterly about Pakhomov's snooping,[20] and in February 1953 about being guarded by his driver. On that occasion Bialoguski reported that

> Petrov was extremely drunk and at one point was lying on the bed in a drunken stupor. [Bialoguski] noted that Koukharenko (also drunk) insisted on accompanying Petrov and later [Bialoguski] was told by Petrov that 'there are some comrades in Sydney who are jealous of my being on good terms with the Australians'.[21]

Bialoguski felt convinced that Petrov was deeply humiliated by the watch his driver had apparently been keeping on him.[22] Again, when the MGB team was beefed up with the arrival in Australia of Antonov (Pakhomov's 'Tass'-MGB replacement) and Kislitsyn, Dr Bialoguski noticed how Petrov took considerable pains to disguise from both of them the full extent and nature of their relationship.[23]

In short, by gradual steps Petrov was drifting into what Bialoguski correctly characterised as a 'double life' in Sydney.[24] In his professional life he had reason to be wary of the eyes of Australian counter-intelligence; in his social life the eyes of his Soviet MGB and 'SK' colleagues. In these two worlds only Bialoguski shared a part. Perhaps, one senses, for Petrov Bialoguski — the ASIO agent — was his first real friend.

The historian Richard Pipes has argued that for the nineteenth century Russian peasant 'the ideal condition was *volia*, a word meaning "having one's way". To have *volia* meant to enjoy licence, to revel, to carouse.'[25] Petrov, in this regard at least a true son of the peasantry, found his *volia* in Sydney with Bialoguski on drink-sodden evenings in cafes and night clubs (their favourites were the California Cafe and the Roosevelt Club) which usually concluded in the early morning hours with cruises around the Cross in search of women. Judging from the extremely detailed reports Bialoguski gave to his ASIO contact, his role in this dimension of Petrov's life in Sydney became clear in the middle of 1952. In March 1952 Bialoguski merely suspected that Petrov picked up girls in the street.[26] By July he was helping Petrov procure women.

> At about 2.30 a.m. Petrov and I spoke to 'Chris' and another girl with a view, (not matrimony). They were reluctant to go. Chris asked me for my card and said she would ring me. Petrov and I went on our own to the car. Petrov refused to go away, and said you go back and talk them into it. I went behind a corner, and then went back to the car and told him that it is all locked up and we can't do anything about it. He was a bitterly disappointed man, and we went for a drive, around the City. Petrov said he knows a place in Pitt Street, Hamilton Street and Hunter Street area. We circled a few times round there and he said that the place is shut.[27]

Some time towards the end of 1951 Bialoguski's work was transferred from ASIO's subversion (BI) to its counter-espionage (B2) branch, and Bialoguski was assigned a new case officer whom he met under conspiratorial conditions, who took down his increasingly detailed reports on Petrov in shorthand.[28] The resulting rather exuberant reports combined observation with surmise and operational advice. Although Petrov never told him directly that he was MGB, Bialoguski assumed it from the first. (Unfortunately for his reputation at ASIO's counter-espionage headquarters he seemed to assume the same thing about the entire staff of the Soviet Embassy.)[29] Moreover, as early as February 1952, Bialoguski regarded Petrov as a likely defector.

> Petrov never indicated that he would like to stay here, but he seems to like many aspects of life here. He likes Canberra and the climate there very much. He took to gardening and enjoys it. He likes what is called a good time. By that I mean drink and the girls, and when he goes to the pub he chats away with the barmaids and the customers and he seems to feel at home. His position is in charge of the Consular Section of the Legation, but he travels freely.[30]

Bialoguski was also generous with his advice to ASIO as to how they might bring Petrov over. In March 1952 he suggested the establishment of an Australian committee, under the chairmanship of a well-known politician or businessman, which might make a formal approach by letter to likely defectors from Soviet bloc countries.

> Say, for instance, if Petrov was to receive a letter like that. Would he go to the Embassy and show it? You know what he would risk if he showed it. If he keeps it he runs a serious risk too.... If he considers he would come to me and say who is this name on the letter, I would hear of it. You won't ever get it if you don't try. You remember Gousenko was one, but remember all the damage he did.[31]

A year later he became convinced that a former head of the CIS and present Commonwealth Film Censor, J.O. Alexander (with whom Petrov had contact through his VOKS role in arranging for the import of Soviet films) should make a direct approach to Petrov offering him asylum and money to defect.[32]

Although under Colonel Charles Spry ASIO had made the study of Soviet Embassy personnel with a view to their defection a central operational objective of the organisation,[33] before mid-1953 the ASIO counter-espionage branch remained far more sceptical than did Bialoguski of Petrov's defector potential. In February 1952 both Bialoguski and a desk officer at counter-espionage had suggested that Petrov be treated as a potential defector, or in ASIO code a 'Cabin candidate'.[34] Two months later the directorate would go no further than to brief its state branches that Petrov and Pakhomov 'should be studied' as possible subjects 'for a planned defection operation'.[35] For its own purposes an ASIO internal memorandum in the same month argued that there was 'insufficient evidence to implement' any suggested plan for an approach to Petrov.[36] In December 1952 ASIO ventured no farther than to conclude that 'from an operational point of view' Petrov's 'freedom of movement outside the Embassy' and 'weaknesses for wine, women and song' were well worth 'noting'.[37]

ASIO's estimation of Bialoguski had not improved with time or acquaintance. Frequent wranglings over money (in September 1952 Bialoguski's retainer had been increased to £10; in March 1953 plus expenses) led ASIO to view him as a 'mercenary'. The professionals at ASIO also clearly resented Bialoguski's operational advice. His plans to approach Petrov through Alexander (which ASIO thought would involve the Commonwealth Government 'in the incitement of a Soviet diplomat to defect') or by formal letter from a prominent Australian (which it thought would provide the Soviets with 'documentary evidence' of Australian action in a defection scheme) were not only dismissed out of hand but held against Bialoguski by the counterespionage directorate. Most importantly Bialoguski's reports on Petrov were at this time consistently treated by the counter-espionage directorate (but, interestingly enough, not by the case officers dealing directly with him) as unreliable. ASIO was unable to dismiss the possibility that Dr Bialoguski might be a participant in the trap it feared Petrov might be preparing for it.[39]

Indeed so deep were these suspicions that some time in 1952 ASIO engaged the services of an agent to keep a close watch on their own agent, Bialoguski. The man chosen was a Pole, S.J. Maruszewski, who went in Australia under the name of George Marue. On September 26 1951 (after the Government defeat in the referendum concerning the banning of the Communist Party) Marue had written to Mr Menzies offering the services of a quasi-intelligence émigré organisation he proposed to form — the International Democratic Alliance — in the common struggle against Communism, but asking in return for a Government subsidy.[40] Marue's letter was passed on to ASIO where his proposal was turned down. Colonel Spry wrote to Menzies:

> I consider that the formation of nationalist organisations or private investigation services to combat subversive activity in this country is most undesirable.[41]

Marue, however, was not to be wasted. By March 1952 an officer of ASIO had made personal contact with Marue and enlisted Marue's services to watch Bialoguski. The later accounts given of the terms of employment by both partners make clear that Marue was led to believe that he was following a Polish Communist and was given no idea of Bialoguski's ASIO connection. Marue informed the Sydney *Sun* that 'he was told by security that Bialoguski was a communist. He said he later discovered he was being used as a double-check on Bialoguski'.[42] Similarly Spry explained to Menzies, 'Marue was never informed at any time of the tasks of Bialoguski by any member of the Australian Security Intelligence Organisation'.[43]

After Petrov's defection, when Marue was dismissed from ASIO service and had turned against both ASIO and Bialoguski, he wrote the following account of his relations with Bialoguski:

> I had been asked by Fred [Marue's ASIO contact] if I would like to get for his Department all the information I possibly could about Dr Bialoguski, who was

known to Fred's Organization as an active Communist and also probably was an agent, working in Australia for the Soviet Union. . . I began to have my meals in the same restaurant as he had his, I often joined his table and we becam(sic) very good friends. . . I watched him very closely when Petrov was coming to Sydney. I had a chance to listen to their conversations, to follow them and to see many things.[44]

By April 1953 the future direction (if any) of ASIO's Petrov operation was unclear. ASIO had encouraged Bialoguski to continue his cultivation of Petrov but were deeply suspicious of his judgment and motives. It had ruled out Bialoguski's schemes for a direct approach to Petrov inviting him to defect but had as yet no Petrov strategy of its own. Undaunted, Bialoguski in mid-April reseized the initiative with fresh proposals for the consideration of both Petrov and ASIO.

To Petrov, Bialoguski suggested an equal share in a partnership he had (genuinely) been offered in a Polish cafe at the Cross, which was a favourite haunt of theirs.[45]

I told Petrov I needed £1000 (he informed his ASIO contact on April 21 1953) to become a partner to George [Chomentowski] in the Adria . . . Petrov said £1000 is a trifle, but you must find out all you can about George, where was he born, has he got any relatives in Poland, and it does not matter much about his politics. I asked him would he be a partner with me, say 50/50, £500 each, and I would sign a separate agreement that this is a fact. Petrov said no agreement is necessary. He would do it on my word, but information about George is vital.[46]

Despite what Bialoguski suspected at the time and believed subsequently,[47] it is almost certain that Petrov treated the cafe proposal not as some private business arrangement between himself and Bialoguski but in the conventional manner of a Soviet intelligence officer. The joint partnership would draw Bialoguski more deeply into intelligence work for the Soviets. Moreover the Adria was precisely the kind of meeting place — centrally located, noisy and busy — required by Petrov for his conspiratorial work in Sydney. Petrov almost certainly told his wife about the proposition and one or the other almost certainly informed Moscow about it. Several months after her defection, when Petrova decided to spill the beans on Bialoguski and let ASIO know that he was indeed a Soviet agent ('We tried to save him, but I did not want to save him. He was double, yours and ours'), her crucial evidence was his involvement in the Adria joint venture.

One paragraph of a letter to Moscow described that Dr Bialoguski wanted to purchase a restaurant but he did not have enough money . . . and asked Mr Petrov if he could borrow £500. Mr Petrov further reported that he considered this matter very important for illegal work, and recommended that a loan of £500 be made to Dr Bialoguski in order that in future the restaurant could be used for illegal work.[48]

Dr Bialoguski's business proposal instantly drew from Petrov a counter-proposal of more doubtful provenance from a professional point of view. Moscow had recently asked Petrov to reopen a litigation in Australia which might involve as much as £30,000. They had permitted a fee of 15% to the lawyer engaged if the suit was successful. Petrov suggested giving him a mere 5% and dividing the remaining 10% 'fifty fifty'.[49] Nothing seems to have come of this. On the other hand a new chapter in the Petrov-Bialoguski relationship — involving joint participation in a variety of business schemes and petty frauds — had opened.

As it happened, ASIO was favourably disposed at least towards the Adria proposal. They briefed Bialoguski to press Petrov for something definite here, although they remained somewhat puzzled about the relationship of the café venture to the news they had just received from one of their many sources inside the travel business that the Petrovs had just been booked on a passage to Moscow. As the following cryptic telephone message between the counter-espionage headquarters in Melbourne and Bialoguski's Sydney contact makes clear, as usual ASIO's thoughts turned to suspicions of Bialoguski's motives and honesty.

> I have got your Director here and we have gone into the matter you are specially interested in . . . the certain business proposition. You should urge [our friend] to, but first of all, are you satisfied he does not know about the early departure of his friend? If he knew about it he would certainly tell you about it![50]

Bialoguski's proposal to ASIO concerned a different matter. He suggested they subsidise the rental of a fashionable flat in Point Piper, whose owner, Lady Poynter, had just departed for the Coronation. He explained the idea and its conspiratorial possibilities, thus, to his ASIO contact.

> If I can I will take it in any case, but if you are prepared to assist with the rent, I will place it at the disposal of Petrov and the couriers, etc. I have mentioned it to Petrov and he was extremely enthusiastic about it.[51]

ASIO was less enthusiastic. They asked Bialoguski to wait for their decision.

At least from Dr Bialoguski's point of view the Point Piper flat proved an immediate and outstanding success. When Petrov visited Sydney between May 3 and 5 he stayed not at a hotel, as had been his custom, but at the new flat. As instructed Bialoguski pressed Petrov for a decision on the Adria proposal and Petrov promised to do his best. Petrov, who at first seemed depressed, told Bialoguski 'in confidence' that he and his wife were shortly to return for two or three months to the Soviet Union. He had managed to pick up some photographic enlarging equipment cheaply through the Czech Consulate (for the purchase of which he borrowed £25/15/- from Bialoguski) which he installed in Bialoguski's flat.

It was only, however, on the evening of May 4 that the value of the new arrangement was fully revealed. At eight Petrov and Bialoguski had coffee at the California, picked up a couple of prostitutes and returned to the flat.

'Petrov went to bed with one. I paid the other £5'. After the girls left, over dinner and two bottles of wine, Petrov opened up to Bialoguski more candidly than ever before about the tensions inside the Embassy. 'As he was getting more drunk he became abusive towards the members of the Soviet Embassy. He said he had no friends there.' Finally at one in the morning Petrov stumbled into bed. An hour later Bialoguski ventured into his bedroom, took the contents of his coat pockets and the wallet from his trousers and meticulously recorded for his ASIO contact the details of his plunder — some counterfeit coins and a variety of business cards and addresses written on scraps of paper, only one of which was to play any part at all in the subsequent deliberations of the Royal Commission on Espionage. He also, however, found an odd note in ungrammatical English, signed by Petrov and addressed to a Mme. R.M. Ollier, offering her greetings from Sadovnikov and Pakhomov and suggesting a rendezvous in central Canberra. This note was to begin a line of enquiry of considerable significance in the future investigations of the Royal Commission and the future politics of the Petrov Affair. At 4.30 that morning, having replaced the papers and wallet, his work was finished.[52] No doubt Bialoguski was euphoric. He believed his information would 'provide the key to the whole Soviet espionage system in Australia'.[53]

The significance of this new development — Petrov's decision to stay with Bialoguski when in Sydney — was not at the time appreciated by ASIO.*[54] Indeed shortly after the Point Piper intelligence *coup* ASIO turned down Bialoguski's request for a subsidy on the flat. Bialoguski now blew up, sending Colonel Spry (whom he had never met) a formal letter of resignation in which he complained of the discourtesy in the refusal of the subsidy (the advantages of the flat had already, he argued, been proved) and, more deeply, of the mistrust that he felt surrounded him in his work for ASIO. 'It has been my impression over a long period that my telephones have been tapped. . . . Your insistence on inspecting my flat in my absence I could interpret only as an indication that you haven't sufficient trust in me'.[55] While Bialoguski's not uncommon suspicions of ASIO telephone tapping may or may not have been misplaced, those concerning the search of his flat were probably well founded. George Marue was later to claim that on one occasion he had indeed 'searched Bialoguski's flat'.[56]

Clearly Bialoguski did not expect his resignation to be accepted. 'I shall be happy', he concluded magnanimously, 'to reconsider my resignation if I can be convinced by you that my doubts and grievances are without foundation'.[57] When it was accepted, he took off post-haste to offer his intelligence services first to the United States (through a Vice-Consul of his acquaintance,

---

* As ASIO's internal history put it: 'On 3rd May, 1953, a development occurred the importance of which for various reasons was not fully appreciated at the time. Petrov visited Diabolo at his recently acquired flat and stayed the night there.' It is interesting that the ASIO history did not mention 'Diabolo's' resignation over the matter, or his trip to Mullin.

Harry Mullin) and then to the Commonwealth Investigation Service (through his original employer there, Bill Barnwell).[58] Mullin informed ASIO of the approach. Barnwell did not.*[59] Dr Bialoguski remained an ASIO agent pending the expected return of Petrov to the USSR. At this point, it was agreed, his resignation would take effect. This episode could not but have deepened both ASIO's doubts about Bialoguski's character, and Bialoguski's growing scepticism about his employer's capacities in the field of counter-espionage.

Petrov was of course unaware of the squabbles he had inspired between his Sydney friend and Australian counter-intelligence. He had problems of his own. On May 18, the day after Bialoguski had approached Barnwell (who had been handing out how-to-vote cards for the ALP in the Senate election), Petrov telephoned Bialoguski from the Oriental Hotel, asking him to come and see him. (Because he was accompanied by his MVD colleague, Philip Kislitsyn, he could not of course stay at Bialoguski's flat). He was 'sick, worried and depressed'. His wife — at the special request of the Ambassador, Lifanov — was now to stay in Australia while he was in Moscow. He was booked to fly alone on May 29. (Despite his womanising, Petrov was a very jealous husband). His eyes also were giving him trouble.

Bialoguski could help with the eye if not the Evdokia problem. He arranged an appointment for him next morning at the surgery of a specialist with whom he shared premises in Macquarie Street, one Dr Beckett. Beckett diagnosed 'neuro-retinitis' and recommended an immediate operation. As Bialoguski explained to his ASIO contact: 'In the event of him neglecting it he could suffer an optic nerve atrophy, with subsequent loss of vision. In plain language the bugger may go blind'. While waiting for Petrov outside Beckett's surgery Bialoguski struck up an acquaintance with Petrov's MVD colleague, Kislitsyn, whom he discovered had been in the past at the Soviet Legation in London. This acquaintance made Petrov distinctly uneasy. Whenever possible he 'whispered' to Bialoguski 'not to be talkative with Kislitsyn and to try to keep away from him'. The fewer the bridges between his two Sydney lives the better.[60]

The new developments in the situation gave Bialoguski food for thought. Petrov was clearly pleased about the postponement of his flight to Moscow. (He had winked at Bialoguski when discussing it over lunch). Most likely, Bialoguski surmised, the neuro-retinitis was self-inflicted. 'Petrov was the type who could easily take some tablets to which he knew he was allergic.' He was 'certain' that Petrov did not wish to return to the Soviet Union. The question troubling Bialoguski now was not so much whether Petrov would defect but whether the gains from Petrov's defection would outweigh the

---

* The first ASIO learnt of this was when Dr Bialoguski published his Petrov memoir in June 1955, and mentioned there his discussion with Barnwell. ASIO wrote to the director of the CIS requesting an explanation of Barnwell's silence on this matter.

losses incurred to Australian counter-intelligence by the blowing of Bialoguski's cover.

Any such move could be dangerous so far as his position was concerned regarding the future, and he felt (his ASIO contact reported) that through his association with Petrov he had made quite a number of important contacts, both within and outside the Soviet Embassy. . . . He also stated that any such move might place a considerable burden on our Government as Petrov was a drunken type of individual and might be hard to place; and that if he did stay it could prove embarrassing so far as Crane's [Bialoguski's] future activities with us are concerned. However, against the foregoing Crane referred to the case of Gouzenko, a low ranking member of an Embassy, whereas Petrov was the second senior member of the Russian Embassy in Canberra.[61]

On balance Bialoguski preferred the defection option. On May 21, after discussing some separate matters with his contact, he appeared anxious to return to the Petrov theme. A direct and 'not roundabout' approach to Petrov offering money and protection from Soviet threats (definitely in that order) had, he believed, a greater than even chance of succeeding. He recommended once again the Alexander option. He was not concerned even if Petrov suspected that he had inspired the approach.

Petrov was not fanatical about the Soviet; he liked the good time he had been having in Australia; and Crane felt that he had it on Petrov as a result of their association.[62]

Bialoguski's reflections did not convince ASIO's counter-espionage directorate to make the direct approach he had recommended. Instead they enlisted Bialoguski to travel to Petrov's hospital bed in Canberra to make the roundabout approach he had warned against. Bialoguski found his ASIO briefing painfully naive.[63] One of the questions he was requested to put to Petrov — on the comparative merits of Australian and Russian hospitals — was apparently designed to prod Petrov into musings about the superiority of Western over Soviet civilisation. Not surprisingly, given his mood and the nature of his briefing, Bialoguski's Canberra trip was a failure. When Bialoguski pressed Petrov for a decision on the Adria he merely confirmed his continued interest, but showed concern when told that Chomentowski had raised the price of the partnership from £1000 to £2000. Bialoguski now thought his interest in the café might be no more than 'wishful thinking'. When Bialoguski asked him for his hospital-based cultural comparison, Petrov conceded that he liked the sisters in Canberra but found the food and medical attention in the Soviet Union superior.[64]

By mid-June Petrov had sufficiently recovered from his eye operation to resume his old life with Bialoguski in Sydney. His Moscow flight had been put back to July 10 and was later — after the dismissal of Beria — cancelled altogether. On the evening of June 16 Bialoguski picked Petrov up at Mascot and took him home. The next evening they met up again, this time outside the Oriental Hotel where Bialoguski found Petrov standing with an 'old prostitute', from whose company he managed eventually to prise him. On the following afternoon Petrov and Bialoguski arrived at the home of Petrov's Australian friends, Alan and Joan Morton-Clarke, Petrov in the expectation (disappointed) of bedding the mistress of the house while the master was away. Later that evening, now in the company of both the Clarkes, Petrov, far gone in drink, tried unsuccessfully to teach Bialoguski how to use the newly installed photographic equipment. Later still, after the Clarkes had departed, Bialoguski once more went through Petrov's pockets, this time discovering a note book with a number of names (including 'Fergus' and 'A.A. Fridenburg') which were later to play a considerable part in the investigations of the Espionage Royal Commission.[65]

It is difficult to know what ASIO's counter-espionage branch (especially its director, Michael Thwaites, who was a member of Moral Rearmament) made of the increasingly lurid Petrov reports Bialoguski's case officer was submitting to headquarters. What is known, however, is that by mid-1953 ASIO's counter-espionage directorate had come to the opinion that their Petrov operation had reached a 'stalemate'. To break it, ASIO now took what amounted to its first major initiative in the Petrov case since the employment of Bialoguski. Strangely enough the catalyst here was a development not in Australia but in the Kremlin.[66] On July 10 news arrived of the arrest of Beria, head of the MVD.* Through its contacts with friendly intelligence services ASIO soon had word of unrest in several MVD stations abroad.[67] It now decided the time was ripe for the direct approach to Petrov Bialoguski had long advocated. However it also decided to by-pass Bialoguski altogether. As the following passage from ASIO's internal history of the defection makes clear, suspicions of Bialoguski played a considerable part in their tactical planning for a Petrov approach.

> The danger of relying on Diabolo as an intermediary in the defection loomed large in view of (a) his evident ignorance of the diplomatic pitfalls, (b) his personal eagerness and acknowledged mercenary interest in the matter, (c) doubts as the reliability of his reports . . . [and] (d) the feeling that, granted the truth of Diabolo's reports, his unscrupulous character, obvious to ASIO, would not have escaped Petrov's notice.[68]

The man ASIO selected to make the approach to Petrov was Bialoguski's Macquarie Street neighbour and Petrov's eye doctor, H.C. Beckett, who Michael Thwaites (with Colonel Spry's authorisation) now flew to Sydney to sound out and brief. Thwaites found Beckett, who had absolutely no previous connection with ASIO, 'genial, relaxed and attentive'. On July 23, during the course of a check-up on Petrov's eyes (which Beckett had asked Bialoguski to arrange) the following curious conversation took place.

---

* After Stalin's death Beria had merged the MGB into the MVD.

(ASIO's history which turned Bialoguski into 'Diabolo' chose a fine old Anglo-Saxon code name for Beckett — 'Frankman').

Frankman: You are going back to Moscow?
Petrov: Yes.
Frankman: I don't know that I would want to go back, with all the changes taking place there — Beria....
Petrov: It is my duty.
Frankman: Don't you like this country?
Petrov: Yes it is a fine — plenty of food — plenty of everything.
Frankman: Why don't you stay here?
Petrov: It is my duty to go back.
Frankman: If I was in your place I'd stay here.
Petrov: It is very hard to get a job like that.
Frankman: Not if you know the right people ... I have friends who know about these things.[69]

After his consultation with Petrov, Dr Beckett immediately reported to Ron Richards, ASIO's New South Wales Regional Director. His message was rather hopeful. Richards conveyed the news later that afternoon to Thwaites via the telephone. 'R/D NSW [Richards] has seen the man whom D/B2 [Thwaites] saw the other day. He has seen his patient and looks somewhat promising but no panic for two or three days'.[70] At the Royal Commission Beckett was to recall that during this conversation Petrov was watchful but impassive, 'like a clam ... poker-faced'.[71]

In fact, Petrov had been far from unmoved by the conversation with Beckett. It did not require his two decades of experience in Soviet intelligence for him to fathom Beckett's Security connection. When he got into Bialoguski's car outside the surgery he instantly warned Bialoguski to be careful of Dr Beckett. 'He is a queer bird. He has some connection with the Security people.'[72] Bialoguski at once informed ASIO of his conversation with Petrov about Beckett. According to ASIO, in general Bialoguski's account seemed accurate except that Beckett was said to have told Petrov 'that he knew a Security chap. Crane reported that Petrov was disturbed, but was interested to see how it develops'.[73]

It was not only Petrov who was disturbed. ASIO wondered whether it might not in fact have been Diabolo who suggested to Petrov Beckett's Security connection; while for his part Bialoguski correctly interpreted ASIO's trust in Beckett (about whom he had not been briefed, let alone consulted) as a calculated snub to him.*[74] In his published account of the Petrov story Bialoguski provided a number of reasons for disapproving the Beckett

---

*After the Petrov defection Bialoguski discussed his Beckett resentments with his ASIO contact. Bialoguski's contact 'pointed out to "CRANE" that if we broke a confidence with Dr Beckett and informed "CRANE" of the matter, we could hardly expect "CRANE" to feel confident that we would preserve his identity. "CRANE" was not impressed with this and said that the circumstances were entirely different.

approach. ('There was no attempt to introduce a social note, no attempt to build up Beckett as a man of wealth and importance, no attempt to give Petrov a feeling of security and reassurance.')[75] But these were largely rationalisations. The Beckett approach differed only marginally from the Alexander option Bialoguski had long advocated. More deeply, ASIO's Beckett gambit represented a cruel blow to Bialoguski's not inconsiderable self-esteem. Even after the defection thinking about it made his 'blood boil'. He began now to ask himself the question, 'why should I do this?'.[76]

The response to Beckett's July approach to Petrov had seemed to ASIO 'not entirely without promise'.[77] To pursue it they asked Bialoguski to arrange yet another redundant eye appointment for Petrov.[78] On August 22, in Beckett's surgery, Petrov now 'spoke glowingly of Russia, and at any attempt by Frankman to steer the conversation towards the advantages of life in Australia, praised Russia even more emphatically'.[79] It must have given Bialoguski a certain amount of malicious pleasure to be able to report to his ASIO contact that Petrov had found Beckett 'much nicer this time'.[80] By late August 1953 Beckett, and only marginally less certainly, ASIO, had come to regard the question of the Petrov defection as a 'dead duck'.[81]

In early September 1953, shortly after ASIO's hopes for effecting the Petrov defection had been thus disappointed, Bialoguski (still brooding on his mistreatment) decided, once again, to put ASIO to the test on the question of his pay. Instead of the present £10 plus expenses (which he claimed were averaging £15 per week) he asked for a simple £25 per week payment to save him the tedium of constant expense applications and relieve him of the anxiety of their discovery one day by Petrov in the flat. After a short delay ASIO turned down Bialoguski's request.[82] As in May he blew up, but this time he set off not to offer his services to the CIS or the USA but to ask for the intervention on his behalf of the Prime Minister, Mr Menzies.

There are two versions of what now transpired in Canberra — that of Bialoguski (published by him in mid-1955) and that of Geoffrey Yeend, Mr Menzies' Private Secretary, written for Menzies in response to Bialoguski's publication. Because of the importance the Petrov conspiracy theorists would later attribute to this meeting it is necessary to outline these versions in some detail.

According to Bialoguski, two meetings took place with Yeend. At the first Bialoguski handed Yeend a sealed letter, addressed to the Prime Minister, requesting an interview on a matter of national importance. At the second Yeend informed Bialoguski that he had been 'deputed by the Prime Minister' to act on his behalf. As 'proof' of this Bialoguski's letter to Menzies 'lay open in front of him'. Bialoguski outlined his complaints against Security exactly as he would have to Menzies and he 'assumed that Yeend would relay exactly what [he] had to say to his chief'. According to Bialoguski, Yeend expressed sympathy for his position and promised to raise the matter (and Mr Menzies' interest in it) when he next saw Colonel Spry.[83]

Yeend's version is somewhat different. According to him once he heard the substance of Bialoguski's complaint (which essentially concerned his treatment by Richards, who he thought was persecuting him) he rejected Bialoguski's request for an interview with Mr Menzies on the ground that 'this was the sort of thing the Prime Minister left entirely in the hands of the responsible officers'. Yeend promised instead to have the matters raised by Bialoguski placed before Colonel Spry and in fact (once he had determined that Bialoguski was indeed an ASIO agent) presented the details of Bialoguski's grievance to ASIO's Canberra head, Colonel Phillipps, who in turn promised to pass them on to Spry. When Bialoguski telephoned Yeend a few days later he was assured that Spry had been informed. Yeend claimed that he 'did not discuss the interview with Bialoguski with the Prime Minister in any way'. In a second memorandum written for Menzies he added that he was 'certain' that Bialoguski had handed him no sealed envelope and had at no stage mentioned the name of Petrov or the possibility of a Soviet defection. He agreed with Bialoguski, however, that he had conveyed to him 'the impression' that he was 'sympathetic' to his case.[84]

With the exception of the dispute about whether or not Bialoguski brought a letter with him to Canberra there is, in fact, no important discrepancy between the versions given by Bialoguski and Yeend of their meeting — and even that discrepancy is of no great import. Even if Bialoguski had brought a letter to Canberra addressed to the Prime Minister and even if he had indeed later seen it lying open on Yeend's desk, this was no ground for Bialoguski to assume, as he did, that the Prime Minister had personally read it. (Bialoguski apparently believed the Prime Minister was obliged to read all the mail personally addressed to him.) Moreover Bialoguski's general assumption that Menzies had taken a personal interest in his case is readily explained. The combination of Yeend's sympathy and his own egocentricity could easily have led Yeend to imply and Bialoguski to infer Menzies' private interest in the affair.

If the precise details of the Bialoguski-Yeend meeting are in doubt, at least its immediate consequence is not. Shortly after the meeting, Colonel Spry (who had of course learnt through Phillipps of Bialoguski's petition to the Prime Minister) let Bialoguski know, through an ASIO intermediary, that his work for ASIO was at an end. Spry made clear to Bialoguski that it was he and not the Prime Minister who was responsible for Australian Security and that his Organization had both known about and deeply resented Bialoguski's offer of service to the Americans. Bialoguski asked whether the decision to remove him from ASIO work was 'irrevocable'. 'Quite irrevocable' was the reply.[85]

When Bialoguski's account of his 1953 trip to Canberra in quest of the Prime Minister was first published in mid-1955 those who already were convinced that Menzies had manipulated the Petrov defection for party political advantage pounced eagerly upon it as a new and vital piece of evidence to support their case. From that day to this the Bialoguski-Yeend (Menzies) meeting has been one of the evidentiary cornerstones of the Petrov conspiracy theory. What the theorists, however, fail to do is to consider the impact on their theory of the actual and immediate consequences of Bialoguski's Canberra trip — his dismissal from ASIO service. Menzies' first act as manipulator of the Petrov defection was hardly likely to have been the sacking of ASIO's leading Petrov agent — the only man who could genuinely advance the cause of the Petrov defection.

The truth is that in September 1953 Menzies was not preparing to take control of the Petrov operation, ASIO was losing belief in it. If anyone had genuine grounds for feeling defensive about developments in the spring of 1953 it was not Menzies but ASIO. In dismissing Dr Bialoguski they had let go a priceless, if infuriating, asset.

3

TERROR AUSTRALIS

It was not Bialoguski's relations with ASIO but Petrov's relations with the Soviet Embassy and MVD Centre at Moscow that would determine his future course and draw him on to his defection. The full truth about the deterioration of those relations will probably never be known. The most that can be done is to piece together an outline account of Petrov's Australian decline from the evidence of the Bialoguski reports and the stories the Petrovs later told to their ASIO interrogators, the Royal Commissioners and to their 'ghost', Michael Thwaites. In it there are, as we shall see, several strands.

The first of these is relatively straightforward — the apparent demise in Australia of Petrov's reputation as an effective Soviet intelligence operative. Prior to his arrival in Canberra Petrov's career had been spent predominantly at a desk in Moscow, in its earlier part in cypher work and in its latter phase on the 'SK' line. Even in his middle period in Sweden he had been occupied only in cypher and 'SK' work. Before Australia his experience of working both in the field and amongst foreigners was extremely limited. Petrov's appointment, while in Australia, as temporary 'legal' Resident represented for him entry into a new realm of intelligence work and was certainly the greatest challenge, thus far, of his career.

What little evidence there is would suggest that Moscow Centre did not think highly of Petrov's work in Australia. In the middle of 1952, only four months after Petrov had been appointed to the Canberra Residency but about one year and four months after his arrival in Australia, Moscow Centre issued an extremely harsh verdict on the work of Pakhomov and Petrov.

> Intelligence work in Australia in 1951-2 was actually at a standstill and has not produced any discernible results. This is explained by the fact that the Australian section of the M.V.D. was not fully staffed, and you and Pakhomov were not working to a definite aim. The absence of a plan of work on the part of the M.V.D. section also had an adverse effect on the state of affairs.[1]

Perhaps Petrov might have consoled himself at the time that the weight of this criticism fell on Pakhomov, who had held the Residency between April

1951 and February 1952, and who was shortly recalled to Moscow. If so, the words of the new MGB officer, Philip Kislitsyn, who arrived in Australia from Moscow at the time of Pakhomov's recall, must have been extremely worrying.

> On being questioned as to the valuation of my work at the M.V.D. Centre in Moscow he told me that my work was not considered to be of the standard expected and was low grade. He did bring to my attention the inefficient handing of 'Yeger' [Anderson of the Clerks' Union] and 'Olga' [Mme Ollier of the French Embassy].[2]

Once again, in early 1953, Moscow issued Petrov with a strong reprimand concerning the indifferent quality of his work in Australia.[3] The sensitivity the Petrov couple still felt about the failure of Petrov's Residency in Australia, even after their defections, seems to have been reflected in their eagerness to reveal to the world the gaucherie, timidity and inefficiency of their MGB-MVD colleagues (Kislitsyn and Antonov) and 'coopted' collaborators (Kovaliev and Kharkovetz).[4]

After the death of Stalin (March 1953) Petrov's private concerns about his standing at Moscow were almost certainly complicated and deepened by anxieties about the turmoil into which the entire Soviet intelligence world had been thrown. Shortly after Stalin's death the Politburo member in charge of Security affairs since the late 1930s, Beria, made what is generally interpreted as a bid for supreme power. His first move was the resumption of direct control over the MGB which, it appears, had slipped from his grasp in Stalin's final year, when Ignatiev had replaced Beria's client Abakumov at its head. To regain control Beria not only merged the MGB with the MVD (of which he became the Minister) but also purged Ignatiev (who is believed to have been a client of Beria's rival, Malenkov) and launched an open attack on the Ignatiev period of MGB leadership by disgracing it for its role in Stalin's final bloody purge, the so-called 'Doctors' Plot'. Manifestly Beria's power bid failed. In mid-1953 Beria was himself disgraced and placed under arrest by his Politburo colleagues. On July 10 his arrest was announced to the world. At the end of the year he was executed alongside a number of leading Soviet Security officers.[5]

The meaning of these complex and bloody changes must have been extremely difficult for all foreign Residencies, and particularly the remote Canberra one, to discern. The disruptions within Moscow State Security, destroyed all predictable lines of command. In 1954 there were, indeed, a number of MVD defections — Rastvorov in Japan; Khokhlov in Germany; and of course, most famously of all, the Petrovs in Australia.

At the heart of the Beria crisis (between April and July 1953) Petrov was on notice of recall to Moscow. At first he was reprieved because of his eye troubles. Later, following the arrest of Beria, his recall was postponed altogether. His MVD offsider, Plaitkais, explained to a British officer that Petrov's flight to Moscow had been cancelled because 'everything [was] upside down at home'.[6] Despite this reprieve, in the context of the disgrace of the MGB, the downfall of Beria and the subsequent purge of the MVD, Petrov's low standing at MVD Centre and the hostility that had opened between himself (and his wife) and the Soviet Ambassador and Party Secretary at the Embassy, must have seemed particularly threatening.

According to both Petrov and his wife the protracted intrigues of the Soviet Ambassadors, Lifanov and then Generalov, and the Party Secretary, Kovaliev, were at the heart of their Australian woes. Petrov was a man of little eloquence but what little he possessed was unleashed in several post-defection monologues to his ASIO debriefers about the perfidies of Lifanov, Generalov and Kovaliev.

> My intention to settle for life in Australia was born approximately in 1952 at the time when Ambassador Lifanov, Kovalev (sic) and others began to hound me and my wife. . . . Their actions were directed to waging war against honest people. . . . We had to go through all this, bearing it on our shoulders and in our hearts. It was very hard to bear all the mockery and all the insults.[7]

According to his wife these intrigues reduced Petrov to 'such a nervous state that he could not speak normally but only with tears. His hands always trembled. I am surprised he did not commit suicide'.[8]

One source of the trouble between Petrov and his colleagues was his wife. As early as mid-1952 MGB Centre warned Petrov about the 'tactlessness' she was showing in her relations with Lifanov and others in the Embassy and instructed him to issue her with a reprimand.[9] As late as April 3 1954 in his phoney suicide note Petrov wrote of the false accusation directed against her 'of being a gossip and the chief culprit in the collective's dissensions'.[10] On several occasions after their defections the Petrovs acknowledged that much trouble had arisen from Evdokia's outspokenness. Sometimes they justified this on formal Bolshevik grounds (the right of Party members to the exercise of criticism); and on other occasions explained it as a consequence of her life-long passion for 'the truth'.[11]

There is no reason to doubt that Petrova's outspokenness within the Embassy and at Party meetings did indeed on occasions land the couple into trouble. To judge by her later performances at the Royal Commission Petrova's honesty did not take the form of compulsive truth-telling but of bursts of passion where caution would be thrown to the winds and even uncomfortable words uttered. Nor is there reason to doubt her claim that on occasion her criticisms (as Embassy Accountant) may have concerned the minor subterfuges over money matters practised by her Embassy colleagues, including the Ambassador. On the other hand the portrait she draws of herself in *Empire of Fear* (which apparently convinced Michael Thwaites) as an island of fiscal propriety in a sea of petty corruption is, as we shall see, somewhat misleading.[12]

There was, however, more to the difficulties surrounding Petrova in the Embassy than her sharp tongue. When she arrived in Australia she was an extremely attractive woman in her prime. Sexuality is frequently a destabilising force in institutions. It was especially likely to be so in the small and inward looking Soviet Embassy colony in Canberra in the early 1950s. Her presence was clearly resented by many of the rather dowdy women (including the wives of both Ambassadors) she rather mercilessly mocks in her portrait in *Empire of Fear*. Her overtly western taste in clothes, music and films, which set her apart from them, was a source of envy and the grounds for one of the earlier intrigues that was set in train against her. (The intrigue concerned an accusation that she had placed a photograph of a film star in too close proximity to the portrait of Stalin on her desk. Evdokia took the accusation extremely seriously. 'I wrote to the Central Committee, insisting on the baselessness of the change. I even enclosed a sketch of the layout of the top of my table.'[13]) Moreover it is likely at least that many Soviet and 'People's Democracy' males competed for her eye.[14] Evdokia believed that her husband's problems with Ambassador Lifanov arose, at least in part, from her rejection of his advances. When she first met Richards of ASIO in Darwin she told him that

> She felt as far as Lifanov was concerned her position was aggravated because he wished to make her his mistress and she had refused. This had resulted in a scene and she feels it was never forgotten.[15]

For his part, Petrov always believed that his Australian decline began in clashes with Lifanov. The first serious dispute appears to have occurred during the Revolution Day celebrations of 1952. More than six months after it had occurred Petrov confided to Bialoguski that he suspected this clash (in association with his many rows with Lifanov over his wife's work load) to be the cause of his recall to Moscow.

> [Petrov] told me that on the 7th November, 1952, the Soviet National Day, there was a party in the Embassy, and the Official on duty had a few too many; and that the Ambassador approached Petrov and asked him to remove this fellow from duty. Petrov refused. . . . On the next day there was a meeting in the Embassy, and the Ambassador charged Petrov with disobeying his lawful order whilst being under the influence.[16]

In *Empire of Fear* Lifanov's hostility to the Petrovs is explained in part in political and in part in biographical terms. Lifanov is said to have resented the Petrovs *qua* MVD officers because their presence 'represented a separate arm of authority which was safely under his control' and because he bore a long grudge against State Security as a result of the arrest of his brother in 1938.[17] Especially given the story of Lifanov's part in Sadovnikov's demise, there is no reason to doubt that Lifanov's hostility to the State Security presence in his Embassy was genuine.

On the other hand, if Lifanov (and later Generalov) needed a weapon in their campaigns, Petrov's fondness for the bottle more than provided them with it. From one point of view Petrov's Residency reads like a long chapter of drink-induced misfortunes. In July 1952 Petrov, driving his new Skoda under the influence,

> narrowly missed running down a Police constable. On arrival at the Embassy, (the constable in pursuit on . . . motorcycle), Petrov disappeared into the Embassy sending out another member to placate the constable and drive the Skoda out of sight.[18]

In November 1952, as we have seen, again while under the influence, Petrov clashed openly with the Ambassador. On Christmas Eve 1953 he overturned his car and almost killed himself on a country road outside Canberra.[19] In early 1954 he returned to Canberra from Sydney by aeroplane in such an intoxicated state that 'the airport officers of A.N.A. carried Petrov from the aircraft to two members of the Soviet Embassy who were waiting in the Airlines waiting room'.[20] By this time at least one Australian Communist do-gooder had reported on Petrov's public drunkenness to the Soviet Ambassador.[21]

There can be no doubt that Petrov's drinking did at the very least contribute considerably to the effectiveness of the Embassy campaign that was waged against him. In one of her outbursts at the Royal Commission, Petrova admitted that several hostile reports had indeed been made to Moscow by Lifanov and Generalov concerning Petrov's drinking, all of which were, she hastened to add, outright lies.[22] Although MVD drunkenness was far from uncommon, its official reporting was another matter. From the point of view of the MGB-MVD, Petrov's drunkenness (if not covered up) would have had to be regarded as a serious security risk and gross indiscipline. From the point of view of Soviet ethics, where personal lapses were invariably interpreted as willful acts of hostility to the State, it would have had to be viewed as a dangerous case of anti-Soviet behaviour. In Petrov's drinking in Australia there was, also, a vicious circularity. His drunkenness, no doubt, sharpened the weapons of his Embassy enemies in their campaign against him. In its turn, their campaign drove him, for consolation, to drink. In the final weeks before his defection, where several drunken incidents are clustered, he had become a truly pathetic fear-ridden figure, whose life seems largely to have passed outside his control.

After their defections the Petrovs claimed to have learned the worst about the Embassy campaign being waged against them through the influence they possessed with the chief cypher clerk, Prudnikov, who is said to have secretly shown to the Petrovs the various reports and cables concerning them sent by the Ambassadors to the Cadre Department of the Ministry of Foreign Affairs and by the Party Secretary, Kovaliev, to the Central Committee. Concerning Prudnikov and his leaks to the Petrovs much, however, remains murky. At the Royal Commission Petrov suggested that Prudnikov's motives in the affair were either 'friendship' or, alternatively, that in passing on these reports, he was fulfilling his role as a coopted 'SK' agent of the MGB.[23]

Characteristically, Petrova was less charitable. Prudnikov was in her view a 'double-dealer . . . [who] instigated the Ambassador and led him on against the Petrovs . . . [who] was obliged to show us what was happening to save his own hide'.[24]

Nor is the content of these leaks quite clear. Petrov at the Commission spoke of two leaked annual personnel reports from Lifanov to Moscow, the first of which commented favourably on Petrov and adversely on Petrova, the second of which commented adversely on both of them.[25] Petrova, as we have seen, admitted that the question of Petrov's drinking was raised in the telegrams of both Lifanov and Generalov. In evidence before the Royal Commission and elsewhere both claimed to have been harshly criticised (as 'enemies of the people') in Embassy party meetings and in reports to the Central Committee sent by the Party Secretary, Kovaliev.[26] According to Petrova the anti-Petrov stories were believed not only inside the Cadre Department of the Ministry of Foreign Affairs and inside the Central Committee but, even more ominously, within the MVD itself.

> We sent off our telegrams (she told the Royal Commission) to the MVD in which we described the whole slander which had been written to the Central Committee. . . . The reply which we received from Moscow to our telegram made us understand that they were believed and we were not believed. That, of course, meant a lot . . . and forced us to be afraid.[27]

Most seriously of all, the Petrovs, at the Royal Commission and in private, gave details of an accusation made after the announcement of Beria's arrest that they were working to establish an anti-Party Beria faction inside the Embassy. A fortnight after his defection Petrov wrote thus to his wife (at the time a virtual prisoner in the Soviet Embassy).

> If you remember Mr Lifarnov (sic) and Mr Kovolov (sic) accuse me in the same method as Beria of organizing a special group directed against Mr Lifarnov and Kovolov.[28]

More precisely, at the Royal Commission, Petrov gave details of a 'telegram of special importance', despatched in July 1953 by Lifanov containing the Beria accusation.[29] Somewhat differently, Petrova claimed that the Beria accusation had been first raised openly at an Embassy Party meeting shortly after Beria's arrest. According to Petrova it was at this time that her husband first discussed with her the idea of their staying in Australia and that he exhibited what she called his signs of 'madness'. 'He could not speak without crying; his hands were always shaking, trembling'.[30] In *Empire of Fear* the Beria story assumed its final and most definitive shape. Here it is stated that Prudnikov first showed them the Beria cable and that 'before his departure in September 1953, [Lifanov] brought his charges into the open at one of the Party meetings which were the battleground for the open part of the campaign'. Here he accused the couple of ' "plotting to form a Beria faction in our Embassy!" '.

Kovaliev backed him up. In spite of our indignant denials, the writing was on the wall. From that point it was either them or us.

Lifanov's object was obvious. He wanted the minutes of the meeting, endorsing what he had said, to reach the Central Committee, to convince Moscow that his quarrel with us was not a personal feud, but had the backing of the Party comrades in the Embassy.[31]

In the context of Soviet politics after July 1953 no more grave accusation could be levelled against the Petrovs than the Beria one. Such an accusation, if made in Canberra and accepted in Moscow, must have appeared to the Petrovs tantamount to a death sentence. There are, however, grounds for feeling a certain scepticism about the Petrovs' increasingly concrete accounts of the Beria accusation of September 1953. In part it is difficult to imagine how, if the Beria charge was made in September in the form suggested in *Empire of Fear*, the Petrovs were able to survive (seemingly unscathed) in the Embassy for another eight months. In Soviet political culture being accused of following a traitor to the revolution was not the kind of accusation that could pass without the immediate demise either of the accused or the accuser. An accusation of this kind was not the first shot in a political campaign but the final act in the purge process.

There is, moreover, no sign of such an accusation or of a Petrov maddened by fear in the Bialoguski reports to ASIO between July and September 1953. As it happened Petrov was in Sydney staying with Bialoguski at the time of the July monthly Party meeting. At midnight on the evening of July 22 Petrov telephoned his wife from Bialoguski's flat. Of their conversation Bialoguski reported thus.

Petrov said how did it go, did they talk about us. He got an answer everything went all right. He explained to me subsequently that there was a meeting at the Embassy and very often he said, the bastards try to put somebody in and they talk about each other. He said he had a row with Kislitzyn over his ... rudeness to Kucharenko. He said he despised the system of putting each other in.[32]

Nor is there any sign in Bialoguski's detailed reports of his August or September meetings with Petrov of any unusual distress. If anything, Petrov was, by September 1953, somewhat more chirpy on the Embassy front than he had been for some time. As he informed Bialoguski his nemesis there, Lifanov, had just received an unexpected notice of recall. Petrov expressed to Bialoguski his confidence of an improvement under the regime of his successor Generalov to whom he offered to introduce Bialoguski as soon as he arrived. 'He hopes', Bialoguski reported, 'that we will get along very well'.[33] Only once after July 1953 did Petrov discuss Beria with Bialoguski and this was merely to offer calmly his cynical opinion that the Soviet announcement of his arrest was a ruse to 'cover up for his absence' and 'mark time till he is caught'.[34]

It is significant that under examination at the Royal Commission

Bialoguski — a shrewd observer of Petrov and an outstandingly accurate witness — dismissed leading questions concerning the role of the Beria accusation in Petrov's decision to defect from Victor Windeyer, counsel assisting the Commissioners.

Windeyer:	Did he seem to you worried for himself because of the fall of Beria?
Bialoguski:	No, I would not say that.
Windeyer:	Did he ever mention to you that an accusation had been made against him in the Embassy in reference to Beria?
Bialoguski:	No, he never said that.
Windeyer:	Did he ever say that he would be marked down as a Beria man?
Bialoguski:	No, he did not say that either.[35]

In Bialoguski's opinion, as we shall see, the turning point for Petrov came not in July or September over a Beria accusation but in November in quite different circumstances.

Most probably the Beria accusation, which grew with time in concreteness and importance in the Petrovs' story of their defection, was an exaggeration based upon the couple's experience of the keenness of their ASIO interrogators to believe it. As we have seen the announcement of Beria's arrest had been the determining factor in ASIO's initial approach to Petrov. Moreover at the opening of the Royal Commission, Victor Windeyer (no doubt under ASIO brief) went so far as to misdescribe Petrov as a 'Beria man'.[36] Petrov had in fact twice encountered Beria briefly in the early part of the war against Germany. He was certainly in no special sense a client of Beria's. It is indeed doubtful if Beria in the early 1950s even knew of his existence. (Naturally it goes without saying that the *fact* that Petrov was not a 'Beria man' offered him no protection from the *accusation*.) For ASIO the Beria line vindicated its tactical judgement in the defection operation and endowed the Soviet Embassy campaign against the Petrovs with a political clarity it otherwise appeared to lack. For the Petrovs it may have been welcomed as a distraction from some of the less dignified aspects of their fall from grace.

For indeed between July and September 1953 the Petrovs were far from acting as a hunted and doomed couple under the shadow of an accusation as grave as that concerning the formation inside the Embassy of a Beria faction. Rather, in these months (with the assistance of Bialoguski in Sydney) they had embarked boldly upon a series of extremely dangerous money making ventures. One of these concerned the recovery of non-existent expenses during Petrov's sojourns in Sydney. On July 23, Bialoguski reported thus.

[Petrov] asked me about giving him a receipt for charges for accommodation. He said he will present it to the Embassy and he will be paid the maximum allowance which is 13/- per day. We went to Penfolds and I got a receipt book ... and wrote out a receipt on carbon paper.... The receipt is for three days accommodation for Mr Petrov at the Kirketon Private Hotel at a cost of £2.8.0. Petrov said he was sorry we did not do it all the time. We went and had a beer on the strength of it.[37]

Later, when other members of the Soviet Embassy were staying at the Kirketon, Petrov asked Bialoguski to make out a receipt from the Buckingham Private Hotel.[38] On the same visit he came up with another scheme, this time inviting Bialoguski to send to the Soviet Embassy grossly inflated bills for medical services.

> He said Mrs Kizlitzin will come on Sunday, to see me professionally.... He told me to charge her £30 ($360) and him [Petrov] £25 ($300), and send the account to the Embassy and it will be paid.

Petrov confided to Bialoguski that he had worked out this scheme 'with his wife who is the Embassy Accountant'. Indeed, he confessed, it was Petrova 'who actually suggested it'.[39]

By far the boldest, most lucrative (and ultimately for ASIO politically embarrassing) branch of Petrovian private enterprise concerned a trade in duty free whisky. The details of this trade can be pieced together from the Bialoguski reports to ASIO and the private papers of Dr Evatt and Eddie Ward. In July 1953 Petrov outlined his scheme to Bialoguski who in turn passed on its details to ASIO.

> At 11.30 a.m. Petrov and I drove to Sussex St. [the premises of Crawford & Co., Liquor Merchants] and picked up some cases of bottled drink, and we drove to my flat where the stuff was unloaded.
> The account for the drinks amounts to £42.6.3 and it is to the Soviet Embassy. Petrov said that next time he is in Sydney he will pay the account, and there is no danger as the account will be received by his wife who won't put it through the books. He took a few bottles for his personal use. I shall try to sell sufficient quantity to cover the bill, at Petrov's request. It is duty free.[40]

This report (and others soon after) reveals the mechanics of the scheme as follows. Petrov brought to Sydney the necessary forms and blank sheets of Soviet Embassy letterhead paper on which Bialoguski typed requests to Australian Customs and to Crawford & Co. (the agents for Bell's Special Whisky) for the supply to the Soviet Embassy of duty free liquor. Petrov and Bialoguski picked the cases up from Crawford's, paying for them with moneys from the Soviet Embassy accounts released by Petrova (without a record on her books), and returned with the cases to Bialoguski's flat, where they were stored. Some of the whisky was consumed by Petrov and Bialoguski (who later complained he had drunk enough with Petrov to last him a life time).[41] A little was given to Petrov's Sydney girl-friends as gifts,[42] while the remainder was sold at bargain prices to a number of Sydney cafes and night clubs. The receipts from sale were used to replace Embassy funds initially withdrawn, while whatever profit remained was presumably divided somehow between Petrov and Bialoguski.

Strangely enough, the sale of the whisky was almost certainly arranged with the assistance of the man whom ASIO had engaged to watch Bialoguski —

George Marue. Subsequently Marue wrote the following account of the Petrov-Bialoguski whisky business and his role in it.

> To get an idea what quantity of imported liquor Bialoguski was able to obtain every month, I bought from him few times in December, 53, January and February, 54 and reported to Fred that I had been able to buy from Bialoguski all together liquor for the amount of £700 ($8,400) — and I also knew that he was selling to other people as well. As I never had so much money that I could pay Bialoguski for the goods delivered C.O.D. I asked him for 3 days credit and he never refused. I had to resell the goods immediately which I did.[43]

There can be no doubt that by the late spring of 1953 Petrov, in his drinking, womanising and private enterprise, had begun to court considerable danger in the way he was managing his double life in Sydney. In evidence to the Royal Commission Petrov later claimed that Moscow had been fully informed about his flatting arrangement with Bialoguski.[44] However soon after his defection, in the privacy of the interrogation room, he had told a different story. 'Nobody knows that I was staying with the Doctor. I took a great risk'.[45] Some of the risks he was now taking were even quite unnecessary. Petrov, for example, with considerable bravado, invited the liquor merchant he dealt with at Crawford & Co., Vahrenkamp, to the 1953 Revolution Day celebrations in the Embassy at Canberra.[46] He was also becoming rather careless with the different false identities he was assuming with the various women he was seeing in Sydney.

> Petrov (Bialoguski reported drolly) said his name was Karpitch and he is a Bulgarian. Miss Edgar remarked that he is a mystery man as he first was Polish, then Bulgarian, and he comes with a little bag from the sky.[47]

4

OPERATION CABIN 12

By late September 1953 Petrov, who had seen the departure of his old enemy at the Embassy, Lifanov, was living in the hope of a revival of his fortunes under the regime of Lifanov's successor, Generalov. On the other hand his Sydney friend, Bialoguski, smarting from his 'irrevocable' dismissal from ASIO but refusing nevertheless to drop Petrov, was living in the hope 'that something would turn up'.[1]

As it happened, the disappointment of Petrov's hopes proved to be the fulfilment of Bialoguski's. The arrival of Generalov on October 3 marked no improvement whatsoever in the fortunes of the Petrovs. As Petrov explained subsequently:

> Mr Generalov saw all these reports about me in Moscow before he came to Australia and when he came out here he must have seen that the whole atmosphere in the Embassy was perfectly normal. Nevertheless he sent home to Moscow an adverse report on me and said that the atmosphere was worse than he expected.

According to Petrov, Generalov submitted his report within three days of arriving in Canberra. 'How could he possibly know what the atmosphere was like after three days?', he enquired plaintively of the Royal Commissioners.[2] As usual the bearer of bad tidings was Prudnikov who showed Generalov's telegram to him. Petrov realised now that the campaign against him extended well beyond the field of Lifanov's personal intrigues and vindictiveness. According to his wife, Petrov now began to live in fear that their home was under the surveillance of Soviet Embassy enemies.[3]

Worse, however, was still to come. On November 20 Generalov announced the immediate dismissal of Petrova from her post as Embassy Secretary and Accountant and her replacement by Vislykha, wife of the Embassy First Secretary. Petrov came limping to Sydney and Bialoguski in panic and despair. The exact reasons for Petrova's sacking will probably never be known. To Bialoguski Petrov attributed his wife's downfall to her criticisms of Generalov within the Embassy and to the bitter hostility that existed between Petrova and Generalova. Her diligence and the scrupulousness of

37

her care for the Embassy accounts had come to nothing! The couple were now completely isolated inside the Embassy. Both contemplated suicide. Petrov informed Bialoguski that it was 'better to work on the roads' in Australia than to 'live in daily fear of your life'. If Bialoguski is to be believed Petrov's brooding on his suffering at the hands of Lifanov, Kovaliev and now Generalov had led him to the formulation, in explanation of his misfortunes, of a primitive theory of the New Class. 'Mr Generalov, another bloody member of the upper caste. They're the new rulers.' Petrov was more than ready to accede to Bialoguski's suggestion that Evdokia's sacking was really a part of the campaign to destroy him. At the time and subsequently, Bialoguski was convinced that Petrova's dismissal as Embassy Secretary and Accountant was the turning point for Petrov in his decision to defect.[4]

Before Petrov brought his terrible news to Sydney Bialoguski had for some weeks been placed in a rather delicate legal situation, cultivating, being cultivated by, and offering assistance to a Soviet intelligence officer without the sponsorship of any counter-intelligence service. His mood in relation to ASIO was no doubt exceedingly black. Indeed at some time prior to Petrov's fateful Sydney visit he had actually (as he admitted under the cross-examination at the Royal Commission of the Communist barrister, Ted Hill) gone to the *Sydney Morning Herald* and begun negotiations about a series of articles on his role as an ASIO under-cover agent. Bialoguski claimed that these articles would primarily have concerned 'Communist front organizations' (presumably exposés of the peace movement), but he also conceded that his trip to the *Herald* was 'partly' at least connected with his cultivation of Petrov. When Hill suggested to him that he had in fact mentioned there the name of Petrov Bialoguski readily conceded that he had.[5]

If ever ASIO's view of Bialoguski — as an unscrupulous mercenary — was to be vindicated by his behaviour during the Petrov Affair it was here. By mentioning Petrov's name at the *Herald* in the context of discussions concerning his own work as an under-cover agent, Bialoguski (whether to avenge ASIO or merely to make money) had placed Petrov's life at considerable risk. Newspapers are, notoriously, institutions which live on leaks and gossip. Undoubtedly Ted Hill knew of Bialoguski's *Herald* visit through some leak, most likely after the Petrov defection, from an employee there. If, however, news had leaked to the Soviet Embassy before Petrov's defection he would almost certainly have been bundled back to Moscow in mortal danger.*[6]

Now that Petrov had come to him with news of Evdokia's sacking,

---

* As Michael Thwaites properly remarks it was indeed something of a miracle, given Bialoguski's garrulousness, that Petrov's proposed defection never reached the ears of the Soviet Embassy. On the other hand what Thwaites fails to consider is that by sacking Bialoguski in September ASIO had greatly increased the likelihood of a Bialoguski indiscretion. ASIO's own reading of Bialoguski's character, as an unscrupulous mercenary, actually provided the best argument for retaining his services not dismissing him.

Bialoguski had to rethink his strategy. In his book on the affair he explicated his situation and the line of his thinking thus.

> What was to be my next move? I thought of the newspapers, or at least of one in particular, because I had contacts with the *Sydney Morning Herald*, but decided against it. I felt that the necessary official imprimatur was lacking. . . . This brought me back again to Security, and the scales were tipped in favour of renewing my contact with the Department by my feeling of friendship and loyalty to North.[7]

For once Bialoguski, in this account of his approach to ASIO on November 23, is less than candid. His account is, in fact, misleading in regard to detail, motives and mood. As the newly released ASIO files on the Petrov Affair make clear Bialoguski telephoned ASIO in order to threaten them. At 4.30 p.m. on November 23 Richards telephoned Colonel Spry with the following blunt and urgent message.

> Bialoguski has informed Gilmour that Mrs Petrov has got the sack from her job at the Embassy and that she and her husband wish to defect. He is willing to assist and bring them to us if we will take him back into his former work, otherwise he will take them to the newspapers.[8]

Richards' telephone call to Spry set the alarm bells ringing inside ASIO. On the following day, November 24, Spry conferred with Thwaites in Melbourne and by telephone with his Regional Directors in Sydney (Richards) and Canberra (Phillipps). Interestingly Phillipps was asked 'to inform Secretary of External Affairs of possible defection'.[9] This is the first evidence of ASIO's involvement of a non-intelligence branch of government in the affair. Strangely enough it appears from the documentary record at least that the Secretary of External Affairs was informed of a possible Soviet defection ten weeks in advance of the Prime Minister. Colonel Spry's military experience had made him very wary of precipitate and unnecessary predictions to those whose trust in his judgement he required.[10]

On November 25 a conference of ASIO's counter-espionage branch was held in Melbourne. The memorandum produced by Colonel Spry as a record of its deliberations bristled with suspicion of Bialoguski. How strong were his grounds for claiming the Petrovs were about to defect? What had he so far told the newspapers he was writing for about 'this possible "defection" and his relations with ASIO?' What did Bialoguski want for himself? Was he in trouble with the police or the BMA (presumably this referred to Bialoguski's abortion practice) or with the Communist Party (certainly this referred to his undercover work for ASIO)? According to Spry's memorandum choosing either to deal with Bialoguski or not to deal with him had its dangers. In the latter case the danger was that Bialoguski may take 'Petrov and Wife to the Press'. In the former the dangers were no less real and certainly more various.

> (i) He may be attempting to discredit us. E.g., Defection may not occur and bearing in mind our past action, Bialoguski may assume that we will make a direct

approach to Petrov, with consequent 'diplomatic fuss'.
(ii) That Petrov has become suspicious of Bialoguski, and is trying out him and/or ASIO. We should remember the case of Dr. Beckett.

Evidently ASIO counter-espionage were still far from discounting the possibility either that Bialoguski was a Communist triple agent or an unconscious dupe whom Petrov was using to lead them into a carefully prepared trap. Even if, however, both these theories were false there was no doubt in ASIO about the moral standards of their former agent. Bialoguski, they warned themselves, 'may use unethical means to produce the bodies'.[11] (This may have been a reference to ASIO's knowledge of a previous occasion where Bialoguski had slipped Petrov a sleeping drug before picking his pockets.)

Clearly ASIO did decide that the risks and potential costs of not dealing with Bialoguski outweighed the risks of dealing with him. On November 26 some time after the Sydney meeting between Spry, Thwaites and Richards, a second memorandum had been prepared as a guide to Richards in his planned meeting with Bialoguski. Richards was to impress upon Bialoguski that 'the Government will not consider granting Petrov and wife asylum if they are (not ...) brought to us'. If the defections occurred without ASIO Bialoguski was to be warned that he would be treated as personally 'responsible' for any harm that befell the Petrovs or any complaints they subsequently raised about their treatment. No 'incitement' to defect could be tolerated. Petrov must be delivered for his protection to ASIO as soon as possible after his defection decision, at which time he would be expected 'to give some clear indication' of good faith towards the Commonwealth of Australia. (Precisely what this might be was not specified.) For his part Bialoguski could expect adequate recompense for his exertions (possibly as much as 'several hundred pounds') but only when the Petrovs were delivered to ASIO and had voluntarily requested 'political asylum in this country'.[12]

On November 27 Richards met Bialoguski, re-employed him and acquainted him with the list of ASIO demands for his future handling of the Petrovs. Bialoguski appears to have accepted the ASIO brief happily enough, although he privately regarded ASIO's warning (that if he failed to deliver the Petrovs to ASIO after their defection he would be held responsible for any harm that came to them) as legal 'poppycock'. In the new financial arrangement there was a certain give and take. Bialoguski's weekly payment was raised to £20 plus any unusual expenses (not the £25 he had demanded) but he was given £50 to cover his costs for the period of his sacking. It was not, as he put it, 'red carpet' treatment but at least he was back.[13]

In reality, Bialoguski's threat of November 23 proved as significant a turning point for ASIO as Petrova's sacking of November 20 had been for Petrov. ASIO and Bialoguski were now formally reconciled and ASIO had completely revised its negative assessment of the likelihood of the Petrovs' defection. Most importantly of all, the Petrov operation was now given the highest priority at ASIO headquarters and placed under the personal control of Colonel Spry and his director of operations, Ron Richards. According to the ASIO internal history:

> From this point until Petrov's defection Richards was in constant touch with the Director-General, reporting each development and discussing each step in the case.[14]

At the other end of the operation Richards from this moment was also in direct contact with Bialoguski who thus no longer made contact with ASIO planners through intermediaries. In early December ASIO rented a safe house in Sydney (initially for a month) in preparation for an imminent single or a double Petrov defection. Their Petrov enterprise was code-named 'Operation Cabin 12'.[15]

At the very moment ASIO, having been aroused by Bialoguski, was preparing itself for a defection, Bialoguski discovered that Petrov had gone slightly off the boil. On the evening of Bialoguski's re-employment Petrov had arrived in Sydney and stayed at the flat. 'He was still a worried man', according to Bialoguski, but 'the note of hysteria which was apparent at our last meeting had gone'. Instead of an imminent defection Bialoguski now reported merely 'solid progress' and a discussion with Petrov where he had indicated his interest in farming in Australia.[16]

Clearly Bialoguski had either exaggerated Petrov's post-November 20 mood or the crisis had passed. Old patterns in Petrov's life, at least in part, re-established themselves. In early December when Petrov travelled to Melbourne ASIO placed him under intense surveillance but noticed nothing of especial operational interest except his fondness for alcohol and the tendency when under its influence 'to waive discretion in his desire for female company, even to the extent of accosting women in the street'.[17]

ASIO and Bialoguski were now forced once more to wait and plan. In the month of December two lines of approach, both Bialoguski initiatives, were tried. On December 12, with ASIO's knowledge and agreement, Bialoguski drove Petrov to inspect an appallingly named chicken farm — 'Dream Acres' — outside Sydney, which belonged to his wife's sister and her husband and which was up for sale. Bialoguski pretended to Petrov to have come into some money recently on the stock market and to want the farm for himself. He asked Petrov to advise him and to pose as the prospective purchaser under the assumed name of 'Peter Karpitch' (which he had previously used in his courtship of Miss Edgar). The aim, clearly, was to whet Petrov's appetite which, according to Bialoguski at least, clearly succeeded. Petrov was very keen. On the journey home from the farm Bialoguski offered now to purchase the farm for Petrov at a cost to himself of £3800.[18] If Petrov did not now suspect that there was more to Bialoguski than met the eye he was a very dim intelligence officer indeed. Most likely he decided upon the willing suspension of his suspicions, and to allow the tide of Bialoguski's plans to carry him along. Unlike the earlier Adria Cafe proposal, in the 'Dream Acres' scheme there could at least be no question but that Bialoguski was now contriving in a scheme for his defection. Between Petrov and Bialoguski a crucial psychological line had been crossed.

Five days after the journey to 'Dream Acres' Bialoguski tried a second gambit — the arrangement of an apparently accidental meeting between Petrov and the man he knew Petrov suspected of being connected with Australian counter-intelligence, Dr Beckett. Feeling himself and not ASIO to be in control of Beckett, Bialoguski's view of the good doctor's usefulness to the Petrov operation was now radically revised. His aim was now to boost Beckett in Petrov's mind, to bring Petrov and Beckett together socially, and to use Beckett as the intermediary through whom Petrov would finally make contact with ASIO. ASIO approved this line of approach. On December 17 Petrov was successfully bumped into Dr Beckett outside his surgery in Macquarie Street. To Bialoguski's satisfaction Petrov and Beckett (who knew nothing of Bialoguski's plans for him[19]) talked heartily. After their chat Petrov expressed a desire for a more substantial meeting. On December 23 Bialoguski conveyed to Beckett Petrov's keenness for a future lunch or dinner and on the 24th, after Beckett had informed ASIO of Bialoguski's approach (of which he wrongly assumed they were ignorant) ASIO briefed Beckett on how to conduct himself in the proposed future meeting with Petrov. If Petrov made 'overtures to stay' Beckett was to assure him 'he could put him in touch with people who could assist him', so long of course as he was 'genuine'.[20]

By late December 1953, in the strange triangular relationship of Petrov, Bialoguski and Beckett, the question of who knew what about whom was becoming exceedingly complicated. According to his own witness Beckett thought Bialoguski was merely a friend of Petrov's and a disillusioned Polish Communist on the point of fleeing to London for musical and political reasons.[21] Petrov and Bialoguski were both quite convinced that Beckett had an ASIO connection. Petrov knew Bialoguski knew he suspected Beckett of this connection. How strongly Petrov also suspected Bialoguski of a similar connection is impossible to determine. Finally, behind Bialoguski and Beckett stood ASIO, to whom both were reporting separately upon Petrov and each other.

Before Christmas 1953 nothing had been consummated on either the 'Dream Acres' or the Beckett front. Petrov had expressed his continued interest in the chicken farm but had asked Bialoguski to wait for his decision until after the New Year. No meeting between Petrov and Beckett, to whom Bialoguski had explicitly mentioned the possibility of a defection, had proved possible before Christmas.

As it happened, Christmas 1953 must have been a dreadfully miserable time for Petrov. Some time in the early morning hours of December 24 his car had overturned on the Canberra-Cooma road and completely burned out. Petrov, who was bruised and cut, knew he had been lucky to escape with his life. He claimed he had been forced off the road by a truck and, not unnaturally given his present state of mind, wondered whether his Soviet colleagues were behind some attempt on his life. Inside the Soviet Embassy he received little sympathy. Petrov had never renewed the insurance policy on the Skoda he had inherited from Pakhomov. Generalov demanded he pay for a replacement with his own money.[22] When he eventually emerged from the Soviet Embassy to speak to the Canberra police about the accident he misled them on a number of points, at least partly because he wished to conceal from them the purpose of his trip to Cooma — a conspiratorial rendezvous with Madame Ollier of the French Embassy.[23] Only an unusually heavy evening in Sydney with Bialoguski to bring in the New Year could temporarily mask his growing despair.[26] Petrov was now a changed man. In early January 1954 someone who knew him well, the United Kingdom Passport Officer, George Hawkins, reported to ASIO that 'Petrov is now much more reticent and has lost his former jovial attitude'. Hawkins noticed that when he lit a cigarette his hands were shaking noticeably.[25]

On Petrov's first Sydney visit after the New Year Bialoguski took a rather sozzled 'Peter Karpitch' to talk again with the rather bemused proprietors of 'Dream Acres'. ASIO had supplied Bialoguski with £50 (Karpitch's holding deposit on the farm) and, for the first time, a wire recorder which Bialoguski was instructed to instal in his car. ASIO were very keen to have a voice record of Petrov discussing his desire to defect, almost certainly not with any intention of using it as a weapon to blackmail him into defection (an unwilling defector would prove a nightmare to any counter-intelligence service) but to safeguard themselves in the case of any future allegation by Petrov of an ASIO 'incitement'. ASIO, as we have seen, still feared a Petrov trap.[26]

From ASIO's point of view the significance of the wire was that they now had in their possession a record of Petrov voluntarily discussing his interest in settling on a farm in Australia. From the point of view, however, of the later history of the Affair the most significant aspect of the wire recording of January 9 concerns the question of dates. When Bialoguski first began to operate the recorder he asked Petrov to indicate at least approximately when he proposed to take over the farm. Petrov responded at once, 'in April', and when asked for something more definite, 'about the 5th'.[27] Although Bialoguski had suggested this date might be too far in the future Petrov nevertheless clung to it. As it turned out April 5 was two days from the date of Petrov's actual defection, which occurred on the day of the arrival of his MVD successor Kovalenok. It is unlikely that this was coincidence. During January Petrov had been informed of his recall to Moscow and at least its approximate date.[28] Judging by the wire recording of January 9 it seems most likely that he had already been informed of the precise date of his successor's arrival and that, through some foggy belief that a proper handover of affairs would minimise the dangers to himself or even because of some residual police-bureaucratic tidiness of mind, had already decided to leave the service of the MVD only after handing its Australian affairs to Kovalenok.

The later conspiracy theory of the Petrov Affair would suggest that Petrov's defection was saved up by Mr Menzies and precision timed for the election of May 1954. The evidence shows not only, as we have seen, that ASIO had high hopes for his defection in July-August and then again in November-December 1953. It also at least suggests that by January 1954 Petrov had already determined that if he defected it would be on the arrival of his successor. It appears that early April had become for him now the one fixed point in his extremely uncertain future.

The morning after their return from 'Dream Acres' Petrov (who was already drinking) came to Bialoguski's bedroom, bearing a *Sydney Morning Herald* article on social conditions inside the Soviet Union as his text, and let forth a torrent on the iniquities of the Soviet system.

> Look at that man! [Malenkov] He and his clique live in luxury, just as the Tsars did, while the masses of Soviet people grovel in poverty! Three million Russians refused to go home after the war. They were better off as prisoners of the Nazis! But if you go to Russia and say these things they'll cut your head off! Look at Beria — killed after he himself had killed thousands. . . . Why shouldn't Russians live and let live, open their frontiers, they can't fool anybody anyway; foreign diplomats can see the whole thing for themselves. I will stay here, I will tell the whole truth, I will write a true story, I will fix those bastards.*[29]

This was the first occasion in the Bialoguski reports in which Petrov's words unambiguously had moved from complaints about Embassy intrigues and personal misfortunes into a thoroughgoing criticism of Soviet Communism. Petrov's early morning tirade of January 10 clearly became (at least after his defection) a cherished record in the files of ASIO's counter-espionage branch, quoted more or less verbatim in ASIO's internal history of the Petrov defection, in the Petrovs' own *Empire of Fear* and, later still, in Michael Thwaites' *Truth Will Out*. It would be a mistake to underestimate the desire inside ASIO's counter-espionage branch to believe that Petrov had defected not merely to save his skin but that he, too, like Kravchenko and Gouzenko before him, had 'chosen freedom'. The Cold War was a time when Western passions ran deep (even inside counter-intelligence agencies) about the genuinely profound moral contrast between the communist and democratic worlds and when defectors were prized as the witnesses to the evil of one world and the promise of the other. While, unfortunately, for his part

---

* I have not been able to locate the original report as submitted by Bialoguski. My version uses where possible the words quoted in ASIO's internal history (the latter half of this quote) and where it has been paraphrased the version published in *Empire of Fear* and *Truth Will Out*.

in this drama poor pickled Petrov was singularly miscast, his performance of January 10 at least gave ASIO B2 branch some heart.

If in the long term Petrov's outburst helped ASIO endow Petrov's defection with a moral dimension it might otherwise have seemed to lack, in the short-term it proved an opportune moment for Bialoguski to offer Petrov help, for the first time quite openly, in making contact with Australian Security. Both Bialoguski and Petrov now looked towards Dr Beckett. The first meeting was arranged for January 15 but at the last minute Petrov pulled out. On January 23, however, Bialoguski was able to get Petrov to dinner at the Becketts'. After Bialoguski discreetly absented himself Beckett offered to put Petrov in touch with someone who could help him to stay in Australia and guarantee him the necessary financial assistance and physical protection. When Beckett (quite coincidentally) spoke of the possibilities in Australia of running a restaurant or a chicken farm Petrov seemed to him 'quite enthusiastic'.[30] Bialoguski, however, a far shrewder Petrov-watcher than Dr Beckett, thought he was still rather 'non-commital'.[31]

Independently Beckett and Bialoguski reported their versions of the dinner to Richards.[32] On January 28 Richards visited Beckett and briefed him. The next time Beckett saw Petrov, if he was convinced Petrov was really 'serious', he was to try and arrange the long awaited meeting between Petrov and Richards. The mood of tense expectancy in the Sydney office of ASIO is reflected in a letter Richards sent down to Colonel Spry by courier before his meeting with Beckett. The position was now, he believed, 'critical'. Petrov had shown 'real signs of anxiety' at Mascot where Richards had watched him on the previous day. 'Our potential guest has sought and received assurances by two people of financial assistance and personal protection when he comes to us.' The future of the operation remained, however, 'tricky and difficult'. Richards thanked Colonel Spry for the confidence being shown in him and informed him of the 'complete silence' he had imposed inside ASIO's Sydney office.

> So far we have steered the operation clear of acts which could be proved provocative and I am most anxious that it should continue that way, particularly in this most crucial stage and bearing in mind the characters we are using and dealing with. I have, therefore, warned all concerned that a careless word could now undo all the work put into the case and, in addition, make the Government and us the target of an embarrassing attack.

In Richards' view the main barrier to Petrov's defection was his wife. Petrov had asked Bialoguski to go to Canberra to sound her out. Despite the dangers (Bialoguski would have to take care not to 'compromise himself'), Richards thought he should go. 'I feel he could handle the situation.'[33] Colonel Spry was not so sure. 'The danger of leaving her in an anxious state of mind, possibly leading to indiscreet talk, is obvious.' On the other hand he believed it might be dangerous to veto the visit if Petrov had his heart set on it. If the visit went ahead Spry thought that Bialoguski's approach to

Petrova should be both 'very general and tentative'.[34] In fact on January 30 Bialoguski's Canberra trip did go ahead. When the prospect of staying in Australia was first raised with Petrova she expressed indignation and commitment to the Soviet cause. Bialoguski believed that in reality, while she had little concern for her father and brother she was deeply worried about what would become of her mother and sister if she defected. He reported that in the formal part of her conversation she praised Marxism-Leninism-Stalinism and in the informal part the dress sense of the British Empire's new Queen.[35] The visit had neither fulfilled Petrov's hopes (of winning Petrova to the defection cause) nor ASIO's worst fears (that Bialoguski might be compromised or the operation blown). After January 30 Petrova remained what she had been before, an enigma and an obstacle.

There was little for ASIO to do now with Petrov but to wait upon his next move. While waiting, however, Colonel Spry decided that the time had come to brief the responsible officers of the Australian Government on the possibility of Petrov's defection. Within ASIO a short briefing paper had been prepared — 'Considerations concerning a possible Soviet defector' — which pointed out that two ASIO sources had recently confirmed the possibility of a request by a Soviet diplomat, believed to be an MGB officer, for political asylum. This diplomat, it was argued, had been in contact in Australia with a 'number of suspect persons' and was considered, if he came over, a likely source of valuable intelligence.[36] This paper was shown to the Solicitor-General and Secretary of the Department of External Affairs (Mr Watt) for comment. In addition, between February 9 and 11, Spry came to Canberra to discuss with them and with the Minister of External Affairs (Casey), the Attorney-General (Senator Spicer) and the Prime Minister the possibility of the Petrov defection.

Strangely enough, the records of these briefings suggest that the Solicitor-General, Professor Bailey, who had served with Dr Evatt under Chifley, was the most 'machiavellian' of the servants of the Crown Spry spoke to in Canberra. Bailey suggested to Spry the value of fear in extracting intelligence information from Petrov. 'Any complaint by him with regard to his protection would enhance his value as a supplier of information to us, and may be a means of obtaining further information.' He was also of the view that asylum should not be offered to Petrov merely to 'save his skin'. He had no doubt that the defection would cause 'high diplomatic and political repercussions' and that therefore asylum should only be offered 'for something we get out of it, viz information on the case etc'. 'The case' he had in mind was the series of leakages to the Soviet Union from External Affairs (during Dr Evatt's Ministry) which had been responsible for the foundation of ASIO.

At least to judge from the documentary record Professor Bailey was the first member of the Australian Government to suggest to ASIO the virtues of holding a Royal Commission into Soviet espionage on the Canadian-Gouzenko model.

As regards possible legal outcome of the information obtained, in the Solicitor-General's opinion a Royal Commission could be a possibility and a fruitful means of propaganda. The Canadian Royal Commission report was referred to.

Bailey and Spry seem to have seen a Royal Commission as a means of alerting the Australian public to the dangers of Soviet espionage, as a kind of school to the nation. It is highly unlikely that the 'propaganda' value Bailey spoke of had for him any party-political meaning, although if either he or Spry had dreamt of the later troubles it is highly unlikely either would have allowed the word to intrude into the record of their meeting.[37]

As might have been expected the response from External Affairs to the possibility of the Petrov defection was considerably less robust than those of ASIO or even Professor Bailey. In a preliminary comment the then secretary of the Department, Alan Watt, had appeared overwhelmingly concerned with the welfare of the Australian legation at Moscow. 'They may', he predicted, 'try to frame one of our people, who may just disappear'. Less drastically the Soviets might terminate the lease on the Embassy in Moscow, withhold supplies from it, or deprive it of 'servants'. To minimise such risks Watt argued that the Soviet Embassy at Canberra must be granted 'access to the parties after the event, in our company'.[38]

Colonel Spry (courtesy of John Fairfax and Sons)

Colonel Spry's February 10 meeting with Watt's successor, Arthur Tange, was slightly less dominated by the social welfare aspect of the defection, although Tange did demand from ASIO 'that if subject or his wife desired at any time to return to the Embassy they would not be forcibly held by us'. The question of Soviet access to the couple would be considered in the Department 'from the point of view of the protocol'. External Affairs agreed that ASIO and not themselves should handle the Petrovs and that no notification of the defections would be given to the Soviet Embassy before they issued a protest. ASIO and External Affairs were at one on the desirability of keeping Immigration out of the affair for as long as possible.[39]

On February 10 Spry went from Bailey to Tange and from Tange to Menzies. This meeting — the first documented record of an ASIO discussion with the Prime Minister on the Petrov case — is of considerable interest because of the later claims of the conspiracy theorists of Menzies' sinister role in the affair and of considerable sensitivity because of Menzies' post-defection suggestion in the Parliament that he had known nothing whatever about Petrov before early April 1954. Because of its significance to the history of the affair the official ASIO record of the meeting is quoted here in full.

On 10/2/54 the Prime Minister was given a preliminary briefing and the question of the evidence of probable defection and subject's membership of M.G.B. were discussed. The Prime Minister was informed by the Director-General that the whole operation had been most carefully handled so as not to give any grounds for a suggestion that the defection had been provoked.

The Director-General stated that the reception of subject had been most carefully planned and every necessary precaution taken and that he was hopeful that nothing would go wrong.

The question of a Royal Commission was discussed and also the Prime Minister agreed that the protection of subject should be undertaken by A.S.I.O. and that there was no necessity to inform Immigration Department for the present.

The Prime Minister was informed of the discussion with the Secretary, External Affairs and with the Solicitor-General and agreed that he would make the necessary statement in due course but that it might be necessary for the Attorney-General to make some statement for him.

He agreed that the statements should not be shown to the Minister, External Affairs, or officers of External Affairs.

Agreed that they should be short and to the point.[40]

The fact that this internal ASIO record of the meeting between Colonel Spry and Mr Menzies is referred to as a 'preliminary briefing' seems to make clear that Menzies had no knowledge or involvement in the Petrov operation at any time prior to February 10. It also makes clear that the idea of the Royal Commission emanated not from Mr Menzies but was suggested to him by Colonel Spry as a result of discussions earlier that day with Professor Bailey. Spry's main objective seems to have been to assure Menzies that ASIO was showing due caution on the diplomatic front and to try and win Menzies' support against the natural departmental enemy of an ASIO operation such as this — External Affairs.

There is no evidence, either one way or the other, of Menzies' personal response to Spry's briefing. In his memoir on the 'Petrov Spy Case' he comments blandly,

> On February 10, 1954, Spry consulted me, told me that a defection was possible, and that the possible defector was probably a member of the M.V.D. . . . It is his memory that he for the first time mentioned the name of Petrov to me. There was no particular reason for me to remember an individual name; and in fact I did not.[41]

Whether Menzies' political instincts were in any way aroused by his discussion with Spry and whether he kept in touch (through Spry) with the progress of the operation between the day of his briefing (February 10) and the defection of Petrov (April 3) cannot be resolved one way or other on the basis of the documentary evidence.

By February 17, one week after the Prime Minister had been briefed by Colonel Spry, five copies of a document of the highest possible security sensitivity had been produced at ASIO headquarters. The document — 'Operation Cabin 12: Necessary Action In Preparation for Possible Defection' — was ASIO's Petrov campaign plan. It represented, in part, the agreements arrived at on February 10 and, in part, weeks of ASIO tactical planning.

Before the coming of the Cold War when Igor Gouzenko had defected in Canada he had found extreme difficulty in finding anyone in authority even willing to receive him and his wife. At the other end of the Cold War the Petrovs' reception was prepared with military precision. The ASIO preference was for Petrov (and if possible also his wife) to defect in New South Wales and to pass there under the protection of Ron Richards who was issued by Spry with a document authorising him 'to receive any person or persons on behalf of the Government of the Commonwealth of Australia seeking political asylum'. Fully equipped safe houses (with everything from wire recorders to whisky) were made ready in both New South Wales and Victoria. If Petrov defected in Canberra elaborate plans were drawn up for ASIO officers of the ACT to deliver him to Richards at a rendezvous point on the Wombeyan Caves Road in Mittagong. The cars carrying Petrov were to be fitted with recording devices and concealed cameras but the ASIO officers were not to be armed. They were instructed not to interrogate Petrov but to obtain whatever information came spontaneously from him and were not, under any circumstances, to let him know 'that he is liable to become a principal witness' in legal action arising from his defection. If he asked about Bialoguski the Canberra officers were to profess ignorance of him. If he wanted to return to his Embassy he was not to be detained by force. Even the manners of the ASIO officers bearing Petrov to the safe house had been pre-determined by headquarters. They were to be 'friendly but official'.

As soon as he defected Petrov was to be given (*pace* Professor Bailey) a guarantee of 'fullest physical protection' and of 'livelihood' in Australia 'so long as his cooperation continued'. If he wished, the Commonwealth would purchase a farm for him ('Dream Acres' was still a possibility) and guarantee him a decent income for two years. (There was as yet no mention of a lump sum payment.) On the other hand, it was to be impressed upon him that he must 'establish his bona fides by giving the fullest information in his possession'.

The campaign plan underlined that the 'primary task' of the whole operation was 'the extraction of intelligence information from him'. Nothing must be allowed to impede this objective. Petrov was to be pumped at once for any information concerning Soviet espionage in Australia 'which calls for immediate action'. In general the material from him was to be obtained in a manner that made it legally usable. In the light of subsequent political allegations it is interesting that there was only one mention in the campaign plan of Petrov as a supplier of 'documents' of intelligence interest. After his defection Petrov was to be asked: 'Is he in possession of any Embassy or other documents?'

The defection of Petrov was to be accompanied by intense ASIO activity throughout Australia. Surveillance was to be mounted against the 'Tass' man Antonov, the Soviet Embassy, John Rodgers of Australia-Russia House in Melbourne, the Australia-Soviet Friendship Leagues, the Communist Party headquarters in each state, and finally against any 'leads' provided as a result of the initial interrogation of Petrov. 'Monitoring' (presumably phone tapping) of Antonov, the Soviet Embassy (on a twenty-four hour basis), Rodgers, Communist headquarters, and of two Control Commission Party members, M.J.R. Hughes and H.B. Chandler, was also to be undertaken. If Petrova defected with her husband their bedroom was to be fitted with a recording device.

Interestingly, at the top of ASIO's lists of those requiring 'surveillance' and 'monitoring' was 'Crane', i.e. Bialoguski. Bialoguski was to be separated from his friend, Petrov, as soon as practicable and warned not to make any statements to the press. In gratitude for his services he was to be paid an 'honorarium' of £500 ($6000), offered a share in the profits of any book about the Petrov story that might be produced and, if he remained useful and cooperative, continued employment by ASIO. All of this was, of course, in reality hush money. Even the earliest of the suspicions of Bialoguski remained alive. One of the lines of interrogation being prepared for Petrov concerned Lydia Mokras and her knowledge of Soviet espionage organisations in Australia.

A short statement on the defection had been prepared which it was now agreed the Minister for External Affairs would deliver. External Affairs had won another point. If the Soviet Embassy so requested, a meeting, limited to half an hour, between the Petrovs and Soviet officials would be permitted.

The meeting was to be recorded and Richards present. ASIO was to be responsible for protecting the Petrovs from any Soviet 'violence' which might break out during the course of this interview.

There is one additional small detail in the campaign plan which reveals the tension and excitement inside ASIO in February 1954. The Commissioner of Police in the ACT was to be briefed about the possibility of a stream of defectors from the Iron Curtain countries descending upon Canberra in the wake of the Petrov defection.[42]

5

END GAME

On February 19 1954, two days after the ASIO campaign plan had been completed, Bialoguski successfully coaxed Petrov into accompanying him once more to visit Dr Beckett, this time with the express purpose of asking Beckett to arrange a meeting for Petrov with his 'friend' in the Security Service. For his role at this meeting Beckett had been briefed by ASIO and primed by Bialoguski.[1] The wire recorder secreted inside Bialoguski's jacket documented that on the way to the Becketts' Petrov revealed to his friend that the official notice of his and Petrova's recall to Moscow on April 5 had been received. Petrov now thought his wife would almost certainly return. 'If it was not for her it would have been a different thing.'[2]

After a round of drinks Dr Bialoguski, on Petrov's behalf, asked Dr Beckett directly whether he could arrange the meeting between Petrov and the Security friend, whom Beckett now named as Richards. Beckett, as a result of his ASIO brief, had one main point to make. 'You must understand that no Commonwealth Government man could possibly approach you — you must approach him — because the international complications could be very serious.' Petrov indicated understanding. Within his earshot Beckett telephoned Richards and a meeting between the two principals was arranged for the following morning in Bialoguski's flat. The meeting, it was stressed, was 'unofficial'; nothing said there would go beyond Richards. After the company had drunk a toast to Petrov's future in Australia (with appropriate accompanying banalities) and Beckett and Bialoguski had completed a discussion on language and culture in Europe (where Beckett revealed his belief in the existence of an Austrian language), Petrov and Bialoguski departed the Beckett home in search of 'some girls'. Once outside, their conversation quickly turned from Dr Beckett to the human condition.

> *Bialoguski*: He is a decent fellow and he is unpretentious. That is the main thing.
> *Petrov*: Yes, he is not out to shoot men of my type . . . . Let a man live, he only has one life. You kill him and everything is finished. Even if he acted like a hooligan, why destroy him?

Bialoguski: Human beings are not saints.
Petrov: They are all rascals, do you understand?[3]

The following morning Petrov was in a 'restless' mood and departed hurriedly on business before the agreed meeting with Richards.[4] Throughout the day Richards remained in contact with Bialoguski by telephone but Petrov did not return to the flat until mid-afternoon.[5] On his return it was clear Petrov would not see Richards on this visit although a quasi-conversation between Richards and Petrov did take place with Bialoguski acting as a go-between. Richards, through Bialoguski, offered Petrov immediate 'assistance'. Petrov, through Bialoguski, declined. However another meeting time was arranged for February 26.[6]

Not a word had yet passed directly between Petrov and Richards but by February 20, at least from ASIO's point of view, some progress, in the form of two indirect telephone exchanges, had been made. Petrov seemed temperamentally best suited to this slow motion march towards a meeting. More importantly Petrov's thinking had made some progress. On the evening of February 20, after he had returned to Canberra, Petrov (apparently unbeknown to his wife) saved from the flames the letters from Moscow Centre of 1952 which the couple, under official instructions, had been required to commit to the MVD furnace.[7] If the Petrovs' evidence on this point is to be believed, by February 20, then, Petrov had already begun to collect the documents for his defection and to do so behind the back of his wife in order that she might not be implicated in his act.

Petrov returned to Sydney not on February 26, as had been planned, but on the 27th. Bialoguski picked him up at the airport, started his wire recorder, and set to work upon him at once. Richards, Bialoguski told Petrov, had now become 'anxious' about his safety. If anything nasty were to befall him in the Embassy there was nothing Security could do to help him. Richards had investigated the conditions of assistance the Commonwealth could offer Petrov. Bialoguski thought them very generous. Richards seemed to Bialoguski a 'responsible person ... fairly young, you know, very sympathetic'. He had 'full authority to speak in the name' of his Government. Above all he was most keen now to speak personally with Petrov. 'He feels responsible for your — how can I express Volodia — welfare.'

Petrov remained uncertain. Perhaps, he suggested, they might meet the next day. When they arrived at the flat (where Bialoguski turned on a radio with the racing results from the Newmarket meeting at Flemington to drown the hum of the recorder) Bialoguski's pressure mounted. It was no use, he said, speculating on the conditions Richards might offer. 'If conditions are not suitable and you decided to go you can say, forget all about, bye, bye and away you go.' Petrov was not so sure. A meeting with Richards would be very 'dangerous'. Bialoguski tried to soothe his fears. 'Nobody has authority to force you to remain here ... Don't think there is any blackmail ... Englishmen are not fools, generally speaking.' Slowly Petrov's resistance was worn away, his curiosity overtaking his anxiety. 'Do you think we can find out everything?' 'Yes, everything.' At 6.25 Petrov finally agreed to allow Bialoguski to telephone Richards and invite him to the flat. At long last he had taken the plunge.[8]

In the early evening of February 27 1954 the first of the meetings between Petrov and Ron Richards prior to Petrov's April 3 request for ayslum took place. The suggestion that something sinister transpired at these meetings has long been a central feature of the Petrov conspiracy theory. As its most influential recent exponents put it:

> The more facts one gathers the more likely the conspiracy theory becomes. . . . The most conspiratorial — and most undocumented — element remains the series of meetings between Richards and Petrov on at least twelve occasions from 28 February (sic) to the time of the defection. It has been suggested they were manufacturing, or at least, embroidering the documents that were to prove so useful to Menzies.[9]

As it happened, during many of the meetings between Petrov and Richards, beginning with the meeting in Bialoguski's flat on February 27, an ASIO wire recorder was employed, on most occasions successfully. Amongst the recent archival releases on the Petrov Affair are not only detailed memoranda of these meetings but also the verbatim transcriptions of the conversations where the minifon was working and cassette copies of the actual wire recordings themselves. It has now become possible to discover precisely what occurred between Richards and Petrov at these meetings. As we shall see the new evidence makes clear beyond reasonable doubt that there was no eleventh hour ASIO-Petrov conspiracy to forge (or tamper with) documents for the purpose of helping Mr Menzies or injuring Dr Evatt. It also makes clear that the version of these meetings given by Richards at the Royal Commission was substantially accurate. On the other hand, the new evidence reveals that, on one central and sensitive issue — the relationship between money and documents — Richards' account at the Commission was significantly misleading.

At the first meeting on February 27 Petrov's main interest was in the conditions the Commonwealth could promise if he (and his wife) should stay in Australia. As had been predetermined by ASIO planners, Richards was authorised to offer Petrov physical protection from Soviet reprisal efforts (Richards thought this kind of protection might be required for two years or longer), a 'new identity', and financial security for the future. A fund of 'several thousand pounds' had been set aside to help establish Petrov on a farm or in a business enterprise of his choice. While Richards did not offer Petrov any specific sum of money at this interview, he did suggest that the assistance to Petrov might be stretched to as much as £10,000 ($120,000), depending on the line of business. 'It is very difficult to say whether it is going to cost £5,000 or £10,000'. Bialoguski, acting in the role of Petrov's legal representative, made the fine print inquiries. Would Petrov's living expenses be deducted from the capital sum? Richards assured him they would not.

What would be the attitude of the Commonwealth to the publication of a book or newspaper series? Richards expressed great enthusiasm for the idea, offering ASIO's assistance 'in writing the story and getting it on the proper market'. An anti-Soviet work from the pen of Petrov was, Richards assured Bialoguski, precisely the kind of guarantee the Commonwealth sought to assure themselves that Petrov's defection was 'genuine' and that he was 'no longer part' of what Richards delicately called 'this other business'.

In front of Petrov, Richards and Bialoguski enacted a political charade. Richards admitted to certain concerns about Bialoguski's left-wing leanings. Bialoguski assured him he would be discreet. Petrov for a moment assumed the role of intermediary between Richards and Bialoguski. The doctor had once, he joked, been 'a fighter for peace' but had been drawn away from such nonsense under his influence. Petrov looked straight into Bialoguski's eyes and assured Richards, 'I will trust him'.

Considerable discussion, naturally, concerned the position of Petrova. Richards, of course, made clear that the same protection and financial security offered to Petrov would be extended to her. But would she stay? Petrov thought she was '50-50'. Had Petrov, Richards enquired, discussed the question of staying with his wife? Petrov claimed that indeed he had. She was, however, concerned about the wellbeing of her parents and brother and sister in Moscow, despite the fact that she had no better grounds for feeling confident of her homecoming than he had. Indeed, Petrov told Richards, much of their trouble stemmed from her 'critical' tongue which had wagged in the Embassy. Richards expressed his concern about the same tongue. Might Petrova give away his secret to the Ambassador? Petrov expressed only limited confidence on that front. It was 'possible but unlikely'. What, then, would happen to him if she talked? 'Oh, they would kill me.' What, Richards asked, would happen to him if he returned to Moscow in the light of the adverse Embassy reports on him? Petrov put his finger, 'like a gun', to his head.

The defection question now remaining to be discussed was not whether but when. Richards on several occasions assured Petrov that if he wished to defect that very evening there would be no delay. Richards had full authority to receive him in the name of the Commonwealth of Australia as soon as Petrov signed the document he had brought with him requesting political asylum. Petrov slowed Richards down. His successor at the Embassy was arriving on April 3 and he suggested to Richards that this was a likely choice for his defection date. Nevertheless he promised Richards a firm decision by the 'middle of March' when, through Bialoguski, he would make contact once again with Richards.

At no stage in their discussions of February 27 was the question of the production of intelligence documents raised let alone made a condition of Richards' offer of protection and financial security. Richards merely asked of Petrov on February 27 that he tell him 'the truth about everything you know', to which Petrov pledged to tell 'the truth — everything'. Somewhat inauspiciously when in the very next breath Richards asked him for his position at the Embassy, Petrov omitted to mention that he was the MVD Resident in Australia. According to Richards' evidence Petrov throughout the interview was in a highly nervous state, sweating freely and laughing at odd and unexpected moments.[10]

On the evening of February 27 a similar thought came independently to Richards and Bialoguski. Petrov, they both believed, needed something more 'tangible' than mere promises of financial security to help him overcome his doubts. Richards discussed this question with Colonel Spry on the evening of the 27th and in person with Bialoguski on the following day. Bialoguski confirmed Richards' prognosis. Petrov should be shown the money that would come to him when he defected. The figure of £5000 ($60,000) which had been mentioned to Petrov on February 27 (at the lower end of the scale of possible help) was by now in everyone's minds. Richards spoke to Spry by telephone again on the evening of February 28. A draft for £5,000, dated March 3, was despatched to the ASIO office in Sydney. When he next met Petrov Richards was prepared to allow Petrov to inspect a far from unimpressive vision of his future in Australia — a bundle of £10 notes amounting to £5,000.[11]

It was not until the evening of March 19 that Richards and Petrov met again, once more through the good offices of Bialoguski, at his flat. Richards found Petrov 'much more composed than on our previous meeting. He was tidy and neat and clean in appearance, and quite sober'. The conversation rapidly took a decisive turn. Petrov told Richards he was now quite determined to remain in Australia. He would return to Canberra after this trip but would stay permanently the next time he came down to Sydney. Richards, as planned, took the £5,000 from his bag and showed it to Petrov. Petrov promised to tell Richards 'everything' when he defected.

Richards, however, pushed him a little further. 'Can you give me any idea what I can expect to learn?' He might have to make what he called 'special arrangements' if the story turned out to be of 'great importance'. Petrov indicated that he understood where Richards was heading. 'I know your position Mr Richards. I can tell you what you want to know.' Richards now laid his cards on the table.

> I said, I think I should make it clear to you that if your information deals not only with your experiences in the Soviet Union . . . but also describes and identifies Australians or others in Australia, who are being or have been disloyal to their country by the helping the Soviet in ways that could have serious effects to the security of Australia . . . you will be provided for and looked after according to the degree of your importance.

Petrov indicated that he understood what Richards meant, but Bialoguski asked for even greater clarity. Richards, in turn, now offered Petrov £10,000 if he could provide ASIO with information on Australians who were involved in Soviet espionage.

> If Mr Petrov is able to give information of real value and interest to me . . . in my main responsibility of giving security to Australia against persons in Australia who work to destroy its present system of government and way of living, he will be rewarded accordingly. It could mean that the £5,000 now available would be doubled.

At this point in the conversation Richards asked Bialoguski to prepare some sandwiches. For the first time he and Petrov were alone. Petrov agreed to a meeting next day 'without the doctor'. Richards asked whether Petrov knew the names of any Australians who had passed intelligence to the Soviets. Petrov indicated that while he knew some names no-one knew them all. 'Some of it was before I came to Australia.' As Bialoguski re-entered the room Richards and Petrov broke off this line of conversation and discussed the details of the defection. Petrov would come to Richards after meeting his successor in Sydney on April 3. When Bialoguski left again they returned to the main theme. Petrov offered to get whatever documents he could from the Embassy. (This was the first mention of documents in the Richards-Petrov discussions). It would not, however, be easy. 'We have special girls doing things with the documents . . . but I have a lot in my head already.'* At once Richards emphasised his interest in documents and reiterated the financial advantages to Petrov if he managed to bring some with him. On the other hand, he warned Petrov not to take any unnecessary risks.

The relationship between money and documents on March 19 differed both from the accusations against ASIO brought down subsequently by Dr Evatt and his supporters — namely that ASIO's £5000 was offered as the purchase price of the documents — *and* from the case maintained by ASIO at the Royal Commission — namely that at no stage was there a money bargain between Richards and Petrov over documents. The evidence makes clear that while, as ASIO maintained throughout the Royal Commission, Petrov would indeed have received £5000 without any documents, on March 19 Richards offered to double his defection lump sum if documents of interest were produced. There was, however, no question whatsoever (as the wilder conspiracy theorists believed) of Richards asking Petrov to produce documents harmful to Dr Evatt or the Labour movement let alone of offering to work with him to 'forge' or 'embroider' documents. Richards made clear to Petrov that what ASIO wanted was documentary evidence of Soviet espionage in Australia. In Canada in 1945 documentary material from Gouzenko had been invaluable in exposing Soviet espionage (and taking action in the courts

---

* Either Petrov was lying here to Richards or he lied subsequently to the Royal Commission on Espionage when he claimed to have collected the 'Moscow letters' of 1952 on February 20, 1954.

against it) and in breaking one of the Soviet's atom bomb spy rings. ASIO no doubt now hoped that documentary material from Petrov might prove as fruitful.*[12]

As arranged, Petrov telephoned Richards next morning and a rendezvous was prepared for midday. Richards led Petrov to an ASIO flat near the Cross and the couple embarked upon their first completely *sans* Bialoguski conversation. As soon as Petrov had inspected the flat for obvious technical aids (of which there were none, not even a minifon recorder) Richards returned to the espionage business of the previous day. Would Petrov be able to inform him 'of the persons in Australia who give secret information to the Soviet Government?' Would he be able to produce 'copies of the reports'? Petrov promised to do what he could. There had been, he informed Richards for the first time, a 'very serious situation' in External Affairs during and after the war. Richards asked if the situation was still continuing. 'Not much now — they are frightened.' Were they 'important people' in External Affairs? After considerable reflection Petrov said that one had been. Was he still in the Department? He was. Had the Australian Communist Party been 'involved in this business'? It had.

At this meeting no names were named by Petrov. Clearly he was holding his vital information in reserve. Almost as an afterthought Richards enquired of Petrov whether there would be a war soon. Petrov thought 'not yet'. For his part Petrov took the opportunity to apologise for Bialoguski's manners. 'The doctor talks a lot about money for me. I am not worried about that — I trust you to take care of me.'

On the evening of March 21 Richards met Petrov for the third time in as many days, once more with Bialoguski in the flat. Much discussion had taken place on the two previous occasions and again now on the position of Petrova. Petrov was most concerned that no publicity be given his defection before his wife's departure for the Soviet Union. He was worried either that she might be killed in the Embassy or used as a hostage by the Embassy to threaten him. Petrov agreed in principle to a scheme proposed by Richards for ASIO officers to make contact with her on the ship taking her home, bearing a note from her husband. Petrov did not discount the possibility that she might defect, at the last moment, in Fremantle. (There was as yet no thought that she might be flown out of Australia.) At the meeting of March 21 it was finally agreed that no efforts would be made either by ASIO or Bialoguski to 'induce her to stay' prior to Petrov's own defection. On the Petrova front Petrov now preferred to allow events to take their course. Clearly the Petrovs had discussed the possibility of her defection (she had recently been in Sydney which had appealed to her) but equally clearly she was playing upon Petrov's darkest suspicions about the treatment the couple were likely to receive at the

---

* The meetings of March 19-21 were not recorded on a minifon. The record of these meetings is contained in a very detailed memorandum completed by Richards on March 22, 1954.

hands of Australian authority. 'My wife says,' Petrov confided to Richards, 'that we are like the Rosenbergs if we stay'.[13]

Only practical details, or so it seemed, now remained to be settled. Bialoguski tentatively agreed to meet Petrov at Canberra Railway Station on April 2 and to drive him to Sydney with his beloved Alsatian, 'Jack', in tow. Richards was alarmed by this development (taken in his absence) and resolved to warn Petrov against it. He was now determined to keep a semi-permanent eye on his valued ward. On March 23, at Mascot airport, Richards passed Petrov a note which outlined a rendezvous in Canberra in two days time.

On Thursday March 25 Richards drove to Canberra. Shortly before nine o'clock that evening he picked up Petrov (and 'Jack' who breathed down Richards' neck from the back seat) and drove around the outskirts of Canberra. A recorder was working, although its sound quality was very poor. Richards had intended to warn Petrov about the dangers of the Bialoguski-'Jack' defection plan, but Petrov's news brought him far greater cause for concern. Petrov made clear he had now decided not to remain in Sydney on his next visit but to return to Canberra with his successor. It would now be two weeks or even more before his defection. Petrov offered Richards some consolation. He would be able, he suggested, to discover from his successor a great deal about the Beria purges being conducted at home. Petrov had more, equally disturbing, news. He showed Richards a letter, written in Russian, which had been sent to the Ambassador and which the Ambassador had shown to him. Its contents suggested to Richards that news of Petrov's coming defection might have leaked.*[14] Perhaps, he speculated, the doctor might have talked indiscreetly.

Richards was by now thoroughly alarmed. The entire defection operation seemed threatened by these new developments. He enquired of Petrov whether he thought the delay was wise. 'I'm worried, you know, I'm worried about you now'. 'What', he ventured 'if my chief thinks that it's a really risky situation . . . and he feels you should make the break next weekend . . . what do you think?' What Petrov thought was far from clear. The more Richards pushed on this question the more Petrov evaded. The most Richards could achieve was an agreement to meet on the following evening, clearly to chew over the same questions again.[15] On that evening and again on the following morning Richards discussed the new Petrov difficulties with Colonel Spry, who was in Canberra.

As arranged Richards and Petrov met on March 26 in an ASIO car at the rear of the Hotel Kingston shortly after seven o'clock. They talked for a little under an hour. Once more the wire recorder was working but on this occasion the sound quality was excellent. In his slow, patient and reassuring manner Richards opened with a theme to which he would return in their conversation

---

* The letter read: 'Part of your maps or plans are being known or disclosed. Zalivin is a very very big foolish man. For this I congratulate you. With regards KH'.

time and time and time again.

> My chief came up today to see me and I told him of the talk we had last night. He thinks that the situation is very dangerous for you, risky, and he thinks ... when you come to Sydney next week ... [you should] stay if you can.

Petrov tried to reassure Richards that there would be no great risk in the change of plan. He spoke vaguely of a defection in two weeks time, possibly sooner. Richards doubted that any additional information he might gather was worth the risk. The longer the conversation went, the more definite did Richards become. 'Every day is dangerous. . . . My advice is go down, do your work, meet these people ... and stay with me. Don't come back.' Petrov, however, would not be budged.

The best Richards managed at this meeting was to get Petrov to agree that he would think seriously about the timing of the defection before their next meeting, arranged for the following Tuesday, March 30. Petrov also agreed, albeit rather vaguely, that at this meeting he would sign the request for political asylum and then talk in person to Colonel Spry, who would be present. There would be no publicity given, he enquired of Richards? 'No, no.' He was also concerned that after his defection the Soviet Embassy would approach Mr Casey, who might order the Australian police to search for him. Richards gave him a brief (and no doubt unconvincing) lesson in Australian federalism. The Australian Minister for External Affairs had no authority to order the state police to do anything. In any event noone would be told of the locality of the safe house. Richards was more concerned that neither 'Jack' nor Bialoguski should be brought to the safe house. Both were too conspicuous and might reveal Petrov's whereabouts to his enemies. Did many people in the Party know him? 'Oh, many, many, many.'

The conversation of March 26 turned from safety to espionage questions. Richards had not been able to discover anything definite about the author of the letter to the Soviet Ambassador. He suggested, however, that there might be some link with a pro-Soviet immigrant, Jan de Lager. Did Petrov know of this de Lager? Petrov claimed he did not. (Again, somewhat inauspiciously for their future relationship, his answer here was probably somewhat unsatisfactory from Richards' viewpoint. ASIO had information that in January 1954 Petrov had spent the night at de Lager's Melbourne home).[16] They also discussed, once more, 'the Case'. Richards showed Petrov a photograph (most likely that of Walter Clayton) which Petrov could not identify. They also discussed again the prominent figure in External Affairs who Petrov had mentioned in Sydney. He was now, Petrov reaffirmed, 'very still'. If Richards hoped for his name on this evening he was disappointed. Later, Petrov promised, he would 'name names'.

During the latter part of the conversation Richards asked Petrov whether there was anything else he would like to discuss. Petrov delicately alluded to a topic of considerable interest — money. In great detail and without the slightest ambiguity Richards made clear again precisely what was on offer. If Petrov defected at this moment, with no more information than he had already delivered, £5000 was waiting for him. He could expect a large sum for writing a book. If, moreover, he brought with him documentary evidence of Soviet espionage in Australia then 'the money we've shown to you . . . will be only a small amount of what we will pay you'.

> If your information is of extreme value and you have something to support it — you may have a report or something like that — then, as I told you before, it could be £10,000.

As they were about to part company Petrov mentioned that he could help 'in another thing . . . not in spies but in other things'. Richards was interested but emphasised that it was 'important if you can help us with spies, you know that, Peter'. 'That' (Richards emphasised the words with considerable *gravitas*) 'is the very important thing'.*[17]

Petrov's procrastination ended on March 31 1954, broken not by Richards' persuasive powers (or Menzies' wizardry) but by the renewal inside the Soviet Embassy of the campaign against him and his wife which, ominously enough, coincided with the scheduled arrival of Petrov's MVD successor, Kovalenok. On March 30 when Petrov and Richards met briefly (Richards had returned to Canberra after the weekend at home) Petrov had still not decided when he would stay permanently in Sydney.[18] On March 31, after an Embassy Party meeting had brought down charges against the Petrovs (which included the charge that Petrova had behaved insolently towards the Ambassador's wife on New Year's eve) Petrov told Richards that his mind had been made up — 'may-be'.[19] Soon after this meeting Petrov discovered that his Embassy desk and safe had been raided by the Ambassador and First Secretary and documents discovered there which were out of place (happily, not *the* documents). On April 1 Petrov, who was by now in a genuine state of panic, told Richards he would travel to Sydney next morning and never return to the Embassy. It was agreed that Richards would also fly next morning to Sydney and that on the evening of April 2 Petrov would at long last sign the request for political asylum (which had been burning a hole in Richards' pocket for a month) and meet finally with the head of Australian Security, Colonel Spry. Even Richards seemed quite confident now that Petrov was ready. When late on the evening of April 1 Petrov scampered from his car Richards spoke the following words into his wire recorder:

> Petrov has just left me. He has left with me a bag and a rifle for me to take down to Sydney tomorrow. He has informed me that he has definitely made up his mind to stay in Australia and will not return to Canberra.[20]

---

* The complete conversation of March 26 is available at the Australian Archives only on tape. The ASIO file of transcriptions of minifon recordings makes available only the first half of the conversation. This does not include the money discussion.

Throughout the night of April 1-2 ASIO cars cruised around the Soviet Embassy and the private homes of its members looking for any unusual signs of movement which might indicate the impending detention of the Petrovs. On the following morning, as planned, Petrov and Richards flew to Sydney.[21] They exchanged a few words at Mascot. It was agreed that Petrov would telephone Richards in the early afternoon and that they should meet at once in the ASIO flat at the Cross where they had first met alone on March 20. When they met there Petrov took from his satchel two white envelopes wrapped in a copy of *Pravda* and showed Richards an assortment of documents — some in Russian, some in English. After Richards had perused them they were returned to the satchel. Petrov mentioned now, for the first time,

On the point of defection

that he was an officer of the MVD. He still, however, did not sign the document requesting political asylum. At four o'clock Richards left Petrov alone at the ASIO flat where he wanted to sleep. At six he returned and Petrov now signed the request for political asylum. Shortly after eight Richards formally introduced Petrov to Colonel Spry.[22] Their conversation began with a discussion of Australian marine delicacies.[23]

Petrov slept overnight on April 2 at Bialoguski's flat. Bialoguski had by now been removed from the centre to the edge of the defection operation. Since March 21 he had known nothing of what had transpired between Richards and Petrov. When Richards turned up at the flat that evening it was primarily to mislead Bialoguski. Richards and Petrov were now conspiring to keep him in the dark about the details of Operation Cabin 12.

On the morning of April 3, again as planned, Petrov left Bialoguski and went to Mascot to greet a Soviet party, which included his successor Kovalenok. Kovalenok's first words on the surface were reassuring. All would be well for him when he returned to Moscow. Petrov, who had been a member of the NKVD-MGB-MVD for more than twenty years responded privately to these assurances with alarm. His worst fears seemed confirmed. An ASIO party, which included Richards, picked him up at Mascot. Petrov, however, had one final official task to perform — a handover of money at the Kirketon Hotel to a Soviet party on its way to New Zealand. Arrangements to drop him off and pick him up were improvised hastily. Richards looked on anxiously as Petrov, document-satchel in hand, left him once again. When he completed his work at the Kirketon, Petrov, suspended for a moment between his past as an intelligence officer and his future as a defector, had a beer or two in freedom. His thirst quenched he returned to the waiting ASIO car (inside which nerves were on edge) and was driven to the safe house on Sydney's north shore. On arrival Richards handed Petrov £5000 and Petrov passed Richards the documents in his satchel. He had now defected.[24]

PART II
Politics

6

THE ANNOUNCEMENT

As soon as he arrived at the ASIO safe house on April 3 Vladimir Petrov, despite his terrible mental state, set down to work. Almost at once he composed a curious letter to the new Embassy Secretary and Accountant, Vislykha, which tied up certain loose ends of unfinished official business (he enclosed a receipt for the £10 he had passed on to his New Zealand-bound colleagues and £6-15-0 in unspent Soviet funds) and then notified the Embassy of his impending suicide. While the substance of the suicide note was, of course, false (designed to throw his colleagues off the scent of his defection) its spirit came directly from the heart. Petrov wrote with deepest feeling about his nervous collapse as a result of the persecution he and his wife had suffered at the hands of Lifanov, Kovaliev and Generalov. 'Let them bathe in my blood.'[1]

At three o'clock in the afternoon the serious business of the defection began. With the assistance of an interpreter (who Petrov privately feared to be a Soviet mole[2]) Richards began to debrief Petrov. The first formal debriefing extended over six hours. At its end Richards had managed, with considerable difficulty, to extract from Petrov twenty pages of handwritten information concerning his life and career inside the NKVD-MGB-MVD, Soviet espionage in Australia and the nature of the documents he had brought with him in his satchel.[3]

Richards was, of course, intensely interested in the documents. As Petrov explained, one group consisted of the letters sent by the MVD* Centre to their Canberra Residency in 1952. Eventually they were to become known as the 'Moscow letters' and to be labelled by the Royal Commission on Espionage as Documents A-F. In the unprocessed form in which they were delivered by Petrov to ASIO on April 3 the 'Moscow letters' were incomprehensible. It would take days of hard labour, translation and complex decoding of words and figures, with the assistance of Petrov, before the 'Moscow letters' would

---

* In general, for the sake of convenience, the term MVD will be used as a comprehensive description of the KI-MGB-MVD in the years of the Petrov's intelligence function in Australia.

67

surrender their meaning. The second group of documents brought over by Petrov were a variety of Russian language notes, extracts of MVD letters and transcriptions of material, in Sadovnikov's and Petrov's handwriting, all originating from the period of the Sadovnikov Residency. These documents were eventually to become known as the 'G' series. Unlike the 'Moscow letters' once translated the meaning (if not the significance) of at least a great deal of this series was relatively clear cut. Many of the Australians who were listed in the 'G' series as of potential value to Soviet intelligence had long been of interest to ASIO, and some of extreme interest. It was probably the lists of names in the 'G' series which initially reassured ASIO that Petrov's documentary material was genuine and that they were not being fed 'disinformation'.[4]

In addition to the 'Moscow letters' and the 'G' series Petrov had brought with him two English language documents, both of which appeared to be of far less significance than the Russian language ones from the espionage point of view. The first of these was a short three page typescript describing those characteristics of the Canberra press gallery likely to be of interest to the Soviet intelligence service — financial situation, drinking and sexual habits, religious affiliations and political allegiances.[5] Petrov informed Richards that this document had been prepared in Canberra in 1951 by a journalist for the Tass-MVD man, Pakhomov. Eventually the profile of the Canberra press gallery was to be labelled by the Royal Commission Document 'H'. Finally Petrov on April 3 handed Richards a long thirty-seven page typescript analysing the American and Japanese penetration of Australia but with a single page included concerning Dr Evatt and the ALP.[6] Petrov told Richards that this document had been composed in 1953 inside the Soviet Embassy by the Australian Communist, Rupert Lockwood, under the supervision of Antonov, Pakhomov's 'Tass' and Security replacement.[7] Eventually the document Petrov attributed to Lockwood was to be christened Document 'J'. 'J' was perhaps the least significant part of the haul Petrov brought with him. Nevertheless, as we shall see, it was destined to haunt the political imagination of Dr Evatt and his supporters and to become the central document in the controversies and conspiracy charges which eventually overtook Australian politics and the Petrov Affair.

From the political point of view the most startling information Petrov supplied ASIO in April concerned the author not of Document 'J' but of Document 'H' — the Canberra press gallery profile.

> The man (Petrov informed Richards) is not a member of the Australian Communist Party, but he is a sympathiser of the Party. He is not now a newspaperman — he is now an important man with the Australian Government. He is a responsible secretary to a member of the Opposition. He is the Private Secretary to Dr Evatt, the leader of the Opposition.

Petrov named the author as 'Frank O'Sullivan'.[8] However, as his description would have instantly revealed to Richards, the author of Document 'H' was not Frank but Fergan O'Sullivan, who was not the Private but the Press Secretary of Dr Evatt. Since his appointment by the Leader of the Opposition in April 1953 ASIO had been concerned about O'Sullivan's Communist connections. He had twice been, as we shall see, the subject of conversations between Dr Evatt and ASIO.[9]

Petrov had handed ASIO *prima facie* evidence that one member of the small staff of the Leader of the Opposition had in the past, while employed on the *Sydney Morning Herald*, supplied apparently valuable information to the Soviet intelligence service in Australia. The ethos of ASIO under the Director-Generalship of Colonel Spry, which derived from his military training and service and the strict separation in the British tradition of the military and political realms, was fundamentally opposed to permitting any party-political consideration to deflect in any way the fulfilment of what it saw as its security duties. Nevertheless after the debriefing of April 3 Colonel Spry and Ron Richards must have been aware of the extreme political delicacy of the information Petrov had passed on to ASIO about the Soviet intelligence connection of Dr Evatt's Press Secretary.*[10] If Mr Menzies were to reveal to the world before the election day, May 29, Fergan O'Sullivan's authorship of the Canberra press gallery profile, the future Document 'H' might play in the Australian election of 1954 a role not dissimilar to the role the 'Zinoviev letter' was believed to have played in the British election of 1924.[11]

On April 4 Colonel Spry, Ron Richards and ASIO's Russian interpreter — with the Petrov documents in hand — left Sydney bound for an interview in Canberra with the Prime Minister. On the journey one of the tyres on the ASIO car in which they were travelling blew out, although luckily before the blow out actually occurred the party had noticed something was amiss and had pulled up by the side of the road. Colonel Spry noticed that the tyre was cut on the inside of the wheel and, such was the atmosphere of tension at the time, suspected the possibility of an assassination attempt.[12]

The meeting with Mr Menzies, which extended over an hour or an hour and a half, went ahead as planned. Unfortunately no contemporary record of what transpired at this meeting has been located in the ASIO or Prime Ministerial files. Subsequently both Colonel Spry and Richards remembered it as an extremely unsatisfactory meeting. The attempted literal translations of the 'Moscow letters' were virtually meaningless. Menzies skim read documents 'H' and 'J' and was, no doubt, told by Spry of Petrov's information about the authors.[13] According to what Menzies later told the Parliament before the Petrov defection he had never heard the name of Fergan O'Sullivan.[14] During the course of the meeting Menzies directed ASIO to prepare translations of the Russian documents 'as soon as possible'.[15]

---

* Richards at the Royal Commission claimed not to see any party-political implications in the information given. In the atmosphere of the Commission by this time he could hardly have said anything else.

It is almost certain that the question of the holding of a Royal Commission into Soviet espionage, mooted as early as February 10, was discussed between Menzies and Spry on April 4. It would be wrong to imagine that Menzies either initiated the idea or imposed it upon a reluctant ASIO. It is Sir Charles Spry's memory that in the post-defection discussions between himself and Mr Menzies he was even keener than the Prime Minister on the idea of appointing a Royal Commission to investigate, in the light of the Petrov defection and documents, the subject of Soviet espionage in Australia. In part this was a matter of precedent. After the Gouzenko defection the Canadian government had established a Royal Commission which had eventually produced an outstanding report on Soviet espionage in Canada which was extremely highly regarded inside ASIO. In part it was a matter of legal necessity. Under the statute of its establishment ASIO had been given no legal power to require of anyone that they must speak to its officers or answer their questions. By agreement with Mr Menzies it was clear that the Royal Commissions Act could be amended readily to give it the power of subpoena. Finally it was in part a matter of public education. Colonel Spry believed that the proceedings of a Royal Commission might alert the Australian people to the reality and danger of Soviet espionage. 'We thought', he explained in 1985, 'that by having the Commission we would awaken Australians "that it can happen here".' On the question of the establishment of a Royal Commission Mr Menzies, although somewhat sceptical at first, required little convincing.[16] The timing of the defection announcement was, of course, ultimately in Mr Menzies' hands.

In the safe house in Sydney Petrov worked steadily with Ron Richards, Leo Carter, John Gilmour and ASIO's Russian interpreter to prepare material for the impending announcement of his defection and the establishment of the Royal Commission of which he was, as yet, totally uninformed. By April 9, through their joint efforts, Colonel Spry was able to despatch to Mr Menzies (via Colonel Phillipps) translations of three of the six 'Moscow letters' and a preliminary list of the Australians who had been allotted code-names by the MVD.[17] When this information reached him on April 11, Mr Menzies — according to what he subsequently told the Parliament — determined finally to ask his Cabinet, due in two days' time, to agree to the establishment of a Royal Commission.[18]

In the five days between April 6 and April 10 ASIO received in outline form — on the basis of questioning inspired in part by information contained in the 'Moscow letters' and the 'G' series and in part by five years of independent investigation — Petrov's story of Soviet espionage in Australia. According to what Petrov now told ASIO the MVD regarded Australia as a country of considerable importance, not primarily (as ASIO had imagined) because of the British atomic tests here but because Moscow thought of Australia as the potential western supply base in the case of war in Asia.[19] By 1954 the MVD establishment in Australia had consisted of five full-time cadres. Petrov was its head; his wife MVD cypher clerk and accountant. Kislitsyn, the Embassy Second Secretary; Antonov, the 'Tass' representative in Sydney; and Plait-kais, a Latvian with responsibility for penetrating the 'anti-Soviet' refugee groups in Australia — were all career intelligence officers. In addition, the MVD had in the Soviet Embassy a number of 'coopted' workers, the most important of whom were Kharkovetz, the Press Attache and Kovaliev, the Commercial Secretary.*[20] The Petrov story of Soviet espionage in Australia will be considered in detail later in this book.

On April 10 Richards enquired of Petrov about the recent difficulties of the MVD in Australia.

> You remember you told me that it was very difficult now to get information, the agents, they are very frightened, very scared. You told me it was for two reasons. You thought we had a good Security Organisation in Australia and the Government had frightened them because of their attitude towards communism generally in Australia. Is that the situation?

Petrov confirmed Richards' summary. 'Yes, that's right.' 'I wanted,' Richards continued, 'to get it clear because it is very important that the Prime Minister should have it clear also'.[21] Petrov's affirmation was certainly music to both ASIO and Prime Ministerial ears. However, how far Petrov was speaking truly and how far telling his hosts what he sensed they wanted to hear, it is impossible to know.

While Petrov was telling ASIO his tale in the Sydney safe house, his absence from Canberra stirred the Soviet Embassy to action. On April 6 Petrova was summoned by Generalov and required to leave her home at 7 Lockyer Street to take up residence inside the Soviet Embassy under conditions of virtual house arrest. Generalov, who had presumably already received Petrov's suicide note, explained that she had to be guarded against kidnap. While she was in the Embassy a party, no doubt including Petrov's MVD successor Kovalenok, ransacked their home in search of evidence.[22] Discreet inquiries were put out to Petrov's Sydney friends concerning his whereabouts. On April 7 Antonov and Plaitkais visited Dr Bialoguski's Sydney surgery but he was not there. On the same day, while under official watch, Petrova reached Bialoguski on the telephone. He immediately informed ASIO of the call. Bialoguski intuited accurately from the tone and cirumstances of the call that she was 'virtually a prisoner' in the Embassy and deduced from the fact that she had called from there that Petrova had not informed the Ambassador of Bialoguski's January 30 conversation with her in Canberra, that is of her knowledge of his role in the Petrov defection. In order further to deflect suspicions from himself Bialoguski approached two of Petrov's Communist contacts in Sydney — Lily Williams of the peace movement and Jean Ferguson

---

* On April 9 Colonel Spry wrote to Professor Bailey suggesting that Kislitsyn, Plaitkais, Kharkovetz and Kovaliev be declared *persona non grata*. Antonov did not have diplomatic status.

of the Australia-Soviet Friendship League — asking for information about Petrov's disappearance. Williams seemed indifferent to Petrov's fate but Ferguson appeared to Bialoguski distressed and anxious.[23] So, too, did Antonov whom he met in the 'Tass' flat at the Cross on the evening of April 8 and later accompanied to the stage of the Sydney Town Hall where the couple listened, in full view of the Sydney Left, to Professors Marcus Oliphant and Julius Stone discussing the dangers to mankind of the H-bomb.[24]

Sometime in the first days after the Petrov defection, two armed couriers — Zharkov and Karpinsky — were sent to Australia with instructions to fly Petrova and, interestingly, Kislitsyn from Australia on the first available commercial aircraft. The couriers set out for Australia from Rome on April 11, five days after the Soviet Embassy in Canberra had become alarmed about Petrov's disappearance.[25]

On April 7 the First Secretary at the Soviet Embassy, Vislykh, approached External Affairs to discuss Petrov's disappearance. He was shown to the Department's Protocol Officer, Francis Stuart. Vislykh asked for Australian assistance in tracing Petrov. Stuart said he would report the matter to his superiors. The following day he was instructed by the Secretary, Tange, to contact Vislykh with the message, 'I have referred the information you gave me; and the matter is now being looked into'. Tange also instructed Stuart not to 'give any undertaking to make specific inquiries'. Concerning the details of the affair, Tange reminded Stuart, 'you can quite easily profess ignorance'.[26] Quite deliberately Stuart had been maintained in the happy position of being able to mislead Vislykh without actually lying to him.

On Saturday April 10 Vislykh approached Stuart once again and demanded an official meeting that evening. Here the first Soviet complaint about the failure of the Australian authorities to find Petrov was delivered. Speaking on behalf of his Ambassador he demanded to know what steps had been taken in the search for their Third Secretary. Stuart contacted Vislykh, as he promised, on April 12 but still had nothing of substance to tell him. He promised, however, that he would make contact again at noon on the following day, April 13. The game of procrastination was coming to an end.[27]

On the morning of April 13 the Australian Cabinet was informed, to its considerable surprise, of the Petrov defection and of Menzies' desire to hold a Royal Commission on Soviet espionage. Unfortunately for the historian Australian Cabinet minutes of the 1950s record only decisions not discussions. Its central conclusions of April 13 were the following:

> It was decided that the Government should immediately amend the Royal Commissions Act to enable the Royal Commissioner to compel the attendance of witnesses etc and that the Prime Minister should make an immediate announcement of the circumstances to the House. The Prime Minister announced that he did not propose to make public the names of any Australians mentioned in the documents until the Royal Commissioner was in a position to deal with the allegations made against them.

Cabinet agreed that this was the proper procedure and did not wish proceedings to be conducted in any way which would suggest a 'smear' campaign.[28]

By April 13 Mr Menzies had of course in his possession the knowledge that Dr Evatt's Press Secretary had been the author of Document 'H'. He also by now knew that Evatt's Private Secretary, Allan Dalziel, had been the subject of MVD study over many years and that another staffer, Albert Grundeman, had been cited as a source of information in Document 'J'. His private resolve that these names would not be revealed before the election had now been translated into a binding Cabinet commitment. It is not necessary, of course, to believe that the motive for the self-denying ordinance Mr Menzies took in Cabinet on April 13 was solely or even mainly one of political honour. Menzies was probably highly conscious that any appearance of manipulation of the Petrov defection for party-political gain exposed him to censure not only from his opponents but also from his friends, for example from the conservative moralists who wrote editorials for Australian newspapers in the mid-1950s. Sometimes in the life of politics, honour and prudence may dictate the same course of action.

Not everything that occurred in Cabinet on the morning of April 13 appears to have been quite so honourable as the decision to suppress the names mentioned in the Petrov documents until after the election. By the late afternoon of April 12 Mr Menzies had decided that the Soviet Ambassador would be officially informed of the Petrov defection at noon on April 13 and that he would make his announcement to the Parliament, during the course of question time, at 2.30 p.m.[29] As late as 11.30 a.m. on April 13 External Affairs cabled this timetable to Moscow.[30] For some reason, however, around lunchtime on April 13 the decision was taken to delay the Parliamentary announcement of the defection from 2.30 until 8 o'clock that evening. Why?

On the morning of April 13, before Cabinet, Harold Holt, who was acting Leader of the House, was informed by Arthur Calwell, the Deputy Opposition Leader, that Dr Evatt would not be in Canberra for the Parliamentary sitting on the evening of April 13, having agreed to attend a function being held by his old school, Fort Street. It appears that the impending absence of Dr Evatt from the House, of which Holt no doubt informed Menzies, determined the change in timetable. As planned the Soviet Embassy was informed at noon on April 13. However, before Dr Evatt's departure from Canberra at 5.30 p.m., the Government had given the Opposition no warning that an important announcement was to be expected that evening. Shortly before it was due, Evatt's office was phoned. As expected the caller was told he was in Sydney. In his stead Calwell was informed shortly before 8 o'clock of what was to take place. Dr Evatt himself did not hear of the Petrov defection until an hour after Menzies' announcement to the House. He was caught badly off balance.[31]

At the best of times Dr Evatt was a prickly and suspicious character. It boded ill that from the first moment of the Petrov defection announcement he felt, not unjustly, that he had been treated dishonourably. While later defenders of Mr Menzies would struggle valiantly to find an innocent explanation for his failure to inform Dr Evatt of the announcement to be made in the House,*[32] one of Menzies' close friends and colleagues, Percy Joske, knew that Evatt had 'some justification for regarding himself as ill-used' over the events of April 13.[33] As for Evatt himself, although he was not aware that the defection announcement had actually been delayed for five and a half hours apparently on his behalf, he never forgave Menzies this original discourtesy.

On the evening of April 13 Mr Menzies told a stunned and silent House of Representatives of the defection of Petrov. His short announcement began with the somewhat inappropriate rhetorical form ('It is my unpleasant duty to inform the House') more usually employed for the outbreak of war or the death of a member of the Royal household. Mr Menzies told the House that Petrov, an officer of the MVD in Australia, had brought important information concerning Soviet espionage in Australia which would require patient investigation by a Royal Commission. He did not propose prematurely to reveal names, although he advised the House that the names in the Petrov documents had contained few surprises for Australian counter-intelligence. Those named would be placed under surveillance pending the conclusion of the inquiry. Menzies expressed unhappiness that a Commission had to be established before the election but was sure that 'all Parties' would agree that there must be 'no avoidable delay' in initiating investigation into what appeared already as 'systematic espionage and at least attempted subversion'. He was pleased, however, to be able to inform the House that 'the growing efficiency' of ASIO in recent years 'has made it much more difficult than in the past for espionage to succeed' and that Petrov no longer believed in Communism since he had 'seen the Australian way of living'.[34] Naturally Mr Menzies' announcement dominated the newspapers which appeared on the morning of April 14.

---

* John Paul argues: 'Giving Evatt any detailed information in advance was to run the risk that he would himself consult the Soviet Embassy and at the conclusion of Menzies' statement make the Parliament the forum for parroting the Soviet Union's line on the whole issue.' Of this it can be said: (1) It was not necessary to give Dr Evatt any detailed information. A warning that something of importance would happen in Parliament that evening would have sufficed. (2) The likelihood that Dr Evatt in April 1954 would 'parrot the Soviet line' on Petrov was negligible. John Paul confuses the post election Evatt — when he had come to believe in a conspiracy against him — with the relatively rational and cautious pre-election Evatt. (3) If, however, Dr Evatt had indeed been foolish enough to parrot the Soviet line in the Parliament on April 13 Mr Menzies' electoral stocks would have risen remarkably. If Menzies even remotely imagined he might have done so he would have probably been delighted to have had him in the House on April 13.

There was at least one Australian resident who had not heard Mr Menzies' announcement or read about it in the press of the following morning — Vladimir Petrov. As we have seen, in March he had expressed the fear that if an announcement of his defection was made before Evdokia left the country she might be used as a hostage to try and force him to return to the Embassy. Before April 13, in addition, he had been given no hint that he would be required to give evidence in public before a Royal Commission. ASIO was extremely anxious about how their charge would react to the news that his defection and the establishment of a Royal Commission had been announced.

Shortly after lunch on April 14 Petrov was shown the morning papers by Leo Carter. There had been, it was now explained to him, no alternative but to announce his defection. If Generalov's version of events had reached the press first 'it would have been bad' for him. Petrov was not told directly of the establishment of the Royal Commission but was expected to discover it for himself in what he read. Carter had been instructed to lead Petrov up the hill behind the second safe house, to which he had been moved on April 10, before showing him the morning newspapers and to keep a very close watch on him for the first hour or so after he had read them. Evidently ASIO feared Petrov might panic and flee their protection.[35]

In the event Petrov took the news relatively calmly. Shortly after reading the front page of the *Sydney Morning Herald* with great interest and seriousness he settled down to a game of chess. When told of the imminent departure of his wife and Kislitsyn he said 'that is bad' and 'spontaneously' wrote her a letter urging her to join him. To ASIO's relief he made no comment at all on the matter of the Royal Commission. His greatest display of emotion came when he saw the photograph in the newspapers of Generalov and 'disfigured' it with a pen. According to his ASIO minders his 'morale' had been boosted when it was explained to him that he had 'the support of both sides of the Federal Parliament'.[36]

This was not entirely the case, at least so far as the Leader of the Opposition was concerned. Already by the morning of April 14 a divide between the position on the defection Dr Evatt felt obliged to adopt for the public realm and his private bitterness about the defection and its timing had appeared. The morning newspapers carried his brief press release of the previous evening in which he offered his Party's full support for a thorough judicial investigation.[37] On the other hand the Commonwealth driver, Gordon McPherson, who took him to Mascot that morning revealed to someone (who was an ASIO informant) that on the way 'Dr Evatt had given the impression that he regarded the "Petrov disclosures" as a lot of bull'.[38] In Parliament on April 14 Dr Evatt repeated his support for the Royal Commission, especially one that could lead to the prosecution of traitors, and stressed the importance of a 'non-party' approach to the matter. Only the expression of his irritation at not being informed of the announcement before going to Fort Street revealed his inner tension.[39] Yet when he phoned Colonel Spry to request an immediate interview on the affair his explosive mood was clear. Dr Evatt complained bitterly about the previous day's events. Spry explained he had been instructed to pass all requests for information to the Prime Minister. Evatt paused and then banged down the telephone. It was the last time Spry and Evatt spoke.[40]

Deep mistrust of Dr Evatt's character (whether justified or not is another question) explains at least in part why he was not told in confidence about the Petrov defection when it occurred; why he was not informed before the election of May 1954 that the names of three members of his staff had been found amongst the documentary material Petrov had brought with him; and why Mr Menzies instructed Colonel Spry not to deal with him directly over the defection. It can, of course, never be known whether the Leader of the Opposition would have been briefed more fully on the Petrov defection if Mr Chifley had been alive at the time or if Mr Calwell and not Dr Evatt had succeeded him. No doubt being treated as an untrustworthy character and in one instance with pointless discourtesy rankled Dr Evatt deeply. Even more importantly for the future politics of the Petrov Affair, in a psychology such as his, personal grievance was rapidly converted to dark suspicions of a conspiracy directed against him.

On April 16 the tension between Dr Evatt's public and private selves was rather startlingly revealed when on the basis of Mr Menzies' utterly innocent exposition to a journalist of the principle of parliamentary privilege (in answer to a question about whether Australia had any equivalent of the American 'Fifth Amendment'), Evatt compared Menzies unfavourably to Joe McCarthy.

> Mr Menzies has . . . made the sly insinuation that members of the Parliament might be called as witnesses. . . . It resembles the 'smear' technique employed by some of Menzies' supporters . . . [He] disclaims McCarthyism in his background statements to the Press. But this much must be said for Senator McCarthy. At least he makes his own charges . . . under his own name.[41]

Not surprisingly or unjustly Mr Menzies characterised Dr Evatt's complaints as 'curious', 'hysterical' and 'meaningless'.

> If Dr Evatt's statement is a fair sample of what he regards as a non-party contribution, then the election should be a pretty lively one.[42]

Although Dr Evatt quickly reined himself in, his outburst of April 16 was the first public sign of the storm that was to come after the election of May 29.

7

EVDOKIA

On the morning of April 15 the Australian press reported the Soviet Ambassador's not unexpected accusation that his Third Secretary had been kidnapped. To reply to this charge Mr Menzies held the press conference which was responsible for provoking Dr Evatt's strange outburst. The kidnapping charge was of course, Menzies told the press, 'ludicrous'.

> It would be singular good luck, if we were contemplating a kidnapping, that we would be able to pick up the victim at the very moment he was walking down the street with some hundreds of documents.

The Soviet Embassy, he pointed out, had not even yet applied for access to Petrov.[1]

On April 15 and 16 Menzies, Tange, Bailey and Phillipps conferred in Canberra on the question of what to do should the Soviets now indeed request access. They decided on a pre-emptive strike.[2] Petrov was determined not to see his Soviet Embassy colleagues. He was not, however, averse to meeting with his wife before her departure.[3] Letters from Petrov to both Petrova and Generalov were despatched on Good Friday, April 16, requesting a meeting with her.[4] Only Bialoguski thought this a bad idea. Petrova, he advised ASIO, was 'far superior mentally' to her husband and would 'have it all over him' when they met. A far better means of answering the kidnapping charge was, he thought, for Petrov to write to Generalov requesting the return of 'Jack'.

> The Soviet Embassy would probably not return the dog and this would make world press headlines and a good deal of public sympathy would go towards Petrov and would tend to show his human feelings — 'the man and his dog' aspect.[5]

In fact a meeting between the Petrovs was not at all to the taste of the Soviets — their sole interest in this matter being now to get her home. Under instructions from Moscow Generalov directed Petrova, on the eve of her departure from Canberra, to sign a letter declining the meeting with her husband. She feared, she was obliged to say, a trap.[6]

By mid-April, through its connections in the travel industry, ASIO was aware that Petrova and Kislitsyn were booked to fly out of Sydney on the BOAC flight of the evening of April 19 in the company of the Soviet diplomatic couriers, Zharkov and Karpinsky.[7] ASIO was, of course, also aware by now that both Petrova and Kislitsyn were MVD officers and had come to believe both to be potential defectors, whose defections might prove of the greatest value to Western counter-intelligence. ASIO had known since the Richards-Petrov conversation that Petrova had discussed the possibility of defection with her husband on several occasions. If now, after her husband's defection, she returned home she faced savage and almost certain punishment. On the other hand, if she did not return she exposed her family to great danger. Clearly self-preservation pushed her in one direction and family loyalty (especially her feelings for her mother and sister) in the other.

Petrov had also made it clear by now that there was an excellent chance that his offsider Philip Kislitsyn might defect. He and Kislitsyn had been great friends in Australia. According to Petrov Kislitsyn's loyalty to the Soviets was doubtful and his relations with Generalov very bad. From an official point of view he was already living dangerously, with a mistress in Moscow whom he maintained in a flat and with whom he corresponded secretly via the diplomatic bag. ASIO and the MI5 team in Australia were undoubtedly excited at the prospect of Kislitsyn's defection. According to Petrov he had seen the 'top secret' material which had been passed to the Soviets by the missing British diplomats Guy Burgess and Donald Maclean. Even more intriguingly he had seen material from 'other people in England engaged in the same operation'.[8] On April 17, under ASIO inspiration, Petrov handwrote a letter to Kislitsyn (a copy of which is in the ASIO archive) urging him to defect.

Philip Vasilievitch.

I write to tell you that I am well and am enjoying the free air of Australia in conditions which I have so often heard you praise. Why do you not join me, instead of going to the hell of life in Russia under this regime, which we both fear and which has betrayed true Communism.

I suppose you realise that in Russia your fate is sealed, after what has happened. Remember Rogov's death after the Canadian affair? Of course they would never send you abroad again, so now is your last chance of escape. And after your close cooperation and friendship with me you will be under grave suspicion. Do you think Generalov will assist you? You will be accused of lack of vigilance, of careless work, of bearing responsibility for my act. You know that you will be punished and eliminated.

I know from your own demeanour that you like life in the free world outside Russia. You will be well received, will be assured complete protection and will have a secure material future. Now choose whether to go to disaster or take the path of freedom.[9]

ASIO and MI5 were determined to make some approach to both Petrova and Kislitsyn before their return to Moscow. Interestingly, in the light of subsequent developments, the evidence of the ASIO archive makes clear that in mid-April a firm decision was made to approach both of them directly, not in Sydney or Darwin, but on British territory at Singapore. The Department of External Affairs evidently thought one Soviet defection in Australia was as much as Australia-Soviet relations or the safety of the Australian mission in Moscow could bear. Petrov's Kislitsyn letter was despatched to Singapore; while concerning Petrova Colonel Spry wrote thus to Mr Menzies on April 26 1954.

> In view of the delicacy of the diplomatic situation as a result of Petrov's defection, it was decided to make the definite approach to Mrs Petrov in Singapore, to ascertain her personal views on this matter.
> The necessary co-operation with the British authorities was established, and a British security officer, after consultation with me in Sydney, flew to Singapore on April 14th, 1954, with letters from Mr. Petrov to his wife, plus photographs showing that he was well and happy. It was also agreed by the British authorities that, should she defect in Singapore, she would be flown back to Australia as soon as possible to rejoin her husband.[10]

The Australian Government was, of course, prepared to receive Petrova at Sydney or at Darwin if at either airport she should approach the Australian authorities and ask for asylum. But the clearest instructions were issued to ASIO and other responsible officers in Sydney and Darwin that they must not in any circumstances initiate an approach to her on Australian soil. On April 17 the Northern Territory's ASIO office was instructed to be at the Darwin aerodrome to meet Petrova's flight and to remain on hand until its departure but was also issued with the following warning. 'You will on no account approach her in any way unless she makes a request for the assistance of the Australian Government'.[11] Similarly, the following reminder was issued to the police, Government officials and ASIO officers who were on duty at Mascot airport for Petrova's departure on April 19. 'Exercise of compulsion by Soviet officials upon Petrova does not of itself give the Australian Authorities the right of interference.' Only if Petrova called out for 'help' or 'protection' could the Australian authorities 'ask' her diplomatic guards to 'desist' from their violence and approach her with an offer of asylum. Only if the guards did not 'desist' from their violence could force then legitimately be employed to prevent them removing her from Australia.[12] On April 19 strict legalism and diplomatic caution dominated tactical planning on the Petrova front.

The plans of April 19 foresaw neither the growing excitement within Sydney's Soviet and East European refugee communities nor the intensity of general public feeling on the question of Petrova's now imminent and well publicised departure from Australia. Amongst Old Australians noone by April 19 was more agitated about the Petrova question than the Federal Member for Mackellar, the volatile anti-communist activist, W.C. Wentworth. On the morning of April 19 the *Sydney Morning Herald* had carried an article of his outlining the punishment Petrova was likely to face on her return home.

If Mrs Petrov returns to Russia (Wentworth concluded) she knows very well that she is going to punishment. Perhaps she chooses this in preference to the reprisals which would fall on her family and friends should she refuse to go.[13]

Wentworth was determined to do whatever he could to ensure that Petrova was given a genuine choice. On the morning of April 19 he attempted to make telephone contact with Mr Menzies and Colonel Spry, in both cases unsuccessfully. At midday, when an ASIO telephonist informed him that Spry would not be available to him at all on that day, he lost his temper and only slightly calmed down when the assistant regional director in Sydney phoned him back to assure him that the Petrova question was 'being considered at the highest possible level at Canberra'. Wentworth was by now convinced that Petrova wanted to stay. If she failed to make that clear at Mascot it would be because she was 'drugged'. His operational advice was to separate her from her guards at Mascot by giving everyone about to board the aircraft there a medical examination or on the flight to Darwin by pressuring BOAC to segregate men and women. By midday Wentworth knew, through his contacts amongst Sydney refugees, that a demonstration at Mascot was being planned for that evening. He would, he informed ASIO darkly, be there to see for himself what transpired.[14]

ASIO was, of course, making its own plans for Mascot. Richards and the External Affairs Protocol Officer, Stuart, would be close by in case Petrova made an appeal for asylum. They planned to wait for her in a room she would have to pass through on her way to the international tarmac.[15] Petrov himself was to be at the airport with his ASIO minders, hidden under the awning of a utility truck, in case Petrova was doubtful as to his well-being and should demand to see him at once.[16] In preparation for this moment he had written a note which would be passed to her by Richards or another ASIO officer.

Doosia, stay here. Trust this man. He is my good friend. Go with him towards the car and you shall be with me.[17]

Shortly after 1 o'clock on the afternoon of April 19 an Embassy car, driven by the Ambassador's chauffeur, Sanko, left Canberra on its way to the airport at Sydney. Petrova was accompanied by the First Secretary, Vislykh, and the diplomatic couriers, Zharkov and Karpinsky. (Kislitsyn travelled in a second car.) For the past thirteen days Petrova had been confined to a single room in the Embassy and treated as a pariah. In the Soviet political culture gestures of friendship for someone who had fallen from grace were altogether too dangerous. Sympathy for her, in the traditional Russian fashion, came only from the humblest menials at the Embassy — the Golovanov couple. Two images of her confinement at the Embassy — of Generalova leering at her in triumph and contempt and of the stoney silence of the Embassy staff at her departure — stayed with her after her defection.[18]

What thoughts passed through Petrova's mind on the journey from the Embassy to Mascot? Clearly uppermost must have been fear at the prospect of the fate awaiting her at Moscow. Petrova later claimed to have pressed Generalov unsuccessfully for a guarantee from the Soviet Government that she would be treated well on her return and to have been threatened by Kovalenok of the camps 'or worse' that awaited her at home. She was also certainly frightened by now of the couriers. Generalov had warned her that they were armed and would shoot if any attempt was made to abduct her. The possibility of an arranged 'accident' on the way home even crossed her mind. What did she think had happened to her husband? It is very hard to believe (as on occasion she was later to claim) that she genuinely feared he had been kidnapped by the Australian authorities. After all he had more than once discussed defection with her in the past. On the other hand she may genuinely have feared that he had come to some harm in the hands of the Australian authorities after his defection. She had lived a far more cloistered life in Australia than Petrov. She had an instinctive grasp of the practices of only one Government — her own — and had warned her husband that the Australians would treat them 'like the Rosenbergs' if they defected. By this time she most likely felt considerable resentment concerning her husband. By his flight — through motives of cowardice and selfishness — he had ruined the (slender) career prospects of both and placed her and her family in the gravest peril. She might well have reflected blackly that she had only married him because of his good career prospects inside the NKVD and his eminent respectability.[19]

By the time she arrived at Mascot on the evening of April 19, her inner turmoil had been stirred by the effects of the brandy she had taken on the way. She felt by now thoroughly frightened and ill. She was greeted by a large and extraordinarily highly charged crowd of Soviet and East European refugees. For these people the Soviet Union was an unspeakably cruel tyranny, which had ruined the lives of family and friends and separated them from their homelands and cultures. There was no element of pretence in the violent anger they directed at the Soviet couriers they believed were dragging Petrova towards imminent death and no element of doubt in their minds that Petrova was being pressed onto the plane against her will and that she wanted to be saved by them.

In the confusion of the moment Petrova was led by the diplomatic couriers to the wrong tarmac at Mascot, for the domestic and not the international flights (thereby accidentally by-passing the room where Richards and his group were waiting) and towards an aircraft bound for some Australian destination. By this time the crowd had broken through police cordons (effective crowd control was an administrative art of the future) and surrounded the BOAC Constellation on the international tarmac. Airport staff manned the fire hoses. Petrova, held so tightly now between Zharkov and Karpinsky that the bruise marks stayed on her arms for several days, was led towards the Constellation. She lost a shoe and asked her guards to retrieve it but they refused and continued on their journey. The noise of the crowd imploring

her to stay in Australia was deafening. Some of the crowd held onto her cloth-
ing trying to restrain her; others struck out with arms and legs at the couriers.
As the Soviet party was climbing the gangway towards the door of the Constellation the crowd managed to separate it temporarily from the plane and
Petrova let out a scream. Eventually she and her guards, with the assistance
of the BOAC crew, were pulled on board. Karpinsky and Zharkov congratulated her on her courage and celebrated the success of their mission with a
beer. Later, Petrova could not recall what she had felt on her slow passage
across the tarmacs at Mascot other than animal fear.[20]

On the evening of April 19 many of the demonstrators were sincerely convinced that they had heard Petrova crying out for help. The more resourceful
among them caused statutory declarations to this effect to be made and
passed on to journalists immediately.[21] The refugee demonstrators, many
radio and press journalists who reported Mascot, and even some Australian
officials involved in the scenes were convinced that Petrova had been badly
let down by the Australian Security officers on the spot. One Qantas official
was reported to have called on Security men for help as he struggled against
the Russians on the gangway of the Constellation.

The Security men (he was reported to say) should have been there to give Mrs.
Petrov asylum when she did not want to leave. I saw several New South Wales security police at the airport, but none attempted to intervene.[22]

Another onlooker who was convinced that Australian Security had failed
Petrova badly was W.C. Wentworth. After the Constellation had departed
he booked a trunk call through to the Prime Ministerial Lodge at Canberra
where, as it happened, the entire Australian Cabinet was assembled for a pre-
election dinner. Wentworth recalls speaking not to Mr Menzies but to Sir
Philip McBride, the Minister for Defence. He outlined the events of that evening and reported his opinion that unless the catastrophe at Mascot was
reversed at Darwin the Government's electoral prospects would be shat-
tered.[23]

More certainly than at any time in the Petrov Affair party-political considerations now dictated the actions of Mr Menzies. The combination of
Wentworth's telephone call and the somewhat alarming tone of the radio
news that evening caused him to call an impromptu meeting of his somewhat
inebriated Cabinet (where the coolness of McEwen won him the name thereafter of 'Don't Panic Jack').[24] Here it was apparently decided to do whatever was possible at Darwin to give Petrova the free choice of whether she
stayed in Australia or returned to the USSR. At 9.45 p.m. Menzies telephoned
Colonel Spry who was with Professor Bailey in Canberra. They discussed
Mascot. At 10.30 p.m. Spry called Menzies, now with ASIO's information
on the events. Richards had assured Spry that 'Mrs Petrov had not called out
for help at any time' and had been 'terrified of the actions of the crowd'.

According to Colonel Spry, Menzies now instructed him,

(a) That contact be made with the aircraft to ascertain the condition of Mrs Petrov, and whether she had indicated if she wished to remain in Australia, or was frightened.

(b) That I should contact Mr Leydin, Acting Administrator, Northern Territory and direct him personally to ask Mrs. Petrov whether she wished to seek political asylum in Australia.[25]

The 'direct approach' to her was now to be made, if at all possible, not at Singapore through MI5 but through whatever Australian resources could be mustered at Darwin. Menzies extended full operational control to Spry. From Mr Menzies' point of view Operation Darwin was probably the most important task he had ever set his ASIO Director-General.

Shortly after midnight Mr Menzies issued a press release affirming the Government's intentions at Darwin, hoping no doubt thereby to take some of the sting out of the morning's Mascot press reports.[26] Then he went to bed. When he awoke the fate of his Government and his own political future — if things went badly at Darwin — might be sealed.

Colonel Spry went immediately to ASIO's small Canberra office. With the assistance of Colonel Phillipps and the Senior Operations Officer at Air Traffic Control at Mascot, Greenleash, Spry sent three questions to Captain Davys of the BOAC Constellation.

(i) What is the physical condition of Mrs Petrov?

(ii) Is she in a state of fear?

(iii) Has she indicated that she wishes to stay in Australia?[27]

Somewhat surprisingly, on board the Constellation the dozing Soviet couriers — apparently believing in the success of their mission — paid little attention to Petrova who was able to move fairly freely around the aircraft. One of the air hostesses, who comforted her, Joyce Bull and a flight steward, Muir, managed to speak to her on several occasions. According to Petrova she told neither directly that she wanted to stay in Australia but she did appeal to Muir for 'help'. She also mentioned that she was very frightened of her couriers, who were armed.[28]

At 2.20 a.m. Captain Davys was in a position to signal his replies to Colonel Spry's questions. Petrova was 'very tired'. She was in a state of fear. She did wish to stay in Australia. Spry at once sent through Air Traffic control at Mascot two supplementary questions. What was she frightened of? Was her desire to stay in Australia known by query or by observation? At 3.10 .m. the Captain replied. 'She was afraid of the armed guards. Her request to stay in Australia had been obtained by direct query.'[29]

Colonel Spry was also in contact that night, by ASIO secret telephone, with the Acting Administrator of the Northern Territory, Reginald Leydin. (The permanent Administrator was on holiday and forfeited, thereby, his place in history.) Shortly after midnight Spry issued Leydin with his riding instructions. He was 'personally to ask Mrs Petrova on arrival whether she wished to stay in Australia', to 'take her under his protection' and get her to sign the necessary asylum papers, held already by the ASIO office at Darwin. 'It would be necessary', Spry instructed Leydin, 'to separate her from her companions, so that she could talk freely and without fear'. He suggested to Leydin the advantages of having seven or eight imposing policemen with him at the airport.[30]

At 3.15 a.m., shortly after he had received the signals from Davys, Spry spoke with Leydin again in the Darwin office of ASIO. The couriers were known, he now told Leydin, to be armed. In order to separate Petrova from them and to prevent one of them from taking a shot at her, Spry advised Leydin to greet the couriers on the Darwin tarmac as soon as they emerged from the aircraft and to use the police, who were themselves to be armed, as a screen between Petrova and her guards. Although Petrova's defection was the first priority, if possible Leydin should also approach Kislitsyn and offer him asylum. The entire enterprise should be effected 'quietly and smoothly' if at all possible. If, however, the couriers resorted to violence, force might be used against them.

At 3.45 a.m. Greenleash of Mascot Air Control telephoned with what Spry instantly understood to be a highly significant item of information. According to section 119 of the Air Navigation Act the carrying of firearms on aircraft flying over Australian territory was illegal. Spry at once roused Professor Bailey from his bed. Happily, Bailey advised that diplomatic privilege did not release diplomats (or diplomatic couriers) from the obligation to 'conform to the local laws of the country through which they were travelling'. A legal basis for the Australian authorities to approach and disarm the Soviet couriers at Darwin evidently existed. Spry called his regional director at Darwin, Barrington, and told him to pass this splendid news to Leydin at once. He also now roused the Secretary of the Department of External Affairs, Arthur Tange, from his bed and invited him to come down to the ASIO office in Canberra to discuss the 'diplomatic repercussions' of the planned operation at Darwin and to wait with him upon events. At best Petrova and Kislitsyn might ask for asylum and the couriers might surrender their arms peacefully. At worst there might be a shootout at Darwin airport between Australian police and the Soviet diplomatic couriers.[31]

At 4.30 a.m. Leydin met with his assembled troops at Darwin airport — Edmunds (the Acting Crown Law Officer), Littlejohn (Superintendent of Police), Tiernan (Darwin Special Branch) and Barrington (ASIO) — and discussed tactics. As agreed, when the Constellation came to a rest shortly after 5 a.m., this party, accompanied by ten armed Darwin policemen, approached the gangway. The couriers were at first unwilling to leave the aircraft with their charges but officials on board insisted that they must leave during refuelling. The Soviet party were the last passengers to alight. As soon as the couriers came to the bottom of the gangway Edmunds approached one of them and Barrington the other, while Leydin drew Petrova to one side to offer her asylum.[32]

As it turned out, the courier Edmunds chose to approach was Karpinsky. Edmunds asked him whether he had been carrying firearms on the aircraft. Karpinsky, a very powerful man, tried to brush him aside. When Edmunds returned to his questioning Karpinsky swung violently at him with his heavy brief bag. Edmunds seized Karpinsky by the shoulder and pushed him away from the aircraft. One of the policemen on the spot, Constable Fay, seized one arm and a second, Constable Davis, who shouted to his fellows that Karpinsky was going for his gun, the other. Karpinsky was by now struggling violently, four policemen upon him. Constable Davis pinioned Karpinsky's arms by slipping his jacket from his shoulders; Sergeant Ryall came from behind and — this moment was immortalised by an *Argus* photographer — placed him in a fierce headlock. Constable Ross now seized the gun from a right hip pocket holster. Karpinsky's struggle was over. He joined his companion, Zharkov, who had merely put up token resistance while being disarmed. An RAAF pilot, Flight-Lieutenant McCluskey, who had observed the struggles, was certain that if Karpinsky and Zharkov had not been disarmed 'they would undoubtedly have used their guns'.[33]

While these scuffles were taking place on the tarmac Leydin was deep in private conversation with Petrova. 'I am', he announced on meeting her, 'the Governor of Darwin. Do you wish to seek political asylum in Australia?' Unexpectedly Petrova groaned and replied: 'I don't know. I don't know'. Caught between fears for her own safety and the safety of her family she proposed that Leydin resolve her dilemma by kidnapping her.

I cannot choose — they will kill my father and mother and my brothers (sic) and sisters (sic).
If you take me by force, alright, but I must not choose. I cannot choose.
Look, they are still looking at me.
Why did you not arrange it at Canberra?
It would have been so easy.

How, she enquired, on a more practical note, would she be able to live in Australia? Where was her husband? Was he not dead? 'Can I see my husband here? Can I speak to him?' If she could speak to him, she added, 'it may be alright'.

Leydin moved from Petrova to Kislitsyn, who had been standing quietly watching proceedings. He complained bitterly about the breaches of diplomatic immunity on the tarmac and the restraint the police had placed upon the Soviet party. Leydin assured Kislitsyn that Petrova and the couriers were entirely free to move about the airport as they wished. He then seized his chance. Would Kislitsyn, perchance, like to remain in Australia? 'Can you', Kislitsyn enquired, 'arrange these things here?' 'Yes', replied Leydin, 'the

Commonwealth Government will make the necessary arrangements for your safety'. 'Very interesting. Very interesting.'[34] According to Leydin, Kislitsyn delivered these words with a straight face; according to the Crown Law Officer, Edmunds, who was on hand, in a sneering fashion.[35] It will never be clear whether Kislitsyn's interest was in the offer of asylum or in the fact that he now possessed tangible evidence of the Australian Government's flagrant breach of diplomatic etiquette.

The Soviet party were now reunited and retired together to the International Lounge. Barrington telephoned Spry with a progress report. Petrova, he informed his chief, could not make up her mind and wanted to be kidnapped. What Arthur Tange thought of the abduction plea beggars the imagination. Barrington was of course advised that 'under no circumstances was [Petrova] to be kidnapped'. Barrington continued. Petrova believed her husband might be dead; only a telephone call from him would reassure her.[36] This was easier to organise than a kidnapping. At 7 a.m. Spry telephoned Richards in Sydney asking him to arrange for a telephone call from Petrov, who was back in the safe house, to be put through to Darwin airport.[37]

The trunk call was booked by Leo Carter from the safe house. Ten minutes of tension passed without result. Carter recontacted the Sydney exchange. There had been, he was told, some delay in Brisbane. Carter said he was calling on behalf of the Attorney-General and demanded 'operational flash priority'. Within a minute the safe house and Darwin airport were in contact. Carter was now told that Leydin was unavailable. Safe house security was now entirely breached. Tell Mr Leydin, he instructed the telephonist, that Colonel Spry is on the phone. Leydin answered. Carter told him that he was speaking on behalf of Spry. Petrov was with him and wished to speak to his wife.[38]

Petrova refused to be parted from her guards and to take the call in privacy in an upstairs room. She took it instead in the Customs office, flanked by the entire Soviet party. Petrov told her he was being well looked after. He implored her to place herself under the protection of the Australian authorities. Petrova answered, 'I know you are not my husband. I know he is dead'. When Petrova emerged from the Customs room she winked at Leydin, but when he suggested they might have a private chat she refused. The person she had been speaking to was not, she told the assembled company, her husband. Leydin had now almost given up hope. He bade his farewells to Petrova. 'Goodbye', he said, 'and good luck'.

Perhaps the wink drew him back for one last try. 'Would you like a short conversation with me?' Petrova this time agreed. In the privacy of his office Petrova said she wished to stay in Australia but refused to sign any papers until she had seen her husband. Spry was contacted urgently. He informed Leydin, through Barrington, that the paper work was not essential. Two witnesses to her request for asylum would do. Edmunds called together the police and some airforce men on the spot and asked them to form a group by the main entrance at the airport. They obscured the view of the Soviet party as Petrova was hurried by Leydin to a waiting car which drove them both to Government House. Throughout the morning of April 20 she sat on the verandah there in a thoroughly depressed state.[39]

The Crown Law Officer, Edmunds, remained at the airport to see the Soviet party off. Kislitsyn complained to him bitterly again, this time about Petrova's abduction. He demanded (successfully) a priority trunk call to his Ambassador and (unsuccessfully) that he be allowed to speak to Petrova and that the couriers' guns be returned to them. He feared, he explained to Edmunds, bandits at Singapore. Around 8.45 a.m. the three man Soviet party reboarded the Constellation and flew off, the couriers to their probable disgrace and Kislitsyn perhaps to punishment or death.[40]

A political demonstration of the ferocity seen at Mascot on the evening of April 19 was itself startling enough to awaken the tranquil democracy of mid-1950s Australia. But with the appearance there of what looked like totalitarian methods on Australian soil the nation rose in indignation. In the still photographs which Australians saw in their morning newspapers of April 20 — of Petrova between Zharkov and Karpinsky — the Petrov Affair transcended politics and curiosity and entered Australian folklore. The nation saw an attractive young blonde woman, weeping and vulnerable, one foot bare, being dragged across the tarmac by two formidable, scowling Slavic gorillas. A durable visual image of what most Australians still believed the Cold War to be about — the struggle between the forces of Evil and Good — penetrated the national consciousness. 'Somehow or other', Melbourne *Herald* columnist, Bill Tipping, commented, 'we reckon we learned more about the Soviet system in these pictures than in all the things about Russia we've ever read or heard'.[41] Within a day twenty-nine cinemas over Sydney were showing a newsreel of Petrova's Mascot ordeal.[42] When the same newsreel was shown in a packed cinema in Melbourne 'anger, resentment and indignation simmered'.[43]

It was indeed fortunate for Mr Menzies and his Government that the national indignation over the events at Mascot on the evening of April 19 was balanced by the mood of national celebration with the radio news on the morning of April 20 of what had transpired at Darwin. In the iconography of national consciousness the newspaper photograph of Sergeant Ryall with a fierce headlock on Karpinsky joined the photograph of Petrova flanked between Zharkov and Karpinsky. At Mascot the forces of Good and Evil had contended; at Darwin Good had triumphed. On the morning of Easter Tuesday Robert Menzies, in a shabby dressing gown, had woken Colonel Spry who was dozing on a sofa in the Lodge. He had good reason to feel gratitude to his Director-General of Security. The friendship between these two men was sealed.[44]

Amongst Australia's major metropolitan dailies only Sydney's *Daily Mirror* proved unforgiving about the events at Mascot. On April 21 it asked in the strongest terms for an explanation of who was responsible for allowing

'.. at Mascot, the forces of Good and Evil had contended'
(photo courtesy of News Limited)

the 'nauseating' scenes there to take place and the name of the person who had misled the Cabinet into thinking that Petrova had left Sydney of her own volition. 'Someone', it demanded, possibly even Colonel Spry himself, 'should be sacked for this'.[45] This tone was found nowhere else in the Australian press and is mainly of interest as an indicator of how the press would

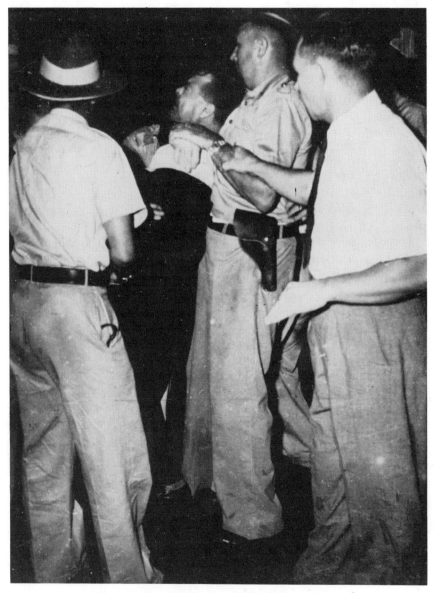

'.. at Darwin, Good had triumphed' (photo courtesy of
Australian Consolidated Press)

most likely have jumped if Petrova's decision at Darwin had been to fly home. For most Australian newspapers Petrova's decision completely salvaged Mr Menzies' reputation. 'When Federal Cabinet intervened to stop the abduction of a terrified and terrorised woman', the *Argus* editorialised, 'it had the whole Australian nation solidly behind it'.[46] According to the *Daily Telegraph* the Government's and Security's 'resourcefulness and deft action thrilled the people of Australia and the rest of the free world'.[47] Morality, the press argued, was far more important than mere diplomatic protocol. Mr Menzies, too, was congratulated on the detailed statement concerning events at Mascot and Darwin (written for him by Colonel Spry) which was released on April 20 to the press. Truth was the best antidote to Soviet propaganda.

Somewhat to the pride of Australians news of Petrova's defection dominated the headlines in the United States and the United Kingdom. Scores of congratulatory telegrams and letters arrived on Mr Menzies' desk. From Britain the Conservative MP, Mr Henry Kerby, thought that 'the fearless Christian action of the Australian Government' had 'lifted high the torch of freedom the world over'.[48] From the United States the trade union leader, Matthew Woll, telegrammed that Mr Menzies' 'courageous lifesaving rescue of wife of Russian diplomat who chose freedom arouses sincerest admiration of . . . liberty loving people everywhere'.[49]

The mood of celebration and triumph, of righteousness vindicated, left the Opposition little room for effective political manoeuvre. The Deputy Leader of the Opposition, Arthur Calwell, misread the post-Darwin national mood very badly indeed with his scathing comments about the Government's bungling at Mascot.

> The Government comes out of this sordid and nauseating business with its battered reputation further damaged. The fact that Mrs Petrov's blood is not on its hands is merely a lucky accident.[50]

Several newspapers scolded Calwell for cynical political opportunism. Dr Evatt's alternative press statement, which supported the actions taken at Darwin to give Petrova the choice of freedom as 'fully justified', made greater political sense. His criticism of the Government was extremely mild. 'It seems strange', his short statement concluded, 'that similar action was not taken much earlier'.[51]

From the point of view of the Menzies Government the only casualty of Darwin was Australia's diplomatic relationship with the Soviet Union. At 4 p.m. on April 23 the Australian Chargé d'Affaires in Moscow, Brian Hill, was summoned to an interview with the Deputy Minister for Foreign Affairs, Mr Andrei Gromyko. Gromyko handed Hill a five page letter which detailed Soviet complaints about recent events in Australia. The Soviet Note complained about the failure of the authorities there to hand over the 'criminal'

Petrov; about the incidents at Mascot where 'obviously selected persons acting in full accord with representatives of the Australian Police' had tried to kidnap Petrova; and about the 'forcible seizure' of Petrova and the 'attacks' on Kislitsyn and the couriers at Darwin. The Soviet Government intended to close its Embassy in Canberra. Gromyko demanded that Hill and the Australian Legation in Moscow leave 'within two or three days'.[52]

The Soviet Government now began a campaign of harassment against the small Australian Legation of Brian Hill and Third Secretaries, Richard Woolcott and Bill Morrison. Without notifying the Australians, Moscow blocked direct cable traffic between the Legation and Canberra. Hill was forced to improvise contact with Canberra with the assistance of the British Embassy at Moscow. Messages from the Australians were sent to the Foreign Office via UK channels which in turn passed them on to the Australian High Commissioner in London for transmission to Canberra. The Legation was not isolated entirely but communication with home had become extremely slow. On April 24 Hill was summoned once more to the Soviet Foreign Ministry. Here, Koktomov falsely accused the Australian Government of preventing telegrams reaching or leaving the Soviet Embassy in Canberra. Until cable communications were restored, and until all Soviet personnel had left Australia, no exit visas would be issued to the Australians in Moscow. Koktomov's manner throughout the interview was 'aggressive'.[53]

In the interview of April 23, Gromyko had threatened that if the Australians had not quit Moscow 'within two or three days' they would lose the protection of diplomatic immunity. Now their exit visas were being withheld. Arrests of one or more of the Australian Legation on some trumped up charge, following the expiry of the 'two or three' days of guaranteed immunity, seemed a distinct possibility. On the evening of April 24 Hill cabled home:

> I do not want you to get the impression that we are now in a state of alarm. Fortunately there is so much to do that we have no time to worry about any possible Soviet moves which in any case we all consider rather unlikely. However, latest developments would seem to me to justify care to ensure that if in any way possible we are not left here in Moscow until all Soviet personnel are out of Australia.[54]

Hill was advised to protest strongly in Moscow about the claims concerning the withholding of cables to and from the Soviet Embassy in Canberra (as Tange already had to Generalov) and to demand 'your full immunities until the time you leave the Soviet frontier'.[55]

The Minister for External Affairs, Richard Casey, arrived at Geneva for the international conference on Korea and Indo-China while the fate of the Australian Legation at Moscow hung in the balance. (Casey who had missed the entire Petrov Affair complained wanly that 'things seem to happen while I am away'.)[56] He raised the question of the treatment of the Australians at

Moscow with Gromyko who, unconvincingly, pleaded ignorance of the matter.[57] The Australian Legation was fortunate that their expulsion from Moscow coincided with the opening of the Geneva Conference. The Soviet Government was probably unwilling to allow their harassment of the Australians to build towards a major diplomatic incident between themselves and the British or even the Americans.

At Canberra the Department of External Affairs was doing all it could to expedite preparations for the departure of Soviet Embassy personnel in the belief that this might assist their colleagues in Moscow. The Soviets demanded a journey by sea but no commercial berths could be found at short notice. On April 26 the Soviet Ambassador was offered the required berths on an Australian migrant ship which was returning soon to Southampton.[58] A meeting of External Affairs, Security and the RAAF convened on the 27th and concluded details. The Soviet party was to be flown to Perth from the RAAF base at Fairbairn by commercial aircraft chartered by External Affairs and driven to the port of embarkation, Fremantle, by the West Australian police.[59] Generalov accepted these arrangements. As late as the evening of April 28, however, External Affairs had still not heard that the exit visas had been issued at Moscow. Tange informed his Minister: 'If exit permits have not been granted . . . we intend to hold the ship until situation has been satisfactorily clarified.'[60]

It was only on the morning of April 29 that news came through, via London, that on the previous day the Australians at Moscow had been issued with their exit visas. No incidents had occurred.[61] On April 29 the Australian Legation left Moscow on a train bound for Helsinki and the Soviet Embassy departed Fremantle on board the *New Australia*. Diplomatic relations between Australia and the USSR had ended.

8

THE ELECTION

After the excitement of Evdokia's defection the Australian nation prepared itself for the relative anti-climax of a Federal election campaign. Certain allegations about the impact on this election of the defection of the Petrovs form the most fundamental and enduring element in the Petrov conspiracy theory. While the conspiracy theorists may differ on many questions of fact and interpretation none would dispute the proposition that Mr Menzies, with the assistance of ASIO, consciously manipulated the Petrovs' defections for the purpose of achieving a Coalition victory at the polls. Insofar as Australian students now know anything at all about the politics of the Petrov Affair, what they 'know' is that Mr Menzies cunningly used Petrov to hold onto a political power that was inevitably falling from his grasp. After the Petrov defections and the election loss the Labor Party soon split. The potency of the Petrov Affair for Australian political mythology lies in the suggestion that the long period of conservative political hegemony in Australia was only made possible by a swindle.

The electoral dimension of the Petrov conspiracy theory consists of three distinct claims which can, at least for analytical purposes, be examined separately. The first of these is that Mr Menzies and ASIO saved up the Petrov defection for the election of 1954. While, it is claimed, Petrov would have been willing to defect at any time over a period of many months, ASIO, on behalf of Menzies, delayed his defection until election eve. In this view Colonel Spry and Mr Menzies, not Petrov himself, were the masters of the defection time-table. 'Although the Government had been aware of Petrov's desire to defect for several months', the *Dictionary of Australian Politics* recently informed its readers, 'the defection was only announced on the eve of the House rising for the forthcoming elections'.[1] Many years earlier Dr Evatt made the same point even more strongly.

> Petrov was nursed and nurtured over a period of years before his defection; ... the object of Dr Bialoguski and the Security Chiefs was that his defection was to take place only if and when required. In fact it is reasonably certain that Petrov would most gladly have defected and sought asylum at least twelve months previously.[2]

The second claim about Petrov's role in the election of 1954 concerns the manner in which the Menzies Government is alleged to have used the Petrov issue during the course of the campaign in April and May 1954. 'Prime Minister Menzies', the *Dictionary of Australian Politics* continues, 'announced the defection and imputed the existence of a widespread communist conspiracy network, reaching the highest reaches (sic) of the Labor Opposition, e.g. the private secretary to the Labor leader, Dr Evatt'.[3] Dr Evatt had himself long ago argued such a view.

> The Zinovieff letter and the political manipulation and propaganda of the German fascists in 1933 *pale into insignificance* before what was done in the name of the internal security of Australia for the purpose of influencing the 1954 general election.
> Those responsible for the Tory victory in the British elections of 1924 or the Reichstag fire manipulation in the German elections of 1933 had at least some small excuse ... because of the period of excitement but in the present case of Petrov the organisation of the affair was ... careful, calculating, cold and callous ...[4]

The third allied claim concerns consequences not intentions. According to this extremely widely held view the Petrov defection turned the election tide in 1954 and was responsible for the victory of the Menzies-Fadden Government at the polls. 'The spy scare', according to Professor Russel Ward, 'was sufficient to arrest the swing of popular opinion against the Government'.[5] The historians of the Petrov Affair, Nicholas Whitlam and John Stubbs, claim even more precision than Professor Ward in their analysis of the electoral impact of Petrov. In what they believe to have been the last published Gallup Poll taken prior to Petrov's defection the ALP commanded 52% support. According to them, after the Petrovs' defection another Gallup Poll, held on May 1, found Coalition support to have soared to 57%. 'There can be', they continue unsurprisingly in the light of these 'facts', 'no question that a strong reason for the return of the Government was the Communist scare, a scare created by the Government itself'.[6]

To assess the Petrov conspiracy theory and to determine the role the Petrovs played in the Australian election of 1954 three separate questions must be addressed. Firstly, did Mr Menzies, either alone or in association with ASIO, save up the Petrov defection until the eve of the election? Secondly, did Mr Menzies or his Coalition colleagues use the defections during the election campaign to destroy the political credit of the Opposition? And thirdly, did the Petrov defections actually determine the outcome of the Australian election of 1954?

The first of these questions can be answered, with least uncertainty, on the basis of the new evidence recently released by ASIO on the Petrov's defections, which has been used extensively in the first section of the present work.

As we have seen between the end of 1951 and July 1953 ASIO had employed an agent, Dr Bialoguski, ultimately with the intention of leading Petrov towards defection. At no time, however, between late 1951 and July 1953 did Petrov and Bialoguski discuss the question of defection openly. In July 1953, primarily as a result of intelligence information which friendly services had supplied to ASIO about unrest in several MVD stations abroad following the demise of Beria, ASIO decided to make an approach to Petrov, with the purpose of inducing him to defect. For this mission they selected not Dr Bialoguski but a more trusted intermediary, Dr Beckett. In July, as we have seen, Beckett broached the question of defection with Petrov. Although he did not rise to the bait, ASIO in July 1953 was not unhopeful that Petrov might change his mind. A second Beckett-Petrov meeting for August was arranged but here Petrov steered clear of any discussion whatever about remaining in Australia. Beckett was now of the opinion that the prospective Petrov defection was a 'dead duck'.[7] The idea that, if in July or August 1953 Petrov had indicated a willingness to defect then ASIO would have advised him to wait several months for the next year's general election campaign, is as implausible as the idea that Mr Menzies might have gone to the polls early if Petrov had defected in the spring of 1953. At this time the Gallup Poll showed that the Coalition Parties were likely to gain 45% and the ALP 54% of the popular vote.[8]

By September 1953 ASIO clearly no longer held out much hope of a Petrov defection. After Dr Bialoguski went to Canberra, in the hope of being able to complain to Mr Menzies of ASIO's niggardly treatment of him, Colonel Spry summarily dismissed him from ASIO service. ASIO's interest in the Petrov defection was only rekindled in November 1953 when Bialoguski contacted them, in part with the news that Petrov and his wife were about to defect, and in part with the threat that if ASIO was not interested he would take the Petrovs to the newspapers. ASIO quickly decided to offer the Petrovs political asylum at once.[9] Its intentions can be demonstrated by a simple detail. In early December 1953 ASIO rented a safe house for a period of one month as the proposed accommodation for the Petrovs should they decide to defect.[10]

Between December 1953 and Feburary 1954 Petrov, however, as we have seen, moved far more painstakingly slowly towards his defection decision than Dr Bialoguski in November had suggested to ASIO he would. In this period ASIO did all it could to lead Petrov towards defection, supporting two Bialoguski initiatives — one tempting him with the prospect of owning his own farm; the other employing Dr Beckett to encourage him to make contact directly with Australian Security. Already in early January, Petrov — in conversation with Bialoguski — had indicated that if he was to defect he would do so in early April, after the arrival of his MVD successor.[11] On February 19 Petrov finally agreed to Beckett's proposal of a meeting with Richards of ASIO, but on February 20 apparently changed his mind. Their first meeting eventually took place on February 27 1954. Richards offered Petrov political asylum, if he wished on that very night.

Between February 27 and April 2 Richards and Petrov were, as we have seen, in frequent contact. The minifon wire recordings of their meetings have recently been released to the general public. Far from revealing an ASIO holding Petrov's defection back what they reveal is an ASIO increasingly anxious about Petrov's vacillation and fearful that, while he dithered, his freedom of decision might be destroyed by some punitive action against him taken by his colleagues at the Soviet Embassy. The wire recordings also reveal that Petrov's procrastination did not finally end until the night of March 31-April 1, on the eve of the arrival of his successor. On that night two events — the chastisement of his wife at a Party meeting and the raid on his own Embassy safe and desk — clinched Petrov's defection decision.[12]

Only if it is believed that ASIO fabricated hundreds of documents after Petrov's defection and destroyed hundreds of others and employed the services of Petrov, Dr Bialoguski, Dr Beckett and Richards (or actors to mimic them) to record a large number of tapes (incidentally containing certain material embarrassing to ASIO) can it now be believed that Petrov's defection was saved up for the election of 1954.

Nor is it possible to believe that Mr Menzies played any role at all in the timing of Petrov's decision to defect. Traditionally Menzies' involvement in the Petrov conspiracy has been traced back to September 1953 when Dr Bialoguski journeyed to Canberra in search of an interview with him. Not only is there no evidence — old or new — that the man Bialoguski saw, Menzies' Secretary Geoffrey Yeend, ever informed Mr Menzies of his conversation with Bialoguski; more revealing, as we have seen, is the fact that the immediate result of their meeting was an act signifying the abandonment of hope in the Petrov defection — namely the dismissal of ASIO's greatest asset on the Petrov front, Dr Bialoguski.[13] Mr Menzies, the newly released evidence shows, was first informed of the possibility of Petrov's defection by Colonel Spry on February 10 1954. If he had been involved earlier than that in the defection planning the description of his meeting with Spry, in an internal ASIO memorandum, as a 'preliminary briefing' would make no sense.[14] Moreover once informed, however keen Mr Menzies might or might not have been for the defection to occur before the election, it is difficult in the extreme to see by what means he could have influenced, one way or the other, the outcome of the delicate discussions which occurred between Richards and Petrov from February 27 until April 2. The evidence reveals beyond reasonable doubt that it was neither Mr Menzies nor ASIO but Petrov himself who ultimately determined the moment of his defection and that there was no time in 1953 or 1954 when ASIO would not have offered Petrov immediate asylum.

Even if, however, it is conceded that neither Menzies nor ASIO saved up the Petrov defection for the election (as the traditional conspiracy theory had suggested) might it not alternatively be argued that Mr Menzies delayed the election until the last legally permissible date in the hope of an eleventh hour Petrov defection? In support of this theory a conspiratorial significance might be attributed to the fact that, on February 10, Mr Menzies received his preliminary briefing on the possibility of the Petrov defection from Colonel Spry and that, two days later on February 12, the Cabinet determined that the election should be held on the last possible day, May 29.[15]

Again, however, the sinister construction of these events crumbles on investigation. Firstly the decision to put the question of the election date to Cabinet on February 12 was not taken after but before the Spry-Menzies conversation of February 10. On February 9 journalists already knew that this was to be an item on the Cabinet agenda of February 12.[16] Secondly, and more importantly, the May 29 election date was the obvious and logical choice for Mr Menzies and his Cabinet, readily explained without reference to a secret hope in Menzies' heart about an impending salvific Petrov defection. By early 1954, for the first time in two years, economic indicators — unemployment, inflation and import levels — were beginning to look favourable for the Government. If an election had been held at any time in 1952 or 1953 the Gallup Polls suggest that the Menzies Government would have been swept from office in a landslide. In February 1954, in a steadily improving economic climate, political logic suggested that the passage of as much time as possible could only improve the once remote chance that a Menzies-Fadden Ministry might be re-elected.

There was, in any case, in mid-February, no possibility of holding an election before, at the very earliest, the beginning of May. The Royal Tour of Australia, by the new Queen and her Consort, was not to come to an end before early April. It was, of course, inconceivable that it should be allowed to coincide with an election campaign, let alone an election. As election campaigns in Australia traditionally continued for three to four weeks, the earliest possible election date by middle February was early May. But as election manoeuvring was difficult to contain to the official campaign period even a date in early May would threaten to undermine the political truce both Government and Opposition Parties favoured for the extent of the Royal Tour. Moreover, ironically as it turned out, in mid-February Cabinet would have been aware that to set an election date for early May, with a campaign beginning at the moment Queen Elizabeth departed Australia's shores, would have exposed the Government to the charge of political opportunism. From every point of view May 29 was a sensible election date, irrespective of whether or not Mr Menzies might privately have dreamt of a Petrov defection.

It appears, then, clear that Mr Menzies neither saved up the Petrov defection for an impending election nor, alternatively, delayed the election until the last possible moment in the hope of an eleventh hour Petrov defection. What, however, is to be made of the second charge — namely that once Petrov had defected he and his colleagues ruthlessly used the fact during the election campaign to discredit Dr Evatt and, through him, the Australian Labor Party?

It is, as we have seen, certainly true that Mr Menzies was very keen to announce Petrov's defection to the world before the Australian Parliament rose for the election on April 14. It would be naive to consider this keenness unrelated to the possible political advantages the defection might bring to the Government parties in the forthcoming election. The Menzies Government had twice unsuccessfully attempted — once by legislation which had been rejected in the High Court and once by a referendum which had been narrowly defeated by popular vote — to dissolve the Communist Party. On both occasions the leading opponent of their attempt had been the present Leader of the Labor Party, Dr Evatt. Evatt had also, more recently, led his party in opposition to the Government's trade union secret ballots legislation, which many Australians regarded as having been crucial in the struggle against Communist industrial power. The Petrov defection and Mr Menzies' revelations of 'systematic espionage and at least attempted subversion' could not but revive in the public mind memories of former battles between the Coalition and Labor over the Communist issue and were likely to convince many Australians that the Government's anti-Communist initiatives had been well-founded. On the evening of Mr Menzies' Petrov announcement many gallery journalists believed the Government's electoral stocks had risen sharply. In the excitement of the moment one, at least, thought the Petrov announcement had already determined the outcome of the election.

> The Communist plot now revealed by one of its leading diplomats (Frank Chamberlain wrote in the Melbourne *Sun*) so completely vindicates the Menzies-Fadden policy that the result of the elections is a foregone conclusion . . .
> Labour men are flabbergasted.
> They thought that Communism was a dead issue. They cannot accuse the Government of arranging the Petrov affair.[17]

Given opinions such as these it would be foolish in the extreme to believe that in mid-April Mr Menzies was either unaware of, or embarrassed about, the political advantages which might be expected to flow to the Coalition candidates in the forthcoming elections as a result of the Petrov defection announcement. This, however, is no great criticism. Despite his irritating habit of pretending never to stoop to mere political calculation, Menzies was, after all, a politician. Machiavelli had long ago commanded the Prince not to squander whatever good fortune Fate might throw in his direction.

Political advantage was, then, undoubtedly one motive propelling Mr Menzies towards a rapid defection announcement. It was not, however, his only motive. If Menzies had not announced the Petrov defection in April (as his critics suggest he should not have) it is difficult to believe that news of it would not anyhow have reached the Australian public — via the Soviet Embassy — before the election of May 29. Earlier that year an MVD officer, Yuri Rastvorov, had defected in Tokyo and been flown to the United States. Within a week of his defection the Soviet Embassy in Tokyo had announced his disappearance, publicly claiming that he had been kidnapped and that he was being held against his will in Japan by agents of American intelligence.[18] If the Soviet Embassy in Canberra had made a similar accusation to the Australian press the Menzies Government would have been placed on the defensive and possibly even seriously embarrassed by Opposition criticism, during the course of the election campaign, that it had behaved over Petrov in a dishonest and secretive fashion.

In the defection announcement and the establishment of the Royal Commission Mr Menzies' misgivings about the character or reliability of Dr Evatt also, again, possibly played a part. By establishing the Royal Commission before the election, even if the Labor Party were to be successful at the polls, Dr Evatt's hands — at least in relation to the broad juridical form of the enquiry into the Petrov material — had been tied. As with the failure to inform him in confidence of the Petrov defection when it occurred or that three members of his staff had been named in the Petrov documents, here again Dr Evatt had some justification for feeling that he was being treated with mistrust.* He was certainly, however, not justified in believing, as he came to, that Mr Menzies or his colleagues had ruthlessly used the Petrov defection and the documentary material Petrov had brought with him for political gain in the election campaign of 1954. If anything, the opposite was the case.

As we have seen, by mid-April Mr Menzies was aware that Dr Evatt's present Press Secretary, Fergan O'Sullivan, was the author of Document 'H' and that his Private Secretary, Allan Dalziel, had been for many years under study by Soviet intelligence operatives in Australia. Moreover, he was also aware by this time that O'Sullivan, Dalziel and Albert Grundeman had been cited as sources of information in Document 'J' — the document Petrov had told ASIO Rupert Lockwood had composed inside the Soviet Embassy in May 1953. If O'Sullivan's authorship of Document 'H' or the fact that he, Dalziel and Grundeman were cited as sources in Document 'J' had been revealed to the Australian public before the election, Dr Evatt would have had some genuine grounds for feeling aggrieved, if not for comparing the Petrov Affair with the 'Zinovieff Letter' scandal or the Reichstag fire incident. In fact Mr Menzies' behaviour gave him no such grounds.

---

* Neither of these last two matters adversely, of course, affected Labor's electoral chances in 1954. Indeed, if anything, the reverse. To judge by the violence of his reaction when he later discovered that O'Sullivan had been involved in Soviet espionage and that the names of Dalziel and Grundeman appeared in the Petrov documents, such knowledge in April or May 1954 may have seriously harmed Dr Evatt's performance on the campaign trail.

A search through the metropolitan press of Sydney and Melbourne in the months of April and May 1954 has revealed only two indirect references that suggest any leakage of information concerning the involvement of Dr Evatt's staff in the Petrov materials. On April 15 the *Sydney Morning Herald* was able to predict, on the basis of what it called 'Canberra sources', that

> people closely associated with politicians would be named in the Petrov case. There is speculation that some members of Parliament may have to give evidence in the inquiry following the disclosure of these names.[19]

As so often in the mid-1950s, the best informed journalist was Alan Reid. Buried in an article of his concerning the Petrov Affair in the *Sun-Herald* of April 18 is the suggestion 'that very important figures are involved — not key in themselves, but key in that they would occupy if Labor were returned to power, posts from which they would have access to vital information'.[20] Clearly one or two leakages had occurred in the early days of the defection. According to Whitlam and Stubbs senior journalists in Canberra in the early 1970s remembered them as having come from the camp of Sir Arthur Fadden.[21] Yet in these leaks no names — either of Dr Evatt or his staff — were revealed. The references were, moreover, buried in such a mass of sensational material that their impact on the electorate was almost certainly negligible.

There was, in addition, to these vague but generally accurate leaks one story which appeared in the Melbourne *Sun* and *Herald* on April 22 which suggested (as it turned out falsely) that Labor parliamentarians were directly implicated in Soviet espionage as 'the dupes of Communist agents'. Not surprisingly, this story, which both these Melbourne newspapers attributed to the 'North American Newspaper Alliance', particularly angered Dr Evatt.*[22] However as no newspaper followed it up it is unlikely, to say the least, to have had any impact on the fortunes of Dr Evatt or his party. Moreover any suspicion that Labor politicians might be directly involved in Soviet espionage was carefully extinguished by Victor Windeyer, Counsel assisting the Royal Commission, at its pre-election Canberra sitting. Windeyer told the Commissioners that there were, in the Petrov documents,

> two or three Members of Parliament mentioned. It is said of them that they are, in effect, worth remembering as possible 'in the dark' informants.... They are not persons whom the public generally regards as of great importance ... to the public life of the country ... [They] sit on opposite sides of the Chamber.[23]

The self-denying ordinance Mr Menzies and his Cabinet swore on April 13 concerning the suppression of names mentioned in the Petrov documents

---

* Dr Evatt later wrote thus about the article in the Melbourne *Sun*: 'On reading the article, I rang up Chamberlain, the representative of the *Sun* at Canberra, and referred to the foulness of the libel on the Labor Party. He gave me clearly to understand that he had been asked by his office in Melbourne to father the message to Melbourne under the Canberra date-line but that he had refused to do so.'

was scrupulously maintained throughout the period of the election campaign. When Mr Menzies was subsequently charged by Dr Evatt and his supporters with the most ruthless manipulation of the Petrov defection for political purposes, he not unjustly reminded his accusers of his decision to suppress the names of Fergan O'Sullivan, Allan Dalziel and Albert Grundeman.

I well remember (Menzies told the Parliament in October 1955) the cynical but wise remark of a former Supreme Court judge . . . 'You may think it is permissible to regard your opponent as a crook; but you must never commit the elementary error of thinking he is a fool'. The right honourable gentleman says . . . I was a crook. But why should he also charge me with being a fool? . . . When I made my announcement to the House about Petrov and the royal commission, I would have been, in the ordinary course, well entitled to quote a specimen of the documents Petrov had brought with him. If I had done this, the names of O'Sullivan, Grundeman and others, directly or indirectly associated with the right honourable the Leader of the Opposition would have become public property.[24]

The fact that Dr Evatt eventually came to believe that the role of Petrov in the Australian election of 1954 made the 'Zinovieff letter' and Reichstag fire incidents 'pale into insignificance' showed — given the suppression of the names of O'Sullivan, Dalziel and Grundeman — an extraordinary absence of balance and common sense.

Clearly Mr Menzies and his Coalition colleagues did not use the Petrov defections in the unscrupulous manner they might have — and in the manner Dr Evatt and his defenders have always suggested they did — in the election of 1954. What impact, however, did the Petrov Affair in fact have in the 1954 election?

As the official campaign opening approached, Australian newspapers began speculating about the likely role of the Petrovs in the coming election contest. Political journalists were generally of the opinion that party-political argument about the Petrov Affair was almost inevitably destined to become a major and possibly even the main issue of the coming campaign. The editorialists, however, had warned the Parties not to allow the Petrov defections to become an election issue. Already both Dr Evatt and Mr Calwell had been chided for introducing a partisan note into the nation's Petrov discussions.[25]

At the official opening of the Coalition's campaign by Mr Menzies at Canterbury Memorial Hall on May 4 both the curiosity of the press gallery and the piety of the editorialists were to some degree satisfied. Everybody noticed that in his speech the name of Petrov had not passed Mr Menzies' lips — as it was not to do for the entire extent of the campaign. On the other hand, in offering the Prime Minister a vote of thanks, the Treasurer and Deputy Leader of the Government parties, Sir Arthur Fadden, rhetorically asked the audience whether, at the time of the Petrov Commission, they would prefer to see Mr Menzies or Dr Evatt in charge of the nation's affairs. According to the Melbourne *Age* after Sir Arthur's remark Menzies looked 'momentarily uneasy'.[26]

Whether or not this was the case, on the following evening two senior Coalition Ministers again made passing reference to the Petrov Affair. In Sydney, Sir Eric Harrison, the Minister for Defence Production, criticised Dr Evatt harshly for representing Communist trades unionists in the courts. 'This man', he added, 'with this record now asks you to let him take charge of the Royal Commission into communist espionage'.[27] On the same night, speaking in Hamilton in support of a young, obscure Western district grazier (Malcolm Fraser) Sir Arthur Fadden — while claiming that he did not wish to deal with the Petrov case — reminded his audience of Dr Evatt's record of appeasing the Communist enemy and warned it that 'only the present Federal Government could be trusted to carry out with the rigour of the law the findings of the Royal Commission on espionage'.[28]

Sir Arthur's hypocritical disclaimer made him an easy target for editorial criticism. Fadden was now chastised, as Evatt and Calwell had been before him, for introducing party politics into the Petrov Affair. The *Sydney Morning Herald* was ironical about his performance; the strongly anti-Communist Melbourne *Herald* openly censorious.

> When Mr Menzies opened his Government's election campaign, he refrained from making political capital out of the circumstances which have led to the setting up of a Royal Commission on the allegations of Soviet-inspired subversion in Australia. His colleague, Sir Arthur Fadden, would be well advised to follow the same line.[29]

On the weekend prior to the election campaign Mr Menzies had advised Liberal Party state branches not to permit any mention of the Petrov Affair to appear in their election material.[30] Politically speaking, a partisan use of the Petrov defections would not only be unfair but might be seen by the electorate to be so. Legally speaking, after the executive council had agreed to form a Royal Commission on espionage, Mr Menzies evidently believed all discussion of the Petrov Affair would involve breaching the rules of *sub judice*.*[30]

After the Fadden-Harrison remarks of May 5 it appears that Mr Menzies acted to enforce a Petrov gag on all Coalition candidates.

> Early in the campaign (he told the Parliament in October 1955) it appeared that some reference had been made on a public platform. I at once communicated with every Government candidate in Australia — as everybody here can confirm — and

---

* Before the election the idea of *sub judice* was taken to such lengths that a group of students from Queensland University were compelled to dismantle a Petrov float they had constructed for a parade. After the election, and the rapid politicisation of the Affair, such early *sub judice* hopes had to be altogether abandoned.

said that as this matter would receive judicial investigation, I wanted it kept out of the political campaign. I have every reason to believe that this request of mine was scrupulously observed.[32]

And indeed it was. Although a defensive Sir Arthur Fadden denied to the press that his Petrov reference at Hamilton had infringed any Coalition agreement, he never again returned directly to the Petrov theme.[33] Nor, after May 6, did any other Coalition candidate. Extraordinarily enough, even W.C. Wentworth more or less held fire on the Petrov front.*[34]

Given that the Coalition had determined not to refer to the Petrov Affair on the hustings it was not, of course, surprising that the Opposition also generally kept silent about it. Dr Evatt was almost certainly privately convinced that the Petrov defection had been timed for the election. Some advice, indeed, came to him — in particular from a conspiratorially minded confidante, R.F.B. Wake, a former prominent ASIO officer with a deep grudge against Colonel Spry — urging him to seize the initiative on Petrov and campaign on the theme of a 'frame up', the theme that dominated the Petrov propaganda being produced in April and May by the Communist Party of Australia.[35] Fortunately for the Labor Party Dr Evatt declined this advice. On May 2 Alan Reid claimed that Evatt had consulted widely in his Party on the implications of Petrov and had come to the conclusion that 'he should watch his public statements most carefully'.[36] Like Mr Menzies Dr Evatt did not mention Petrov during the course of his campaign.

To show that the Petrov defections and their implications went almost entirely undiscussed during the course of the 1954 campaign is not, of course, to show that it played no role in influencing the outcome of the election. While Coalition candidates after May 5 avoided the Petrov Affair altogether in their campaign, it is also true that they played the Communist issue very hard in the election of 1954. Labor, the electorate was told time and again, had successfully frustrated the Coalition's attempts to have the Communist Party banned and unsuccessfully tried to frustrate Coalition legislation for trade union secret ballots. Nevertheless despite this Labor opposition, under Mr Menzies' anti-Communist regime Australian industry and the Australian nation had prospered. Under Mr Chifley and Dr Evatt the Communist Party had almost, during 1949, brought the nation to its knees. One of the Liberal Party advertisements in Victoria argued that 'THE COMMUNIST CONSPIRACY WAS THE GREATEST CHALLENGE TO PROGRESS AND SECURITY DURING THE EIGHT YEARS OF FEDERAL LABOR GOVERNMENT.... DON'T GIVE THE REDS A SECOND CHANCE'.[37]

The Coalition not only played the Communist issue hard, it also played it very personally. Dr Evatt might not be, it was argued, a Communist himself

---

* The 'less' here concerns a reference by Wentworth on May 7 to Dr Evatt's appointment of Dr Burton 'a young Communist sympathiser', as Secretary of the Department of External Affairs.

or even a Communist sympathiser but he was certainly the most powerful asset the Communist cause had ever had in Australia. The electorate was asked to judge Dr Evatt by consequences not intentions. The central moment in Coalition anti-Evatt propaganda came when Sir Arthur Fadden launched the Country Party's campaign. Fadden addressed to Dr Evatt a list of '13 questions'. His list began uncontroversially by asking Evatt whether he had been appointed Attorney-General on October 7 1941 and ended by asking him whether he had opposed the Government's secret ballots legislation 'the most potent weapon yet placed in their hands to combat Communist domination'. In between it enquired of him whether he had released well-known Communists from war-time internment; whether he had paid for an overseas trip for the Communist leader, Ernest Thornton, 'out of taxpayers funds'; whether he had represented Communist trade unions in the High Court; and whether he had campaigned 'vigorously against the Menzies Government's constitutional referendum designed to provide safeguards against Communist espionage, sabotage and subversion'.[38]

In general the superior metropolitan press — the *Sydney Morning Herald* and the *Age* — steered clear of endorsing the more strident aspects of the Fadden-Wentworth-Gullett anti-Communist campaign, finding (as we shall see) other grounds on which to base their support for the Coalition. On the other hand, the more popular press of Sydney and Melbourne, the *Daily Telegraph*, the Sydney *Sun*, the Melbourne *Herald* and *Sun*, all strongly and indeed enthusiastically supported the Fadden tone. In the final week of the election campaign the *Daily Telegraph*, evidently fearing a Coalition electoral defeat, even (this was unusual) briefly gave the Communist issue a pre-eminent place in the case of the return of the Menzies Government.[39]

Clearly Dr Evatt and the Labor Party were deeply concerned about the role the Communist issue might play in determining the election outcome. On the day after Fadden's challenge to him Dr Evatt — in one of those characteristic public storms where emotion overcame prudence — made an impassioned broadcast over national radio in which he spoke of his opponents as the 'vilest liars', 'smearers and slanderers' in the world. His voice, according to the *Age* report, was 'trembling with anger'. On this evening Evatt almost broke his self-imposed Petrov taboo. 'Very odd things', he told an audience at Dandenong, 'have been happening in the Australian Parliament in connection with the timing of important events'.[40]

In general, in order to answer the charge of frustrating Mr Menzies' anti-Communist programme, the ALP adopted for the 1954 election a very strongly anti-Communist line of its own. While the Coalition merely talked of Opposition to Communism, the Chifley-Evatt Labor Government, it claimed, had acted. Under Menzies, Dr Evatt pointed out, no Communists had been arrested or imprisoned, whereas under his Attorney-Generalship several had been.[41] Why, Arthur Calwell asked on numerous occasions, had the Menzies Government issued passports to Communists to allow them to travel to China during the Korean War?[42] Why was a well-known Communist leader, Laurie Aarons, even now meeting with other Communists in Indonesia?[43] When, Stan Keon continued, would Casey clean out the 'nest of traitors' in the public service he had spoken of two years earlier?[44] The most effective weapon against Communism in the trade union sphere, Labor claimed, had not been secret ballots but the long, persistent organisational struggles of the Industrial Groups. The Coalition might pretend to oppose Communism but they, in fact, secretly needed to preserve it, in order to have it on hand for election campaigns.[45] All Communists knew that the greatest destroyer of Communist hopes in Australia would be a strong and effective Labor Government — a Government of the workers.[46] As the campaign drew to a close ALP anti-Communism was an increasingly frequent aspect of its advertising. In his final remarks to the electorate Mr Menzies actually made no reference to the Communist issue, while Dr Evatt reminded voters that 'the Labor Party fights and has always fought Communism'.[47]

Communism was, then, an issue in the election of 1954 as it was in every Australian election between 1949 and 1969 and as it certainly would have been in 1954 whether or not the Petrovs had defected. It is, of course, likely that the Petrov defections gave it a greater prominence and sting than it might otherwise have assumed in the campaign, although, as we shall see, it was certainly not the most important 1954 election issue. It is also likely that when in 1954 the politicians cried Communism the people thought Petrov and that, to some degree, thinking of the Petrov Affair and its implications aided the Coalition with its strongly anti-Communist rhetoric and programme and harmed the Opposition with its more ambiguous record on the issue.

It can, of course, have done no harm to the Government's electoral prospects that in the middle of the penultimate week of the campaign the newspapers were again dominated by the Petrov Affair, this time by reports of the first three days' hearings of the Royal Commission on espionage,* held in a specially redecorated concert hall in Canberra before a tense and expectant audience which included a large part of the diplomatic corps and sixty Australian and foreign journalists. It would, again, be naive to believe that Mr Menzies and his colleagues were unaware of the possible political advantages of a pre-election sitting of the Royal Commission. On the other hand, in fairness to them, it must be pointed out that the Government, in the latter half of April, came under considerable newspaper pressure to convene the Royal Commission with the least possible delay. In the week following Petrova's defection the Melbourne *Herald* ran what amounted to an editorial campaign on the need for an early Commission and, even before that, a press interview with the Petrovs. 'For the peace of mind of our own people', it editorialised on April 20, 'the start of the Commission's tasks should be

---

* What precisely transpired at these hearings will be a matter for the succeeding chapter.

expedited'.[48] On April 23 it ran a front-page editorial hostile to the Government entitled 'End All This Secrecy'.[49] Three times in the week following Darwin the *Age* editorialised on the same theme. 'There should not be', it argued, 'a moment of avoidable delay in telling the people in broad outline what it was that Mr Petrov disclosed to the Government'.[50] On April 23 even the most 'left-wing' political commentator to be found in the metropolitan dailies, Peter Russo of the *Argus*, argued for all haste in convening the Petrov enquiry. 'The sooner the Royal Commission gets down to business the sooner shall we be able to see the Petrovs in correct dimension.'[51] It is perhaps, in the circumstances, unreasonable to have expected Mr Menzies to forego the political advantages of an early Commission sitting in order to run the risk of serious editorial and possibly even Opposition criticism.

It is certainly true (as we shall see and as Dr Evatt subsequently argued) that in the pre-election hearings of the Commission evidence which might have embarrassed the Government was withheld — most importantly that Petrov had been paid £5000 on his defection. (Whether it was withheld for that reason is another matter.) But it is also true that material which would certainly have damaged Dr Evatt and Labor — the names of the author of Document 'H' and the sources of Document 'J' — was likewise deliberately withheld. Moreover, as we have seen, in these hearings Windeyer made a point of assuring the Commissioners and through them the public that no Labor parliamentarians were implicated in Soviet espionage. The fair-mindedness, the solemnity, even the dullness of the first days of the hearings (where the Petrov couple had not been called to give evidence) more than satisfied even the strongly anti-McCarthyist Melbourne *Argus*, which supported Labor during the campaign.

> There was an air about the opening session of the Royal Commission on espionage yesterday that should have done Australian hearts good. . . . In some hands, this investigation *could* become a heresy hunt . . . Australia is lucky that its judicial system is modelled on the British system, which is about as decent and honest an instrument of justice as any that mankind has yet devised.[52]

In the election campaign of May 1954 it cannot be emphasised too strongly that it was not Communism, let alone Petrov, that was the dominant issue. The overwhelming issue, which in reality swamped all others, was Dr Evatt's startling proposals — made in his campaign opening on May 6 — for the extension of the Welfare State in Australia. In brief Dr Evatt promised, if Labor were elected to office, to abolish the means test on old age pensions within the life of a single Parliament, to increase at once the rates of old age, invalid, widow and repatriation pensions and child endowment, to provide a form of universal medical insurance, to increase Commonwealth finance for road building and to provide, through the Commonwealth bank, housing loans at 3% repayable within 45 years. He pledged to cut sales tax on certain items (in particular home furnishings) and even to make certain cuts in direct taxes. His programme, he claimed, could be financed through eliminating Government 'waste and extravagance', from an expected budget surplus, through loans raising and by diverting the cost of the Commonwealth works from annual revenue to the Loans Fund. In his campaign opening Dr Evatt did not offer any overall cost estimate of his programme, let alone an itemised account.[53]

Shibboleths of the past — in particular all discussions of socialism and all undertakings to nationalise certain industries — were carefully avoided. (He signalled clearly, for example, that bank nationalisation would not be revived.) In pledging the abolition of the means test*[54] and arguing that it penalised thrift, and in appealing to the needs of the home buyer, Dr Evatt was both employing Liberal rhetoric and attempting to outbid the Coalition in the quest for the 'middle class' electorate. In his campaign Dr Evatt tried to move his party from the Age of Chifley to the Age of Whitlam in a single stride. His programme of 1954 was a bold and dramatic gamble.

With the metropolitan press of Sydney and Melbourne Dr Evatt's basket of promises went down like a lead balloon. Almost with one voice (if not one tone) the editorials argued that the Evatt programme was little more than a cynical attempt to bribe voters. Australians no longer believed in Father Christmas. How were the costs of Dr Evatt to be met? Was Australia now destined to return to the inflationary spiral from which it had so recently and so painfully escaped? The Sydney *Sun* thought Dr Evatt's 'fairy floss' proposals would drive Australia into a 'bottomless pit of inflation'.[55] The Melbourne *Herald* compared the Menzies-Fadden 'business-like management' with Dr Evatt's 'wild cat finance'.[56] The *Sydney Morning Herald* thought Evatt's election speech 'the most irresponsible ever delivered to Australian voters'. The *Age* spoke in the *lingua franca* of the metropolitan dailies when it commended voters to ask themselves 'whether it is wise to risk a growing stability and prosperity . . . for a shadowy future in which the prospect of a return to inflation looms large'.[57]

Dr Evatt's campaign speech provided Mr Menzies with the opening he needed. Dr Evatt's proposals were, he announced, 'the most disgraceful' he had encountered in twenty-six years of political life, an insult to the character and intelligence of Australians, certain (if implemented) to plunge the nation to economic ruin. A high offical of the Treasury had, on his instruction, made

---

* Within Labor ranks there were undoubtedly misgivings about Dr Evatt's promises, although during the election, even on the means test, only the longstanding anti-abolitionist, W.M. Bourke, actually broke ranks. In March, before the ALP election programme was finalised Bourke had made a very strong speech against abolition. His opposition to means test abolition went back at least to September 1953. Bourke was associated with the Movement and his breaking ranks during the election probably played some small part in the later decision of Dr Evatt to attack it. Opposition to the means test was by no means restricted, however, to pro-Movement ALP members. Their nemesis, Kennelly, was also reported to have opposed Dr Evatt on this question in September 1953.

an estimate of the cost of Evatt. The figure he had arrived at, Mr Menzies told an audience in Brisbane, was £357,800,000 ($4,300,000,000).[58] Three days later Sir Arthur Fadden, in his campaign opening, provided a rather devastating critique, from the Treasury point of view, of what he called 'Dr Evatt's crack-pot financial revolution'. Evatt's pledges would cost the people an additional 40% to 'the total tax revenues in the present year'. The money would have to be raised either by credit expansion, the use of the printing press and consequent inflation, by diverting loan funds from the States, or by vast increases in direct or indirect taxes.[59]

Labor, through Calwell and Senator McKenna, naturally promptly provided alternative costings to the Coalition's 'faked figures' and attempted to demonstrate the fiscal responsibility of their Leader's strategy.[60] Nevertheless for Coalition candidates Dr Evatt's Welfare State programme provided the most promising line of attack. Some, taking their lead from the Prime Minister,[61] linked Dr Evatt's profligacy with the anti-Communist motif by suggesting that Communism would feed upon the inflation and economic ruin Labor would visit upon the nation. Alternatively, Sir Eric Harrison told an audience of seven which gathered to hear him at Mitcham, that under Labor living standards would fall to those of Russian peasants,[62] while W.C. Wentworth thought Dr Evatt might prove the Australian Kerensky.[63]

There is also, however, no doubt that certain Government members and supporters feared the electoral impact of Dr Evatt's promises.[64] As the campaign neared its end one pro-Coalition newspaper — the *Sunday Telegraph* — panicked and called upon Mr Menzies to 'get in and fight', that is to say to offer the electorate something more tangible than his record of steady and responsible economic management.[65] The Prime Minister refused to join in what he called a public 'auction'. He could not help it 'if the Australian electors care to abandon solid prosperity and security for a wild-cat policy which will eventually destroy them'.[66]

On May 29 Australians went to the polls. Some 50 per cent of the electorate supported the Labor Party and some 47 per cent the Coalition.[*67] (A little over 1 per cent voted Communist and a little under 2 per cent for independent candidates.) Because of the closer concentration of Labor voters the Coalition was returned to Government although with a reduced majority. After the election of 1951 the Coalition had 69 seats in the House of Representatives

---

* According to the final result 50.03% of valid votes were cast for the ALP. In fact, this figure slightly exaggerates the real level of Labor support. In 1954 six constituencies were uncontested, five of them 'belonging' to the Coalition and one to Labor. Moreover in three contested constituencies there were no Coalition candidates, only independents and Communists. If the potential Coalition voters had not been, as it were, statistically disfranchised, Labor would have polled slightly less than the magical 50%.

and Labor 52 seats; after the election of 1954 64 and 57 respectively. If five additional Coalition seats had gone to Labor, Dr Evatt would have been Prime Minister with a majority of two in the lower House.[68]

It has long been an article of faith of Dr Evatt's supporters and Labor stalwarts that the result of the 1954 election was determined by the Petrov defections. In 1974 Nicholas Whitlam and John Stubbs attempted to prove this faith was not unfounded by reference to the Gallup Polls. According to them, following the Petrov defections, there occurred 'a complete reversal of the drift of public opinion'.

> Before, the Labor Party had every chance of forming a new government . . . the last published opinion sample had shown the Opposition party commanding 52 per cent of the vote. Now a Gallup Poll published in the *Sydney Morning Herald* on 23 May showed a remarkable switch in popular sentiment. The survey, which had been completed on 1 May, indicated that the Menzies Government had the support of 57 per cent of the voters.[69]

If the facts indeed were as outlined by Whitlam and Stubbs the case about the role of the Petrov defections in the election of 1954 could be closed. In reality their case rests upon two obvious errors. What they claim to have been the last Gallup Poll taken before the Petrov defection announcement was taken in mid-February 1954. It revealed support for Labor (including, as Gallup always did, the Communist vote) at 52 per cent and support for the Coalition at 47 per cent. In late March 1954 (apparently unbeknown to Whitlam and Stubbs) Gallup polled the nation again. It now discovered that support for Labor (including the Communist Party) had declined to 49 per cent, while support for the Coalition had actually increased to 49 per cent, with 2 per cent of the voters preferring independent candidates.[70] In late March 1954 — before the announcement of the Petrov defection — support for the Coalition (at least as measured by the usually accurate Gallup) was actually considerably higher than it proved to be at the election of May 29.

Even if Whitlam and Stubbs are wrong, then, in their first contention — that the ALP had a clear electoral lead until the Petrov defection announcement — what is to be made of their second contention, namely that after the Petrov defections a Gallup Poll taken on May 1 showed Coalition support to have soared to an extraordinary 57 per cent of the popular vote? Surely this, by itself, should constitute proof that the Petrovs swung the election. The trouble here is that the 57 per cent claim is sheer fiction, based upon a misreading of a Gallup Poll finding, published not (as the authors claim) in the *Sydney Morning Herald* but the *Sun-Herald* of May 23 1954. What this article showed was that in fifteen city electorates which had voted solidly Liberal in 1951 (seven with a poll of less than 55 per cent, eight with a poll of between 57 and 61 per cent) 57 per cent of the voters on May 1 and 56 per cent on May 15 intended to vote Liberal in the coming election. This level of support, Gallup estimated, would be sufficient to return the Government to power. Apparently either Mr Whitlam or Mr Stubbs took in the headline of the article ('Gallup Poll Favours Return of Government') and glanced at its statistical table but omitted to read it.[71] From this misreading the Petrov myth was proved for a new generation of students!

The following statistical table — which combines electoral results and Gallup Polls — may help begin to chart the ebb and flow of opinion between the Representatives election of April 28 1951 and that of May 29 1954.

	Liberal-Country Party	ALP*	Others
April 1951 — Election, H. of R.	50	49	1
August 1951 — Gallup	49	50	1
October 1951 — Gallup	45	54	1
February 1952 — Gallup	47	52	1
May 1952 — Gallup	43	56	1
October 1952 — Gallup	40	59	1
February 1953 — Gallup	39	60	1
May 1953 — Election, Senate	44	54	2
June 1953 — Gallup	45	54	1
September 1953 — Gallup	45	54	1
December 1953 — Gallup	48	51	1
February 1954 — Gallup	47	52	1
March (late) 1954 — Gallup	49	49	2
May (early) 1954 — Gallup	50	49	1
May 21 1954 — Gallup	48	51	1
May 29 1954 — Election, H. of R.	47	51	2

From this table the following (necessarily tentative) conclusions can be drawn. During the second half of 1951, following the so-called 'horror budget', Coalition support declined sharply, although it had improved slightly by early 1952. In late 1952 and in particular in early 1953, in an extremely serious economic climate (with unemployment, inflation, taxation increases and import restrictions only the largest problems) Coalition support declined to probably the lowest level — 39 % — experienced by the non-Labor parties since the Great Depression. By the May 1953 Senate elections Coalition support was beginning to pick up, although not yet sufficiently to save the Coalition from landslide defeat at a general election. This remained the position in the spring of 1953.

---

* All ALP statistics here include the Communist vote. This was the Gallup practice of the 1950s, based on the fact that at this time the Communist Party invariably directed their preferences to the ALP.

By December 1953, for the first time in more than two years — as the austere Menzies-Fadden economic policies began to bear fruit — the Coalition appeared to have some real chance of success at the next general election. This possibility was made clear to the nation by the solid Country Party victory at the Gwydir by-election, where the Coalition vote almost returned to its 1951 general election level.[72] In February 1954 the Gallup Poll recorded a slight swing back to the Labor Party. (On this Poll the entire statistical base of the Petrov-turned-the-election case rests.) However, in late March 1954, at the climax of the triumphal Royal Tour, Coalition prospects looked extremely good — with the conservatives and Labor both polling at 49%, enough to secure a comfortable Government victory. After the defections of Petrov and Petrova the Gallup Poll of May 1 showed a marginal (1%) increase in support for the Coalition, although no percentage decline at all in Labor support. Possibly — and this is as much as can be ventured — the dramatic events were responsible for delaying the drift back to Labor of some of the support the Coalition had gathered during the Royal Tour. It appears that during the official election campaign of May some support did move back to Labor, although, as it happened, not quite sufficient for it to secure victory. Perhaps the number of swinging voters attracted by the Evatt programme was larger than the number of those fearful of its consequences. Perhaps the passage of time dulled the temporary pro-Coalition effects of the Royal Tour and the Petrov dramas, with the electorate returning, roughly, in May 1954, to the position of December 1953.

In the rise of the Coalition from the dismal 39% of February 1953 to the 48% of December 1953, a level of support which more or less held until the election of May 1954, clearly the dominant underlying factor was the perceived success of Government economic policy. By late 1953 and early 1954 all the major indicators — inflation, unemployment and import levels, trade and budget balances — were looking favourable. (On the eve of the general election even the pro-Labor *Argus* felt compelled to congratulate what they hoped would be the outgoing Menzies-Fadden Ministry on its economic achievements.[73]) The movement of opinion to the Coalition in March and April 1954 appears, at least on a survey of the Polls, to have begun not with the Petrov defections but with the Royal Tour. The standard case, that these defections were solely responsible for turning a certain Labor victory into a narrow defeat, is at best a vast and misleading over-simplification.*

---

* Except, of course, in the trivial sense that in *any* close election any number of particular issues can be claimed to have determined the election's outcome.

9

THE ROYAL COMMISSION

Conventional wisdom now tells us that Australia in the early 1950s passed through not only an anti-Communist but also a 'McCarthyist' period of its history.[1] According to this wisdom the Petrov Affair was 'the culmination of Australia's McCarthy era' and the Royal Commission on Espionage 'a cold-war spectacular',[2] conducted 'in an atmosphere more akin to that of a "show-trial" in Moscow than to judicial procedures in a democratic country'.[3] Characteristically, at the end of its short entry on the Petrov case the *Dictionary of Australian Politics* advises its readers to refer to 'McCarthyism'.[4]

The McCarthyist interpretation of the Petrov Affair in general and of the proceedings of the Royal Commission in particular by no means, however, represents merely the retrospective judgment of a later generation of Australians on a former, supposedly shameful, period of their nation's history. Within three days of Mr Menzies' defection announcement to the Parliament, Dr Evatt — on the flimsiest of pretexts — had, as we have seen, compared the Prime Minister's political style unfavourably to that of Senator McCarthy. Even more strikingly (if less importantly), within one day of the announcement of the intention to establish the Royal Commission the Australian Communist Party already 'knew' that it would be thoroughly McCarthyist in style and motive.

> Menzies (the *Guardian* observed on April 14) will try to turn it against the Communists, Labour Party leaders, trade union officials, church dignitaries, scientists, University professors, journalists — against anybody who stands as the least barrier to the frightful American plans for atomic war.[5]
> As the McCarthy inquisitions in America show, no citizen is safe from these fascist style witch-hunts.

The McCarthyist interpretation of the Petrov Royal Commission actually preceded not only its deliberations but even its creation.

There are many misconceptions about the atmosphere of Australian political life at the time of the Petrov Affair, but none more obvious than those concerning McCarthyism. At the time the Petrov Affair broke Senator McCarthy was in the United States already a spent force, locked in a losing battle with the Eisenhower administration over his latest wild charges about Communist influence in the U.S. Army.[6] In Australia McCarthyism was by now an accusation and not a political movement. Both mainline Laborites (who were overwhelmingly strongly anti-Communist) *and* Coalition conservatives considered McCarthyism an illegitimate species of anti-Communism, where due process of law and cool judicial sifting of evidence had been sacrificed to highly sensational and politicised hearings before cameras and where reputations and careers had been destroyed by false accusation, innuendo and smear. It was precisely because McCarthyism was an accusation (from which the entire liberal political culture recoiled) that the Australian Communist Party tried to tar all anti-Communist activity with the McCarthyist brush, and that the Labor Party tried to label the Coalition brand of anti-Communism (as opposed to its own democratic brand) as McCarthyist in nature. For many Australians in the mid-1950s — on both the Left and the Right — McCarthyism was a peculiarly American phenomenon which demonstrated, by contrast, the superior maturity of the British legal-political tradition to which we were, fortunately, the heirs.

The Royal Commission on Espionage was established by the Menzies Government in a general political atmosphere best described as anti-McCarthyist anti-Communism. Of this atmosphere let two small examples suffice. At the first Cabinet where the Petrov defection was discussed it was, as we have seen, resolved to suppress all names mentioned in the Petrov documents before the Royal Commission was formed. The reason was to avoid — and here the language was self-consciously anti-McCarthyist — any suggestion of a 'smear campaign'.[7] Similarly in the 'Act relating to the Royal Commission on Espionage', which passed through the Parliament in August 1954, it was made an offence punishable by a fine of £500 or one year's imprisonment for an employer to dismiss an employee on the grounds of his appearance before the Royal Commission. The onus of proof here rested on the employer.[8] In establishing the Royal Commission the Menzies Government strove to create an independent and impartial judicial tribunal which would investigate Soviet espionage in Australia and its connection with the Australian Communist Party, whilst avoiding what it regarded as the excesses of McCarthyism. Whether or not the Government and the Commission it established succeeded in this ambition is, of course, another matter, to which, directly or indirectly, a considerable part of the succeeding analysis in this work will be addressed.

Somewhat inauspiciously, even the creation of the Royal Commission on Espionage was enveloped in a series of minor difficulties and controversies. One of the first actually arose from the decision of the Menzies Government to consult with the Opposition (Dr Evatt and the Labor Leader in the Senate, Nicholas McKenna) on the Commission's terms of reference. Dr Evatt appears to have prepared for this meeting with some enthusiasm and — at least to judge by the short paper he wrote in preparation for it — in a somewhat hawkish frame of mind. The Commission would be, he wrote, 'the most important which has ever been held in the history of Australia'. Its terms of reference must be carefully drawn in order not to 'nullify or prevent any subsequent prosecutions for treason, subversion or any other crime against the security of the people of Australia'. Without such 'safeguards' the Commission was in danger of degenerating into a 'farce'. In order to help write the terms of reference and to prevent the Commission becoming a farce Dr Evatt requested full access to the Petrov documents and statements.[9] Unsurprisingly — given their contents, the nature of the enquiry and the Government's view of Dr Evatt's untrustworthiness — Dr Evatt's request was turned down. At once Senator McKenna, on behalf of Evatt, wrote to the Attorney-General, Senator Spicer, expressing a regret 'that our full cooperation with the Government has not been reciprocated'.[10] Clearly Dr Evatt was offended. Eventually he came to regard his one Petrov meeting with the Government as a 'pretended consultation', while his supporters appear to have forgotten it ever took place.

Dr Evatt would have liked some part in the selection of the Royal Commissioners. He was, however, excluded from this process. Nevertheless, it proved even more difficult than settling the terms of reference. As Colonel Spry was soon to discover Mr Menzies' first choice for the Commission was Australia's greatest jurist, Sir Owen Dixon, who in 1954 was Chief Justice of the High Court and at the height of his powers. Before the Royal Commission was appointed Sir Owen, who was a friend of Colonel Spry, told him in confidence that while in principle he was opposed to High Court judges sitting on Royal Commissions he had thought very carefully this time about whether he might make an exception. Like Dr Evatt, presumably Sir Owen Dixon thought of the Royal Commission on Espionage as of supreme importance. Eventually he decided against becoming the sole Commissioner.[11] (In August 1955 a speech he delivered at a law conference suggested that he was relieved that this had been his decision.)[12]

In lieu of Sir Owen Dixon, Mr Menzies decided to approach three Supreme Court judges (Dr Evatt had actually suggested the need for an enlarged Commission) — Mr Justice Owen of New South Wales, Mr Justice O'Bryan of Victoria and Mr Justice Philp of Queensland.[13] Only the Owen appointment — who was made Commission Chairman — proceeded moderately smoothly. When Mr Menzies approached the Victorian Labor Premier, John Cain, his request was passed on to the Victorian Supreme Court. Its head, Sir Edmund Herring, reiterated the longstanding (although not invariable) reluctance of the Victorian Court to permit its members to serve on Royal Commissions.[14] There is no evidence that this refusal rested on anything other than adherence to strict legal principle. In the absence of supporting evidence it is fanciful in the extreme to claim (as pro-Evatt historians invariably do) that the Victorian reticence to release a Supreme Court judge for service on the Petrov Royal Commission was motivated by some hostility to Mr Menzies' handling of the political aspects of the Petrov Affair.*[15] In Mr Justice O'Bryan's place the Government chose Mr Justice Ligertwood of the South Australian Supreme Court. By no stretch of the imagination can this appointment be seen as anti-Labor. Ligertwood had twice been chosen to serve on Evatt-appointed Royal Commissions, once clearing Eddie Ward of a corruption charge.

Mr Menzies' approach to the Queensland Labor Premier (and future DLP Leader and Australian Ambassador to Dublin) Vince Gair turned into something of a diplomatic disaster for the Government. According to the story Menzies told the Parliament, when he approached Mr Gair with a courtesy request to release a member of the Queensland Supreme Court for the Commission he already had Mr Justice Philp firmly in mind. Gair, however, believed (or claimed to believe) that the choice of judge had been left to Queensland. Gair approached the Chief Justice of the Queensland Supreme Court, who selected Mr Justice Townley for the job. Menzies, however, wanted Philp not Townley. As soon as he learnt of the mistake he telephoned Gair and, then, Townley. To Mr Justice Townley he explained the confusion and offered his apologies for any embarrassment it might have caused him. According to Menzies Townley accepted his explanation in good humour.[16] It was, however, election season. Apparently Mr Gair could not resist revealing to the press that Mr Menzies had 'rejected' the offer of Mr Justice Townley's services on his Royal Commission.

Unwittingly, then, two very characteristic anti-Communist types of the 1950s — Sir Edmund Herring, an Anglophile conservative, and Vince Gair, an Irish-Australian larrikin — prepared the ground for one of the more improbable elements in the Petrov myth, namely that Mr Menzies had experienced great difficulties in 'finding judges willing to serve on such a highly politicized body' as the Royal Commission on Espionage.[17]

Other major Commission appointments proceeded with less publicity than that of the judges. At least in part on Sir Owen Dixon's recommendation, Victor Windeyer Q.C., an Establishment lawyer and a leader of the Sydney

---

* Thus Messrs Whitlam and Stubbs: 'Recognising the political overtones of the Petrov affair, they chose to restrict their activities to the due process of law; they said that "in British countries", except in rare cases, judges "retain the confidence of the people" because they adhere to interpreting the relationship between the law and the Queen's subjects. Then, in a pointed attack on the handling of the Petrov affair, the Victorian judges declared: "Parliament, supported by a wise public opinion, has jealously guarded the Bench from the danger of being drawn into the region of political controversy"'. This "pointed attack" was actually an exact quotation from a letter written by the Chief Justice of the Victorian Supreme Court, Mr Justice Irvine, to the Victorian Attorney-General. Its date was August 14, 1923.

Bar, was chosen as Counsel assisting the Commisson. When Colonel Spry, who had served under him in the Sydney University Regiment, heard from Sir Owen of his appointment his heart sank just a little. Windeyer had a fine legal brain and was a man of high virtue, but he was an Equity lawyer. Spry had hoped for the appointment of a leading criminal barrister for the purpose of cross-examining the key witnesses ASIO planned to call.[18] Not even Windeyer's assistant, George Pape of the Melbourne Bar, had much experience in the criminal law. As Secretary to the Commission — the pivotal administrative post — Kenneth Herde of the Prime Minister's Department was chosen. Concerning him also there were doubts. In the past, and again on this occasion, ASIO had experienced Herde's great keenness to retain the services on his secretarial staff of a particular female typist, and of a certain deviousness of approach on his part to ASIO investigations of this lady. While ASIO assumed Herde's motives were probably innocent, an internal memorandum at least broached (but did not press) a more disturbing Security possibility.[19]

The last major Commission appointment passed almost without controversy or misgiving. On Mr Justice Owen's recommendation the Commission decided to appoint a Russian translator and interpreter of the highest reputation and of assured impartiality. Owen suggested someone was needed who had never worked for Australian Security. Colonel Spry's investigations led to Major Birse, an Englishman who had been brought up in Czarist Russia, who had interpreted for Winston Churchill at Teheran and Yalta and who had been rewarded with both a British CBE and a Soviet Order of the Red Banner.[20] Only Dr Evatt, who resented the fact that Major Birse had arrived in Australia on May 28 (on the day before the election) could find any ground for hostility to this particular appointment.[21]

On May 3 1954 — on the day before Mr Menzies launched the Government's election campaign — the terms of reference for the Royal Commission and some major appointments to it were approved by Executive Council. Although ultimate authority and daily decision-making now passed from the Government to the Commissioners and their assistants one very important meeting did take place, on May 9, between the Government and the Commission. This meeting was attended by Mr Menzies, the head of his department Allan Brown, Victor Windeyer, Colonel Spry and Professor Bailey. Here a number of decisions of considerable importance for the deliberations of the Commission and the future politics of the Petrov Affair were taken.

The most pressing, but ultimately least important, concerned the question of the press conference with the Petrovs which had been planned for the following morning. Windeyer told the meeting that Dr Evatt had telephoned him and expressed the view that to hold such a conference might constitute contempt of the Commission. Windeyer had spoken to Owen who thought Evatt had a case. Mr Menzies decided at once to cancel the press conference.[22] That evening Colonel Spry explained to the managing editor of the *Age* that the interview had been cancelled because of the likelihood that Dr Evatt would make of it 'a political issue' and because the question of contempt of the Commission might arise.[23]

From the point of view of the future politics of the Petrov Affair the most important decision taken on May 9 concerned the problem of whether to disclose to the Commission the fact of the £5000 payment ASIO had made to Petrov on April 3. On this matter, as Windeyer's letter to Menzies of September 1955 makes clear, he and Spry were in fundamental disagreement.

> I informed you that I had learnt from Spry that Petrov had been paid £5,000. I think you did not earlier know of this. Spry had said to me that he considered this should not be publicly revealed as it was contrary to well established principle in the United Kingdom as well as Australia ever to publish details of the expenditure of Secret Service funds. I told you of this and said that to me the amount seemed small in the circumstances, but that I considered its payment was certainly relevant and should be disclosed, the only question in my mind being the proper way to bring it before the Commission. As Spry and I had somewhat differing views, I asked your opinion. You said you considered it was a matter to be proved and proved publicly, and that this should be done later in its proper setting when Petrov was examined.[24]

Simply put Mr Menzies' Solomonic judgment determined that the public criticism which might arise from the disclosure of the Petrov payment would not be heard until after the election. There were no plans to call Petrov at the Commission's pre-election hearings at Canberra.*[25] Although Dr Evatt's subsequent rage at the non-disclosure of the £5,000 payment before the election was certainly disproportionate to the offence, his suspicions were not in this case entirely baseless.

By far the most important decisions, however, taken on May 9 concerned the question of publicity. Mr Menzies expressed to Windeyer the view that in his opening address to the Commission (before the election) no names should be named. He then raised the question of whether or not the Royal Commission should be held in secret or in the open. Windeyer informed him that Owen preferred an open inquiry.[26]

Clearly the decision on this matter was fundamental to the social impact of the future proceedings of the Commission. Important considerations and examples pointed in different directions. A secret inquiry would breach the ingrained judicial principle that justice must be seen to be done and dash the hopes held in ASIO and the Government that the Royal Commission might instruct the public on the dangers of Soviet espionage. Moreover it was also clear that secrecy bred gossip and rumour. There were, however, on the other hand, very serious civil liberties' objections to an open Commission. Almost inevitably even quite innocent persons mentioned in the Petrov documents would be harmed by being called to appear in public as witnesses. It was at

---

* As it happened, however, Richards was called at Canberra. He was just as competent a witness to the £5,000 payment as Petrov, but was not in fact questioned about it.

least in part for this reason that the Royal Commission on which the Petrov inquiry was modelled — the Gouzenko inquiry in Canada — had been held entirely *in camera*. Eight years after its completion the transcript of its proceedings (which had been flown in early May to Australia by a Canadian diplomatic courier) was still classified 'top secret'.[27]

No doubt all these considerations were present to the mind of the Commission, the Government and ASIO in early May. However, if Mr Windeyer's memory of the meeting of May 9 is accurate, Mr Menzies' decisive opinion was delivered with some levity and on pragmatic rather than principled grounds. Mr Menzies felt that while an *in camera* Commission might be more 'effective' it would prove a political disaster. 'The press in Australia would never cease protesting if it were sought to hold the whole inquiry in private.'[28] And not only the press. In the Parliament on August 12 1954 two Labor members, Dr Evatt and E. James Harrison, even criticised the article in the Royal Commission on Espionage Act which permitted the holding of some *in camera* hearings[29]. Mr Menzies political instincts were undoubtedly well-founded.

The Royal Commission opened its hearings in Canberra's Albert Hall on May 17. In the first half of May benches, bar tables and witness boxes had been hastily constructed,[30] while some borrowed dignity was brought to a Hall more customarily employed for dances and concerts than Royal Commissions with velvet curtains and tasselled ropes from the nearby Parliament.[31] More seriously, careful provision was made for the sixty international and Australian journalists who descended upon Canberra. At short notice the Commonwealth Department of Post and Telegraphs installed a large number of telephones and teleprinters. 'Experienced pressmen with a world reputation', Allsopp of the Parliamentary Press gallery wrote to Kenneth Herde, 'told me they had never seen a better set-up for press coverage in any part of the world'.[32]

The Canberra hearings at Albert Hall were entirely dominated by Victor Windeyer, who addressed the Commission for two and a half days in a manner some described as deliberate and others as painfully tedious. He began where the meeting of May 9 had ended, on the question of publicity. The quasi-judicial nature of the Commission, the fact that Parliament appeared to believe that the Commission it had established would be held in public and the citizen's right to be informed about a matter as serious as Soviet espionage all pointed, in Windeyer's view, to an open Commission. With this reasoning Mr Justice Owen concurred. He intended, he informed the world, to conduct his Commission, as far as possible, in public. No one, however, Windeyer continued, would be named at all until investigations had proceeded farther.

Windeyer's opening remarks balanced anti-McCarthyism against anti-Communism. The Commission was engaged 'not in a heresy hunt but in an investigation of acts prejudicial to the security and defence of Australia'. He could not emphasise too strongly his conviction that the Commission must in no way interfere with 'freedom of thought'. Individuals must be protected from 'malicious gossip or ignorant speculations'. He already felt in a position to state that certain people, whose connections with the Soviet Embassy had been completely proper, had been named in the Petrov documents.

> We do not appear here to attack or to shield or to defend anyone.... Where the facts lead and whom the truth may hurt, we feel, is not our concern. We shall, however, endeavour to avoid saying anything which could be used by the malicious to smear anyone's reputation.

This was a strange beginning to a 'show-trial'.

On the other hand Windeyer certainly had no qualms about indicating his hostility to Communism. The most promising field of recruitment to Soviet espionage in Australia were 'adherents of Communist doctrine and Communist sympathisers'. For persons even of high intelligence but 'no firmly anchored religious beliefs' or 'inherited loyalties' the doctrine of Communism appeared capable of instilling great 'devotion' and 'self-sacrifice'. He stressed that in Australia recruitment to Soviet espionage work occurred from ideological rather than pecuniary motives. The ethic of Communism — where evil means were justified by the good ends they were believed to serve — seemed to Windeyer 'to make what other persons would call treachery . . . easy and acceptable'.

Windeyer turned from his sociology of espionage to the Petrovs. It ill-became those who sympathised with Communist treachery, he said, to sneer at a couple who had 'dramatically and completely' renounced allegiance to their homeland. In explaining their defections Windeyer placed far greater emphasis on the Petrovs' fears of the retribution which awaited them at home than on their attraction to the Australian or democratic way of life which Mr Menzies had stressed in Parliament on April 13. However Windeyer's own portrayal of Petrov as a close personal associate of the fallen Beria was misconceived. Windeyer reminded the Commission of the need to scrutinise the Petrovs' evidence with the greatest care but reminded the nation that they deserved 'friendly understanding'. Their decision to defect, he pointed out, had earned them 'the implacable enmity of the rulers of Russia and of Russian sympathisers'.

At Canberra, Victor Windeyer presented the nation for the first time in its history with an authoritative outline of Soviet espionage in Australia. Apparently it not only could but did happen here. The MVD team in Australia during Petrov's Residency had comprised, Windeyer pointed out, five full-time and two coopted workers. It ran old agents, sought to recruit new ones and tried to plant Russian 'illegals' in this country. The MVD team was charged with building a Soviet 'fifth column' in Australia and with obtaining, by clandestine means, secret information especially concerning Australian foreign policy. This last matter, Windeyer suggested, might prove the most important and delicate of the entire Commission. Evidence would be presented concerning leakages from External Affairs which had occurred before the Petrovs' arrival in Australia. The Petrovs' evidence on this matter would, necessarily, be hearsay, although one of the documents Petrov had brought with him appeared to include what Windeyer somewhat self-consciously described as a 'spy ring'. In recent years, due to the vigilance of Australian 'counter-intelligence', leaks from Government departments had greatly if not entirely 'dried up'.

Windeyer proceeded to the Petrov documents. Most time was spent on the 'G' series and the mysteries of interpreting the documents which he believed to be by far the most important part of the Petrov haul — the Moscow Letters. ('These are strange fields in which we find ourselves', a somewhat bemused Owen remarked.) Petrov had also, however, brought with him two English language MVD documents, which appeared to be the work of Australians. One (formally now christened Document 'H') was, he said, a three page type-script composed between February 1951 and mid-1952, passed on to Pakhomov and containing short accounts — 'not all entirely creditable' — of the political leanings and social habits of a variety of Australian journalists. The other (christened Document 'J') was a thirty-seven page document which, according to the Petrovs, had been typed inside the Soviet Embassy. One section concerned Japanese and another American interests in Australia. A third part, 'of rather little consequence' Windeyer thought, commented on 'certain trends in politics'. The information contained in Document 'J' did not appear to Windeyer 'to throw any direct light on the subjects of the inquiry'. On the other hand it did cast what he called 'a glaring light' on 'the depths to which one person . . . descended, to act in a way which it was thought would be of help to a foreign power'. What most impressed him about 'J' was its 'malicious foulness' and the gratuitousness of much of its scurrilous matter. To prove his point Windeyer dwelt for some time on the stories of embezzlers, sexual perverts, dipsomaniacs and syphilitics who inhabited its pages. Taken all in all Document 'J' was, he said, in the one memorable phrase of the Canberra hearings, 'a farrago of facts, falsities and filth'.[33]

There were two Australians who immediately recognised from the newspaper reports of the Canberra sittings of the Royal Commission on Espionage that they were in deep trouble — Rupert Lockwood and Fergan O'Sullivan, the authors, respectively, of 'J' and 'H'. Their responses, however, to this knowledge were markedly different.

Rupert Lockwood was a prominent Communist Party activist and journalist. Shortly after the Canberra hearings, presumably after consultation with the Party leadership, he set about writing a pamphlet which he called

'What Is In Document J?' and which he published under his own name on June 19.

> I am (he wrote) the author of certain writings that appear to have been labelled as Document J, but I do not overlook the possibility of some mix-up of documents. . . . As the author of material stolen by Petrov, I hasten to bring before the public a survey of this material as far as it can be recalled so long after it was written.

In somewhat less scurrilous terms than in the original, Lockwood's pamphlet summarised a considerable part of the political and some of the sexual matter found in 'J'. Strangely enough Lockwood appeared a little sensitive to Windeyer's charge of 'malicious foulness'. 'At no time', he argued, 'did I write nor have I written "filth"'. Nor was he a Soviet 'agent' or 'spy', although for struggling to transform Australia into 'the kind of society the Soviet Union is achieving' he would make no apology. Lockwood referred also to the list of sources which appeared in 'J'. To these people, he wrote, 'I owe an apology for any possible embarrassment that may follow Petrov's action in supplying their names to the Menzies Government's Security Police'.[34]

It is interesting to speculate on the motives of Lockwood and the CPA in the publication of 'What Is In Document J?' In part they probably hoped

Rupert Lockwood (courtesy of Herald and Weekly Times)

for a propaganda coup. For once, it could be predicted, a Communist diatribe against American imperialism and its Australian lackeys would be likely to be devoured (if only for its curiosity value) by the non-Communist reader with relish. In part, as the Commissioners came to suspect, Lockwood and the Party might have hoped to force the Royal Commission to publish Document 'J', if only to vindicate the justness of Windeyer's description of it and to demonstrate that the sequel was a pallid imitation of the original. If they had so succeeded the Commission hearings were likely for some months to be absorbed in listening to the Australian anti-Communist Right defend itself against Lockwood slanders. Finally in identifying himself as the author of 'J' Lockwood may even have been preparing the legal ground for the defamation action which the Party's legal men, Hill and Laurie, were soon to initiate for Lockwood against Windeyer.

Rupert Lockwood, then, responded to the knowledge of his involvement in the Petrov Affair with defiance and bravado. Fergan O'Sullivan responded with fear and shame. For a fortnight after the Canberra hearings Dr Evatt's Press Secretary kept secret from his employer all knowledge of his authorship of 'H'. Only on June 3, five days after the election, did he pluck up the courage to make his confession to Evatt. Why, Mr Justice Philp would later ask him, had he not confessed to Dr Evatt sooner? Confessing to a man like Evatt O'Sullivan replied, no doubt truthfully, was not an easy matter.[35] Dr Evatt's reaction to O'Sullivan's news was predictably and characteristically explosive and violent. He dismissed O'Sullivan from his service at once. A letter from him formalising the situation, which was sent on June 4, reveals the spirit in which the Leader of the Opposition received the intelligence of his youthful Press Secretary's even more youthful indiscretion.

> The statements made by you to me late yesterday afternoon in my office and repeated this morning, in the presence of your father, Mr P.G. Evatt and myself, have amazed and disgusted me as they obviously did your own father.
> Although the matter disclosed by you related to a period when you were on the staff of the 'Sydney Morning Herald' at Canberra, and before you became Press Secretary on my staff, I have no alternative but to treat you as immediately suspended from the performance of all duties.[36]

The shattering news Fergan O'Sullivan brought on June 3 could not have come for Dr Evatt at a less propitious time. His psyche seemed peculiarly unable to cope with set-back and peculiarly vulnerable in the face of failure.*[37] On June 3 he was still reeling from the shock of the election loss, particularly severe because it was unexpected. (An eleventh hour *Argus* poll had

---

* Throughout his public career Dr Evatt's fragile ego had required the sustenance of frequent reference to the genuinely extraordinary story of his life's triumphs. In his memoir Evatt's Private Secretary, Allan Dalziel, recalls how when he first stood for the Parliament Dr Evatt's electoral propaganda included a detailed list of the honours, awards and prizes he had collected while a student at the University of Sydney.

predicted a comfortable victory.)[38] Dr Evatt's post-election press release of May 30 was bitter and graceless.

> The Government did not win the election fairly. . . . Throughout the campaign it resorted to the smear and hysteria technique adapted from the police states of Germany and Russia. In spite of that, Labor outnumbered Government votes by more than 250,000. Yet Labor did not win the election.[39]

The same mood dominated a lunch he took with the editor of the *Sydney Morning Herald*, J.D. Pringle, towards the end of the week following the election.

> I was appalled (Pringle later wrote) by the deterioration of his mind. He blamed his defeat on a conspiracy. . . . At one moment he accused Menzies and the Australian Security Intelligence Organisation who, he firmly believed, had timed the defection of Petrov . . . so that Menzies could use it against him. . . . At another moment Evatt blamed 'certain forces' in the Labor Party which were plotting against him. . . . His mind seethed with plots and conspiracies.[40]

It is, unfortunately, uncertain whether this lunch occurred before or after the O'Sullivan news. It cannot therefore be known whether Dr Evatt's frame of mind at his lunch with Pringle reflected the consequence of his interview with O'Sullivan or the mood in which it was to be received.

Fergan O'Sullivan and his counsel, F.J. Meaher (courtesy of News Limited)

Certainly, however, this much can be said. Before O'Sullivan had come to him Dr Evatt was convinced that the Petrov defections had determined the election result. Now on June 3 he discovered that a member of his own staff was to be centrally implicated in the Petrov inquiry. Dark questions and sinister possibilities surfaced in Evatt's mind, demons from whose grip he would not be freed for the remainder of his life. Who after all was this Fergan O'Sullivan? Who had prompted him to apply to join the Evatt staff? What was his connection with Evatt's Coalition political opponents? What was *Fergan O'Sullivan's* connection with 'Catholic Action'? What was his connection with the Petrovs and ASIO? Had he been planted upon Dr Evatt by his enemies in order to destroy him? Over the next few weeks Dr Evatt's mind turned these questions about O'Sullivan into possibilities and the possibilities into established facts. He now came to see with a terrifying certainty the connections between apparently unconnected persons and events. Progressively from this moment, Dr Evatt, a man whose life had been devoted to Justice, Reason and Scholarship, abandoned himself to the darkest suspicions concerning real and imagined enemies and to an absolute faith in his powers of intuition. Psychologically speaking, O'Sullivan's confession to him of the authorship of Document 'H' appears to have broken through some dam which held back the flood waters of his paranoia. Politically speaking, this is the turning point of our story. Without Dr Bialoguski there may have been no Petrov defection. Without Dr Evatt there would have been no Petrov Affair.

One week after Dr Evatt had dismissed Fergan O'Sullivan from his service the Royal Commission held its first brief post-election hearing. Here Major Birse was introduced formally to the Commissioners while Windeyer indicated the need for more time before the hearing of evidence could begin in earnest. When the Commission reassembled he proposed that the Petrovs should be called to give general evidence concerning their own MVD histories and the MVD establishment in Australia. After their evidence, he suggested, the Commission should turn its attention to the question of the authorship of the English language Documents 'H' and 'J'. He proposed that the Commission meet next on June 30 in Melbourne. To all Windeyer's suggestions the Commissioners agreed.[41]

Considerable excitement was aroused by Vladimir Petrov's first public appearance since his defection. (Much to Mr Menzies' annoyance, on the morning of June 29 both the *Argus* and, in self-defence, the Melbourne *Sun* broke the embargo which had been placed on the publication of his photograph.[42]) At the beginning of the day there was what one journalist called 'a wild scramble for seats' in the High Court at Melbourne.[43] Throughout the first day of his evidence Petrov remained tense and impassive; at its end he appeared exhausted.[44] For five sessions of the Commission — between

Petrov leaves the Royal Commission, July 1954
(courtesy of Herald and Weekly Times)

June 30 and July 6 — he spoke of his life in the service of Soviet intelligence, of the general structure of the MVD, of its operations in Australia and, in extremely general terms, of his decision to defect.[45]

As a witness, even under Windeyer's friendly questioning, Petrov seemed neither forthcoming nor overly scrupulous. When, for example, Windeyer asked Petrov on how many occasions he had met Richards he first replied rather vaguely 'twice in Canberra' and 'once in Sydney'.[46] That evening

Richards took him through a detailed chronology of their pre-defection encounters.[47] The following morning Petrov happily acceded to Windeyer's suggestion that there had been in fact twelve meetings.[48] Once or twice in the opening examination Petrov was just a little defensive. When Windeyer asked him whether he had enjoyed his visits to Sydney he evidently smelt an unintended rat. These visits were 'always', he snapped back, 'connected with our work'.[49] On July 6 Petrov gave the Commission certain evidence that was to prove of great value to the enemies of the Petrovs and ASIO. He had received £5,000 from Mr Richards at the moment of his defection. Immediately Windeyer led him through a detailed account for the Soviet salary and savings he had forfeited by his defection. 'I suppose', Mr Justice Ligertwood interceded, 'that the point of all this, Mr Windeyer, is that £5000 was a very meagre compensation'.[50]

When on July 6 Evdokia Petrov stepped into the Melbourne Courtroom her pretty face was already famous throughout the land. But it soon became clear that there was more to her than that. After some initial uneasiness her presence, theatricality and sexual magnetism quickly came to dominate the Court. According to Ronald McKie, the most perceptive journalist to report the Commission proceedings, she played upon 'the emotional wires' of the audience that morning 'with the ease of a harpist'. The male reaction to her was 'immediate and violent'. After Evdokia smiled at her intepreter, Major Birse was, McKie thought, 'an emotional wreck', his bald pate blushing with pleasure.[51] In the course of three days in the witness box she told the story of her life in the MVD, and in particular the story of her defection, with a vividness altogether beyond the capacity of her husband. Windeyer had to work very hard to prise information from Vladimir. By the time Evdokia was in full rhetorical flight, in her description of the dramas of Mascot and Darwin, she had come to resent any interruptions on the part of Windeyer or the Commissioners.[52]

The natural and expected enemy of the Royal Commission was, of course, the Communist Party of Australia. From the moment the defection was announced the Party produced an unending stream of propaganda pamphlets and articles in the Party press — the *Tribune* in Sydney and the *Guardian* in Melbourne. The Petrov defection was a Menzies election stunt.[53] Petrov was a Beria man, a traitor to his country and (this was before he became a forger) a thief of Embassy documents and moneys.[54] At first Petrova's defection was a kidnapping;[55] later it was to become a Hollywood melodrama staged with Petrova's complicity.[56] The Royal Commission itself was certain to be, and later had indeed become, a McCarthyite forum.[57]

Yet Party activity was not restricted to saturation propaganda. As early as May, though its phone taps and surveillance, ASIO had discovered that

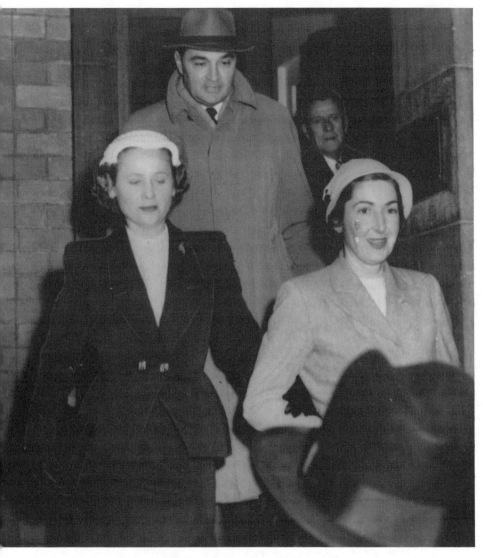

Petrova leaves the Royal Commission (Ron Richards in the background)
(courtesy of Herald and Weekly Times)

the Party planned to thwart the proceedings of the Royal Commission. It had overheard and observed a series of conversations and meetings between John Rodgers of Australia-Russia House, Ted Hill and Ted Laurie of the Party and Brian Fitzpatrick of the Council for Civil Liberties concerning the initiation of legal action against the Commission. A figure of £150 ($1800) had been mentioned as the cost of buying the advice of a leading silk, Maurice Ashkenazy. Ashkenazy's advice suggested that only a defamation action might halt its proceedings.[58] The Party may have despised 'bourgeois' justice but it was far from inept at exploiting the ponderous and intricate mechanisms of the law for its political purposes.

By early June ASIO also knew of the likely tactics the Party lawyers would adopt at the Royal Commission. On two occasions John Rodgers had dined in Sydney with Dr Bialoguski. He had sought to enlist Bialoguski as a witness to Petrov's drinking and womanising. They discussed an apparently notorious incident which had occurred at Bialoguski's flat where Petrov had made an unwelcome pass at Lily Williams of the peace movement. 'Everything possible must be done', Rodgers told Bialoguski, 'to destroy Petrov's credit'. Bialoguski, of course, kept ASIO informed of his talks with Rodgers. Indeed, on the second occasion, as they dined in the Adria Cafe (which he and Petrov had once dreamt of purchasing) his trusty minifon recorder was in action.[59]

When Ted Hill arrived on the first day at the Melbourne hearings and applied successfully for leave to appear for Rupert Lockwood (who had, as it were, named himself in his pamphlet as the author of Document 'J') none of ASIO's expectations about likely Communist behaviour were to be disappointed. On June 30 Hill interrupted the examination of Petrov with legal argument concerning the irrelevance of 'J' to the terms of reference of the Commission. A number of times he was overruled, and eventually silenced.[60] On July 7 and 8 he interrupted the examination of Petrova with an argument suggesting that as his client had just initiated a defamation action against Windeyer (over his Canberra comments) for the Commission to proceed with the Lockwood case before that action was settled would constitute a clear contempt of the High Court. By the replication of this defamation process, Owen pointed out, the entire Commission could be aborted. 'That possibility', Hill returned, 'certainly strikes no horror into me'. Already an odd kind of camaraderie was developing between the Communist barrister and his class enemies, the Commissioners. After protracted legal argument Hill was again eventually overruled.[61]

The Party had two further legal tricks up its sleeve. In the April legislation concerning the Royal Commission on Espionage only a single Commissioner was mentioned. A writ was issued in the High Court on Lockwood's behalf alleging that the Letters Patent establishing the Commission, which included the names of *three* Commissioners, were invalid.* In the same legislation the power to subpoena witnesses was granted the Commission but, curiously enough, no provision was made for punishment if subpoenaed witnesses refused to answer questions. In the July sittings two Communist witnesses appeared at the Commission with sealed lips. It was clear that the legislation establishing the Commission — with its defamation, subpoena and Letters

---

* At a weekend sitting of the High Court Mr Justice Fullagar (on July 11) brought down an interim ruling against Rupert Lockwood's attempts to halt Royal Commission proceedings.

Patent loopholes — needed considerable redrafting. On July 12 Mr Menzies promised that as soon as Parliament assembled for its August sitting a new Act concerning the establishment of the Royal Commission would be presented.[62]

The first witness who had refused to answer questions at the Commission was Rupert Lockwood. Lockwood claimed that his answers would be 'used to frame criminal charges' against him. Owen assured him that nothing said at the Commission could, in fact, be used against him in court. Lockwood, however, would not be budged.[63] Given his silence the Commission was obliged to prove his authorship of 'J' by means other than sworn confession.

The evidence presented on this question between July 8 and 14 was so overwhelmingly convincing that were it not for the fact that Dr Evatt's entire conspiracy theory rested upon the contention that Lockwood had not authored 'J' it would hardly even be worth summarising in detail here. On April 3, the Commission learned, Petrov had told Richards that he knew through Antonov and his wife that Rupert Lockwood had typed 'J' in the Soviet Embassy. The Commission learned that when she had defected Petrova had confirmed her husband's story. She had been on duty in the Embassy when, over three days, Antonov had supervised its typing and had handed her the finished pages. She had seen Lockwood frequently during this time and now in the Commission successfully identified him by sight. From a contextual analysis of 'J' it was clear that it had been written after May 20 1953 (there was a reference in it to a *Tribune* article of that date) and before June 2 1953 (when it was written the Coronation was still in the future). Certain hotel registers were subpoenaed for the Commission. They showed that Lockwood had been a guest at the Kingston Hotel, which was directly opposite the Soviet Embassy, between May 22 and 25 1953. The author of Document 'J' referred to himself as a former editor of a now defunct newspaper, the *Daily News*. Evidence was brought proving that Lockwood had, indeed, once held this post. The author of 'J' claimed to have been involved in certain disputes within the Australian Journalists' Association concerning J.H.C. Sleeman and Frank Browne. The minute books of the New South Wales district of the AJA were subpoenaed. They revealed that Rupert Lockwood had indeed been involved in these disputes. Inspector Rogers, the most experienced handwriting and type-writing expert in the New South Wales police force, was called to the Commission. He had spent a week examining Document 'J'. Rogers gave evidence that 'J' had been composed on two typewriters. Both these particular machines had been used to type official letters from the Soviet Embassy. (A bundle had been handed him for study). He also gave evidence that the capital letters in the margin of 'J' (the references to sources) had been written in the same hand as Rupert Lockwood's passport application and customs declaration.[64]

Throughout this phase of the Royal Commission Ted Hill (although he did not exactly admit Lockwood's authorship) made no attempt, when questioned directly on this point, to deny that his client was the author of 'J'.[65] Lockwood had, after all, published a pamphlet on June 19 admitting to being its author. Even Rupert Lockwood himself, who had on July 9 vehemently denied that he had accepted money and brandy as a reward for writing it, would not, when the thirty-seven pages of Document 'J' were physically handed to him on July 12, go so far as to deny it was his work.[66]

After the evidence on the authorship of 'J' was complete, Ted Hill rose to cross-examine Petrov. As had been planned by the Party he set about the task of character assassination. Petrov was, Hill's questioning suggested, a thief (who had stolen Embassy documents) and a liar (who had written a false suicide note and signed a false 'act of destruction' for the 1952 Moscow Letters). On April 3 he had betrayed both his country and his wife, abandoning her to her fate. What, Hill inquired, had Petrova said to him after their reunion? Had Petrov been faithful to their marital vows? More recently, Hill continued, had he not cast his friend Prudnikov into direst peril by revealing at the Commission the role he had played in leaking the Ambassador's cables to the Petrovs? Did Petrov care nothing for what became of him? Had not this man even abandoned his Alsatian dog?

Already Ted Hill had prised from Petrova the admission that both Lifanov and Generalov had cabled Moscow about Petrov's drinking.[67] He threatened future evidence which would show Petrov was a drunk. Several times he had appeared under the influence at the Adria Cafe and at the flat of a person the Commission typists called 'Dr Belovusski'. Finally and most seriously, on the basis of the £5000 payment to Petrov, Hill suggested that between February 27 and April 2 some sinister bargain had been struck between Richards and Petrov. In return for handing over documents had he not been promised political asylum and £5000? Was not money Petrov's real motive in this sordid affair?

Throughout Hill's prolonged assault on Petrov's character the Commissioners showed a remarkable leniency, only occasionally stopping a line of inquiry being pushed. (After Hill had questioned Petrov for some time about the quality of his marriage Owen finally protested. The Petrovs would not be put 'on the rack' in his court.) Hill's demolition of Petrov was, it should be remembered, on behalf of a client who had refused to answer all questions. As Lockwood had, moreover, not even denied writing 'J' it was hard to see how Petrov's 'credit' as a witness (Hill's invariable pretext for his attack) was of any concern to him. Once more, this was a strange way to conduct an anti-Communist 'witch hunt'. Throughout the barrage Petrov ducked and weaved, answering honestly where he could but, if necessary, stonewalling or lying. He had never been drunk. His marital relations were perfect. There had been no discussion with Richards where money had been offered in return for documents.[68]

On July 14, after Ted Hill's savage cross-examination of Petrov, Windeyer announced that evidence concerning Document 'J' had concluded. The Commission now transferred its attention to Document 'H'. Fergan O'Sullivan was called. On his first appearance he refused, like Lockwood before him, to answer questions.[69] On his second appearance he confessed to being the author of 'H'. The portraits of the gallery journalists had been given to Pakhomov, he claimed, to help Pakhomov place pro-Soviet articles in the Australian press. Why would information about journalists' extra-marital affairs or drinking habits assist Pakhomov here? O'Sullivan was not sure. What had he meant when he described certain journalists to Pakhomov as 'politically reliable'? He had meant, O'Sullivan answered, reliable from the point of view of the ALP. He was shocked to discover that Pakhomov was an intelligence officer and that his little typescript had been despatched to the MVD Centre at Moscow.[70]

Precisely because O'Sullivan had been appointed as Dr Evatt's Press Secretary in April 1953 this case seemed, from the espionage point of view, far more serious than the Lockwood case. Petrov gave evidence that a Party 'talent scout', Rex Chiplin, had recommended O'Sullivan to Pakhomov. The Moscow Letters revealed that MVD Centre had been extremely interested in him in 1952, while in April 1954 Petrova had heard from Kovalenok (Petrov's successor) that for Moscow the cultivation of O'Sullivan had the highest priority. In the case of an Evatt Prime Ministership the Soviet intelligence service might have an agent at the heart of the Australian Government.

It was with such considerations in mind that the Commission turned, late on the afternoon of July 15, to the question of the appearance of Fergan O'Sullivan's name in the list of 'sources' at the end of Document 'J'. Under Windeyer's examination O'Sullivan admitted that he had drunk with Lockwood at the Kingston Hotel. He was certain, however, that it had not been in May 1953 but sometime after July. O'Sullivan was then shown page thirty-five of 'J'. He had been, he now discovered, listed as a source for certain information about difficulties Dr Evatt was supposed to have experienced in acquiring a visa for the United States and about big business donations to the ALP election fund. O'Sullivan denied possessing such information, let alone passing it on to Lockwood. Mr Justice Owen pointed out that O'Sullivan had also been named as a source in 'J' for a story about a Security file photograph of another Evatt staffer. Windeyer added that a third member of the Evatt staff — one Albert Grundeman — had also been named as a source in Document J.[71]

Shortly before the Commission adjourned for the day Mr Justice Owen returned to the question of Document 'J' and the Evatt staff.

We think it is right that we should say that we do not find anything in this document which reflects on the Leader of the Opposition. What disturbs us is that the document quotes as sources on various matters, some of which are of a confidential nature, three members of the secretariat of the Leader of the Opposition, including, in that three, O'Sullivan.[72]

As it turned out these were probably the most consequential words to be uttered by Mr Justice Owen during the course of his distinguished life in the law.

10

CONSPIRACY MOST FOUL

Ever since the fateful interview with Fergan O'Sullivan on June 3 Dr Evatt had known that his name was certain to be involved in the Royal Commission on Espionage. Soon after it he had revealed to Victor Windeyer that O'Sullivan was the author of Document 'H' and had enquired of him whether any other associate of his was likely to be called as a witness to the Commission. 'Perhaps wrongly', Windeyer later confessed, 'I told him that that was so'.[1] Now, on July 15, the expected had happened: the Commission Chairman had indicated that three members of the Evatt secretariat were listed as 'sources' in Document J.* Not surprisingly, the radio news on the evening of July 15 and the morning headlines of July 16 were dominated by this new sensation.

Dr Evatt, who had been on an exceedingly short Petrovian fuse since early June, now exploded into action. At once he telegrammed the Prime Minister demanding his rights as Leader of the Opposition to be supplied with all the information 'adversely affecting my staff'.[2] He also telegrammed the Secretary of the Royal Commission.

> I . . . feel it is my bounden duty to protest at once at the making of the defamatory and injurious imputation reflecting on members of my staff. This statement has been given the widest circulation by press and radio. . . . The course taken in naming persons by obvious reference to a small group is quite opposed to the basic procedures of justice. . . . No notice having been given injury to individuals is immediate and may be irreparable.

As Dr Evatt requested, on the morning of July 16 his protest was read into the Commission's record.[3] Mr Justice Owen — perhaps somewhat surprised by the violence of its tone — reminded the world that he had already made clear that nothing in 'J' reflected adversely on Dr Evatt himself and that on the previous afternoon Ligertwood had pointed out that O'Sullivan had

---

* Two of the three were known from the words of the Commissioners and counsel to be O'Sullivan and Grundeman. The third could have been either Byrne or Dalziel, both of whom had been mentioned by O'Sullivan on July 15 as members of the Evatt staff.

133

denied he was a source for 'J' and Philp that the 'allegations as to the source of information may be entirely untrue'. He had, he added, made clear at the opening of the Commission that their enquiries could not possibly hope to proceed 'without mention from time to time of the names of persons who will have no warning'. Dr Evatt's staff would be given an immediate opportunity to answer the claim in 'J' that they had provided its author with information.[4] None of this, of course, satisfied Dr Evatt. On the same day he prepared a statement for the press and radio which denounced the Commission in the strongest terms. 'At the commencement of the enquiry', he wrote, 'the Commission boldly nailed its colours for the mast of just procedures and no "McCarthyism"'. But was not this singling out of 'one or two members of the staff of the leader of one political party' (out of the one hundred names listed as sources of 'J') 'the quintessence of "McCarthyism"'?[5]

Within the Evatt camp there were certain tactical differences about how best to answer the 'charge' that Dalziel and Grundeman had supplied information to Lockwood. Dr Evatt's younger brother, Clive (a silk and a highly controversial New South Wales Labor politician, who had been recently relieved of his Housing portfolio by the Cahill Government) wanted to accept the Commission's invitation, to fly to Melbourne at once and to represent there the 'injured parties', Dalziel and Grundeman. To judge by his later account of the matter Dalziel favoured this approach. Dr Evatt, however, would have none of it. He intended to represent them himself. Faced with the determination of his 'boss and political chief' Dalziel felt no option but to 'defer'.[6]

Despite his frequent public declamations about the McCarthyist smearing of his staff, in reality in mid-July Dr Evatt's overwhelming interest was not in their vindication (which of course could best have been achieved by an immediate Melbourne appearance) but in the exposure of what he now understood to have been the true meaning of the Petrov defection. The naming of Dalziel and Grundeman gave him an opportunity to place himself at the centre of the inquiry and to transform it from an investigation of espionage into an investigation of political conspiracy. For this he needed evidence and time. On July 21 the solicitors acting for Dalziel and Grundeman wrote to the Secretary of the Commission requesting access to Document 'J' (which Evatt was by now convinced would provide the clue to the conspiracy which had been mounted against him) and the deferral of the appearance of Dalziel and Grundeman for a further four weeks.

We understand that the present arrangements are that the Commission will sit in Sydney on August 2nd next. We ask that the date for our clients' examination be fixed for the 16th August next. We ask for this extension of time as senior counsel will probably be retained, and it may also be necessary to request permission to call a number of witnesses other than themselves and to cross-examine a number of witnesses who have already given evidence.[7]

As it turned out, Dalziel who, if Clive Evatt had had his way, might have been called on July 19 and cleared his name in a matter of minutes, found himself compelled — because of Dr Evatt's deeper concerns — to wait until September 13 before being invited to take the stand.

In the first fortnight of August 1954 the Royal Commission was in the process of transferring from Melbourne to a permanent home in Sydney and in recess.* Temporarily the focus of the Petrov Affair moved to Canberra where the Parliament elected on May 29 had at last assembled. Here, in the second week of August, the Petrov Affair emerged unambiguously as the central issue of Australian politics. The precipitant was the revised 'Act relating to the Royal Commission on Espionage' which Mr Menzies brought into the Parliament on August 11.

The Menzies' bill was a complex piece of legislation aimed at closing the loopholes in the former Royal Commissions Act which Communist Party legal activity had already skillfully exposed. The new Act revised the Letters Patent, with the names of the three Commissioners included. It protected the Commissioners and Counsel from the possibility of defamation actions being launched against them. It prescribed stiff penalties for witnesses who failed to answer questions put to them during the course of the Commission's proceeding. The new Act (as we have seen) provided protection from wrongful dismissal for witnesses called before it. Equally, it provided that the Commissioners and the proceedings should be protected from all manner of disruption and insult. According to Section 24(e) anyone whose words or writings brought the Commission 'into disrepute' could be charged with a criminal offence and, if found guilty, fined up to £100 ($1200) or imprisoned for up to three months.[8]

Mr Menzies' revised Royal Commission on Espionage Act was debated behind the closed doors of the Labor Party's Parliamentary Caucus on the morning of August 11. This was the first Caucus discussion of Petrovian matters since April 14. It proved to be the beginning of a series of astonishingly bitter Petrov or Petrov-related Caucus sessions which, at the end of two months, had torn the Federal Parliamentary Party apart. On the morning of August 11 Dr Evatt moved in Caucus an executive recommendation that the Party 'should oppose clause 24 sub-clause E in the committee stages and, if defeated, that the Party should support the Bill'. The official minutes of Caucus, which are, here as elsewhere, far from revealing about either the content or tone of debate, recorded merely that Dr Evatt argued 'that the Bill in its present form would close down any opposition to the Commission — whether

---

* The Royal Commission ceased its Melbourne hearings on July 27. It announced on that day that it would reassemble at the Darlinghurst courthouse in Sydney on August 9. However, due to the indisposition of Mr Justice Owen (who had injured himself one evening when going to the assistance of his wife) it did not in fact reassemble until August 16.

it was just or false — which would be classified as a criminal offence'. Calwell seconded the motion and debate ensued. Clearly, the anti-Communist right-wing of the Party opposed the Evatt-Calwell motion. John Mullens, seconded by Ted Peters, moved that the debate be adjourned until seven that evening. That afternoon Mullens discovered that the protective powers of 24(e) were closely modelled upon Dr Evatt's own Conciliation and Arbitration Court Act of 1947. At 6.30 the Party executive reversed its stand. When Caucus reassembled at seven o'clock Dr Evatt brought with him a new executive motion. The Party should not oppose any part of the bill, although members were to be accorded the right to speak on 24(e). Apparently Eddie Ward moved that the new executive recommendation be disregarded. After bitter debate Ward's motion was lost and the executive recommendation carried. When the meeting had concluded, with feelings high, Leslie Haylen — a member of the Party's left but no friend of Ward — approached Ward and told him to stop 'beating his own chest' and to stop acting as if he were the Party's leader. Ward, a former minor prize fighter, struck out at Haylen and Haylen struck back. Their Caucus colleagues separated them. That evening journalists found several Labor men still shaken by the incident. On the morning of August 12 the newspapers carried detailed accounts of the previous evening's fisticuffs and the previous day's Caucus debates. Clearly, by this time, the Petrov Affair had Labor nerves on edge.[9]

On August 12 Dr Evatt rose in Parliament to speak on the Royal Commission on Espionage Act. Unbeknown to his Caucus colleagues he intended to use the occasion to begin his public exposé of the Petrov conspiracy. For the most part this new Act, he argued, merely replicated legal powers of existing legislation. Why then had it been introduced? 'One of the reasons', he suggested darkly, 'may be that the question asked of Lockwood was about his authorship of a document known as Exhibit J'. At once, the Speaker, Archie Cameron, stopped Evatt in his tracks. Cameron ruled that there could be no debate on any matter at present being heard before the Royal Commission. Calwell moved dissent from this ruling. Apart from the defection of W.C. Wentworth — who apparently felt so strongly about his right to speak his mind on Soviet espionage that he ignored the entreaties of his Coalition colleagues and crossed the floor — Calwell's motion was defeated on Party lines. Dr Evatt had been robbed of his chance to begin in Parliament his exposure of the Petrov conspiracy. When debate resumed attention was stolen by W.C. Wentworth, who accused Dr Evatt of an 'underlying pro-Communist bias'* throughout his public life,* and by Eddie Ward, who raised with some effect, Mr Menzies' difficulties with Vince Gair.[10]

---

* For his troubles he was accused by Dr Evatt of being an 'agent provocateur' and a 'dirty little liar' and by Reg Pollard of being a 'dirty mongrel'. When asked to withdraw his remark Pollard apologised 'to the mongrel'. At least Pollard's parliamentary insults were bi-partisan. On the previous day he had suggested to his anti-Communist Caucus colleague, Stan Keon, that he join the French Foreign Legion.

Blocked in the Parliament Dr Evatt resorted to the press release. For the first but by no means the last time, the nation now learned the outline of the Petrov conspiracy theory which had taken possession of the Leader of the Opposition. One of the keys to the Petrov Affair, Evatt argued, was the payment — in advance of the delivery of any documents — of £5000. These documents had been 'bought for the purpose of unduly and improperly influencing [the] people of Australia at the general elections'. Why had Mr Menzies not informed the Parliament of this payment on April 13? Why was 'this vital fact' suppressed before election day? Had any intermediaries bargained with Petrov 'during 1953'? What moneys were, even now, being paid to the Petrovs?

> I believe (Dr Evatt concluded) that when the tangled skein of this matter is finally unravelled the Petrov/Menzies Letters case will rank in Australian history as an equivalent to the notorious Zinovieff letter or the burning of the Reichstag which ushered in the Hitler regime in 1933.[11]

Dr Evatt's press release was too much for Menzies to bear. Late on the evening of August 12 he rose to speak in the adjournment debate. The Evatt production was, he said, evidence of a 'grave state of panic' and closely reminiscent of the Communist line of the Commission. One by one Mr Menzies answered Dr Evatt's charges. He had not told the House of the £5000 payment on April 13 because he knew nothing of it then. He had not in fact learned of it until May 9. He reminded Dr Evatt that many facts had not been publicly revealed before the election. If he had revealed what he knew of O'Sullivan and Dalziel Dr Evatt would not be in the House now. Menzies said he did not know whether or not ASIO had used an intermediary in the Petrov defection. But how did 'people suppose the Government is to fetter Communist activities unless it has secret agents'? Of course the Government was now supporting the Petrovs financially. It would have to be 'half-witted' not to do so. As for Dr Evatt's theory that the Petrov defection had been used to influence the election, had he not personally ordered every Government candidate to refrain from Petrov comment?

> I say to the House and the country (by these words Mr Menzies landed himself in much later trouble) that the name of Petrov became known to me for the first time on Sunday night, the 11th April, I think, or the preceding Saturday night.

And as for Dr Evatt's theory that the Petrov documents were forgeries Mr Menzies asked Hansard to record the eloquent and embarrassed silence of the Opposition benches. By the time he arrived at the Zinoviev letter and Reichstag fire analogies Menzies was positively crowing with the pleasure of the chase.[12]

As he rose in his place Dr Evatt seemed relieved to have finally provoked a Petrov confrontation with the Prime Minister. 'At last', he began, 'the oracle has spoken'.[13] As Dr Evatt repeated his conspiracy charges he was continuously taunted from the Government back benches in what the *Sydney*

Morning Herald called 'one of the most merciless spectacles the House of Representatives has ever seen'.[14] According to the *Age* the adjournment exchange on the evening of August 12 was 'probably the most bitter personal debate' that had ever taken place in the Parliament 'between a Prime Minister and an Opposition leader'.[15] The uneasy Petrovian political truce, which had sealed the lips of Menzies and Evatt in May, had at long last formally ended. Between the Prime Minister and the Leader of the Opposition — between whom there existed an utterly genuine and fully reciprocal passion of loathing — the Petrov Affair would now be an open fight and, most likely, a fight to the finish.*[16]

Following the Menzies-Evatt clash of August 12 rumours circulated freely about the possibility that Dr Evatt might personally represent his staff before the Royal Commission when it resumed its sittings on August 16. Dalziel told journalists that the decision rested not with himself but with his solicitor, Mr Barkell; Barkell told them that thus far he had certainly not engaged Dr Evatt.[17] In August 13 and 14 the press carried stories of the deep concern within the parliamentary party about the possibility of Dr Evatt's appearance at the Commission and of the failed attempt, mounted by the anti-Communist right, to convene an extraordinary Caucus to debate the matter.[18] Obviously Dr Evatt was determined to do whatever he could to conceal his intentions from his Caucus colleagues and to prevent them from making moves to bar his passage to the Royal Commission. Only on the actual morning of his appearance did he despatch to all members of the Caucus an explanatory tele-gram.[19] Caucus was not asked for a decision but presented with a fait accompli. On the day of his appearance the sparring partners of last week — Ward and Haylen — offered public support for his decision, while Ward and Senator Ashley turned up at the Commission in an obvious gesture of solidarity with their leader.[20] At least for the moment even the misgivings of the Labor right were buried.

On the morning of August 16 the nation — perhaps by now becoming somewhat addicted to the dramas that almost inevitably followed Dr Evatt — turned its eyes to the Darlinghurst courtroom in Sydney. From the moment of his arrival at the Commission, until the moment of his involuntary depar-ture on September 7, Dr Evatt totally dominated its proceedings. Even before the morning tea break on August 16 he had accused Victor Windeyer of mak-ing 'propaganda' and smearing the reputation of an innocent lady (June Bar-nett) and had lectured the Commissioners on constitutional law and on how, in the interests of justice, they might best conduct their proceedings.[21] 'Do

---

* The conflict was not without a lighter side. On August 13 Dalziel challenged the Prime Minister to a character trial before the elders of the Presbyterian Church, to which they both adhered. When asked for his response to this novel proposal Mr Menzies smiled and said 'No comment'.

you not think you can rely on us', Mr Justice Ligertwood enquired, 'to do justice to the witnesses . . .?'[22]

In order to grasp the meaning of Dr Evatt's strange and often obscure three week performance at the Royal Commission it is necessary to understand what it was that he had already come to believe about the Petrov Affair. As we have seen, in mid-August Dr Evatt was unshakably convinced that there had been a conspiracy — involving Petrov at one end and the Menzies Government at the other with ASIO in between — to harm him and the Party he led in the election campaign of May 1954. Petrov had sold, and the Government through ASIO had bought for £5000, certain documents amongst which were to be found some malicious forgeries. Already it was clear to him that the central document in the conspiracy was 'J'. As the world had discovered in mid-July, three members of his staff had been named as 'J' sources. Evatt believed that 'J' had been brought into existence and bought and sold in order to damage him. For this purpose the names of two loyal members of his staff — Dalziel and Grundeman — had been wickedly inserted into it. The third (disloyal) member — Fergan O'Sullivan — had been not a victim but an active participant in the conspiracy. At his most charitable he was willing to believe that O'Sullivan had been blackmailed by Petrov (on the basis of his authorship of 'H') into inserting the names of Dalziel and Grundeman and details about the affairs of the Evatt camp into Document 'J'. At his least charitable he believed that O'Sullivan was a conscious anti-Evatt agent planted upon his staff by ASIO.[23]

For all these core beliefs Dr Evatt in mid-August as yet possessed no evidence. He entered the Royal Commission with a dual purpose: to expose the conspiracy and to acquire the evidence by which its existence could be proved. Until the early hours of each morning during his Commission appearance Dr Evatt perused the documentary material he had prised from the Commissioners with an attention to detail worthy of Sherlock Holmes. Unlike Holmes, however, his reasoning was not empiricial. For three weeks he threw himself into the evidence in a feverish hunt for clues which might confirm a truth which had already been revealed to him.

On the first day of his Commission appearance, Dr Evatt's overwhelming determination was to be granted access to the whole of 'J' — the evidentiary cornerstone of his conspiracy theory — and not merely, as the Commissioners had intended, that part which concerned his clients. He also wanted to be provided by the Commission with an expert in typewriting and handwriting who could assist him to test what he called 'J''s 'genuineness'. The Commissioners were somewhat puzzled about what Dr Evatt might mean by this. 'Do you say', Ligertwood asked, 'that [Lockwood] did not compose the document?' Not exactly that, Evatt replied.

It may be that Lockwood is responsible for most of it. It may be that there have been some additions to it. It may be that there have been some interpolations in it. That aspect has never been examined, and cannot be examined until the whole document is checked.[24]

On the afternoon of August 16, as he commenced upon a cross-examination of his former Press Secretary, Dr Evatt began to reveal to the Commissioners who he believed responsible for the mysterious 'additions' and 'interpolations' he had predicted might be discovered in the Lockwood document. Did not Fergan O'Sullivan's authorship of 'H' place a 'potent weapon' in Petrov's hands? Could this fact not have been used to O'Sullivan's 'ruination'? Could it not equally have been used to embarrass the Leader of the Opposition? And could it not have been used by Petrov to blackmail O'Sullivan himself? Evatt then moved to fresh ground. Already that day Windeyer had established that O'Sullivan had been in Canberra in May 1953 and had, while there, drunk with Lockwood and Grundeman in the Hotel Kingston. Dr Evatt now asked O'Sullivan whether he had not visited the Soviet Embassy at this time and whether he had not told Grundeman that he was going to a film screening there. O'Sullivan agreed that this might have been so.[25]

Dr Evatt was very wary of revealing his hand prematurely to the Commissioners. However surely his suggestions about possible 'interpolations' in 'J', about O'Sullivan's vulnerability to Soviet blackmail and his movements in May provided a clear enough indication of where he was heading? 'I submit that I have carried the case far enough to show a right . . . to see Exhibit "J"'.[26] No doubt the Commissioners were still rather puzzled. All they would offer Dr Evatt on the afternoon of August 16 were photostat extracts of twenty-three of 'J''s thirty-seven pages which were deemed of possible relevance either to Evatt's clients or to O'Sullivan.[27]

On the following morning Dr Evatt at once renewed his application to see 'J' in its entirety. He hoped to see the original document but demanded as a bare minimum a photostat copy. He needed, he said, to examine 'the typing; the arrangement'.[28] Moreover it was 'vital' that he should be able to inspect the headings and side-letterings.[29] Tempers were now becoming exceedingly short. When Windeyer innocently reminded the Commissioners that one of the pages under discussion was the one — J35 — which concerned 'Dr Evatt', Evatt intervened in anti-McCarthyite indignation. 'Never mind names; do not introduce names. I will introduce names'.[30] Soon he accused Windeyer of deliberately creating a 'political . . . atmosphere' at the Commission. Windeyer, for his part, bitterly resented Dr Evatt's attacks upon his honour.

> What concerns us . . . is that our motives have been attacked. It has been suggested, and it is suggested, that I have sought to suppress . . . parts of the Document for some political purpose. Your Honours know from the parts of the Document I gave to my learned friend yesterday how unfair that suggestion is.

Owen was also rather shaken by the Evatt attack. Although, he said, he believed it was the wrong thing to do he, was slowly coming to the conclusion that 'J' might have to be published in its entirety. 'The imputations which are constantly being made' seemed to him 'almost beyond endurance'. Philp disagreed. If it was 'unjust' to publish J 'why should we be affected by malicious criticism of us'?[31]

On the morning of August 17 Ligertwood could not yet even fathom why Dr Evatt was so keen to examine the whole of 'J'. 'I am afraid I am', he confessed, 'a little dull. The Chairman says he understands what you are at . . . I do not'. Beyond the ears of the Commission's stenographers Ligertwood now conferred with Owen. Clearly Owen told his brother that Evatt believed O'Sullivan had interpolated political material into 'J'. He was, however, he admitted, 'only guessing'. Perhaps Dr Evatt had overheard their conference. Generously he reassured Owen. 'It is a well-based guess'.[32]

At least the Commission now knew what it was they were being invited by Dr Evatt to investigate. From the morning of August 18 the attention of the Commission was focussed on a single question, namely whether (as everyone had believed in July) Rupert Lockwood was the sole author of 'J' or whether (as Dr Evatt had now alleged) O'Sullivan had shared in its authorship. Mr Justice Owen soon christened this new possibility the 'two hands theory' of 'J'; Dr Evatt described it as 'the root of everything'.[33] Evatt also now felt able to declare his hand openly. Two persons at least, he submitted, had been involved in the authorship of 'J'. 'J' had been produced for what he called a 'local blackmailing purpose'. It had nothing whatever to do with espionage (and had never been despatched to the Soviet Union) and everything to do with politics. For the first time at the Commission, on the morning of August 18, he allowed the word 'conspiracy' to pass his lips.[34]

Grundeman was now called. Although he admitted that he and O'Sullivan had drunk with Lockwood in the Hotel Kingston in May 1953 he denied having supplied to Lockwood any of the information attributed to him in 'J'.[35] O'Sullivan was recalled. Under the examination of his counsel, J.A. Meagher, he denied absolutely having had anything to do with the composition or typing of 'J'. Dr Evatt, in the course of his short cross-examination, produced no evidence or argument which even remotely indicated any reason for his conviction that O'Sullivan had part-authored 'J'.[36]

On August 19 Rupert Lockwood returned to the witness box. In early July, as we have seen, he had refused to answer any questions put to him at the Commission (except to deny he had received money and brandy for writing 'J') on the grounds of a potential 'frame up'. Now Lockwood answered questions relatively freely. His evidence took almost four days to complete.

It was indeed true, Lockwood now affirmed, that he had gone to the Soviet Embassy with Antonov in May 1953 and, over three days, completed some typing work there.[37] If he had believed that anything he composed was destined for the eyes of the Soviet Government, let alone the Soviet intelligence service, he would have 'fainted with horror'.[38] He could see nothing wrong with supplying Antonov with details about the location of Australian airfields (which might be used to wage war on the peoples of Asia) or the names of ASIO agents.[39] Why, he was asked, had he gone with Antonov (who was, like him, a Sydney resident) to the Canberra Embassy to do his typing? It was, Lockwood replied vaguely, 'a convenient place'.[40] Apart from the question of the £30 and the three bottles of brandy was not his account of this matter, Mr Justice Owen asked him, identical to the story told to the Commission by Petrova? Lockwood thought for a moment and asked whether he might inspect the transcript.[41]

Despite these admissions, from the very first moment of his August appearance Lockwood was determined to deny that the actual document before the Commission was his work.[42] 'J' — the document he had been shown in July — was thirty-seven pages long. He had left one hundred and fifty pages of prepared material with Antonov and had typed a further fifteen or twenty pages in the Embassy.[43] Lockwood was now asked by Windeyer to read 'J' carefully and to mark the passages which he definitely believed were his work and those which were not. The Commission adjourned for two hours. When Lockwood returned he claimed that some of the material in 'J' had been 'recast' and some was definitely not his. He had, however, made only a few 'emergency and inadequate markings'. He refused to indicate any passages in 'J' which were definitely his and for the most part — except for the page concerning Dr Evatt, J35, which he called 'the classic example' — which were not. Here or there in a 'recast' passage a sentence or a phrase of his might be found. He had no confidence in this tribunal. He feared a trap.[44] While he was willing to admit that the content of 'J' might be 'strongly similar' to the material he had supplied to Antonov and that the side-lettering resembled his handwriting, he felt now that he could inform the Commission with confidence that 'J' was not his work. He had not, in fact, typed one word of it.[45] From this position, throughout the Royal Commission hearings of the matter (which were to extend into October!) Rupert Lockwood would not be budged.

On August 20, during the course of Lockwood's testimony, Dr Evatt was granted access to Document 'J' in its original form and in its entirety. At the commencement of the next sitting day, August 24, he announced in triumphant mood that a weekend of study had led him to the inescapable conclusion that 'J' could not possibly be the work of Lockwood. Unlike Lockwood's polemical writings, which displayed a certain felicity, 'J' was full of 'gibberish and rubbish', a 'literary monstrosity'. Dr Evatt — whose literary essays had won him several prizes while at University — informed the Commissioners that style was to the scholar what the finger print was to the policeman.[46] In 'J' moreover certain 'historical howlers' appeared and certain phrases were used for which Lockwood could not conceivably have been responsible.[47] As his examination of Lockwood later that day made clear, the historical howler which the author of *Rum Rebellion* had in mind was the description of D'Arcy Wentworth as a 'sexual pervert'. The phrase he believed Lockwood could not conceivably have used was 'right wing *clerical* group'. Not surprisingly, Lockwood was more than happy to accede to the propositions Dr Evatt put to him about his fine style, historical integrity and vocabulary. He agreed that without evidence he would never have described W.C. Wentworth's ancestor as a 'sexual pervert'.* He had indeed noticed that 'J' was not in his style, had a 'different swing' to it. 'A man at least', he proposed, 'gets to know his own style'. And as for the word 'clerical' — although it might perhaps 'slip' into his writing on occasions — it was certainly a term foreign to him.[48]

By now Dr Evatt appeared to believe he was well on the way to having proven 'beyond doubt and peradventure' that the whole of 'J' could not have been the work of Lockwood. His submission was that there had been 'a deliberate conspiracy to injure the Leader of the Opposition by defaming his staff' through their appearance in 'J'. He submitted, moreover, that Fergan O'Sullivan had been the author of at least part of 'J'. On the morning of August 25 Dr Evatt declined the persistent invitation of the Commissioners to indicate who, besides O'Sullivan, had participated in this anti-Evatt conspiracy. Everything would soon 'unfold'. He asked Their Honours to be 'patient'. He bitterly resented the 'remarkable statement' made that morning by O'Sullivan's counsel, Meagher, who had asked Dr Evatt — the champion of anti-McCarthyism — to reveal which parts of 'J' he was alleging were written by O'Sullivan and to extend to him some notion of 'fair play'.[49]

In order to test Dr Evatt's 'two hands' theory of 'J' Inspector Rogers was recalled to the Commission on August 25. He had spent the last four days examining 'J' and typewriting specimens from Lockwood and O'Sullivan. Rogers had arrived at three main conclusions. The uniform nature of the paper on which the whole of 'J' had been typed and the persistence throughout it of certain idiosyncracies of typing style — the use of the double-dash, the irregularity of paragraph spacing, a repetitive apostrophe error and the abundance of parentheses — had convinced Rogers that 'J' had been typed by one person. When he compared the typing in 'J' with other pieces of Lockwood's work — which the Commission had, in Lockwood's presence, taken from his office at the *Maritime Worker* — he had discovered these same characteristics. None of them had appeared in the specimens of O'Sullivan's typing which Dr Evatt had supplied to the Commission. Moreover, as he had previously testified, in his view the handwriting in the margins of 'J' was the same as that which had appeared on Lockwood's passport application, hotel registration form and customs declaration. His conclusions were clear. One person had typed 'J' and that person was Lockwood.[50]

---

* In *What Is In Document J*, Lockwood had written thus: 'One of Mr Windeyer's references to "filth" in "Document J" apparently refers to D'Arcy Wentworth ... I will go further here than anything said in the document, and describe D'Arcy Wentworth as a brutal flogger, torturer, sadist, racketeer and inhuman trafficker in the labor of sick convicts.'

On August 26 Inspector Rogers was due to complete his evidence but was ill. The Commission might have adjourned for the day had not Dr Evatt asked for Richards of ASIO to be recalled to the stand. Apparently that night Dr Evatt — who was reported to be working on 'J' until three each morning — believed he had made a discovery (concerning the width of the staple or pin marks on J35) which might prove to be a turning point in the Commission's investigations. The matter, he told the Commissioners, could not wait. 'The reason why the urgency is so great', he said to the complete bewilderment of everyone present, 'is to protect the condition of evidence — physical evidence'. The matter on which Dr Evatt interrogated Richards concerned the precise manner in which 'J' had been stapled when it had been passed to him by Petrov. Richards thought that the sections concerning America and Japan had been stapled separately. Four of the five pages of sources had, so far as he could remember, been stapled together. One was loose. J35 was 'attached to nothing ... But it had the appearance of having been attached to something'. 'It had what?' When exactly had the document been handed to Richards? At whose house? ('Dr Evatt!', Owen exclaimed.) When J35 had been handed over was the present tear on it? Dr Evatt's suspicions were by now aglow. He feared that Richards might be tampering with the crucial clue to the conspiracy — the staple/pin marks at the head of J35 — even as he stood in the witness box. 'Are you touching portions of the original ...?' 'DR EVATT!' On the morning of August 26 Dr Evatt proposed formally to the Royal Commission that J35 had been torn from some other document and fraudulently inserted into 'J'. To his 'two hands' theory he had now added his 'ring in' refinement.[51]

On August 27 Dr Evatt was let loose upon Inspector Rogers. At first he sought Roger's assistance over the staple/pin marks on J35. Rogers could not offer him an opinion one way or the other. He was not, he pointed out, a staple expert. 'There must be', Owen warned, 'less laughter in the court room'.[52] With little satisfaction on the staple front and perhaps disturbed by the fact that all of Rogers' typewriting and handwriting evidence pointed to Lockwood as the sole author of 'J', Dr Evatt now raised a new possibility — forgery. If someone had in his possession specimens of Lockwood's typing and writing would it not have been a relatively easy matter to give 'J' the appearance of Lockwood's work? Meagher rose to his feet. Was his client now being charged with forgery? If so he demanded a trial by jury. In front of Evatt the Commissioners speculated about what was in the doctor's mind. Owen thought the logic of his position entailed the allegation that O'Sullivan was the forger. Philp thought that he might merely be talking of some 'hypothetical forger'. The trouble was, Meagher suggested, that Dr Evatt would not 'come out into the open and say what ...'. He was cut short. 'I will come into the open, and I am not going to be intimidated by anybody.'[53]

There were many bizarre moments in the Evatt performance at the Royal Commission but none so bizarre as his exchanges with Inspector Rogers during his attempt to prove 'J' a forgery. Let one example suffice. Dr Evatt thought the side-letter 'Y' in Document 'J' was uncharacteristic of Lockwood's hand. Lockwood's Y's were tailed 'U's; this looked more like a tailed 'V'. Did this not point inescapably to forgery? Rogers begged to differ. In his view the 'Y' in 'J' bore the mark of Lockwood, but even if Evatt was right why would a forger make such an obvious error as this? Because, Dr Evatt returned, he had no example of a Lockwood 'Y' to forge. There was an 'AX' and an 'AZ' later in the document but no 'AY'! Was it not clear that towards the end of his labours the forger had lost his nerve?

Rogers: I do not agree with you, Doctor.
Evatt: What do you mean, you do not agree? ...
Rogers: I understood that you had been putting to me for the last quarter of an hour that he was a very shrewd, cool, calculating forger.
Evatt: And he is a very wicked man if he is a forger.
Rogers: If he is, by the time he reaches 'AX' he says to himself 'I have made a possible mistake in using that "Y"', and it seems to me he would have enough brains not to use the 'Y' again, but to remove the 'Y' he had made.[54]

Touché!

Lost in the mysteries of staple marks and forged 'Y's, Dr Evatt was now proposing parallel theses concering the authorship of 'J' — the older 'two hands — ring in' thesis and the newer 'forgery' thesis. Noone — neither he, nor the Commissioners, nor the Counsel assisting — had noticed the simple fact that Dr Evatt's theories were not only equally implausible but also mutually contradictory. If the whole of 'J' was, as Dr Evatt had maintained, a forgery how could he also maintain that J35 was a 'ring in' page which had been torn from somewhere else and wickedly smuggled into it? Everything was by late August getting out of hand.

There is a strange intimacy, almost an unworldliness, in the proceedings of a courtroom during a complex hearing. Nevertheless there could be no doubt that the world was unusually interested in what was transpiring at the Royal Commission on Espionage. While it was very difficult for the politicians in Canberra to gauge what the citizen might be making of the rather bewildering daily reports of Dr Evatt's fresh charges of 'sinister payments', 'blackmail', 'forgery' and 'conspiracy', there was in late August, on both sides of the House, evidence of political unease.*.

Within the Labor Party this unease came to a head on August 25 at the first Caucus meeting held since Dr Evatt had entered the Commission. The

---

* And on both sides with reason. A Gallup Poll taken at the end of August showed that 40% of people disapproved of Evatt's appearance at the Commission and 31% approved. However it also showed that 49% believed the £5000 payment to Petrov was wrong and only 23% that it was right.

meeting, in Evatt's absence, was chaired by Arthur Calwell. At its opening he moved an executive motion, that 'it be left to the Leader's own judgment as to how long he should remain at the Commission and as to when he should resume his Parliamentary duties'. Although seconded by Senator McKenna, the motion was generally considered to be inspired by Eddie Ward. It provoked heated debate. What was most evident was that opposition to it extended well beyond the anti-Communist right. The Party Whip, Fred Daly, complained that as Dr Evatt had not bothered to consult his colleagues before his Commission appearance he could not expect their retrospective approval now. Dr Evatt should place loyalty to the Party above loyalty to his staff. Daly was supported in debate by Albert Thompson, an aged Salvation Army trade unionist, and by Senator Kennelly, whose dislike for Dr Evatt was only exceeded by his dislike for the 'Movement' Catholics in the Caucus. Only Ward was reported to have spoken spiritedly in favour of the executive recommendation. Tom Andrews' motion to refer the matter back to it — an obvious snub for Evatt and setback for Ward — was carried 37 votes to 30.

Some members of the Caucus clearly wished to push even further against Evatt. Galvin moved and Joshua (the future leader of the Anti-Communist-ALP) seconded a motion formally authorising Calwell 'to act as Leader during the absence of Dr Evatt'. Most likely Calwell interpreted this as an attempt to push him into a leadership challenge. He was, however, not yet ready to burn his bridges to the left. He ruled the motion out of order. According to Alan Reid's intelligence, Caucus on August 25 concluded with a furious foreign policy argument between Eddie Ward and the rising star of the anti-Communist element of the ALP, Stan Keon. Ward accused Keon of allowing someone Alan Reid coyly described as 'a mysterious background personage' to dictate policy to him. Keon told Ward that a soapbox at the Domain was not the place from which to formulate an ALP policy on foreign affairs. In late August, it was clear, that a majority of the Labor Caucus disapproved of the circumstances of Dr Evatt's appearance at the Royal Commission. More ominously it was also becoming clear that Evatt's appearance there was bringing the Party's deeper ideological conflicts to a head.[55]

Unease at Dr Evatt's Royal Commission appearance was not restricted to the Opposition benches. Mr Menzies was also by late August more than a little worried. At this time he wrote a long and extremely significant 'draft' letter — which is to be found in the Prime Ministerial file on the Affair — in which he spoke from the heart about certain Petrovian concerns.

I cannot pose (Menzies' letter began) as a master of the contents of Document J, but I rather gather the impression that it is not of the highest intrinsic moment and that a Royal Commission which did not more than prove the authorship and source of Document J might not have got very far. Yet for weeks, the public has read about nothing but Exhibit J. My experience is that people are getting very tired of it and that they are wondering whether the whole Petrov incident is not a 'mare's nest'.

Mr Menzies was convinced that Dr Evatt was engaged in a 'political excursion'. He wanted to represent the whole affair as a conspiracy and himself as a 'lover of justice' who courageously shook the Commission up. 'Quite frankly, I think that so far he is having a considerable measure of success in the public mind'. It would indeed be an 'unpleasant irony' if the 'ultimate public reaction' were to be against a Government which had quite properly instituted an enquiry into Soviet espionage and the Petrov documents.

What, then, Menzies asked, could be done? In his view it should be made plain that Dr Evatt was not defending Dalziel or Grundeman at the Commission but himself and that he was not even remotely fulfilling the role of the disinterested advocate there. Mr Menzies would regard it as 'a grievous injury' if Evatt was to be permitted to have it both ways.

> If Evatt wants to defend himself or to prefer charges of a political nature, he should be put into the box as a witness and cross-examined as any other witness would be.

It was 'cold comfort' to Menzies to know that 'months hence' the Commission would dispose of Evatt's charges in its report. In his view Evatt at the Commission was attempting to consolidate his leadership of the Labor Party and was not 'half so concerned about the ultimate findings' of the Commission as 'about repairing his fortunes in the intervening period'. He hoped that as soon as the 'J' enquiry had concluded — and surely it was not the most important aspect of the case — the Royal Commission would prepare an interim report, and one 'in terms which the man in the street can understand'.

> [Dr Evatt] would regard it as the ultimate triumph if he could create a state of innuendo in which I felt it necessary to become a witness myself. He would then have converted a Royal Commission into Espionage, . . . into a political dog-fight. To put it quite crudely, if there is to be such a dog-fight, I will undertake to win it; but only if Dr Evatt's right to cross-examine me is reciprocated by my right to cross-examine him. This would no doubt add to the gaiety of nations and would certainly occasion me no physical or nervous discomfort, but it would destroy the whole purpose of the Royal Commission and would, therefore, do a great disservice to the nation.[56]

Mr Menzies' draft letter of late August is of the greatest interest. In general Menzies kept his thinking about the political dimension of the Petrov Affair extraordinarily well concealed. This letter — written at a critical moment, a fortnight into Dr Evatt's Royal Commission appearance — is almost the only existing evidence in which Mr Menzies' anxieties about the Affair are frankly expressed and in which he can be glimpsed thinking politically about it. Unhappily nothing in the letter, or in the file where it is to be found, indicates to whom it was written.* For the student of the Petrov Affair it raises two

---

* The most likely candidates would appear to be Professor Bailey, the Solicitor-General or Kenneth Herde, the Secretary to the Commission. It is, however, not even certain that it was ever sent to anyone.

intriguing but unanswerable questions. Did the practical and angry advice it offered become known — by direct or indirect means — to the Royal Commissioners themselves? If so, did its suggestions influence the way in which, in the first week of September, they were to resolve their Evatt problem?

On the morning of September 1 Mr Justice Owen's patience with Dr Evatt was finally exhausted. For more than a day the Commissioners had been listening to Dr Evatt's cross-examination of Petrova. While, for some reason, the chemistry between them had drawn from her the most bitter public statements she was ever to make about her husband's conduct — he had deceived her terribly; even now she could not bring herself to discuss with him the false suicide note; if she had known of his defection plans she would have handed him over to the Soviet authorities in the Embassy — nothing she said to Dr Evatt threw even the palest light on his conspiracy charges.[57] Where and when would it all end?

> You were permitted (Owen's challenge began) to appear here, Dr Evatt, for two persons, and you are entitled to ask such questions as we think proper. We are not prepared to allow you to ask questions the relevance of which to your clients we are unable to see. My colleagues and I wish to know from you, after the lunchtime adjournment at half past two, what is the conspiracy to which you have made many allusions, and who you allege are the conspirators in addition to O'Sullivan.[58]

After the luncheon break Dr Evatt pronounced his conspiracy charges formally. Document 'J' was not Lockwood's work but a concoction and a forgery. There had been a 'foul and most serious conspiracy' to insert the names of Dalziel and Grundeman into it in order to damage their master, the Leader of the Opposition and, through him, the Labor Party. The forgery had been produced, Dr Evatt now made explicit for the first time in the enquiry, in order to influence the outcome of the May Federal election. He introduced to the Commission the two evidentiary jewels in his political conspiracy crown. Had not the Movement newspaper in Melbourne, *News Weekly*, boasted in its April 28 1954 edition that as early as January 28 1953 it had tipped its readers off about the coming Petrov defection? His plans were, 'an open secret' then, (at least in certain circles!) fully fifteen months before their implementation on the eve of the election. And had not the *Sydney Morning Herald's* parliamentary correspondent written on April 6 that if Mr Menzies hoped to win the coming election he would have to pull one or two rabbits from the hat he had worn with such aplomb during the Royal Tour? The Petrov Affair had been, Dr Evatt claimed, 'one of the basest conspiracies known in political history'.

But who precisely, the Commissions asked Evatt, did he allege had been involved in this conspiracy? The 'centre' of it was, of course, Evatt replied, Petrov himself. Fergan O'Sullivan, who had been blackmailed by Petrov, was his main assistant. Petrova, while perhaps not a main initiator of the conspiracy, had nevertheless supported it. Mr Justice Ligertwood was not satisfied that Dr Evatt's list of conspirators was yet complete. 'You suggested that it was a conspiracy for political purposes.' Dr Evatt knew where Ligertwood was heading. Did he refer to Security? Evatt was strangely cautious now. While he would not allege that anyone in ASIO was involved in the political conspiracy he did charge Richards with having been 'negligent' in not testing for forgery the documents he had bought from Petrov for £5000 and of having 'uttered' them untested to the Government. Questioned on the point Dr Evatt declined to charge Colonel Spry even with negligence. He was never to be asked whether his charges extended to Mr Menzies.[59]

On the late afternoon of September 1 the Commission solicited the opinions of counsel assisting it on the Evatt conspiracy charges. Ted Hill had long declined to support the O'Sullivan aspect of the Evatt case. On the other hand he took great pleasure in alleging, without qualifications, that Richards had been a fully active participant in the Petrov conspiracy.[60] For his part Meagher protested vehemently. In the course of his career he had never encountered such wild and baseless charges as those now being made against his client. What moral and, for that matter, financial redress, he wondered, would Fergan O'Sullivan have against Dr Evatt? For the present Meagher received only some minor comfort from the Commissioners. Owen stated that at least thus far 'no evidence' whatever had been presented to show that O'Sullivan had typed or authored any part of 'J' while 'very, very strong evidence' had been presented to show that he had not.[61]

Finally Windeyer arose. What he said came very close to the bone. 'Nobody', he remarked, 'unless he was suffering from some sense of persecution which completely warped his reason' could, after reading 'J', possibly believe that it had been produced in order to harm Dr Evatt. Nonetheless, he conceded, the grave conspiracy charges would have to be answered. There existed, he now revealed, within ASIO 'contemporaneous reports, diaries and other records, including in some instances . . . tape recordings . . .' concerning the defection. He proposed that these records might be shown to the Commissioners — and, he stressed, to the Commissioners alone — as final proof of the baselessness of Dr Evatt's charges. Richards would also have to be recalled and more evidence taken about ASIO's Petrov operation than was strictly justified by the canons of national security interest.[62] On Colonel Spry's insistence ASIO was to be represented before the Commission by its own counsel — the leader of the Sydney Bar, Sir Garfield Barwick.[63] Its officers had already made contact with Doctors Bialoguski and Beckett in preparation for their Commission appearances.*[64] The nation was on the

---

* Bialoguski was very keen to make an appearance at the Royal Commission. On the other hand he, the consummate cynic, was convinced that Dr Beckett wanted an imperial and also possibly a papal honour in return for his appearance as a witness at the Commission.

eve of learning in detail, if not in its entirety, the strange story of Operation Cabin 12.

Dr Evatt was far from discouraged by the confrontation of September 1. On the following day he made application to call a new witness — Dr Charles Monticone, a New South Wales Government interpreter and part-time handwriting expert — to give evidence on the question of the side-lettering in 'J'. There were, he maintained, grave objections to Inspector Rogers' evidence.[65] On September 3, however, Mr Justice Owen turned down Dr Evatt's Monticone request. While the question of the handwriting in the margins of 'J' might be crucial to Dr Evatt's conspiracy allegations it seemed to Owen to be assuming an undue importance in his Commission's hearings. Had not Lockwood himself even admitted that the side-lettering closely resembled his handwriting? In the end, no matter what expert opinions were presented, the Commissioners would have to make up their own minds on the Lockwood handwriting question. In reality the refusal of the Monticone request was the first clear sign that the Commissioners were determined to retrieve their enquiry from Dr Evatt's control.[66]

The inevitable crisis between the Commissioners and Dr Evatt arrived almost at once. On Friday September 3 the Sydney *Sun* unexpectedly broke the story of the arrest and repatriation — on the basis of the Petrov's evidence — of an attractive, western female diplomat, a reference of course to the Second Secretary at the French Embassy, Madame Rose-Marie Ollier.[67] For several weeks Kenneth Herde and the French Ambassador to Australia, Louis Roche, had been discussing a joint announcement of Mme Ollier's arrest and the release of the transcript of the *in camera* Ollier hearing which had taken place in Melbourne on July 20. Now, on the afternoon of September 3, M. Roche invited Herde to an interview. He intended, in the light of the *Sun* story, to make a public statement on the Ollier arrest. He had no objection if the transcript of the Commission hearing was also to be published. At 6.30 p.m. Herde contacted Owen by telephone. Owen agreed to immediate publication.[68] The morning newspapers of September 4 were dominated by the Madame Ollier sensation. The first Petrov spy had apparently been caught.*
An enraged Dr Evatt threw himself into retaliatory action. On September 5 the front page of Australia's leading Sunday newspaper, the *Sun-Herald*, carried the story of his chivalric defence of Mme Ollier and his attack upon the dastardly conduct of M. Roche. One sentence in Dr Evatt's statement particularly stuck in the throats of the Royal Commissioners.

> Today [Mme. Ollier] will find herself defamed throughout the world as a spy apparently on the say so of two paid informers who, on their own admissions, have been treacherous to both Russia and Australia.[69]

---

* The Ollier case will be discussed in detail in chapter XII. Mme Ollier was eventually acquitted by the French military tribunal.

Dr Evatt outside the Royal Commission (courtesy of John Fairfax and Sons)

When the Commission resumed its sittings on Tuesday September 7 Dr Evatt was informed that his leave to appear at the Commission was under consideration. How could Dr Evatt justify the gross impropriety of the remarks he had made about two witnesses appearing at the Commission? Dr Evatt explained that he had been acting perfectly properly in his role as Leader of the Opposition. This was precisely where the problem, according to the Commissioners, lay. Was it not becoming daily more obvious that there existed a fatal incompatibility between Dr Evatt's legal role as counsel for his staff and his political role as Leader of the Opposition? Even at the Royal Commission it was quite unclear whether he was appearing for his staff or for himself. He seemed, moreover, to lack altogether the disinterestedness required of an advocate. Dr Evatt hotly contested the Commissioner's arguments about his conflicting responsibilities. Nevertheless, if they required him to 'choose between his two roles' as advocate and political leader he would unhesitatingly choose the former. While he did not apologise for his weekend statement about the Petrovs he did promise that nothing resembling it would occur in the future.

After protracted argument it became evident that the Commissioners were not to be deflected from their decision to remove him from their Commission. Dr Evatt appeared hardly able to believe what was happening. He had done nothing else over the 'last four of five weeks' than prepare for his case. Now, just as he was about to begin a renewed cross-examination of Richards, which he believed might prove decisive, his leave to appear was being threatened. Strange things, stranger than he had ever before experienced, had been happening at this Royal Commission. 'I feel more deeply about it than I appear to indicate'. Nothing other than 'an absolute determination, as far as determination of heart and head and hand can go to get to the truth of the matter' was driving him on. Was it not evident that he was now being opposed by the equal determination of Richards and — he hinted darkly — 'perhaps of others' to prevent the truth emerging? With some genuine pathos he begged the Commissioners to reconsider their decision. They would not. Before lunchtime on September 7 Dr Evatt involuntarily and his juniors voluntarily had departed the Commission. After lunch, in ersatz indignation, Ted Hill followed suit.[70]

11

THINGS FALL APART

On September 8, on the day after his expulsion from the Royal Commission, Dr Evatt returned to Canberra for his first Caucus meeting in a month. Here he delivered to his colleagues an uninterrupted and highly dramatic speech (which extended to some hour and a quarter) on the Petrov Affair and its historical significance. This case was, he told them, the most important of his life. It involved one of the most diabolical conspiracies in political history. When the truth was finally revealed the Menzies Government would fall. During his discourse Dr Evatt revealed to the Caucus — as he had to the Commission — that *News Weekly* had boasted that it had known of the impending Petrov defection as early as January 1953. Clearly Petrov had been nurtured by Security for more than eighteen months. At least on some of his Caucus colleagues of the left and the right the hint of some sinister connection between Security and the Movement would not have been lost.

According to the *Sydney Morning Herald's* sources during his Petrov address Dr Evatt 'was trembling and almost tearful with emotion'. Although the atmosphere in Caucus must have been electric, he was heard out in silence. When he had concluded, well after the time the meeting had been scheduled to end, Eddie Ward — apparently in defiance of the wishes of the parliamentary executive — attempted to move a motion of confidence in his leadership. Caucus tensions now exploded. As Dr Evatt tried to close the meeting, several members — including Stan Keon and Albert Thompson — rose to their feet demanding the right to speak to Ward's motion; others exhorted him to withdraw it. The Labor left (who enthusiastically supported Evatt's Petrov crusade) and the right (who abominated it) exchanged abuse. Thompson and Ward — who for the second time in a month raised his fists in Caucus on the Petrov question — almost came to blows and had to be separated.[1]

Uproar followed Dr Evatt from the Caucus room to the floor of the House. During question time on September 8 he repeatedly shouted his opinion that Australia had become a 'police state', before the Speaker, curiously ruling such language unparliamentary, obliged him to withdraw.[2] Later, during a speech by Fred Daly, Dr Evatt was observed thumping the table with his fist and muttering: 'Tell 'em about the Petrov Commission — that is what they are frightened of!'.[3] On September 9, outraged by headline reports of the previous day's Caucus eruption, he hurriedly convened a press conference in his office. For forty minutes he shouted at reporters and denounced the enemies — 'the treacherous liars' — in his midst. The story of the clash between Eddie Ward and Albert Thompson was a 'deliberate lie' being peddled by those he called paid and unpaid 'informers' inside Caucus in order to injure him. The previous day's meeting had in fact been the quietest he had experienced 'in ten years'. As he had revealed the 'inside story' of the Royal Commission to his party, his audience had been, he said, 'enthralled'.[4] Dr Evatt ended his week by issuing a fifteen hundred word press release which called upon Mr Menzies to dismiss the present Royal Commission and replace it with a new five man tribunal to investigate his conspiracy charges.[5] By now several of his Labor colleagues feared he was experiencing some form of nervous collapse. Since Sydney he had appeared 'thinner, white-faced, strained, unpredictable' and, above all else, 'fanatical on the subject of the Petrov Commission'.[6]

In the second week of September, as Dr Evatt wrought his havoc in Canberra, the Royal Commissioners — without the presence of Dr Evatt and his juniors or of Ted Hill — experienced some few days of rare tranquillity. As Windeyer had promised, their time was absorbed in the details of Operation Cabin 12, with the perusal of the evidence which it was hoped would refute once and for all Dr Evatt's conspiracy charges. In the privacy of their chambers the Commissioners were shown for the first time the voluminous and lurid reports on Petrov which Bialoguski had dictated to his ASIO contacts and ASIO's internal records of the defection, including the minifon recordings. In open hearings they listened as Ron Richards and Doctors Beckett and Bialoguski outlined, for the first time to the Australian public, the true story of ASIO's Petrov operation.*[7] By the end of this week the Commissioners were more convinced than ever that Evatt's charges were 'fantastic'.

---

* There was considerable outrage — either mock or genuine — about the role the two doctors had played in the Petrov operation. The Communist Party tried to exploit this feeling by circulating to many Australian doctors a letter condemning their behaviour. It also produced a cyclostyled pamphlet entitled 'Doctors of Honour not Common Informers' purporting to come from 'a panel of doctors'. The leaflet began thus: 'Revelations that two Macquarie Street doctors recently departed from all precedent in the medical profession to become willing agents of the Security police have caused much disquiet in the Australian medical profession'. Not only the left professed indignation. In the Victorian parliament the leader of the splinter Liberal party made a snide remark about the ethics of New South Wales doctors. There were even rumours that the matter might be referred to the Australian branch of the BMA. On September 15 an officer of ASIO visited Dr Beckett. He was told that 'during the week after he had given evidence at the Commission not one of his wife's friends had contacted his wife by phone as they usually did . . . it was very apparent that her friends viewed her with some suspicion and barely spoke to her'.

Ron Richards took the stand on September 7 and remained there for almost three days.[8] In general his evidence was outstandingly accurate. Before his appearance he had committed to memory even the finest details of the history of the defection. The tale he told will be familiar to readers of the opening section of this book. Richards did not even shrink from the mention of at least some matters which were by now certain to bring aid and comfort to the enemies of ASIO and the Government. Recently Mr Menzies had informed the parliament and the nation that he had known nothing of Petrov before April 11 or 12. Richards, however, informed the Commission that he and Colonel Spry had made their Petrov journey to Canberra on the afternoon of April 4.[9] Within three weeks of Richards' evidence the intrepid Eddie Ward (in a parliamentary question) and the equally intrepid Brian Fitzpatrick (in a pamphlet) had brought this discrepancy to the attention of the parliament and the nation.[10]

There was, however, one extremely delicate subject — the precise relationship between money and documents in the pre-defection negotiations with Petrov — where Richards' customary frankness deserted him. During the course of the evidence he gave between September 7 and 9 Ron Richards maintained, quite truthfully, that the £5000 would have been paid to Petrov even if, on his defection, he had brought over no documentary material.[11] What, however, he consistently concealed from the Commissioners throughout his testimony was that on two occasions before Petrov had defected ASIO had offered him an additional £5000 if he managed to bring extremely valuable documentation of Soviet espionage with him. Readers will recall the following words of Richards to Petrov in Canberra on March 26.

> If your information is of extreme value and you have something to support it — you may have a report or something like that — then, as I told you before, it could be £10,000.[12]

At best — as the following exchange demonstrates — Richards' handling of this issue was casuistical.

Philp: Now did Petrov try to raise your bid in any way?
Richards: No
Philp: £5000 was the first sum you had mentioned to him: did he endeavour to get you to raise the bid?
Richards: No. I can say quite clearly that Petrov at no time ever stated an amount of money that he wanted.[13]

Quite so. It was, of course, Richards and not Petrov who had 'raised the bid' from £5000 to £10,000 and who had 'stated an amount of money' that was on offer. In claiming throughout his evidence that there had never been so much as a hint of a bargain between himself and Petrov over money and documents Richards, at least in his public evidence, clearly misled the Commissioners.*[14] As ASIO understood, in the conspiracy atmosphere of September, a belated admission of even an entirely innocent bonus-payment-offer to Petrov in exchange for documents would have presented ASIO's enemies with a quite devastating weapon.

As Dr Evatt had revealed at the Commission on August 30,[15] the anti-Petrov camp planned to call Dr Bialoguski as a witness, chiefly to expose to the world details of Petrov's notorious Sydney night life. No doubt to their considerable surprise, during the course of his testimony, Richards revealed Bialoguski's work for ASIO and his pivotal role in the Petrov defection.[16] Despite the fact that being named before the Commission ended his long and lucrative career as an ASIO penetration agent inside the peace movement and pro-Soviet émigré organisations, Bialoguski was far from unhappy with the new situation. One career might be drawing to a close, but another — as Australia's most famous spy — was opening up. He had already written the first pages of his book on the Petrov Affair. An appearance at the Commission would do this new career no harm and would most likely bring to him, as he told Gilmour of ASIO, 'prestige and material advancement'.[17]

Dr Bialoguski prepared for the Royal Commission with characteristic enthusiasm and cynicism. Aware that he was likely to be questioned by hostile counsel about Petrov's drinking he informed Gilmour that he intended to admit that 'towards the end Petrov drank quite a lot'.[18] He was, however, he pointed out, studying medical texts in order to be in a position to refute authoritatively any suggestion about Petrov being an alcoholic.[19] Bialoguski's Commission appearance was hemmed in by one advance promise of silence. Months earlier, when Bialoguski's ASIO identity had been revealed to Petrov (who either felt or feigned surprise) Bialoguski had solemnly promised an anxious Petrov that he would never reveal to anyone the details of their joint womanising. As Bialoguski at once told ASIO:

> I ... said that our escapades with the girls were entirely our private affair and that I had not said anything to the other Security men about this aspect ... [Petrov] promised his full co-operation and was only too glad to hear that I had not passed on the information to Security about the women aspect.[20]

He did not, however, need to promise anyone that he had no intention of telling the Commission about the whisky trade he and Petrov had in the past conducted.[21] When he took the stand on September 9 and 10 Bialoguski exuded self-confidence. Thirty years later Sir Charles Spry would remember him as a 'magnificent witness'.[22] If anything his performance overshadowed Richards'. Extremely neatly he turned the tables on the left by informing the Commission of John Rodgers' attempt to recruit him as a witness in the anti-Petrov cause.[23] In the absence of cross-examination by hos-

---

* The Commissioners were handed the minifon tapes which should have included the entire March 26 discussion. However if they relied on the file of minifon transcripts they would not have read of the money talk of March 26. The transcription of that conversation is incomplete.

tile counsel during the initial instalment of his evidence, the only banana skin thrown in his direction came from Petrova, who evidently loathed him. On the eve of Dr Bialoguski's Commission appearance she informed her ASIO minders that this man had been all along a genuine double agent — 'yours and ours'.[24]

On Monday September 13 the anti-Petrov legal caravan (minus Dr Evatt) returned to the Commission in preparation for Sir Garfield Barwick's cross-examination of Allan Dalziel and Albert Grundeman. As soon as he took the stand Dalziel absolutely denied the truthfulness of the single mention of him in 'J'. (Dalziel had been named as a source of information concerning a certain American professor, Kluckhohn, who was quoted as saying that Russian studies in Australian universities were pro-Soviet.) Dalziel swore on his Presbyterian honour that he had never met Professor Kluckhohn in his life (although he had once attended a lecture he had given). He attempted at least to support Dr Evatt's negligence-uttering charge against Richards. Why, he inquired of the Commission, had Richards not approached him on the Kluckhohn matter before handing 'J' to the Prime Minister? Owen, in his turn, asked Dalziel what conceivable difference such an approach could have made. Did Dalziel seriously suggest that even if Richards had discovered the Kluckhohn error (one of hundreds of factual matters in the Petrov documents) his duty was not to pass 'J' to Mr Menzies but to return it to Petrov?

Under cross-examination Dalziel readily admitted that the reference to him in 'J' was totally innocuous, and less readily that 'J' may not have been brought into existence in order to harm him or, through him, his political chief. Even so he did complain bitterly about the fact that for two months his name had been 'bandied about' the land as a source for 'J'. Politely Mr Justice Owen reminded him that he had been offered but, through Dr Evatt, had refused 'an opportunity to give evidence within three of four days of the first mention of his name'. In further cross-examination both Dalziel and Grundeman admitted that they had no idea who had composed 'J'. Grundeman saw no reason to suspect Fergan O'Sullivan of involvement in an anti-Evatt conspiracy. Nor, in reality, did Dalziel, although he tentatively ventured that O'Sullivan's Irish ancestry might explain some innate predisposition for conspiracies.[25] As everyone was soon to discover, sectarianism was alive and well in Australia.*[26]

---

* When Evatt attacked the Movement (see below) there was an almost immediate chorus of Protestant anti-Catholicism on the 'neither Moscow nor Rome' theme. The president of the Methodist conference, Reverend Manefield, argued that Catholic Action had been 'white anting' the Labor Movement for years. 'We need', he said, 'neither Moscow nor Rome to tell us how to maintain and extend our democratic way of life'. A leading Presbyterian, the Reverend McEvoy, went even further. He reminded the nation of a recent report from his Church which had warned of 'the determination of the Roman Catholic Church to dominate the life of the people of Australia'. This question required 'vigilance and action'. It was not for nothing that the *Sydney Morning Herald* editorialised even-handedly on October 23 on the theme of 'Sectarianism: A Taint on the Nation'.

By the evening of September 13, no doubt to his considerable dismay, Dr Evatt had discovered that, under the powerful cross-examination of Sir Garfield Barwick, neither of his staffers had been able to sustain the conspiracy charges he had propounded to the Commission on their behalf.[27] Most probably Evatt was furious with them both, especially the more intelligent Dalziel. In his curiously ambivalent Evatt memoir Dalziel recollected accurately that at the Commission he had failed to support the conspiracy theory. It was 'of course', he argued, unreasonable to have expected him 'to maintain the position that Dr Evatt of his own volition had decided to pursue'.[28] A member of Dr Evatt's Petrovian salon, the solicitor Bert Barkell, was later to recall that at this time Evatt did not trust Dalziel. Indeed he trusted noone. In the evocative language of another member of the salon, Leslie Haylen, Evatt appeared now to have 'some demon behind him, which was going to get him'.[29]

Late on the afternoon of September 13 Rupert Lockwood was recalled, yet again, to the witness box. For the best part of two days Sir Garfield, with some assistance from Windeyer and the Commissioners, struggled to compel him to admit he was the author of 'J'. Lockwood, however, proved an altogether tougher proposition than the Evatt staffers. Many of the extremely close textual similarities between 'J' and his pamphlet 'What Is In Document J?' were drawn by Barwick to his attention. He was confronted with his failure in Melbourne to deny his authorship of 'J' or to have noticed, from Windeyer's Canberra address, that while 'J' had 37 pages he claimed to have left 170 pages of typing at the Soviet Embassy. Why, he was asked, did he and his Party claim before Dr Evatt's intervention that 'J' was 'stolen' and after it that it was 'forged' and 'fabricated'?[30] All in vain. Time and again Sir Garfield Barwick appeared on the point of landing his catch just before Lockwood, displaying either dialectical virtuosity or an apparent inability to understand elementary laws of logic and evidence, wriggled off the hook. 'It is almost like trying to cross-examine someone', Barwick expostulated at one harrowing moment, 'in another language'. Although Owen thought the answer to the question of the authorship of 'J' was 'as plain as a pikestaff',[31] he had to admit that Lockwood was 'the best witness at not answering a question' he had ever observed.[32]

After lunch-time on Tuesday September 14 Windeyer invited counsel for Dalziel and Grundeman to begin their cross-examination of Richards. Gregory Sullivan and, in sympathy, Ted Hill politely declined. The Royal Commissioners on Espionage and counsel assisting them had been sullenly chasing the conspiracy hares let loose by Dr Evatt in August for the past five weeks. Now the counsel who had committed them to this ludicrous chase had refused to join them! Owen thought Sullivan's refusal to cross-examine Richards, whom he had charged with gross negligence, unprecedented; Sir Garfield Barwick thought that unless Sullivan at once withdrew the charge against Richards he would 'stand disgraced'. For his part Ligertwood intended to ignore the conspiracy charges — which were, he thought, being used for some 'ulterior purpose' — and begin at long last to investigate espionage. Did Sullivan agree that Dr Evatt's conspiracy charges lapsed with his unwillingness to cross-examine Richards? The hapless Sullivan did not agree.[33]

That evening Gregory Sullivan must have conferred with Dr Evatt. As soon as the Commission assembled on the following morning, he announced that Dr Evatt intended to apply on the following Monday (September 20) for leave to reappear at the Commission. He would then conduct the cross-examinations of Richards, Bialoguski and Petrov. He would also be calling the Prime Minister as a witness. This Inquiry, Ligertwood suggested, 'is getting out of hand'. 'Someone', Philp added, 'is trying to make fools of us'. Owen instructed Sullivan to begin his cross-examination of Richards at once. Sullivan again declined. He had not, he said, had time enough to prepare. Not time enough? Mr Justice Owen thought five weeks more than sufficient. 'The thing is becoming farcical.' 'That is what I have thought', Philp observed sombrely, 'for weeks'.[34]

On the morning of Wednesday September 15 — as the Commissioners and Sullivan clashed over him — Dr Evatt had more on his mind than his planned return to the Royal Commission. Caucus was due to meet. After its last meeting — which had erupted after his Petrov speech — he had publicly described certain of his right-wing colleagues as 'paid informers' and 'treacherous liars'. An announcement now of any intention to return to the Royal Commission might have ignited once more the combustible material in Caucus. Some cunning was required.

Given the nature of Dr Evatt's recent observations on certain unnamed colleagues, it was somewhat strange that the mood of Caucus on September 15 was predominantly conciliatory. Several addresses, which *Age* sources had called 'moving', were delivered on the theme of Party unity.[35] For once the Caucus minutes reflect the meeting's tone.

> Mr T. Burke* asked Dr Evatt to make a statement in relation to press reports dealing with leakages from Party meetings. Dr Evatt made a statement and added that, in the interest of the Labor movement and Party solidarity generally, all members should join together to prevent all sources of leakages from the Party which were damaging the movement. If that were done, *a great improvement in Party unity could result*. He suggested the meeting should, by agreement, terminate in that spirit and that intention.[36]

Some members at least believed these appeals for unity had 'brought Caucus closer together than it had been for several weeks'.[37] Towards the end of the

---

* Somewhat quixotically, Tom Burke (a right winger and father of the present Premier of Western Australia) had stood against Dr Evatt in a leadership ballot at the first Caucus after the May 29 election. He had scored a commendable 20 votes, but then had lost his position on the parliamentary executive.

meeting Ted Peters tried to raise the Petrov question for discussion, but Dr Evatt — most likely with the support of the majority in Caucus, who hoped that the Evatt-Petrov troubles could now be put behind them — refused him permission. Caucus adjourned before the scheduled closing time.*

Before most members had left the Caucus room someone rushed in with details of an item on the midday radio news. Dr Evatt intended to apply to return to the Royal Commission! Many were astonished and angered. They felt that if he had signalled his Commission intentions at Caucus a large majority would have flatly refused him permission. When Peters had raised the Petrov question why had he remained silent? Even his closest Caucus supporters had not been consulted. While appealing movingly for Party unity, he had privately treated his colleagues with duplicity and contempt.[38]

Dr Evatt's mind, however, was already elsewhere. During the luncheon break at the Commission apparently he consulted by telephone with his legal representatives there. After lunch, Gregory Sullivan announced that his leader would not now wait until next Monday but would next morning apply for permission to reappear as counsel at the Commission.[39] That afternoon Dr Evatt cancelled an important engagement — to propose the toast alongside Mr Menzies at the opening of the Rum Jungle uranium plant — and flew to Sydney.[40] The following morning, as he strode into the Royal Commission, he was cheered enthusiastically by a large Communist crowd which had gathered in support of him. This was the anti-Menzies united front in action. Ten uniformed policemen were rushed to Darlinghurst. Inside the courtroom Dr Evatt at once applied for leave to appear as counsel for Dalziel and Grundeman. Mr Justice Owen at once refused. If anything, he said, Dr Evatt's behaviour since his removal — and in particular his public call for the dismissal of the present Royal Commission and its reconstitution — had strengthened his conviction that the decision of September 7 had been wise. Undeterred, Dr Evatt applied for permission to appear as counsel representing himself. He was advised to reapply in the unlikely event of him being called as a witness before the Commission. During his pleadings a young pro-Evatt interjector was forcibly removed from the courtroom kicking and screaming.[41]

Before final judgement on the Evatt application was pronounced, Mr Justice Ligertwood — who had in the past felt some friendship for Dr Evatt — offered some personal advice.

> During the week-end I spent some considerable time going through Mr Richards' evidence and Dr. Bialoguski's evidence, and also Security documents; and I tell you this for your own good: that your suggestion that there was any conspiracy against the Labour Party is just fantastic.[42]

---

* According to the *Sydney Morning Herald* at 12.30; according to the official minutes at 12.55.

Unsurprisingly, if unhappily for himself and his Party, Ligertwood's words fell on determinedly deaf ears. For the next three days of sittings Dr Evatt was forced to content himself with a courtroom seat at the elbow of his juniors and Ted Hill from where he gave his advice in a stage whisper. Somewhat mysteriously, after the Friday sitting Gregory Sullivan departed the Commission. The main burden of Dr Evatt's conspiracy charges now fell upon the young shoulders of his nephew (the future Royal Commissioner on 'Agent Orange') Philip Evatt.

With only the hostile cross-examinations of Richards, Bialoguski and Petrov still to come the end of the testimony in the Evatt conspiracy hearings was at least now in sight. As it happened, five Commission days were to be devoted to this final phase. Ted Hill appeared now to be enjoying himself immensely. Using the courtroom as his forum, he threw grave allegations at the Petrovs, Richards and, above all, Bialoguski. According to Hill Petrov, Petrova, Bialoguski and certain persons unknown had conspired to forge certain documents and sell them to the highest bidder — as it turned out Richards of ASIO, who had paid £5000 for them. The conspirators' purposes were to injure his client, Lockwood; to win for themselves money and asylum; and, most importantly, to destroy the 'Labour movement' during the course of an election campaign. Petrov was not an intelligence officer at all but a treacherous Third Secretary. He had been admitted to the Canberra hospital in May 1953 not because of eye trouble but due to abuse of drink and drugs. He had double-crossed his wife by fleeing to ASIO behind her back. Not that one could have sympathy for her. Petrova had, according to Hill, staged the Mascot and Darwin melodramas in association with Australian Security and a pro-fascist émigré mob. When she had said of her husband that he had cheated her she was referring to his double-cross and failure to drive the price of the forged documents above £5000. And as for Dr Bialoguski — a man whom Hill was to describe as a 'disgrace' to the medical profession and humanity — was he not an international spy with pro-Nazi leanings? Surely noone could seriously believe it an accident that he had left the Soviet Union in the year of Barbarossa and Japan in the year of Pearl Harbour! From the nature of his cross-examination Hill appears to have had his eyes not only on the next week's headlines in *Tribune* and *Guardian* but also the next day's in the *Age* and *Sydney Morning Herald*.[43]

Mr Windeyer, in particular, was becoming acutely sensitive to the potential propaganda uses of the espionage Commission. Before lunch on September 17 he recalled that he had remarked to Colonel Spry that a mere £5000 to bring over Petrov made him 'a very cheap prisoner'. Perhaps some thought of an impending *Tribune* headline (on the lines of — 'Petrov a prisoner, QC tells Commissioner') spoiled his lunch. When the Commission reconvened he advised the world that his words had been uttered in jest. 'My allusion to prisoners this morning was not intended to suggest that Mr Petrov had been kidnapped.'[44]

Even more immediately discomfiting to ASIO than Ted Hill's general accusations was the evidence which now emerged of the kinds of accurate information which had somehow leaked to the anti-Petrovian camp. On September 16 Gregory Sullivan had inquired of Richards whether in the late spring of 1953 ASIO and Dr Bialoguski had quarrelled over money and whether, as a result of these quarrels, Bialoguski had been sacked. Richards was obviously caught badly off balance. To his knowledge there had been, he said, no quarrel or dismissal.[45] Later that day ASIO instructed its Canberra director, Colonel Phillipps, to inquire discreetly of Geoffrey Yeend about the possibility of some leakage from his files.[46] It soon, however, transpired that this was not the source of the leak. During his cross-examination of Dr Bialoguski, Ted Hill asked whether he had not, as a result of some argument with ASIO last October, taken his story to the *Sydney Morning Herald*. Sir Garfield Barwick tried to close down this line of questioning with, however, only partial success. While Owen allowed Hill to ask and Bialoguski to confirm that he had indeed mentioned Petrov at the *Sydney Morning Herald*, he instructed Bialoguski not to answer Hill's question about whether this trip arose as a consequence of his quarrel with ASIO.[47]

Perhaps even more alarmingly, on September 21 Philip Evatt asked Petrov whether Dr Bialoguski had, on occasion, forged 'receipts' for him and whether there was not in his Sydney flat 'a large quantity of liquor' which had been 'bought on what we might call the "diplomatic frank".'[48] As yet no explicit charge about a Petrov-Bialoguski line in the duty free whisky trade had been laid. Nevertheless, in a fortnight, Dr Bialoguski informed ASIO that he had discovered that George Marue (ASIO's one-time watch on him) was threatening to sell information concerning not only Bialoguski's illegal jewellery and abortion practices but also concerning the whisky trade to the anti-Petrov forces.[49] For ASIO new storm clouds appeared to be gathering.

On the late afternoon of September 21, as the 'J'-conspiracy testimony was at long last drawing to a close, two pieces of evidence — both crucial to the Evatt case — were tendered. One was Dr Monticone's short written opinion on Lockwood's handwriting and the writing in the margins of 'J'. This seemed at least to Windeyer so 'far from the point' and so 'extravagant' as to be virtually worthless. After reading it the Commissioners could not but agree. The other was the *News Weekly* article of January 28 1953, which had been introduced to the Commission by Dr Evatt and subsequently reintroduced by Ted Hill and Philip Evatt. Each had tried to use it as proof that Petrov had already made his mind up to defect fifteen months in advance of his actions. Did this not show Petrov had been saved up for the election of May 1954? When Owen read the by now famous article he commented at once that it had not in any way predicted Petrov's defection. It was certainly, he thought, not worth bothering about.[50]

Although ASIO shared Mr Justice Owen's view and knew of course that it had not been based — as the anti-Petrov camp asserted — on information it had supplied to *News Weekly*,*[51] nevertheless it despatched a field officer to its Melbourne office for an interview with the editor on the circumstances of the article's appearance. Ted Madden had caused all the *News Weekly* trouble by vainly boasting to his readers after the defection that 'we tipped you off'. He was now only too happy to cooperate in defusing the matter. The little article, Madden pointed out, had appeared some twenty one months ago. So far as he could recall

> some time after the ALP had taken control of the Federated Ironworkers' Association and the Federated Clerks' Union, he was informed by an official of one of these Unions, possibly Laurie Short, that the name of Vladimir Petrov had been found on an addressograph in the office of one of the Unions concerned.[52]

News Weekly denied now in its columns that it had had, in January 1953, any knowledge whatsoever of Petrov's impending defection.

After the morning tea break on the final day of the conspiracy testimony, Tuesday September 21, Dr Evatt left the Darlinghurst courtoom to fly back to Canberra. Given the way he had deceived his colleagues at the previous week's meeting it was hardly surprising that here now Labor's Petrov cauldron, which had long been simmering, finally boiled over. Evatt's chief accuser was the Member for Fawkner and once *News Weekly* editorial board member, Bill Bourke. Bourke accused Dr Evatt of doing the Communists' work for them at the Commission and of being their greatest asset. Evatt's conspiracy charges were ridiculous and would not hold water. The adulation he was receiving from the Communist press was sickening. Ted Hill was merely Rupert Lockwood's junior counsel. Dr Evatt, it was well known, had even frequently conferred with Hill in Hill's chambers. Last week he had lied to Caucus about his Petrov intentions. Bourke spoke for some ten minutes. His words apparently shocked many of his colleagues.

Formally Bourke was speaking to a motion Ted Peters had proposed and Tom Burke seconded.

---

* ASIO's Petrov file for February 1953 shows that its Melbourne office had noticed the *News Weekly* article and speculated about (but did not pursue) the question of who might have supplied *News Weekly* with information about a Soviet Third Secretary's industrial activities. The memorandum thought 'it may be significant that this article more or less' coincided with a Petrov visit to Melbourne. ASIO however had had Petrov under surveillance 'during business hours' and had noticed nothing untoward. 'If based on Petrov's visit', it continued, 'the report would appear to have emanated from a source with casual access to certain overt activity conducted by Petrov in his official capacity ... the article would otherwise appear to refer to political gossip unrelated to Petrov's visit to Melbourne, and perhaps even to Petrov'. This piece of evidence in the ASIO file alone proves false one of the most crucial and durable elements of the conspiracy theory, namely that the *News Weekly* article of January 1953 revealed Movement involvement with ASIO in the plans for the Petrov defection.

That the Leader do not appear as a Counsel at the Petrov Royal Commission nor make any further public statements on its operation or constitution without the consent of the Parliamentary Labor Party expressed by the Caucus.

Both mover and seconder, however, distanced themselves somewhat from the scathing tone of Bill Bourke's remarks. (The fine psychological line between those right wingers who would split and those who would not was here prefigured.) Reg Pollard rose to Dr Evatt's defence. There were some members in Caucus, he said, who 'were not fit to lick the Doctor's boots'. Had not Bill Bourke given succour to the Liberal Party during the last election by his attack on Labor's means test proposal? Had not he and his mates 'run dead' during the anti-Communist referendum? Dr Evatt could not be blamed for the content of the Communist press. Pollard was supported by Senator Ashley of New South Wales and Gil Duthie of Tasmania. Bill Edmonds pushed further. He informed Caucus — which was by now in uproar — that before this meeting he had been asked to support a plot to replace Dr Evatt with Arthur Calwell. All eyes now turned to Calwell. At once he disclaimed any knowledge of this plot. Indeed he thoroughly supported his leader's call for Ted Peters to withdraw his censure motion. Ted Peters withdrew. With several members — including the Movement's John Mullens still clamouring to be heard — Dr Evatt closed the discussion once and for all.[53]

Tactically Dr Evatt had won a victory at the Caucus on September 22. In August Caucus had resisted the left's attempt to have his appearance at the Commission approved retrospectively. In September it had resisted the right's attempt to condemn it. The uncompromising quality of Bill Bourke's anti-Communist denunciation of Evatt — which had gone too far even for some of his right wing friends — had most likely swung the feeling of the Caucus centre to Evatt's side. Dr Evatt, who had promised his colleagues that he would never again miss a parliamentary day on behalf of Petrov, had retained his freedom to speak his mind on the Petrov Affair. He had not yet, however, silenced his Movement enemies within the Caucus.

On Monday September 27 the Royal Commission reconvened for the addresses from counsel on the conspiracy aspect of their hearings. Philip Evatt initiated proceedings. He outlined the by now familiar theory of his uncle that 'J' had been forged by the Petrovs and Fergan O'Sullivan in order to harm Evatt's staff, through them Evatt, and through him the Labor Party at the elections. Mr Justice Philp asked him why if O'Sullivan had helped concoct 'J' he had inserted his own name in it as a source. 'Whoever heard of a conspiracy to fabricate a document in which one of the conspirators puts his own name as one of the fabricators? I mean it is really Alice in Wonderland'.[54] Not only that, Meagher chipped in. O'Sullivan was apparently even cunning enough to have misspelt his own name — 'Fergun' not Fergan — in the 'J' sources page.[55] Philip Evatt argued further that the Moscow letters (which included an instruction to Petrov to prepare a document on American penetration in Australia) had in turn been forged by Petrov in order to lend to 'J' some bogus aura of authenticity. Owen now disagreed with his brother's choice of literary analogy. 'The only men who could go justice to this ... are Gilbert and Sullivan'.[56]

What was the evidence that 'J' had indeed been forged? Evatt referred first to the suppression of Dr Monticone's evidence on the handwriting in the margins of 'J'. This might have, Evatt argued, proven 'beyond all doubt' the question of forgery. Owen replied that in reality it was a mercy to Monticone that they had not published his worthless and 'irresponsible' statement. Even Lockwood had conceded that the handwriting in the margins of 'J' closely resembled his own. What, however, Evatt asked, was to be made of the crucial 'Y' in 'J'? On this basis alone the forgery and hence the conspiracy could be proved. Ligertwood had, however, as usual, done his homework. He pointed out that in an example of Lockwood's print subpoenaed for the Commission one 'Y' in SYDNEY had been a tailed 'V' and the other a tailed 'U'.[57] 'This is becoming fantastic', Owen observed. 'To think that anyone should be charging O'Sullivan with writing Exhibit J on piffling material of this sort.'[58] Was there not anything more substantial? Philip Evatt referred to the intrusion into 'J' of certain un-Australian expressions — namely 'clerical' and 'diplomatic frank'.[59] Did this not indicate the Russo-Irish origin of 'J'? Unfortunately for Evatt Lockwood had already conceded that the word 'clerical' might occasionally 'slip in' to his writings; while, as for 'diplomatic frank', strangely enough Philip Evatt had himself used this expression one week earlier in his cross-examination of Petrov.

The Commissioners finally asked Philip Evatt to consider the question of motive. Surely if the intention of 'J''s forgers had been to injure Dr Evatt and the Labor Party there would have appeared in it what Philp called some 'red hot stuff'. And surely, Owen added — in what was in reality the most knockdown argument of all — if 'J' had been produced in order to influence the election was it not strange that during 'the last federal elections ... it was never used'?[60]

After lunch on Tuesday September 28 Philip Evatt was succeeded by Ted Hill. He addressed the Commission for more than two days, systematising and exaggerating the accusations he had thrown at the Petrovs, Bialoguski and ASIO during his final cross-examinations.[61] In reality, as Mr Justice Owen shrewdly observed, his speech was not concerned with convincing the Commissioners of his case.

> Mr Hill, it may be an unjust suspicion in my mind, but I cannot help feeling that what you are addressing to us is not intended for our ears but is intended for some other audience.[62]

Unjust or not, shortly afterwards Ted Hill's 'brilliant address to the Petrov Commission' was published by the Communist Party as a threepenny pamphlet entitled *The Petrov Conspiracy*.[63] Perhaps the Party aspired to make

it the Antipodean version of Dimitrov's speech before the judges at the Reichstag fire trial.

Hill was followed by Meagher. There was actually no evidentiary case
against O'Sullivan for him to refute. Instead, in his full Irish voice, he coined
a Windeyerism. The case against his client was no more than 'a farrago of
fantasy, fatuity and futility'.[64] He was more interested in inquiring whether
the protection against defamatory actions accorded counsel at the Commission extended to counsel whose leave to appear had been withdrawn,[65] and
with turning Dr Evatt on himself by charging him with 'the dirtiest piece of
smearing that I have seen in this community'.*[66] After Meagher had concluded, before lunch on October 1, the judges, by now rather exhausted,
retired to their respective homes for a very long weekend.

They resumed the following Wednesday to hear the concluding addresses
of Sir Garfield Barwick and Victor Windeyer. Rarely in the history of Australian law can so much legal acumen have been devoted to proving so self-
evident a question as the authorship of 'J'. Barwick and Windeyer observed
that all known facts — from Lockwood's presence in the Soviet Embassy at
the time 'J' appeared to have been composed, to the most intimate details
of his early life which appeared in the sources in the first person — supported
the theory of his authorship of 'J'. The fact that Petrov's evidence about 'H'
on April 3 had proven accurate gave reason to believe his story of 'J'.
Petrova's account of how she had seen 'J' produced had been confirmed in
every detail but one (the brandy) by Lockwood himself. If 'J' was a 37 page
forgery based on 170 pages of his work was it not inconceivable that Lockwood would not have noticed this fact in Melbourne — where he was given
'J' to read — and announced it to the Commission? Had not his barrister
Ted Hill even virtually conceded at Melbourne that Lockwood was the author
of 'J'? (At Melbourne he had said 'My client freely says that he did in fact
write a document which, it may be, was Document J'.) Had he not also agreed
that the document Lockwood had written was 37 pages? ('I understand from
the Transcript that there are thirty-seven pages in it.')

If 'J' was not Lockwood's work but a forged 37 page condensation of an
original 170 pages, how came it that in his own pamphlet 'What Is In Document J?' no matter was attributed to 'J' which did not in fact appear in it?
How could Lockwood know with such precision what parts of his 170 pages
would not be incorporated in the forged condensation? Such a coincidence

---

* Dr Evatt, not surprisingly, answered Meagher at once. It was he not O'Sullivan who had been
smeared. In this press release he hinted in public for the first time about his darkest suspicions
of O'Sullivan being an ASIO plant on his staff. 'I also feel it quite likely that O'Sullivan
"planted" himself on my staff in April 1953. The evidence discloses that the Prime Minister,
Spry and Richards knew that O'Sullivan was the author of Exhibit "H" in April of this year,
yet they deliberately refrained from informing me of this fact. Further, Security Service
refrained from informing me of the fact that O'Sullivan was in touch with Petrov in July 1953
during my absence abroad ... when they should, and I believe did, know of it'.

was simply beyond all rational possibility. Moreover why should anyone have gone to the trouble of forging an entire 37 pages of 'J' — a task which involved a painstaking replication of Lockwood's polemical, handwriting and typewriting styles and which would have taxed even a master forger — when they could have just as readily slipped one forged Evatt page into the original 170 pages? And to what end was this vast and wicked task supposed to have been deployed? Apparently to the attribution of an 'innocuous' remark to Dalziel and some 'tap-room political gossip' to Grundeman and for some electoral purpose to which, manifestly, 'J' had never even been used![67]

At the end of the addresses of Barwick and Windeyer every rational person who had been in the courtroom must have known that Rupert Lockwood had authored 'J' and that Dr Evatt's conspiracy charges — which rested exclusively upon the proposition that he had not and that 'J' had been forged — were a fantasm of his strange imagination. As the judges retired to prepare their interim report on the first phase of their hearings what must have been troubling them was not the identity of the author of 'J' but the fact that their Commission, which had commenced its work five months before, had as yet hardly even embarked upon the investigation of Soviet espionage in Australia.

At the beginning of October, as the conspiracy hearings drew to a close, Dr Evatt arrived in private at a momentous decision — perhaps the most important of his political life — to declare war upon the Movement.*[68] Most directly he was, of course, responding to the violent attack made upon him by Bill Bourke on September 22 in Caucus which, on September 29, John Mullens, who was even more closely associated with the Movement than Bourke, had tried unsuccessfully to renew.[69] Dr Evatt was thoroughly convinced by now of the existence of some sinister connection between ASIO and his Movement enemies in Caucus. Was not the *News Weekly* article of January 1953 proof of this connection and of their joint involvement in the Petrov conspiracy? In coming to his final decision Dr Evatt must have been

---

* Before the Petrov Affair Dr Evatt's relations with the Movement had been far from hostile. In 1952 he had formed a *de facto* alliance of sorts with the Industrial Groups behind which stood the ideological and organisational power of the Movement. Between 1952 and mid-1954 Dr Evatt's major opponents within the Labor Party were on the left. At this time Dr Evatt opposed giving Communist China a seat in the United Nations. This was a major symbolic question dividing right and left in Australia. Moreover he was also a strong supporter of the ALP Groups. In August 1953 Dr Evatt referred to Communist losses in the unions 'not as Industrial Group successes, but as Labor Party victories'. Before the election of May 1954 Evatt went out of his way to meet, flatter and bid for the support of the driving force behind the Groups, Mr B.A. Santamaria, a man who was not a member of the ALP. It was Dr Evatt's single-minded determination to unmask the Petrov conspiracy which drove him rapidly leftwards during the spring of 1954.

influenced by the atmosphere within the salon which formed around him during the Sydney Royal Commission hearings, which comprised secular anti-Catholic Actionists like Leslie Haylen and left-wing Presbyterians, like the Reverend Keith Dowding and Allan Dalziel. He was certainly, too, influenced by the journalism of Alan Reid who, in the Sydney *Sun* on September 21 and 28, had written (for the first time openly in the Australian press) about the Movement and about B.A. Santamaria, who was portrayed by Reid as a brilliant but alien Mediterranean figure, a 'Svengali' of the ALP right or, alternatively, a medieval monk of the anti-Communist Crusade.[70] Finally, he was also by now predisposed to being profoundly affected by the text of a most striking speech which had been delivered by B.A. Santamaria earlier that year to the Movement, which was circulating widely on the left in early October and which had been pressed upon Dr Evatt by one of Santamaria's targets in it, the Catholic anti-Grouper J.P. Ormonde.*[71]

On the morning of October 6 the Australian nation read about the existence of small group of 'subversives' within the Labor Party, directed from outside it and centred upon *News Weekly*, who used 'methods which strikingly resemble both Communist and Fascist infiltration of larger groups . . . calculated to deflect the Labor movement from the pursuit of established Labor objectives and ideals.' 'This group', Evatt had learned from loyal supporters, 'intended to assist the Menzies Government, especially in its attempt to initiate in Australia some of the un-British and un-Australian methods of the totalitarian police state'. Their activities had caused 'a rising tide of disgust and anger' within the Party. Their activities had sapped Mr Chifley's 'health and strength'. They interpreted 'tolerance' as 'weakness'. 'A serious position' existed. Dr Evatt announced that he intended to bring this position to the attention of the Federal Executive and Federal Conference.[72]

Dr Evatt's statement of October 5 was a direct consequence of the impact of the Petrov Affair on the Labor Party — on the one hand of the genuine fury felt within the anti-Communist right about Evatt's Petrov behaviour and on the other of Dr Evatt's dark suspicions about the hidden connections and

---

* It is far from difficult to see how Santamaria's speech 'The Movement of Ideas in Australia' could be used to stir anti-Movement and even anti-Catholic sentiments in the ALP. In this speech Santamaria is centrally concerned with the growth of anti-Grouper and anti-American feeling inside the ALP. However in his analysis he interweaves religious and political categories in an extremely odd way. The political tendencies he identifies and opposes are described as a species of political 'agnosticism', a state of mind where there are no 'absolutes' and in which the choice is not *between* Moscow and Rome but for *neither* Moscow nor Rome. What might be entailed, within the Australian political context, in choosing 'Rome' is not made clear. Moreover, Mr Santamaria's speech is very much written from the point of view of a movement whose ultimate loyalties are to the Church but whose members have been driven, through these loyalties, to a somewhat reluctant involvement in the affairs of the ALP. It was also said that many Laborites were offended by Santamaria's suggestion that a pro-American 'Curtin legend' should be consciously created as an antidote to the present, objectively harmful, 'Chifley legend'.

purposes of the Movement as manifest in the Petrov conspiracy. His state-ment set in train a protracted political struggle which, within a matter of months, had split the Labor Party and which, for the succeeding eighteen years, kept it from office at Canberra. As Robert Murray has shown, by the time of Dr Evatt's statement, throughout the ALP — within the Federal and state parliamentary parties and executives and within the trade union move-ment — often quite delicately balanced armies of Groupers and anti-Groupers had massed.[73] The Petrov Affair did not, of course, create these armies and was only one of the issues (which concerned jobs almost as much as values) over which they contended. It did, however, create the political condition for the Evatt statement of October 5. In turn, Evatt's statement set these armies in motion. Irrespective of Dr Evatt's attack on the Movement there would have been prolonged struggle within the Labor Party between the Groupers and anti-Groupers. There may, however, have been no all-out war and, possibly therefore, no split.

On October 6 Dr Evatt was answered, not by any of his primary Victorian targets but by the branch secretary, Dinny Lovegrove. It was Lovegrove's response which indicated the centrality of the Petrov Affair to both sides in the new political struggle Evatt's somewhat Aesopian statement had precipi-tated. 'Dr Evatt's attack', Lovegrove claimed on behalf of his branch, was 'motivated' by his Royal Commission difficulties. The Victorian branch was 'the victim of a diversionary tactic'. Months before the Petrov defection a non-Victorian Labor Parliamentarian (in fact, Kim Beazley) had raised dis-turbing doubts about the loyalty of Evatt's staff. There was no 'conspiracy against the Labor Party'; there was, however, a genuine 'conspiracy against Australia' already revealed at the Royal Commission. Those involved in this conspiracy should be 'exposed and dealt with according to the law . . . irrespective of whether they have any connections with any party or Parliamentary leader'.[74] On the following day, not surprisingly and not unjustly (for such insinuations went well beyond any evidence yet presented to the Commission) Dalziel and Grundeman threatened Lovegrove with legal action.[75]

In August Dr Evatt had revealed to the public the role played by ASIO and Mr Menzies in the Petrov conspiracy. On October 7 — in his reply to Dinny Lovegrove — he now revealed that the conspiracy extended even into the heart of his own party. Evatt pointed out that his statement had made only passing reference to the Petrov Affair. Why did Lovegrove's response dwell upon it? 'The reason is obvious. The group controlling Lovegrove . . . deeply resented my public appearance before the Commission.' Why did they resent and, indeed, fear his search for the truth about Petrov? The clue lay in the *News Weekly* article of January 28 1953. This article revealed that the Petrov defection was 'the culminating point in a most carefully planned operation' which had 'extended over more than two years' and which had been 'cold-bloodedly' timed for the May election. 'The matter', however, 'went further still'. 'What I have said shows the association of the outside group . . . with some part at least of the elaborate organisation for the Petrov affair.'[76] In case the penny had not yet dropped Dr Evatt announced to the nation on October 9 that his Movement enemies, who he was now referring to as the 'Santamaria-McManus-Keon' group, had for a long time been in 'closest touch' with Australian Security. The sinister association had, indeed, been 'forged' in order to 'discredit the Labor movement on the eve of an election'.

> The closeness of the link between this anti-Labor group I have mentioned and the Security Service will be (he now promised) cleaned up.[77]

Dr Evatt had, of course, first to weather the non-Movement storms to be expected in Caucus. Before it met on October 13 it was being widely anticipated that Evatt's antics would now finally bring on the long awaited challenge from Arthur Calwell. If Calwell stood it was also expected that Allan Fraser — an independently-minded leftist — would put up for the deputy's position (most likely against Ward). When Caucus met, Senator Cole of Tasmania called for a spill of all the leadership positions. Dr Evatt, as party chairman, refused to accept Cole's motion. Notice of such a motion was, he argued, required. Calwell — who many believed could have had the leadership that day if he had fought Evatt's ruling — once more remained silent. Strong attacks were launched that day upon Evatt but neither from Calwell nor from his Caucus targets — Keon, Mullens and Bourke.[78]

During the following week support for the Calwell-Fraser leadership bid dissipated. Before Caucus met on October 20 many newspapers already knew that it would fail; some even predicted (wrongly) that Senator Cole's motion would be withdrawn.[79] At this Caucus, Evatt's Movement targets now gave voice to their true feelings. Bourke outlined the Petrovian challenge he intended to argue against Dr Evatt before the Federal Executive. Keon called his leader a 'sectarian monger' and threatened him with a defamation writ. Most bitterly and dramatically John Mullens demanded to know what charges Dr Evatt — the 'smear merchant', the bogus civil libertarian — intended to prefer against him. He accused Evatt of preparing a 'Moscow trial'. Above the tumult he warned his colleagues that if they still wanted Evatt as leader they were 'gluttons for punishment'. An open vote was taken on the spill motion. In the excitement Evatt leapt on to the Caucus table; he and Eddie Ward began recording names. Even after five New South Wales members crossed to the anti-Evatt side in a gesture of indignation at the Ward intimidation, the Cole motion was lost 54 votes to 28.[80]

Dr Evatt had survived as Party leader. At the end of the following week he had won a second round of his battle with the Movement. After a special meeting on October 27 and 28 the ALP Federal Executive decided not to censure Evatt for his statement of October 5 but to conduct an investigation into its Victorian branch.[81] For this meeting Dr Evatt had prepared a 6,000 word statement, some half of which was devoted to the Petrov Affair and the involvement of his Movement enemies in it.

Those controlling *News Weekly* were, early in 1953, in close contact with Security and Bialoguski. It is significant that in Caucus I was bitterly attacked by W.M. Bourke for having caused Bialoguski to give evidence.... Mr Mullens showed a foreknowledge of [a] confidential and supposedly secret exhibit ... Those controlling the 'Movement' ... hailed the Petrov case in order to advance and support their own extremist policy. It was dangerous to them if the defection of Petrov proved to be not spontaneous but part of a carefully organised ... plan for election purposes.[82]

By an exquisite irony, Federal Executive met that day in the very hotel where, a year and a half earlier, Rupert Lockwood, Fergan O'Sullivan and Albert Grundeman had — so fatefully for Dr Evatt and his Party — drunk and gossiped together.

On October 28 Dr Evatt moved from the Hotel Kingston to the Parliament for the debate with Mr Menzies on the interim report of the Royal Commissioners on Espionage on the conspiracy phase of their hearing. The Royal Commissioners had, of course, reported that Rupert Lockwood had typed Document 'J' and that Dr Evatt's charges about the forging of 'J' by the Petrovs and Fergan O'Sullivan were totally baseless. Because of the appearance of his secretaries' names as sources of 'J', Dr Evatt had 'apparently ... conceived the theory that he and the political Party which he leads had been made the victims of a political conspiracy'. Charges of 'blackmail, forgery, uttering, fabrication, fraud and conspiracy' had followed, one upon the other, with 'bewildering variations'. All had been proven, on the evidence, false. The Security Service had been maligned by Dr Evatt. His charges were certain to cause 'disquiet in Australia' and might even 'shake the confidence of other friendly nations' in its integrity. They should not have been persisted in when they had proved groundless. ASIO's officers had acted with 'high intelligence and complete propriety in difficult and delicate circumstances'. There was only one point in their report which was incorrectly stated. The evidence, they argued, established 'beyond question' that the '"bargaining for documents" to which reference was made so often by counsel existed only in imagination'.[83]

Dr Evatt initiated, on the evening of October 28, what the *Argus* would call 'the great debate' on the Petrov Affair.[84] Showing unexpected restraint and a greater clarity than had been mustered at any time during his Royal Commission appearance, Dr Evatt outlined to the House his familiar case about the genesis of 'J' and the deeper meaning of the Petrov defection. Old wounds were reopened. Why had Menzies allowed him to fly to Sydney on April 13? Why had noone informed him 'for months' that O'Sullivan had authored Document 'H'? More importantly, why had Mr Menzies misled the House on April 13 into believing that the Petrov defection was a sudden and spontaneous flight to freedom? Petrov, it was now known, had been nursed by Security for two years and had even to be bribed with £5000 before he would defect. Dr Evatt expressed the deepest regret at the decay of the tradition of the apolitical intelligence service which had been established by the Chifley-Evatt Government and their appointment of Mr Justice Reed to head ASIO. ASIO had contrived at the Petrov defection and his so-called disclosures in order to assist the political opponents of Labor at the election. The Petrov Affair was, he told the Parliament, 'one of the greatest cases in the history of Australia . . . fundamental to our lives'. For Dr Evatt, the interim report far from settled the conspiracy question. Much detective work remained to be done. In the fullness of time, he was convinced, the truth would out.

Mr Menzies replied at once. He 'deplored' the fact that the interim report was to be debated at all (noone in the House had heard the evidence on which the judgments had been based) but conceded that, in the circumstances, it was unavoidable. At a rhetorical level his speech — the first he had given on the Petrov Affair since August 12 — was thoroughly devastating. After defending the honour of the Royal Commissioners and dwelling in particular on their war service, Mr Menzies outlined and then indignantly repudiated eight separate Evatt allegations of serious misbehaviour or conspiracy on the part of the Royal Commissioners themselves, Australian Security, the Australian and French Governments, the Petrov couple and even against a former staffer of his own, Fergan O'Sullivan (about whom, Menzies revealed, ASIO had actually warned Evatt in late 1953). Menzies reserved his sharpest words for the attack that Dr Evatt had launched upon the reputation of ASIO. By his attack Evatt had inflicted upon ASIO a degree of damage that even a century of Communist propaganda could not have achieved. Menzies' final words were calculated to turn the knife in Labor's deep and self-inflicted Petrovian wounds.

> I cannot help wondering how many of the great army of Labor supporters in Australia, who fear and dislike Communism, and who are its pledged enemies, have enjoyed the spectacle of their leader . . . playing the Communist game.[85]

Mr Menzies was not — as Dr Evatt fervently believed — the mastermind of the Petrov Affair or the engineer of the process of self-destruction which was already well advanced within the Labor Party. He was, however, to be its chief beneficiary. At the time the interim report was being debated the electoral stocks of Labor — as measured by the merciless Gallup — had fallen to their lowest point in almost twenty years.*

---

*	Lib-CP	ALP	IND
May 29 H. of R. Election	48	51	1
September (Gallup)	52	48	—
October (Gallup)	53	47	—

PART III
Espionage

12

THE CASE

From the Bolshevik seizure of power in 1917 to the present day espionage has been a fundamental aspect of Soviet international behaviour. Although espionage is, of course, a highly traditional method of statecraft and one practised to some degree or other by almost all states, it is probably true to say that no modern state has placed greater emphasis on espionage as a weapon of its foreign policy than has the Soviet Union. At the time the Petrovs defected the reality of Soviet espionage had already penetrated, but was still capable of shocking Western public opinion. The Petrov defections occurred not in a public vacuum but after a series of highly publicised and disturbing espionage cases: the Gouzenko defection in Canada and the subsequent arrest of the 'atom bomb spy', Alan Nunn May; the trial and execution of the Rosenbergs in the United States; the mysterious disappearance from Britain in 1951 of the diplomats, Donald Maclean and Guy Burgess.[1]

By the time of the Petrovs' defections at least the basic structure of the Soviet system of espionage was becoming familiar to Western counter-intelligence services. While the story of Soviet espionage before the mid-1950s is vast and in its fine detail highly complex, the fundamentals of the system — as they had become known to Western counter-intelligence services — can be outlined relatively simply.* For most of its history Soviet espionage had

---

* In Soviet history State Security has been subject to frequent administrative reorganisations and name changes. For all but five months (in early 1941) of the period between 1934 and 1943 the entire State Security Service, including its foreign section, was integrated in the People's Commissariat for Internal Affairs (NKVD). During 1943 a separate Commissariat for State Security (NKGB) was formed which, in 1946, became a Ministry (MGB) which was administratively separate from the Ministry for Internal Affairs (MVD). As we have seen, between 1947 and 1951 an attempt was made to create a unified foreign intelligence branch (KI) by combining the GRU with the foreign bureaux of the MGB. In late 1951 this experiment was abandoned. Once again all political intelligence (both foreign and domestic) returned to the control of the MGB. (Military intelligence had been quickly restored earlier to the control of the GRU.) In 1954 the MGB was merged by Beria into the MVD. After his demise the merger was undone and a Committee for State Security (KGB) created in 1954. The KGB/MVD division has survived to the present day.

been conducted in foreign countries by two strictly separate agencies of state. Foreign military intelligence gathering had been the responsibility of a bureau which was part of the intelligence branch of the Red Army, the GRU. Foreign political intelligence gathering had been the responsibility of one section of the Soviet State Security service.[2] In turn, the military and political intelligence branches had been divided abroad, wherever it proved possible, into strictly separate compartments known in Soviet intelligence jargon as the 'legal' and 'illegal' apparatuses. The 'legal' branches of Soviet espionage — military and political — were under the control of official Soviet representatives, both diplomatic and non-diplomatic. In addition the Soviet intelligence service attempted to plant upon foreign soil 'illegal' officers, whose connections with the Soviet Union were completely hidden. For these 'illegals' contact with Moscow Centre was, of course, far more difficult than for the 'legals' who could use the diplomatic bag, the radio and even the telegraph office to send their coded messages home. On the other hand, for the counter-intelligence service of a host country the discovery of the 'illegal' apparatus posed a much greater problem. Experience had shown that in time of war the 'illegal' officer might provide the greatest and indeed perhaps the only intelligence asset available to the Soviet Union. There had been no greater hero of Soviet intelligence than the 'illegal' GRU officer who had penetrated Japanese military circles during the Second World War, Richard Sorge.[3]

For both 'legals' and 'illegals' in the military and political fields the essential, although by no means exclusive task, was, of course, the gathering of secret information.* By the mid-1950s the Soviet intelligence service had managed, in certain cases, to recruit agents who, in turn, had managed after their recruitment to find their way into the most sensitive and trusted positions in a target country. The most triumphant Soviet intelligence drive had been at Cambridge University in the 1930s. As a result the Soviet service had agents inside the British Foreign Office (Donald Maclean and Guy Burgess) and inside its counter-intelligence services (Kim Philby and Anthony Blunt).[4] More usually, however, the Soviet intelligence service had found means of extracting information from those already employed in sensitive diplomatic, defence or scientific posts. On some occasions (as for example with the cypher clerk at the Foreign Office in the 1930s, Captain King)[5] money appears to have been the primary means of recruitment. More commonly, however, as the Canadian Royal Commission into the Gouzenko affair had concluded, the recruited agent was a non-mercenary 'progressive' who had been drawn into intelligence work through a faith in Soviet socialism or a hatred of his or her own society.[6]

---

* As we have seen, when Petrov arrived in Australia in 1951 he was actually at first solely concerned with 'SK' and 'EM' work, that is to say with the surveillance of Soviet personnel in Australia and the penetration of anti-Soviet émigré organisations. At this time KI and MGB work abroad was controlled by separate apparatuses.

Contacts between the Soviet intelligence service and their agents inside Western government departments or research establishments were made essentially in one of two ways. Sometimes agents met their 'legal' or 'illegal' Soviet controllers directly.[7] Sometimes they met with a non-Soviet intermediary, often recruited into Soviet intelligence after previous experience in the underground apparatus of the local Communist Party. These intermediaries passed agents' information to a Soviet intelligence officer, who in turn despatched it to Moscow Centre. In the United States Whittaker Chambers had fulfilled such a role; in Canada Fred Rose* and Sam Carr; and in Australia, it would appear as we shall see, Walter Clayton.[8]

By the mid-1950s there had been for Western counter-intelligence three major sources of detailed information about the working of the Soviet espionage system. Firstly, the captured records of German intelligence had revealed a great deal about the operation of the Soviet system in wartime Europe.[9] Secondly, by 1948, a significant amount of wartime and early postwar radio traffic between outposts of the Soviet intelligence service and Moscow Centre had been deciphered by an Anglo-American team. Information derived from this source was largely responsible for uncovering the atomic spies — Klaus Fuchs and the Rosenbergs — and for initiating at least (through information which revealed Donald Maclean's involvement in espionage activities) the detection of the Cambridge circle.[10] It was also, as we shall see, responsible for uncovering the existence of a serious security situation in Australia. The third crucial source of information about Soviet espionage for Western counter-intelligence were, of course, defectors from the service itself. Amongst the most significant non-Soviet defectors were the Englishman, Alexander Foote and the American, Whittaker Chambers.[11] More important, however, were the Soviet defectors — most significantly, Alexander Orlov of the NKVD, Walter Krivitsky of the GRU (both of whom had defected in the late 1930s during Stalin's 'great terror') and Igor Gouzenko of the GRU.[12] After 1945 there had been no Soviet intelligence defections until the first half of 1954 when, following the purge of the Beria circle inside the MVD, Rastvorov in Tokyo, the Petrovs in Australia and Khokhlov in Berlin (all members of the MVD) defected within weeks of each other.

It was really only in October 1954 that the Australian Royal Commission on Espionage was able, after having finally disposed of the Evatt conspiracy charges, to embark upon the serious part of its investigations. By now the Commissioners had acquired a small library on the history of Soviet espionage and had had flown to them by safe hand from Canada a copy of the transcript of evidence which had been presented in 1946 to the Gouzenko

---

* The Fred Rose in Canada is no relation of the Fred Rose who was involved in the Royal Commission's hearings in Australia.

Royal Commission.[13] By October the Commissioners were aware of certain chronological and analytic boundaries within which their inquiry would of necessity fall. Clearly the starting point for their inquiry would be 1943, the year in which the first Soviet diplomatic mission to Australia and the first MVD and GRU Residencies had been established. Both the Petrovs knew at least a little about the MVD Residencies of Makarov (1943-1949) and his successor Sadovnikov (1949-51). In addition, Petrov had brought with him some valuable documentary material (the 'G' series) from the period of Sadovnikov. Unfortunately neither Petrov nor his wife appeared to know anything of the scope or nature of GRU operations under Colonel Zaitsev (1943-1947) or his successor Gordeev (1951-1953).

More surprisingly, it soon became clear to ASIO and then to the Royal Commissioners that the most interesting and sensitive aspect of their investigations would concern not the period of the Petrov Residency itself but the light the Petrovs might be able to cast upon an earlier case of Soviet espionage in Australia — a series of leakages from the Department of External Affairs, which had occurred during the Makarov Residency.*[14] Knowledge of these leakages had been very largely responsible for the decision taken by the Chifley Government in 1949 to create a Security Service.[15] Revealingly enough, within this new service, ASIO, these leakages and the investigations into them (which were still being pursued in 1954) were known simply as 'the Case'.[16]

For the Australian Government 'the Case' had come to light in early 1948 with the arrival of a powerful MI5 team. The team was at first led by Sir Percy Sillitoe, the head of MI5. It included Roger Hollis of MI5's Soviet counter-intelligence section, who appears to have visited Australia twice in 1948 and 1949 and, as a permanènt representative, Robert Hemblys-Scales.[17] The MI5 contingent presented to the Australian Government progressively throughout 1948 and 1949 evidence of certain material concerning the passage to the MVD headquarters at Moscow which had been sent originally from London to Canberra. They were able to convince the Australian Government and even the doubting Thomases within it — like the youthful left wing Secretary of the Department of External Affairs, Dr John Burton — that leakages of British material had indeed occurred and that the source of these leakages had indeed been members of the Department of External Affairs in Canberra.

According to the MI5 evidence one source of leakage was Jim Hill, the brother of Ted. In the secret evidence he gave to the Royal Commission Dr Bur-

---

* Colonel Spry wrote thus to Windeyer on June 2 1954: 'I do feel that as a general principle, it is of prime importance to firstly expose the ramifications of the ring which successfully operated during the period 1945-1948. The period 1949-1954 can then be described, according to Petrov, as a time when persistent attempts at espionage were, generally speaking, not very successful.'

ton recalled the following conversation with Roger Hollis concerning Jim Hill.

Windeyer: What was the information which it was suggested or said that Hill had wrongly disclosed?

Burton: From memory it was something fairly remote from Australian policies, some information, I think, of British policy in relation to some Southern European ... or Mediterranean country.... It could have been even the Middle East.

Windeyer: Did you investigate that matter closely yourself?

Burton: Well, as far as one could. The information was not complete in any way. I was given a telegram number which was a correct number, I think, from memory.[18]

Burton appears to have been convinced by the evidence presented to him by Hollis that Jim Hill had indeed passed information to 'a person who seemed to be an MVD agent'. Naturally he and certain others to whom the MI5 team spoke would have been curious to know how MI5 had discovered these leakages. Dr Burton's testimony again makes clear that hints had been dropped by MI5 about the existence of a British mole inside the MVD. The reason given 'for the secrecy' was, he dimly recalled, 'that if any of this information ever became public the source of the information would be prejudiced'.[19]

In fact the MI5's source on the Canberra leakages was not a British mole inside the MVD but information which had been derived from the work of the Anglo-American cryptanalytic team headed by Meredith Gardner in an operation code-named 'Bride'. Part of the material the group had managed to decipher by early 1948 had been some radio traffic passing between the MVD office in Canberra and Moscow Centre.[20] The fact that such a breakthrough into MVD radio messages had occurred was, in 1948, a matter of the greatest possible sensitivity. For this reason many members of the Australian Government to whom MI5 talked about the External Affairs problem were deliberately misled about how knowledge of the leakages had been acquired. Chapman Pincher, whose sources of information inside Anglo-American intelligence circles are excellent, has recently explained the situation thus.

The Anglo-American team deciphering intercepted K.G.B. radio traffic passing between Moscow and the K.G.B. out-station in the Soviet Embassy in Canberra secured information which proved that the Soviets were making a major espionage effort in Australia.... Hollis was a key figure in the [MI5] delegation and was selected to deliver the detailed information about the K.G.B. penetrations in Australia and the names involved. Because the breaking of the Soviet codes had to be kept secret he was required to present the information as though it came from a spy.[21]

According to the evidence Dr Burton gave to the Royal Commission the British information passed to the MVD by his colleague, Jim Hill, was in itself regarded by MI5 as insignificant. It was, Burton remembered, 'the method' of its passage to the MVD which had been of concern to MI5.[22] If indeed MI5 had led Burton to believe that all the material which had made its way from Canberra to Moscow Centre was insignificant, they had seriously misled him. By early 1948 several members of the Defence Department and Australian Military Intelligence at least — including Sir Frederick Shedden, Brigadier Chilton and Colonel Spry — were thoroughly aware that the Canberra leakages had involved at least some material of great sensitivity.

The most significant of these of which MI5 had firm evidence — from the deciphered Canberra-Moscow MVD traffic — was of a highly classified report which had been prepared in May 1945 for the British Chiefs of Staff by a defence committee known as the Post-Hostilities Planning Staff. The report was entitled 'Security in the Western Mediterranean and the Eastern Atlantic'.[23] In the latter half of 1945 this report had been sent from Whitehall to Canberra to a joint Defence-External Affairs Department Committee known as the Defence Post-Hostilities Planning Committee. This paper is now available to the public under Britain's thirty year rule. In 1945 it would have been of more than passing interest to Soviet military planners.

The paper on 'Security in the Western Mediterranean and the Eastern Atlantic' discussed the strategic interests of the British Empire in the area bounded by Sicily in the East, the Azores Islands in the West and North Africa in the South. It expressed the conviction that threats to British interests in this region over the next ten to fifteen years could only come from a hostile Italy and/or rearmed Germany. It discussed in some detail the need for the closest possible military cooperation with France, the maintenance of the traditional alliance with Portugal, the 'vital' nature of American military assistance in the region and the importance of leading Italy away from friendship with the USSR. Perhaps more importantly it provided detailed information about the way in which British military planners intended to defend their interests in this region. If Italy were to be 'overrun' Britain and her allies should, it argued, occupy Sicily and Sardinia at once. Bases in the Azores were 'essential'. If Spain were friendly or neutral at time of war Gibraltar was crucial to Britain but if she were hostile Gibraltar would be useless. To defend the Straits of Gibraltar radar facilities and airfields in French and Spanish Morocco and in the Tangier Zone might be required. And so on. The paper outlined, in short, the strategic and tactical assumptions of British military thinking concerning the Western Mediterranean. Even the fact that British military planners regarded this region as beyond the range of direct Soviet influence for the next fifteen years was, presumably, from the point of view of Soviet strategists, worth knowing.[24]

In February 1948 an Australian investigation into the source of this leakage was undertaken by the Controller of Joint Intelligence, Brigadier Chilton. Chilton was charged, at least in part, with discovering who had delivered this paper to the MVD.[25] His labour was far from time-consuming or difficult.

It soon transpired that the paper on security in the Western Mediterranean had been in the private possession of the External Affairs Department's representative on the Defence Post-Hostilities Planning Committee between November 15 1945 and February 19 1946 and again between March 6 and 28 1946.[26] Somewhat alarmingly it also soon transpired that at the same time this man had had in his possession another of the British Post-Hostilities Planning Staff papers, which concerned the defence of India and the Indian Ocean. If this document had found its way to Moscow Centre it would have doubtlessly been of even greater interest to Soviet military planners than its Western Mediterranean counterpart. The assumption of this paper was that 'the USSR is the only major power which would be capable of threatening our interests in India and the Indian Ocean by 1955'. It admitted frankly that the British position in India was expected 'to be vulnerable to Soviet strategic bombing' from bases in Russian Turkestan and that a Soviet advance through Persia and Afghanistan might prove irresistible. It canvassed in some detail the political and military policies the Planning Staff wished to pursue in Persia and Afghanistan as a counter to possible Soviet moves in these areas of vulnerability.[27] By early April 1948 Chilton was able to report his findings to the Secretary of the Defence Department, Sir Frederick Shedden. On April 7 Shedden wrote to Dr Burton about the External Affairs man in question. Burton replied curtly that this man was 'well known by many officers who all maintained that there was no reason to believe papers held by him would not be in safe custody'. At this time Shedden sent a report to Mr Chifley on the matter.[28]

The man in question was Ian Milner. Milner was a New Zealand Rhodes Scholar who had studied at the universities of Oxford and California between 1934 and 1939. In 1940 he was appointed lecturer at the University of Melbourne and established there its Department of Political Science.[29] He became in addition a leading member of the University's Communist Party branch. After the ban on the Communist Party was lifted in 1942, while Milner did not exactly advertise his Party membership he certainly did not disguise it.[30] An acquaintance of his at the University (who in 1954 told his story to ASIO) remembered the Milner of this period as 'an affable, pleasant personality who made friends quickly' and who was on first name terms with his students.

In the classroom he selected and 'cultivated' students, and after inviting them singly to his home on a social basis, would subsequently invite them to Communist Party study groups or Communist Party branch meetings.
These meetings (during the C.P. ban) were held in a rear room of the North Melbourne Town Hall and in the Communist Bookshop near the North Melbourne Town Hall.[31]

During the war Ian Milner's activities attracted some attention of the various Security Services. In the file handed on to ASIO in 1949 details are recorded of his pro-Soviet writings (including a defence of the Soviets in the University newspaper, *Farrago*, on the charge of having murdered Polish officers at Katyn Wood) and of his lectures for the Australian-Soviet Friendship League.[32] When Milner, for example, visited Tasmania in mid-1943 on a lecture tour, a Deputy Director for Security there, one P.L. Griffiths, concluded that he was a 'superficial young man' whose head 'swims with the fumes of Communistic wine'. Somewhat sourly Griffiths concluded that the performance of this young lecturer 'was another illustration of the deterioration of academic standards in Australia'.[33]

This was not, however, the general view. Late in 1944 — which was culturally speaking the time of greatest pro-Soviet feelings in Australia, the time when even Robert Menzies was a vice-president of the 'Sheepskins for Russia' movement[34] and when anti-communism was almost exclusively the preserve of Catholic loyalists or Security officials — Milner secured a position in the Department of External Affairs in Canberra. There were certainly two protests at his appointment — from Professor Bland, who had read an article of Milner's in *Australian Quarterly*, and from a Miss V.A. Leeper who wrote of him as a 'known Communist'. On the other hand, Milner received favourable references from Sir John Medley, the Vice-Chancellor of Melbourne University, and from Professors Crawford and Boyce Gibson, of History and Philosophy. His passage from Political Science at Melbourne University to External Affairs at Canberra was smooth.[35]

In 1945 Ian Milner was given the responsibility of representing his Department on the newly established Defence Post-Hostilities Committee. (Its first External Affairs representative, Paul Hasluck, was abroad during most of 1945.)[36] Participation in the work of this Committee provided Milner with access to the top secret reports of the British Chiefs of Staff Post-Hostilities Planning Staff. Records of the Committee show that on September 24 1945 at the request of its secretary, George Legge, he returned five British planning papers on the occupation of Germany and Austria and on the future of what was called at the time 'World Organisation'.[37] On November 6 Milner requested — in view of what he called their 'important relationship' to the 'responsibilities' of his department — three further British Post-Hostilities papers.[38] On November 15 George Legge sent him two of the three he had requested, concerning the Western Mediterranean and India. Legge informed him that the third — entitled 'Security of the British Empire' — was not, at present, available.[39] As we have seen, it was one of these papers which had made an appearance in the deciphered Canberra — Moscow MVD radio traffic. This paper was the one which had been in Milner's possession for some four months.

Either late in 1945 or early in 1946 Milner came under the suspicion of an Army Officer, W.J. Matthews, who was attached to the Post-Hostilities division of External Affairs. Matthews noticed Milner removing from the Department and taking with him to Melbourne for a weekend a 'top secret file concerning International Peace Treaty negotiations'.[40] Matthews appears to have spoken of his concerns with Colonel Spry, who was at the time Director of Military Intelligence. In 1954 Spry recalled Matthews telling him that when Milner had been asked to produce a certain missing document he had been 'unable to do so, but 36 hours later produced it without explanation'.[41] If Dr Burton's testimony at the Royal Commission is to be relied upon, during 1946 the suspicions within his Department about Milner became more general. According to Burton, Milner was edged out of the Department at the end of that year because of his associations with the Communist Party.[42] In early 1947 Milner moved from Canberra to take a position in the United Nations at New York. His application for secondment from External Affairs was refused.[43]

It was hardly surprising that when, in early 1948, MI5 told the officials of the Australian Government about the leakage to Moscow of the paper on the Western Mediterranean, Milner's responsibility was readily apparent. What was more surprising was Dr Burton's response. When the Milner leak was brought to his attention by Sir Frederick Shedden, Burton defended Milner as a 'safe security risk'.[44] Apparently Burton interpreted Shedden's Milner letter as a tactical ploy in the bitter inter-departmental war that was at the time being fought out between External Affairs and the Defence establishment.*[45]

By 1948, then, MI5 information had convinced the Australian Government that a serious situation had existed within the Department of External Affairs, at least in its early post-war years, and that two of its officers, Ian

---

* Burton became convinced of the existence of a group within the upper echelons of Australian intelligence, whom he called the 'gnomes of Melbourne', who were set upon subverting the democratic processes in Australia. This view was to gain some currency amongst other members of the ALP but clearly originated from Burton. There is no other evidence for the existence of the 'gnomes of Melbourne' and it may well be that the myth of their existence arose out of Burton's frustrations with the battles between External Affairs and the defence establishment. Burton's statements on the 'gnomes of Melbourne' were revived in the early 1970s and formed a subplot of *Nest of Traitors* but neither the findings of the Royal Commission nor any evidence in that book does anything to give substance to what appears to have been simply a myth created by Burton. By the time of the Petrov defection Dr Burton had some grounds for bitterness. He had by now failed to gain a seat for the ALP in the House of Representatives. Moreover, in the House on May 27 1952 W.C. Wentworth had accused him of being responsible for leaking a draft commercial treaty between Australia and the United States to the *Tribune* journalist, Rex Chiplin. In his reply to Wentworth, while Richard Casey did not (as is commonly believed) support Wentworth's accusation, his careful remarks did not rule out the possibility. In his reply Casey made his fateful remark about the existence of a 'nest of traitors' in the Australian public service. The Labor Party never let Casey forget this remark and frequently asked, thereafter, whether the nest had been uncovered yet. The Royal Commission on Espionage spent much time investigating this particular leakage to Chiplin. It was learned that the leak came from the Department of National Development. They cleared Burton completely from any responsibility for it. Dr Burton also appeared in the 'G' series as one of 'K's contacts. Petrov however did not believe him to be a former agent of the MVD or source of information to it.

Milner and Jim Hill (who had actually been a student of Milner's at Melbourne University) had been responsible for leaking certain information which had somehow found its way to the MVD's Moscow Centre. One consequence of this knowledge was a thorough Security review and, eventually, the establishment of a Security Service based upon the structure of MI5. Such a service was not only required, the Defence establishment argued, to investigate the 'Case' and to try and prevent the emergence of further cases. It was also required if Australia was to be able to convince its allies that it could, once again, be trusted with intelligence information passed on to it. Before 1948 (as Sir Charles Spry had told the author and as a declassified American report of the 1950s has documented) the United States military decided to ban 'the transmission of classified information to Australia because of that country's unsatisfactory security situation'.[46] When Brigadier Chilton gave his secret evidence to the Royal Commission on Espionage, at a time when the intelligence relationship with the United States had been restored after a searching American investigation of our security system,[47] he made it clear that 'there would be very grave consequences for Australia's defence if Australia were not careful with secret information entrusted to the Commonwealth by other friendly powers'.[48]

There was, in the late 1940s, another pressing problem for the Australian Government. What was to be done about Jim Hill? Unlike Milner, who was an employee of the United Nations and chiefly resident in New York,*[49] Hill was still a member of the External Affairs Department and resident in Canberra. According to the testimony of Dr Burton, Roger Hollis discussed the problem of Hill with him in 1949. Burton agreed to Hollis' proposal that Hill be posted to London to work at the Australian High Commission. From here MI5 could keep an eye on him. In London Hill appears to have been cultivated by a member of MI5. On June 6 1950 (according to Burton while attending a football match) Hill was told by his MI5 contact of their suspicions concerning him. In September, after a mere seven months in London, he and his family sailed home. Shortly after arriving in Australia Jim Hill told Burton, who had by now resigned from External Affairs, about his curious encounter with British counter-intelligence.[50] In February 1951 he was transferred from External Affairs to a position in the Attorney-General's Department. Some two years later, he resigned from the public service and moved into private legal practice.[51]

---

* There is some evidence in the ASIO files that the FBI were keeping an eye on Milner in New York. Meetings with a woman there, presumed to be a Soviet intelligence worker, were noted. When news arrived that Milner intended to take a holiday in Australia in late 1949 Brigadier Chilton wrote to the first Director-General of ASIO, Mr Justice Reed. Milner was now placed under intense surveillance but nothing of security interest appears to have been discovered.

By this time his former teacher and colleague, Ian Milner, had moved to Prague. One month after Hill's June 1950 meeting with MI5 in London, Milner applied for leave from his post in the United Nations and travelled east. According to Milner, he went in search of a cure for his wife's rheumatism at a Slovakian spa. Fortunately Milner soon found for himself a position in the English Department at Charles University.[52] From that day to this he has remained a resident of Czechoslovakia.

At the time the Petrovs defected the foregoing represented, roughly speaking, ASIO's state of knowledge about the two men for whom there existed solid evidence of involvement in the leakages of British material to the MVD in Canberra. After April 1954 ASIO was, of course, more than a little keen to hear of what additional light the Petrovs might be able to shed on 'the Case'. They did not have long to wait. On the day of his defection Petrov told Ron Richards the following story.

> Between 1945 and 1948 there was a very serious situation in Australia in the Dept. of External Affairs. The Communist Party here had a group of External Affairs officers who were giving them official information.
> The members of the group were bringing out copies of official documents, which they gave to a Communist Party member.
> This Party man gave the documents to Mr Makarov at the Soviet Embassy.
> The documents described the Australian foreign policy and also contained a lot of information about American and English foreign policy.
> I do not know the name of the Party man who at the time reported to Makarov — but his code name was 'Klod'.[53]

Petrov's first statement revealed at least that it was not only the western intelligence services that had attached importance to the post-war leakages from External Affairs in Canberra. What details, ASIO wondered, could Petrov and, later, Petrova give them concerning 'the Case' and, in particular, concerning Jim Hill and Ian Milner?

The first thing that ASIO must have noticed was that in the Sadovnikov documents Petrov had brought with him there appeared to be a reference to Jim Hill. Document 'G2' (as it became called) listed as one of the contacts of 'K' someone who was code-named 'Tourist'. In Document 'G3' Wilbur Christinson (sic), whose code-name was 'Master', was described as the 'husband of the sister of "Tourist"'. 'Master' was, in fact, readily identified as the Sydney physicist, Wilbur Norman Christiansen. As Christiansen had married the sister of Ted and Jim Hill, 'Tourist' was obviously the code-name of either Ted or Jim. As, however, of the two brothers Jim alone had travelled widely, as he worked in External Affairs and as he had already been identified in deciphered cable traffic as a source for the MVD it was all too obvious that he was 'Tourist'.[54] Unhappily for ASIO, beyond his appearance in the

Sadovnikov documents under a code-name and as one of 'Klod's' contacts, neither of the Petrovs could shed any light on his post-war activities. Both husband and wife claimed never even to have heard of him.[55] Jim Hill himself made a brief appearance before the Royal Commission. Not surprisingly, while he admitted having been interviewed in London in 1950 concerning the leakages from External Affairs, he denied absolutely having been involved in them. Because of the extreme secrecy still surrounding the fact that an MVD code had been deciphered, the Commissioners were unable to reveal to Jim Hill during his appearance at the Commission or to the Australian public in their final report, either the certainty or, of course, the source of ASIO's knowledge of Hill's involvement in 'the Case'.[56]

Both the Petrovs knew more of Ian Milner than they did of Jim Hill. The first extended post-defection Milner discussion took place between Petrov and Ron Richards on April 9. Richards took up a passing reference Petrov had made to an officer of External Affairs 'who went to Korea and then disappeared'. Petrov remembered the man's name as 'Williams or something'. Could it have been Milner? 'Yes, that's him. He is in Prague.' Petrov, on April 9, claimed to know very little about him; nonetheless he gave Richards some interesting information. Some four or five months ago, Petrov recalled, Moscow Centre had cabled him concerning Milner. According to Petrov, Milner wanted to go home to New Zealand to 'live with his parents'. Petrov had been asked to discover Milner's reputation inside the External Affairs Department. Petrov knew that Milner had once worked at the United Nations, serving for a time in Korea; that he had fled to Prague and was presently still there; that he could not stay in Australia because 'he was in trouble'; and that he had been 'an important agent' of the MVD, 'active before my time'. His code-name was 'Bur'.[57]

On May 21 Petrov added some information to his original statement about Ian Milner. After consulting a Russian dictionary he had discovered that 'Bur' was a Russian term for an instrument used for drilling deeply beneath the earth's surface, roughly translatable into English as 'bore'. According to Petrov Milner had rendered the MVD 'valuable assistance' in New York by supplying them with information about the Australian delegation at the United Nations. He now doubted that Milner had been recruited in Australia. If Milner had been in contact with Sadovnikov Petrov believed he would have heard about it. (In fact there was no question of Milner being associated with Sadovnikov. If he had been active in Australia it would have been during the Residency of Sadovnikov's predecessor, Makarov.) Petrov also revealed now that in late 1953 he had, through the good offices of the Secretary of the Australian-Soviet Friendship Society in Sydney, Jean Ferguson, met with the *Tribune* journalist Rex Chiplin who had agreed to report to him on Milner's present standing in External Affairs. A week later Chiplin had provided Petrov with some biographical information on Milner but was unable to say what the attitude would be in Australia to his returning to New Zealand.[58]

There, according to Petrov, the Milner matter had rested.*[59]

In August and September ASIO questioned Petrova separately about Milner. While she confirmed her husband's story about the MVD cable and the approach to Chiplin she added a number of interesting details. According to her the MVD cable made it clear that Milner had passed extremely valuable information to 'Klod' who had, in turn, passed it to Makarov. Petrova recalled that Milner had left External Affairs because of the discovery of some document having gone missing. She was convinced that Chiplin had discovered Milner's standing in Australia through the use of a contact inside the External Affairs Department. Finally, she claimed that the purpose of Moscow's inquiry regarding Milner was not, as Petrov had claimed, to assist him to return home to live with his parents but to plant him as 'a Soviet agent' in New Zealand.[60]

On November 22 ASIO confronted the Petrovs with the discrepancies of their Milner tales. Petrov was extremely angry with his wife. In his second formal Milner statement he reiterated very strongly that he had no idea why Moscow Centre wanted to help Milner to return to New Zealand. He had been given no information that Milner was part of the 'Klod' group. He had not inquired of Rex Chiplin how he had discovered Ian Milner's present reputation within External Affairs. His wife's statement was, he claimed, 'both inaccurate and dangerous'.[61] After consultations with her husband Petrova rewrote her statement. According to Redford of ASIO she was in a black mood. As she had demanded a copy of her husband's statement as a model for her own, and as she was in spirit 'stubborn and un-cooperative', Redford advised Richards to disregard altogether her second Milner statement.[62] Why Petrov should have regarded her first one not only as 'inaccurate' but also 'dangerous' was never to be explained. In this case, as in several others, as we shall see, there is at least some reason for suspecting that Petrov — perhaps through some fear of MVD reprisals — had told his ASIO debriefers less than the whole truth. According to a member of the ASIO safe house team, who spent many months living with the Petrovs, Petrov on the one hand was very anxious about giving evidence to Australian authorities which indicated he had damaged Australian security and, on the other, was obsessed by the details of the assassination of Trotsky which, years before, he had read about in one of the most secret files held in the NKVD archives.[63]

During their proceedings the Royal Commissioners heard some evidence about the Milner matter in secret session. Dr Burton testified briefly to the

---

* When Rex Chiplin was called before the Royal Commission he admitted to two meetings with Petrov (presumably because he had wrongly assumed they had been observed by ASIO) and to having discussed Milner with Petrov during one of them. He denied, however, having been asked to make inquiries about Milner inside External Affairs or, indeed, that he had any contacts there. Especially given what they regarded as the mendacious quality of his evidence on other matters, the Royal Commissioners, in their final report, saw no reason to accept the truthfulness of his evidence on Milner.

MI5 suspicions of him.[64] Brigadier Chilton revealed the outlines of the inquiry of early 1948 to him.[65] In addition the Commissioners read the Petrovs' conflicting statements about Milner and, towards the end of the sittings, were shown a series of top secret ASIO files on 'the Case'.[66] In their final report they concluded that before his United Nations posting and his flight to Prague, Milner had been 'in possession of secret documents in circumstances which gave rise to grave suspicion as to the use he had made of them'. On the balance of possibilities they concluded that he had, as Petrova had first claimed, passed the information which had reached the MVD to the Australian Communist Party agent known as 'Klod'.[67]

On the day of his defection Petrov actually associated neither Ian Milner nor Jim Hill with 'Klod'. He did, however, name as part of this 'Klod group' another member of the External Affairs Department.

> One of Klod's group was (he told Ron Richards on April 3) Ric Throssell . . .
> Throssell had a code name 'Ferro' . . .
> He has served abroad for External Affairs in the Soviet and also in South America.
> He is not active now — he is very still. I think he is afraid.[68]

Because Throssell was a current member of the Department of External Affairs his case was probably the most domestically sensitive matter which the Royal Commission was obliged to handle.*

Ric Throssell was the son of the military hero Hugo Throssell VC and Katharine Susannah Prichard who was both a much loved writer and devoted member of the Communist Party of Australia.[69] In 1943, while serving with the Australian armed forces, the young Throssell had been selected as an External Affairs cadet. During 1944 and 1945 he had worked in the Department's Post Hostilities Division, at one time alongside Jim Hill and under the direction of Ian Milner. In October 1945 he had been sent to Moscow as Third Secretary and had spent a year there before returning to work in Canberra. In February 1949 Throssell received his second posting abroad, to Rio de Janeira. In mid-1952 he returned from Brazil to Departmental work in Canberra. Nine months later, Ron Richards of ASIO sought an interview with him. As a result of this interview Colonel Spry wrote to the Minister for External Affairs informing him that Throssell had been assessed as 'not constituting a security risk to the Commonwealth'. Spry's letter to Casey seems to make clear that nothing in the deciphered MVD traffic, which had implicated Ian Milner and Jim Hill, implicated Ric Throssell.[70] There the question of Throssell rested — until the defection of the Petrovs.

According to Petrov, he had become aware of Throssell at first in conversations with fellow MVD workers Pakhomov and Kislitsyn and later in a cable

---

* As we shall see, Ric Throssell was eventually cleared by the Royal Commission

about him from Moscow Centre. Sometime early in 1952 Pakhomov had told him that Throssell was in Brazil and was, he thought, 'acting as our agent'. In late 1952 or early 1953 Kislitsyn also told Petrov that Throssell had been 'an agent'. He had, he said, learnt of his activities while working on the Australian desk of the MVD.[71] Canberra cabled Moscow informing them of Throssell's return to Australia. Moscow Centre cabled back with an account of Throssell's history and an instruction to attempt to bring him to life. Both the Petrovs, in their separate testimony, recalled that this cable had made clear that 'Ferro' had been a member of 'Klod's group' and had, during the war, passed valuable information to him. According to their memory the cable suggested that Throssell had believed he was merely supplying information to the Party in Australia. Petrova, but not Petrov, thought the cable had made it clear that Throssell had been active for some time in Brazil but had become frightened. She told ASIO that 'one of his group had attracted the attention of security' and 'come under notice'. One officer of ASIO thought it highly likely that word of Hill's interview with MI5 had reached Throssell. After the Moscow cable Kislitsyn was assigned the task of contacting and reactivating Throssell. In this task, both the Petrovs claimed, he had failed dismally. According to Petrova when Petrov's successor, Kovalenok, arrived he told her that one of his three or four major assignments was on the 'Ferro' front.[72]

In February 1955 Ric Throssell appeared before the Royal Commission. He had never, he maintained, during the course of his career in External Affairs, divulged official material to any unauthorised person. He could not explain the origin of the MVD Centre's or the Petrovs' 'misinformation' about him. When in Moscow, he remembered, he had been befriended by a young woman, Lidia Mertsova, whom he had met when looking up a Soviet literary official who was an old friend of his mother. While he had later heard that this Lidia was regarded by Australians with knowledge of Moscow as 'one of the YMCA boys' (that is a member of the NKVD) at the time of their close friendship Throssell had not even suspected her motives. Even now he doubted his colleagues' stories. Throssell claimed that he had not heard about the suspicions which surrounded his good friend Jim Hill until some time in 1953. He had never been a member of the Communist Party and was uninterested as to which of his relatives, friends and acquaintances were. He appeared uncertain even as to whether or not his own mother was a member of the Party. Others' political affiliations were no concern of his.[73]

The temper of the Commissioners' report on Ric Throssell was very far indeed from the McCarthyism of Left-wing mythology. Having listened to the testimony of the Petrovs and Throssell, they concluded that 'only remote hearsay assertions' existed concerning the information he was supposed to have divulged to the MVD via 'Klod'. Whether it had been given directly or indirectly, willingly or unwillingly, had been 'left in the air'. Even its date of transmission was quite uncertain. They thought 'it would be wrong to hold that [Throssell] had been a member of "Klod's" group or that he had willingly given any information'. In arriving at these conclusions the Royal Commissioners' logic was the antithesis of McCarthyist. They actually regarded Throssell's many Communist associations through his mother and wife, in Sydney and in Canberra, to be a factor which weighted the scales in his favour.

> It is quite possible (they concluded) that in the circle in which Throssell lived in Canberra he may have let drop information which he himself did not regard as important and may not even have been conscious of giving, but which was regarded as important by a Communist group which included 'Klod', and through him was passed to the Moscow Centre.[74]

As we have seen, during their interrogations the Petrovs frequently spoke about a former MVD agent in Australia code-named 'Klod'. Both knew that 'Klod' had been a member of the Australian Communist Party and the channel through which leakages from the Department of External Affairs had passed to the first MVD Resident in Australia, Makarov. Neither, however, knew who 'Klod' in fact was.

It did not take long for ASIO and the Royal Commission to discover his identity. In the 'G' series of documents (part of which were intelligence notes made by Sadovnikov) while there was no mention of 'Klod' there were frequent references to someone known as 'K'. 'G2' was headed 'Contacts K'. It listed eleven contacts, six of whom had either a direct or indirect connection with the Department of External Affairs. Even from this clue it seemed likely that 'K' was 'Klod'. 'Klod' was, after all, known to both the Petrovs as the Party man who was the MVD's contact point with External Affairs. One of 'K's' contacts was referred to in 'G2' as 'Tourist'. As we have seen, 'Tourist' was readily identified as Jim Hill's MVD code-name. A second contact was referred to as 'Sestra-Franciska Bernie'. This gave ASIO their first important clue as to the identity of 'K'.[75]

At the time of Petrov's defection ASIO already knew a great deal about Frances (not Franciska) Bernie. Miss Bernie had been employed by Allan Dalziel to work as a typist in Dr Evatt's Sydney office at the end of the Second World War. Her formal employer was the Department of External Affairs. During the initial investigations of 'the Case' she had made an appearance, under a code-name, in the radio traffic between Canberra and Moscow Centre.[76] During 1953 she had been interviewed by ASIO on a number of occasions. (ASIO used the fact that she had allowed her name to be put forward as a referee in a naturalisation application as their initial ground for interviewing her.) After having been offered an immunity from prosecution, Frances Bernie confessed that she had, while working at Dr Evatt's office in Sydney and as a youthful member of the Communist Party, taken documentary material she thought might be of interest to the Party to its offices at

Marx House in George Street, Sydney. Invariably the person to whom she passed her information was a Party cadre, Walter Clayton, who was in fact a member of the Party's Central Committee and Control Commission. In her ASIO statement Frances Bernie said she had brought information from the Evatt office to Clayton on some six occasions. She claimed not to be able to remember a great deal about the kind of documents she had passed to Clayton, although she knew that much of it was External Affairs material which had passed through the Sydney office. On one occasion, Bernie recalled, she had given Clayton documents which concerned on UNRRA Conference held at Lapstone in February 1945. Frances Bernie told ASIO that she believed the material she was giving Clayton was destined merely for the Communist Party in Australia. She had been acting at the time as a dedicated Party member. Although she maintained that she did not hide her Party membership from Dalziel and others at the office in Sydney, noone there of course knew that she was passing information to Clayton. Frances Bernie claimed that she ceased her clandestine work in early 1946.[77] In October 1954 she repeated the story she had already told ASIO to the Royal Commissioners.[78] Her tale was probably sufficient by itself to convince the Commissioners that 'K' would most likely turn out to be Clayton.

More evidence was soon presented to them on this question. In 'G4' (which was a note in Petrov's handwriting, which he said was copied from a paper of Sadovnikov's) the following reference occurred.

Mr C.R. Tennant 'K'
50 Bundarra Road, Bellview
Hill, Sydney.[79]

At the beginning of their investigations ASIO considered it likely that this C.R. Tennant was 'K'. In an ASIO interrogation brief of May 27 there is speculation about an espionage group 'operated by Tennant under the direct control of Makarov'.[80] Before the Melbourne sittings ASIO interviewed both Charlie Tennant, who must have been more than a little surprised to discover he was suspected of heading a spy ring, and his wife Lula. Lula told ASIO and, subsequently the Royal Commission, that during the war she had joined the Communist Party. Some time in 1942 or 1943 she had been approached by Walter Clayton who asked if he might use her address for some correspondence he was expecting. She agreed. Letters which arrived in her post box under the address of 'Sutherland c/- C.R. Tennant' would be passed on to him. According to the first instalment of her evidence this arrangement lasted until 1947; according to the second, until 1945. Naturally Lula maintained that she had no idea that she had been used as a conduit for correspondence from the Soviet intelligence service to Clayton.[81] The combined stories of Frances Bernie and the Tennants left little room for doubt about the identity of 'K'.

There was, however, still further evidence on the matter. In 'G7', in a paragraph which provided a potted summary of the Party history of the Melbourne University biochemist, Jack Legge, it was said that 'when the Communist Party was in an illegal situation, "K" used the house of Legge, J. for the publication of the newspaper *Tribune*.'[82] When Jack Legge was called before the Commission he readily admitted that he had been a longtime Party acquaintance of Clayton (with whom, he claimed, he had discussed Marxism and the problem of science under capitalism) and that during the wartime ban on the Communist Party his home had been used as a distribution point for *Tribune*. Legge was uncertain whether or not Clayton had been involved in this operation.[83] Clearly there could not be the slightest doubt now that 'K' was Clayton.

During the proceedings of the Royal Commission two further minor but interesting incidents concerning Clayton's involvement in leakages from External Affairs came under discussion. The first was raised by Jack Legge's cousin, George. George Legge was, when he appeared to give his evidence before the Commission, a former member of the Department of External Affairs who had, in 1953, been involuntarily transferred to the Department of Commence and Agriculture. Ostensibly Legge was transferred because of an incident in which he had been found guilty of drunken driving. In reality he had been transferred on security grounds. As Colonel Spry explained to Mr Menzies on July 3 1953, ASIO had come to view his cordial private relations with members of the Canberra Communist Party branch (especially Fred Rose) and the Soviet Embassy (especially Petrov) with grave misgivings. Legge had accompanied Petrov on a fishing trip and had been involved in several heavy drinkings bouts with him. ASIO doubted his discretion under these conditions and feared he might easily be compromised by the MVD.[84]

After his defection Petrov told ASIO that while George Legge had in fact given him no information he had indeed been cultivating him. Legge was known to Moscow Centre by the code-name 'Ribak' — the fisherman.[85] For his part George Legge had not taken his transference kindly. He believed the Petrov defection presented him with an opportunity of vindicating his innocence.[86] Perhaps in support of this cause he proved a very helpful and forthcoming witness at the Royal Commission. The most interesting story he told there concerned Walter Clayton. Legge revealed that in 1948 (when he was a member of External Affairs) cousin Jack and Clayton had paid a visit to George's dwellings in Canberra. Clayton was presented to him as the Party's foreign affairs expert. He asked George Legge to provide him with information from the Department which would help keep the Party's foreign policy 'on the rails'. Although Legge did not inform his superiors of Clayton's approach he did, he said, reject it out of hand.[87] From this story the Commissioners acquired at least one further piece in the Clayton — External Affairs-MVD jigsaw puzzle.

The George Legge evidence suggested that Clayton's intelligence function had extended at least until 1948. A final piece of the jigsaw suggested that in fact it might have extended until 1950. In 'G2' there was mentioned, as one of 'K's' contacts, a female Party member who was about to go to work in External Affairs after having finished the course at the Department's 'school'.[88] Although neither a real or code-name was supplied this description fitted a member of the Department already well known to ASIO. During 1953, while making security investigations of External Affairs people being posted abroad, ASIO had interviewed June Barnett. She told them that she had joined the Communist Party during the war and had for a short time after it belonged to a branch in the Melbourne suburb of Camberwell. In 1949 she had been selected as an External Affairs cadet and in early 1950 had gone to live in Canberra. Here, through George Legge, she had been introduced to the Communist Party organiser Fred Rose and had begun to visit his home regularly. At Easter time in 1950, while dining at the Roses, a member of the Party from Sydney, previously unknown to her, had called upon them. June Barnett agreed to accompany this man for a stroll. During it, the Party man had suggested to her that she might supply him with information she came upon during her Departmental work. According to Miss Barnett she refused the offer at once although, like her friend George Legge before her, she did not tell anyone in the Department about the approach. She did, however, tell ASIO the full story when interviewed in 1953.[89] At the Royal Commission June Barnett was unable to identify Walter Clayton — either from a photograph or, when he eventually appeared at the Commission, in the flesh — as the Party man who had made contact with her in Canberra. All that she could say was that Clayton was not dissimilar in appearance to the man she had met at the doorstep of the Rose's Canberra home five years before.[90]

During the Royal Commission on Espionage Walter Clayton went to ground; public calls for help in discovering his whereabouts proved fruitless. However, as the Commission was drawing to a close he suddenly emerged from his hiding place on Broughton Island.[91] He had, he told the Commissioners, been deeply shocked and angered to hear himself being referred to on the ABC radio news as the leader of a spy ring. He had decided to present himself before the Commission to 'clear his name'.

It was, of course, hardly surprising that Clayton denied all knowledge of 'the Case'. Clayton appeared to have been well briefed by the Party for his Commission appearance. By now it was clear that no direct evidence showing Clayton had met with Ian Milner or Jim Hill was likely to be presented to the Commission. To the very best of his knowledge (this was his invariable verbal formula) Clayton affirmed that he had never met with Milner or Jim Hill in his life. He agreed that he had once used the Tennants as a post box but only, he claimed, during the period of the wartime ban on the Party which had been lifted in 1942. He had not the faintest idea how his contact address had found its way into the MVD safe at Canberra. Clayton conceded that he had once accompanied Jack Legge when Jack had visited his cousin in Canberra but regarded as preposterous George Legge's memory of an improper approach for information. He also conceded that he had once known a Miss Bernie — a splendid lass, he recalled — but denied absolutely receiving any confidential information from her. What use had the Party of the working class for 'little bits of paper'? If anyone, he said, had offered him secret documents he would have refused the offer. The Party had always, he informed the Commissioners, to be 'vigilant' against 'provocation'. He admitted that he would be most delighted to meet representatives of the country of his dreams — the Soviet Union. Sadly, however, he confessed, he had not met with a Russian national in the course of his life.

In general, Walter Clayton's performance at the Commission was spirited and insolent. Considerable time was absorbed in listening to examples of his soapbox rhetoric and to his cock and bull stories* of the various dummy bank accounts and false addresses which littered his recent past and seemed to be associated with a somewhat comic attempt to construct a safe house at Baulkham Hills for the illegal apparatus of the Party. Windeyer's rather gentle cross-examination failed utterly to interfere with his pleasure or shake his composure.[92]

The Royal Commissioners concluded that, to put it mildly, Clayton's evidence was not to be relied upon. They were certain, of course, that Clayton was 'K' and that 'K' was 'Klod'. In MVD communications 'K' or 'Klod' had been linked with no fewer than eight members of the Department of External Affairs. One of these — the typist Frances Bernie — had confessed to passing information to Clayton. The Petrovs, at one time or another, had maintained that they had heard from Moscow Centre that both Ian Milner and Ric Throssell had been the sources of information which had been passed via 'Klod'. Jim Hill, who had been identified as a source of leakages by cryptanalytic intercepts, was listed by Sadovnikov as one of "'K's" contacts'. One member of the Department, George Legge, had testified to an improper approach by Clayton; another, June Barnett, had given evidence which, in association with the same Sadovnikov note, strongly suggested a similar approach. Unsurprisingly, given this evidence, the Royal Commissioners came to the conclusion that Walter Clayton had been, during the 1940s, a 'principal channel' for the transmission of serious and damaging leakages from the Department of External Affairs to the MVD in Canberra and thence to Moscow.[93]

---

* Almost literally cock and bull. Clayton claimed to have given power of attorney to a land agent, R.J. Williams. In return Williams claimed to have sold Clayton's private property at Baulkham Hills without his knowledge. The funds, Williams testified, were invested in the purchase, on Clayton's behalf, of thirteen cows. There were no receipts for this purchase. Williams maintained, however, that he could locate the cows by sight from a herd in a relative's paddock.

Walter Clayton (courtesy of News Limited)

13

THE PETROV RESIDENCY

When Petrov defected it must have appeared to ASIO that many of the questions of most fundamental interest to it were on the point of being authoritatively answered. Who were the most important Soviet agents in Australia? What sources did the MVD possess in Australian Government departments? Had the MVD established agent relationships with foreign Embassy staff in Canberra? Was an 'illegal' Soviet intelligence apparatus active in Australia? What was the relationship between the MVD and the Communist Party of Australia? What was the nature of MVD operations in the émigré communities from the Soviet bloc? Had Soviet intelligence penetrated ASIO? What was the MVD's assessment of ASIO's effectiveness? From April 3, 1954 ASIO faced the happy prospect of private, extended and frank discussions with the former head of the Soviet intelligence service in Australia on matters of mutual interest. At £5000 the Petrov defection must have appeared to ASIO a singular bargain; after Petrova joined her husband doubly so.

Almost the first broad line of questioning which ASIO put to Petrov about his own Residency was an extension of 'the Case'. ASIO was of course most anxious to discover whether the leakages from External Affairs which had occurred during the 1940s had been completely plugged. At once Petrov assured ASIO that indeed they had. In his initial debriefing the stories Petrov told Ron Richards suggested that during his Residency the MVD had failed almost totally in its efforts to penetrate the Department of External Affairs. As we have seen while Petrov had informed Richards that there existed within the Department a former Soviet agent — Ric Throssell — he also made it clear that since Throssell's return from Brazil he had been 'inactive' and 'very still'. In Petrov's view he was frightened. Both Petrovs agreed that the efforts to revive Throssell, or indeed even to make contact with him since his return to Australia in 1952, had failed.[1]

After the 'Moscow letters' were deciphered and interpreted ASIO became aware that in January 1952 Petrov had been instructed by Moscow Centre to study and cultivate a second member of the Department, a certain F.J. McLean, code-named 'Lot'. According to Moscow 'one of our trustworthy agents describes McLean favourably and considers that he could supply valuable information'. Before the end of the year the MVD in Canberra had sent Moscow some details about their cultivation of 'Lot', although what their message might have contained is far from clear.[2] In his first ASIO debriefing Petrov described 'Lot' as 'a very important man'[3] but in his later debriefing and evidence before the Royal Commission Petrov maintained that he had neither met McLean nor had his station received any information from him. He had no idea who the 'trustworthy agent' had been who had been convinced of McLean's potential value to the MVD.[4]

Petrov informed ASIO that during his Residency he had made the acquaintance of two other members of the Department of External Affairs — both of whom were discussed in the 'Moscow letters' — but denied that he had derived any intelligence benefit from either. One was the former head of the Consular and Protocol Section, Alfred Body ('Gost'). Body and his wife had dined with the Petrovs in the line of duty. Moscow Centre hoped to be able to utilise Body for 'in the dark', that is to say unwitting, information. According to Petrov Moscow's hopes were in vain.[5] The Royal Commissioners concluded after hearing the evidence that Body was a man of 'character and integrity' who had done nothing whatever to deserve his mention in MVD communications.[6] The second External Affairs acquaintance of Petrov's was George Legge. As we have seen, Petrov had drunk with Legge in Canberra and had gone with him on a fishing trip. After his defection Petrov told ASIO that he was cultivating 'Ribak' under instructions from Moscow Centre. The cultivation appears to have been barren. Petrov claimed he had got nothing from Legge, while Legge regarded his relationship with Petrov as so innocent that he planned to use Petrov's defection as the means by which he could clear his reputation. Petrov's attempted cultivation of his friend, 'Ribak', seems to have been half-hearted at best.[7]

According to Petrov when he had been asked to conduct some serious business with External Affairs (concerning the standing of Ian Milner) he had turned at once to Rex Chiplin of *Tribune*. Petrov told Ron Richards that Chiplin had some contacts — 'two chaps' — inside the Department. Not surprisingly, ASIO was more than a little interested to know who these contacts were. Petrov insisted that he had made no inquiries of Chiplin about his contacts and had therefore no idea as to their identity.[8] It is hard to see how Petrov's account of the Milner-Chiplin incident could have failed to strike ASIO as curious. A year before his talks with Chiplin over Milner, Petrov had been reprimanded by Moscow for transmitting External Affairs information which had been gathered by Chiplin without identifying Chiplin's sources.*[9] Had Petrov genuinely failed to absorb the meaning of this reprimand? Was he really so incompetent or uninterested in his work that he had

---

* 'When receiving information you should ascertain and inform us about the source from whom Chiplin receives information, and not merely its contents, as you did when dealing with the question of exchange of enciphered material between the governments of Australia and America.'

failed to inquire of Chiplin as as to the identity of his sources in External Affairs? Or, alternatively, was Petrov telling ASIO considerably less than the whole truth about his activities in Australia?

The question of Petrov's reliability was raised most starkly in the case of Bert Chandler, a case in which the question of the MVD's penetration of both the Department of External Affairs and ASIO appeared to be involved. Chandler was (like Walter Clayton before him) a member both of the Communist Party's Central Committee and its disciplinary and security section, the Control Commission. On July 17 1953 he had assumed considerable importance for ASIO after two officers of Australian intelligence (Redford of ASIO and Watson of the CIS) had raided his Sydney home. The search was formally launched after the publication of an article on the monarchy which had appeared in the *Communist Review* and which was deemed subversive. It turned into an extremely profitable fishing expedition for ASIO. There were, in particular, two prize catches. In one of Chandler's wardrobes the investigators discovered a list of ASIO car number plates and of the names and addresses of certain members of ASIO in Sydney. Under a pile of soiled linen in another wardrobe they discovered some typed extracts taken from the secret political diary of the Minister for External Affairs, Richard Casey. These two items proved that the Party had in the recent past penetrated ASIO and appeared to indicate the high likelihood that it had a mole somewhere inside the Department of External Affairs.*[10]

What was more uncertain was whether either of these documents, or indeed others deriving from the same sources, were ultimately destined for delivery to the Soviet intelligence service. There was not the slightest doubt that both these documents were of potential interest to the MVD. In the MVD in Canberra a list of ASIO number plates would have been of considerable assistance in their permanent cat and mouse games with ASIO surveillance teams. In the MVD in Moscow the carefully chosen extracts from the Casey diaries — which dwelt upon Anglo-American tensions over ANZUS and discussions of uranium mining — would have been read with relish.[11] ASIO in July 1953 was obliged to ponder seriously the possibility that Chandler might be a major channel for the passage of material from External Affairs or ASIO to the MVD. In a letter of July 31 concerning recent developments in 'the Case', Colonel Spry informed Mr Menzies of the Chandler raid.

> Secret documents of high value as political intelligence were found in the home of H.B. Chandler in the search on 17th July 1953. There are good grounds for believing that Chandler is the Chief Security Officer of the Communist Party, and that he may have taken over Clayton's intelligence role.[12]

---

* As the Casey diary had been circulated on a restricted basis in External Affairs but typed in the Post-Master General's Department it was at least conceivable that the leak had sprung from there.

After July 1953 there was probably no single contemporary relationship which interested ASIO more deeply than that between Chandler and the MVD. In ASIO's detailed tactical preparations for Operation Cabin 12 Chandler's name was near the head of the list of priorities for phone tapping.[13] Naturally, soon after the Petrov defection, ASIO planned to interrogate him on the Chandler matter.

Four days after his defection Ron Richards asked Petrov whether he knew Chandler. Rather disconcertingly Petrov replied thus.

> I don't know him. Charles Brezland I know. He is in the Eureka League. I don't know Chandler.

The following day, however, Petrov spoke differently. While discussing with Richards his knowledge of Party members he volunteered another statement.

> I know Hughes here. I met Sharkey and Dixon at Kafka's, also Mr Chandler, Maher, Henry and Blake. That was the only time I met them. I have not met them conspiratorially. I have not met Chandler in a conspiratorial way.[14]

It is possible that in his first statement Petrov had confused Chandler with his son, who was indeed active in the Eureka Youth League. It is clear, however, that even in this second account of his relationship with Chandler Petrov was not telling the whole truth. At the Royal Commission Chandler (who was hardly likely to exaggerate his acquaintanceship with Petrov) admitted to having met with him on at least three occasions.[15] More importantly there was something rather odd about Petrov's detailed denial of conspiratorial meetings with Chandler, of which he had not been accused. Listened to with a Freudian or even a policeman's ear Petrov's Chandler answer of April 8 inevitably suggested the possibility that there was some dimension to his relationship with Chandler which he was anxious to conceal. For the moment, however, the Petrov-Chandler matter was allowed to rest.

In early May 1954 ASIO discovered that Chandler had suddenly flown out of Australia with a one way ticket to Hong Kong.[16] As Chandler's passport was currently endorsed for travel to Communist China, ASIO thought it highly likely that he planned an extended sojourn there. Shortly after his departure ASIO observed Ted Hill paying a call on his wife, Mary. After this visit Mrs Chandler 'appeared to be very upset'. ASIO guessed that Hill might have informed her that her husband was likely to be away from Australia for a long time. Like Mary Chandler, ASIO was itself very unhappy about the prospect of Chandler's Chinese vacation.[17] Although the Solictor-General, Professor Bailey, thought it 'a terrible thing to withdraw a person's passport under such circumstances', Colonel Spry strongly and, as it turned out, successfully urged upon the Government precisely this course.*[18] On May 9,

---

* At the time the Menzies Government was facing an election and under attack from the ALP for its weak–kneed attitude to Communist foreign travel. The withdrawal of Chandler's passport was an aspect of a general pre-election toughening of policy in this area.

when Chandler was interviewed by Australian officials in Hong Kong, his passport was impounded. Shortly thereafter he returned to Australia to wait upon the Petrov inquiry.[19] When ASIO intercepted a telephone call between Ted Hill and Bert Chandler after the Sydney opening of the Royal Commission they learned that Hill 'was of the opinion that Chandler might be a very worried man'.[20] In early July Chandler was formally advised by ASIO that his presence would be required at the Royal Commission.[21]

Between July and September, while the energies of both ASIO and the Royal Commission were absorbed in Dr Evatt's conspiracy charges, there was no time for work on the Chandler case. However, in late September, it came into focus once more. ASIO's Royal Commission section now perused the Chandler material carefully. At least one of its officers came to the conclusion that Petrov was not telling them the truth about his relations with Bert Chandler. In an internal ASIO memorandum he pointed to the contradiction between Petrov's comments of April 7 and April 8. More importantly, however, he referred to a passage from one of Bialoguski's Petrov reports which indicated the strong probability that Petrov had met with Chandler under conspiratorial conditions.

> Bialoguski met Petrov as arranged at 7.00 p.m., 13 February 1953, and at Petrov's request drove him to the Rose Bay Flying Base.... Petrov told him to park in a particular place, then suggested a walk in the park. They walked in the park parallel to the backs of the parked cars. Bialoguski noticed motor car no. ADM 375 (registered in Chandler's name) with its door open, and two young men in the front seat looking at them. Petrov stopped, told Bialoguski to meet him at the Kirketon at 9.00 p.m. and quickly entered the car, which drove off at high speed.... On 14 February, 1953, in explaining his appointment of the previous night, Petrov told Bialoguski that he had a meeting with Trade Union representatives. He said 'One can do some good work here if one goes about it quietly'.

It seemed likely that the two young men in Bert Chandler's car were his sons, two of whom were indeed deeply involved in work for the Party. Although Bialoguski's report did not prove that Petrov had met with Chandler on this or other occasions the evidence was at least suggestive. In his memorandum the ASIO officer argued that the report seemed 'to indicate that Petrov has had some contact with Chandler and is concealing same'.[22]

Bert Chandler was called before the Royal Commission in early December 1954. Detailed evidence concerning the ASIO-CIS search of his home in July 1953 and its results were taken in camera from Messrs Redford and Watson.[23] Ron Richards outlined to the Commissioners the painstaking but ultimately unsuccessful investigations ASIO had conducted in its attempts to locate Chandler's External Affairs and ASIO sources.[24] When Chandler testified he claimed to be entirely ignorant of the documents discovered in his family's wardrobes. Neither Petrov (who was not called to give evidence in this case) nor Chandler were interrogated by Windeyer about their relationship. When, however, Mr Justice Owen asked Chandler, almost in passing, whether he knew Petrov, Chandler admitted that he had met him on some three occasions although always, he hastened to point out, on a purely social basis.[25]

It would appear from the Commission transcript that Chandler's counsel, Ted Hill, could hardly believe his ears when, on December 6, Windeyer's examination of his client concluded and Chandler was asked to step down from the witness box. 'Your Honours', Hill interceded, 'might I just raise a couple of matters? There was some suggestion that Petrov might be involved in this; Mr Chandler was asked some questions about meeting Petrov'. Owen pointed out to Hill that the only suggestions raised thus far had concerned social meetings between them.

> I do not want to pursue the matter now, [Hill returned] but I do not want it to be taken that if some subsequent matter arises I should not have the right to cross-examine ... I was only directing my remarks to some ultimate evidence that may arise, if it does.[26]

As it happened, Hill's 'subsequent matter' and 'ultimate evidence' never arose. In June 1954 Chandler may have been 'a very worried man' but in the fullness of time he discovered that his anxieties on the Petrov front were needless. While it is doubtful whether ASIO ever really believed Petrov's Chandler story there is no evidence that he was pushed hard on this matter even in the privacy of the interrogation room. Only once or twice in the memoranda of interrogations is there evidence of ASIO attempts to lead Petrov into a Chandler admission. At the end of a long questionnaire put before him in December 1954 ASIO asked, 'Did Petrov send the two Chandler documents to Moscow?' Petrov was shown the documents. He claimed never to have seen them, or the material contained in them, before.[27] ASIO was never to be able to move beyond circumstantial evidence to discover certainly whether Bert Chandler, who appeared to have sources inside External Affairs and ASIO, and Petrov, the head of the MVD in Australia, were linked. As with many aspects of the post-defection investigations into the Petrov Residency, the Chandler case, which had once looked so interesting and full of promise, was concluded in muddle and uncertainty.

The Chandler case had, of course, raised for ASIO a question of considerable interest to it, namely how far Australian Security had been penetrated by the MVD. At first Petrov spoke of only two cases where information emanating from ASIO had reached the MVD. Petrov had learnt from Pakhomov that a former officer of the Clerks' Union (when it was under Communist control) and a present executive of the peace movement, Geoffrey Anderson (code-named 'Yeger' — the huntsman) had given information in the late 1940s to Pakhomov's Tass-MVD predecessor, Nosov. 'Yeger' told Nosov that Australian security was mounting a major surveillance against him. As a consequence of this information Nosov, who did not have diplomatic immunity, was sent home. Petrov claimed that he did not know the name of Anderson's security contact. During his own Residency the efforts made to draw 'Yeger' more deeply into the MVD net had failed.*[28]

According to Petrov's initial evidence, during his Residency he had made only one attempt to penetrate ASIO. In early 1952 Petrov learned through Pakhomov that Rex Chiplin had discovered details of an ASIO surveillance plan. Petrov asked Jean Ferguson of the Australia-Soviet Friendship Society to arrange a meeting, under conspiratorial conditions, with the Party's security head, Jack Hughes. At this meeting Petrov asked Hughes to outline to him the Party's resources inside ASIO. Hughes mentioned a typist who worked inside ASIO who had supplied some information to the Party through her Communist boyfriend. He also told Petrov about a PMG technician who installed listening devices for ASIO and was in the habit of giving the Party the names of people whose telephones were tapped. According to Petrov, Hughes did not tell him the name of either of these sources and argued that neither would be suitable for utilisation by the MVD. Petrov now claimed to have cabled Moscow with the news that 'the Communists have very poor sources in the Security for our contact purposes'.[29]

ASIO appeared to be somewhat unconvinced that these two stories had exhausted Petrov's knowledge. During a private debriefing session in April 1955, Gilmour pointed out to him that there were three instances of information derived from Security in the Sadovnikov documents he had brought with him. If the same source still existed inside ASIO the safety of he and his wife might be at risk. Could he tell ASIO nothing more about attempts at penetration? Petrov searched his memory once more. Suddenly he recalled another, exceedingly odd, story. In 1948 or 1949 a pro-Soviet member of Australian Security had approached Lifanov, the Ambassador, and offered him a list of the entire Australian Security staff. Fearing provocation Lifanov had rejected the offer but had taken down 'a few names'. Subsequently he had pointed this man out to Petrov at a concert in Canberra's Albert Hall. He was, Petrov remembered, grey-haired and fiftyish with a name that began with the letter 'M'. Although Petrov believed that 'M' had by now resigned from Security he and Pakhomov submitted a plan to Moscow for his utilisation. Moscow approved. Unhappily, Petrov was unable to contact 'M'. The

---

* The Moscow letters of 1952 made it clear that the MVD Centre was hopeful that Anderson might become an active agent and dissatisfied with Petrov's efforts to recruit him. In 1953 Petrov farmed the Anderson case out to Antonov but he too had made no headway. Petrov claimed to have spoken with Anderson once, but only with regard to a proposal to bring Shostakovitch to Australia for a peace rally. Anderson was called before the Royal Commission but, as so often, without significant results. Considerable time was, however, devoted to a diverting side incident — Anderson's role in the attempted hire of a private plane to defy passport control and fly a delegation to the Peking Peace Conference of 1952. Bialoguski became involved in this scheme through his public position as Vice-President of the New South Wales Peace Council and his private role as an ASIO agent inside the peace movement. He subsequently wrote about it in his book *The Petrov Story*.

plan died a natural death.[30] At this point Petrov's small repertoire of ASIO stories appears finally to have been exhausted. On both the External Affairs and ASIO fronts, if Petrov was to be believed, his Residency had achieved next to nothing.

From the espionage, political and, indeed, human point of view the most interesting story the Petrovs revealed to ASIO and the Royal Commissioners concerned the Second Secretary at the French Embassy in Canberra, Madame Rose-Marie Ollier, code-named 'Olga'. In September 1954, as we have seen, at the moment the Ollier case became public in Australia, Dr Evatt — playing the role of Emile Zola to Ollier's Captain Dreyfus — proclaimed himself the champion of her innocence. After Evatt's intervention the Ollier case emerged as the symbolic test of the Petrovs' credibility as witnesses to Soviet espionage in Australia. Over Mme Ollier, as over Document 'J', the friends and enemies of the Petrovs divided. The case was, however, more genuinely serious. Mme Ollier was the only person to be arrested as a consequence of the Petrov Affair.

After Petrov's defection ASIO's information about Ollier's involvement with the MVD was derived from a variety of sources. In the six 'Moscow letters' of 1952 which Petrov had brought with him three made mention of Mme Ollier. The letter of January 2 1952 made it clear that 'Olga' had been in touch with the MVD in Australia for two years and that during that time she had agreed 'to give us assistance'. On the other hand, Moscow Centre was thoroughly dissatisfied with the achievements thus far of its Canberra station on the 'Olga' front. Sadovnikov had not taught her 'the ways and means of agent's work'. Pakhomov, who had inherited the task, seemed content to discuss questions of international relations with her. It instructed Petrov to lift Pakhomov's game. Pakhomov should make every endeavor to discover her work routine in the French Embassy and in particular the details of the cipher section, where Ollier worked. Pakhomov was required to meet her under clandestine conditions well out of Canberra. As soon as possible she should be pressed for oral and then written reports on the cables flowing into and out of her Embassy. If she was to return to Paris on leave Pakhomov should arrange for a meeting between her and an MVD representative six weeks after her arrival.[31]

During the first six months of 1952 Moscow Centre was displeased with the rate of Pakhomov's progress. In a letter of June, written shortly after his recall to Moscow, it wrote to Petrov about the 'purposeless manner' in which Pakhomov had conducted discussions with 'Olga' and his 'stubborn refusal' to raise the question of the ciphers. Petrov was to take over the case himself. Secret meetings should be arranged every three to four weeks. Olga was to be told that she could serve the cause of mankind by handing over secret information about the anti-Soviet machinations of Western imperialist ruling circles. A payment of £75 for past services was authorised.[32] (Although such a payment appears never to have been made, sometime in early 1952, according to Petrova, a wrist watch was presented to her by the MVD.)[33]

During the succeeding twelve months Petrov's cultivation apparently made no progress. As we have seen during the night of May 4 1953, Dr Bialoguski had rummaged through Petrov's pockets after the MVD Resident had dropped into a deep and drunken sleep in the Point Piper flat. Bialoguski had come upon a handwritten note from Petrov to Mme Ollier proposing a rendezvous. The text of this note (which was never delivered) makes clear that Petrov had not yet established the connection with Olga long ago required of him by Moscow.*[34]

According to the evidence the Petrovs gave to their ASIO debriefers and to a secret session of the Royal Commission, Petrov handed Mme Ollier a second note in May 1953 suggesting a date and place of meeting — Young's Department store at Queanbeyan — in four week's time. Ollier arrived at this rendezvous. At this meeting the couple agreed to meet at the same place and at the same hour of day, 8 p.m., each month. In order to minimise the risk of counter-intelligence surveillance or telephone interception, the date of the monthly meeting was pre-arranged by a simple system: adding the figure 5 to the number of the particular month (hence January 6, February 7, etc.).

Petrov claimed that he met with Mme Ollier on some seven or eight occasions between June 1953 and March 1954. Although he tried to obtain from her information about the French cyphers — Moscow's overwhelming interest — and asked her for information about the contents of the Embassy's cables, both the Petrovs agreed that she had given nothing of value in either area. On the other hand, Ollier appeared to have been more forthcoming with information about Australian involvement in the French wars of Indo-China. Both agreed that sometime, either in late 1953 or early 1954, Mme Ollier had informed Petrov of a shipment of arms that was being sent to Indo-China from Australia on board the *SS Radnor*. Moreover on December 24 1953 they claimed that Petrov and Ollier had made special arrangements for a rendezvous in Cooma. The purpose of this meeting was to hand over details of the types of armaments Australia was sending to the French in Indo-China. Ollier here told Petrov that she was unable to get hold of the list which was locked in the Ambassador's safe. According to Petrov's story both he and Mme Ollier had arrived hours late for this meeting — Ollier because she had

---

* It read: 'Dear Mrs Ollier, Many regards from Mr Sadovnikov and Mr Pakhomov. We have to continue our meetings and make the best for interests. Would you be so kind and let me know when we could meet each other and at what place would suit you. In my opinion we could meet tomorrow evening at 7 p.m., at the Melbourne Avenue bus stop where you can pass in the car.' This particular note was never handed to Mme Ollier. Petrov rewrote it, this time suggesting the Queanbeyan rendezvous.

left Canberra much later than planned; Petrov because he had almost killed himself when his car had left the Canberra-Cooma road. They had met, almost by accident, around noon. As we shall see, the precise details of this particular meeting were to assume subsequently an unexpected importance.[35]

Shortly after the Petrovs had given their evidence to ASIO about Mme Ollier a representative of the Department of External Affairs approached the French Ambassador in Australia, M. Roche.[36] (Because of the privileges of diplomatic immunity there could be, of course, no question of ASIO interviewing Ollier.) Although M. Roche was of the opinion that his Second Secretary might have been guilty of stupidity rather than espionage, his Government decided to order her to leave Australia at once. On May 18 M. Roche summoned Mme Ollier. 'You are', he informed her, 'compromised'. Her immediate departure was required. Ollier responded with fury. She told her Ambassador she must be allowed to stay and fight to vindicate her innocence, for the good name of France and to support those of her Australian friends who she assumed were about to be, like her, falsely accused of wrongdoing. The Royal Commission was, in her opinion, 'a frame up'; the Petrov Affair an electoral stunt. She threatened to seek political asylum in Australia (!) or in the embassies of India, Ceylon or Indonesia. Roche advised her to go quietly and to write a book on L'Affaire Petrov. It would be, he said, 'le best-seller' of the year. On May 19 M. Roche spoke with Keith Waller of External Affairs about Ollier. If she were allowed to travel to Sydney alone he feared that 'she may skip'. He was by now of the opinion that 'her mind had gone'.[37]

With considerable misgivings Mme Ollier did eventually agree to depart Australia on May 21 on board the *Québec*, which was bound for Noumea. Shortly after arriving there, however, she changed her mind and purchased a Qantas ticket to Australia. The Governor of New Caledonia was compelled to cancel her flight.[38] Frenzy turned to depression and ill-health. Mme Ollier now quietly waited upon her fate in one of Noumea's hotels. At the end of July a representative of French Security — Colonel Ramier — visited her. Ramier had been fully briefed on the affair in Australia by ASIO. Over two days he took from her, in a manner which she described as violent,[39] a detailed statement concerning her relations with the last three MVD Residents in Australia — Sadovnikov, Pakhomov and Petrov. Mme Ollier admitted to Ramier that she had met secretly with both Sadovnikov and Pakhomov on several occasions. According to her, Sadovnikov demanded secrecy in their five or six rendezvous in the countryside because he 'feared scandal-mongering on the part of his colleagues'. (As ASIO later discovered there was a rumour in Canberra diplomatic circles that Mme Ollier's relations with Sadovnikov and maybe even Pakhomov and Petrov had a sexual dimension.) Sadovnikov had departed her life suddenly and without explanation. Before his departure Pakhomov had presented her with a wrist watch as a memento of their friendship. Mme Ollier strenuously denied that she had given either any information of intelligence value.

After Pakhomov came Petrov. Although Mme Ollier claimed to have felt an instant 'antipathy' for him, his persistence had 'intrigued' her and eventually overcome her resistance. An acquaintance, under clandestine conditions, was arranged. She acknowledged that on a number of occasions they had met at Queanbeyan at the time and place and by the method (the month plus five) that the Petrovs had outlined to ASIO. She also acknowledged that she had met Petrov by special arrangement at Cooma on December 24. She was certain of the date because of her vivid memory of Petrov's physical and mental state after his car accident. He appeared to be wounded and to be a defeated individual. Like Petrov she thought they had met around midday. She agreed that at their meetings Petrov had pressed her very hard — in neither case successfully — for information on the French cyphers and on the armament types going from Australia to Indo-China. She also agreed that she had told Petrov about the arms shipments being loaded in New Zealand and Australia onto the *SS Radnor*. Although there were some discrepancies concerning dates, on all matters of substance the Ollier statement to Colonel Ramier and the Petrovs' statements to ASIO coincided.[40]

On August 22, 1954, Mme Ollier was placed under arrest by the French authorities in New Caledonia and two days later confined to a cabin on board the *Tahitien* which brought her to metropolitan France for her investigation and trial before the Military Tribunal. At first Mme Ollier was served with a writ of investigation under article 75 of the French penal code, which concerned treason and carried a possible penalty of death, and articles 103 and 104 which concerned damage to the security of the State. Eventually, after preliminary hearings in Paris, all charges under article 75 were dropped.[41] There could be little doubt that Mme Ollier had behaved strangely and improperly in maintaining clandestine relations with three members of the Soviet Embassy in Canberra (who turned out to be the three successive MVD Residents in Australia). On the other hand, the only information Petrov had claimed she had disclosed concerned the arms shipment on the *SS Radnor*, which had anyhow become public knowledge in Australia by early April 1954.[42] At the time when the charges against Mme Ollier were reduced and she was released from custody, Paris was in the grip of a far more serious espionage scandal.[43] In mid-1955 the charges against her were further reduced — from endangering the security of the State to 'failing to notify superiors of improper questions put by Petrov'. Her trial before the Military Tribunal was still some months distant.[44]

By the time Mme Ollier had set foot on French soil, her case had become of central importance to the politics of the Petrov Affair in Australia. As we have seen, in early September 1954, after a press leakage, the Royal Commission and the French Ambassador had released a joint statement about her. The transcript of the *in camera* hearing of July 20 was simultaneously released. Dr Evatt — who was a personal friend of Mme Ollier and who was at the time dominating the Royal Commission with his conspiracy charges — leapt at once to her defence. Mme Ollier, Evatt declared, was a French Resistance heroine*[45] who had fallen victim to Vichyite elements in France and a criminal conspiracy in Australia. Was it not 'worse than McCarthyism' that she had been 'defamed throughout the world as a spy' on the basis of possible forgeries in the Moscow letters and the 'say so' of two 'treacherous ... paid informers'.[46] As we have seen, this final statement of Dr Evatt's was part cause and part pretext for his removal from the Royal Commission.

The Ollier case was from this moment thoroughly politicised. By the queer political logic of the situation, Dr Evatt, in tying his reputation to the innocence of Mme Ollier, had tied that of ASIO, the Royal Commission and the Menzies Government to the accuracy of the Petrovs' account of the MVD's cultivation of her. On October 1, Dr Evatt revealed to the Australian public new evidence which 'proved' that the Petrovs had after all being lying about Mme Ollier. In his evidence Petrov had claimed to have met Olga in Cooma around noon on December 24. Evatt, through another friend and champion of Ollier (Senator Dorothy Tangney) released to the press a statutory declaration from the proprietors of a hotel in Eden which claimed that Mme Ollier had lunched at their establishment at 12.30 p.m. on Christmas Eve. Eden was some three hours from Cooma by car. As Mme Ollier could not possibly have been at Cooma when Petrov said she was, he had obviously lied on this point. And if he had lied here was it not likely that his entire evidence on the Ollier matter was false?†[47]

ASIO and the Royal Commission were placed in an exceedingly odd situation by Dr Evatt's new Ollier campaign. They knew — or at least came to know when the Ramier report reached them — that the Petrovs had not lied over Cooma or any other matter of substance concerning Mme Ollier and that Evatt's allegations were not only false but could be easily proved to be so on the basis of evidence in their possession. Not surprisingly, ASIO sought permission from French Security for the release of parts of the Ramier report. When their request was turned down, the Australian Embassy in Paris raised this question 'at the highest levels' of the French Government.

[Mme Ollier's] position (the Embassy was informed by Canberra) was given such wide publicity here that the public generally will probably treat Ollier as test case for credit of Petrov as witness and for assessment of Commission's conclusion.[48]

---

* According to the Ramier report Mme Ollier had actually spent the war in the relative security of the French Embassy of the Lebanon.

† After the Evatt press release of October 1, ASIO took Petrov through his account of the events of December 24 once more. Petrov now arrived at 10.30 a.m. as the approximate time of meeting. Strangely, however, Mme Ollier confirmed to Colonel Ramier that the Cooma meeting had in fact taken place around midday.

The French Government proved unsympathetic to the Menzies Government's domestic embarrassments. It absolutely opposed any release of material from the Ramier report in advance of the conclusion of Mme Ollier's trial.[49] When the Royal Commission reported on the Ollier matter it was obliged to restrict itself to obscure statements about unnamed evidence confirming the Petrovs' stories beyond doubt. Until the archives of the Royal Commission were opened in 1984 both the existence and the contents of Colonel Ramier's report of interrogation of Mme Ollier were unknown in Australia.

In its final report the Royal Commissioners argued that the Petrovs' evidence concerning Mme Ollier had proven entirely accurate. In the Ollier case, they pointed out, the MVD had been playing for very high stakes indeed. 'If . . . the MVD could, unknown to the French, get the key to their communications, the security not only to France but of the whole Western world might well be in jeopardy.' Nevertheless, they concluded, in their quest for the French cyphers or indeed for any other important secret information from Mme Ollier, the MVD had been almost entirely unsuccessful. 'The results obtained from [their] laborious and persistent efforts', had been, here as elsewhere, 'negligible'.[50]

In June 1952 Moscow Centre had instructed Petrov to deploy the resources of his Residency to the task of establishing an 'illegal' Soviet intelligence apparatus in Australia.

> The aggravation of the international situation and the pressing necessity for the timely exposure and prevention of cunning designs of the enemy, call imperatively for a radical reorganization of all our intelligence work and the urgent creation of an illegal apparatus in Australia, which could function uninterruptedly and effectively under any conditions.

This was regarded as a 'top priority' task into which all Soviet 'cadre workers' and 'collaborators' of the 'legal' apparatus and reliable Australian agents should be drawn. The Soviet workers were, however, warned to be careful to avoid spreading panic amongst the agents. 'They should not interpret our preparations as a sign of inevitable war in the near future.'[51]

When this stern and emphatic letter of instruction reached Petrov there was in Australia already an obvious candidate for the post of 'illegal' Resident — an immigrant from Czechoslovakia, one Vincenz Divisek (code-named 'Pechek'), a former wartime agent of the Soviet intelligence service. During 1941 Divisek — a man of joint Czech-German parentage — had been conscripted to the German Army and sent to the Russian front. According to the story he told ASIO, Divisek had deserted in the Ukraine and had spent the next two to three years in a succession of Soviet prisoner of war camps, where he had performed small services for the Soviets as an informer on his fellow prisoners. In 1943 or 1944 he was taken from a camp to a house on the outskirts of Moscow and given a crash course under the general direction of a certain Soviet intelligence officer, Captain Medvedev. In late 1944 he and another Czech, one Adolf Stas, as wireless operator, were parachuted into Czechoslovakia. He and Stas built networks within Prague and sent back to Moscow details of German troop formations and war production.

According to Divisek, his work for Soviet intelligence ceased after the Soviet-American liberation of Czechoslovakia. He was decorated by the Benes Government for his services and rewarded with ownership of a small hotel in the Sudetenland, expropriated from its German owners. In 1948, after the Communist *coup*, Divisek claims that he decided to leave Czechoslovakia (he had lost the ownership of the hotel, which was nationalised) and to emigrate to Australia where his wife's sister lived already. After his application to emigrate had been made Divisek claimed to have received an unexpected visit from Captain Medvedev. In return for a passport and exit visa, he agreed to make contact with Soviet intelligence in Australia shortly after his arrival here. A plan of meeting — in front of the Governor Phillip memorial in Sydney's Botanical Gardens — was arranged in an MVD flat in Prague.

When Divisek arrived in Australia he was convinced by his English brother-in-law to go with his story to the Commonwealth Investigation Service. This he did. At first he was taken seriously. At least two attempts were made to have Divisek, or a CIS officer dressed to look like him, meet his MVD contact. These attempts fell through. Eventually Australian Security began to lose interest in his case, coming to believe that Divisek might be a Czech Walter Mitty who had exaggerated or even invented his Soviet intelligence history.[52]

When Petrov defected ASIO learned at once that this was far from the case. In the 'G' series documents ASIO discovered a note with Divisek's code-name, a contact address for him in Australia and an accurate account of his war-time entanglement with the Soviet intelligence service.[53] According to both Petrov and his wife, Moscow Centre had been greatly interested in re-establishing contact with Divisek. On one occasion Pakhomov had gone to a hotel where Divisek was thought to be employed, but found he had moved on. On another occasion Petrov himself had been instructed by Moscow to go to a park in Sydney for a meeting which they claimed to have set up with 'Pechek'. Divisek, however, failed to show up. (At the Royal Commission Divisek claimed not to have received the letter of invitation to the rendezvous from Moscow Centre.) Petrov appears now to have abandoned his attempts to contact Divisek. Shortly before his defection Petrov had been asked by Moscow about the efforts that had been made over the past year to contact Divisek. There had been none. Petrov's successor, Kovalenok (an expert on the 'illegal' line, from the MVD's Fourth Directorate) who arrived in Australia fully five years after Divisek, had before him the task of making the initial liaison between 'Pechek' and the MVD in Australia.[54]

Inevitably the Divisek case threw a rather unflattering light on the efficiency of the MVD Residency in Australia and its guiding hand — Moscow Centre. Despite the brave words about the imperative need to establish a strong illegal apparatus in Australia, the actual efforts made by the MVD, both before and after June 1952, to re-establish relations with Divisek — a most obvious illegal asset, a trained intelligence officer who had been sent to Australia with the blessing of his wartime Soviet controller — had been desultory at best. Moscow's interest in the matter appeared to have been intermittent. Moreover so centralised was the ethos of the MVD that it did not even seem to have occurred to Petrov that he might assume the initiative himself in the Divisek case.

Only one really practical step for the creation of the illegal apparatus seems to have been taken by Petrov as a consequence of the instruction of June 1952. There existed in Soviet Consular files the record of an old Russian woman in Sydney — Kasanova — who longed to bequeath her small house in the suburb of Newtown to her son (who lived in the USSR) and who had begged the Soviet authorities to allow one of her Soviet relations to come to Australia to care for her in her old age. In April 1952, in his consular capacity, Petrov had become involved in this case. In the company of Dr Bialoguski and Kasanova's solicitor, Camille Dezarnaulds, Petrov had assured her that her wishes as expressed in her will would be respected. (Kasanova apparently feared that tenants of hers had designs upon her property.) In November 1952, Petrov was instructed by Moscow Centre to develop this case for an intelligence purpose. Under the guise of a concern for her health Petrov and Bialoguski paid Kasanova a second visit. Petrov but not Bialoguski knew that Moscow was considering sending a 'grandson' to live with her. The grandson would in fact be an intelligence officer who would work on the illegal line. It was Petrov's task to discover whether Kasanova had photographs of her real grandsons. He discovered that she did not. According to Petrov, he cabled this information to Moscow, advising that if Kasanova's son could be neutralised the scheme had every chance of success. Petrov claims to have heard nothing more of the matter.*[55]

A failed rendezvous with Divisek and a visit to the home of Kasanova almost exhausted Petrov's account of the steps he had taken in response to

---

* There were two further references in the Petrov documents which appeared at first of some relevance to the question of the establishment of the illegal apparatus. In the Moscow letters of 1952 there were references to the MVD's interest in the further utilisation of a strange Armenian immigrant named Daghian. As Daghian had on several occasions acted as sponsor for Russian émigrés in China ASIO suspected he might be involved in a scheme to implant illegals here. Petrov, however, denied that the MVD had had any success in recruiting Daghian to serious work. According to Petrov's evidence Moscow was also interested in making use of a pro-Soviet Australian dentist, Dr Clive Sandy — a peace delegate to Peking and Prague in 1952 — for importing illegal intelligence workers to Australia. Document 'G 18', a summary of one of the letters of 1953, named Dr Sandy as of value 'on illegal workers'. According to Petrov, however, he had not even approached Dr Sandy on this matter.

Moscow's stern exhortation to build an illegal apparatus in Australia as a question of highest priority. When Petrova was asked at the Royal Commission to write down the names of the persons who had been recruited by the MVD in her time into illegal work, she was able, after reflection, to think of only one name. This was a man who had supplied forms from the Department of Immigration and who had discussed with Petrov the purchase of a restaurant for conspiratorial purposes. As it turned out, the name of Petrova's candidate as the single recruit on the illegal line during the time of her husband's Residency was an agent on the payroll of Australian counter-intelligence — Dr Bialoguski![56]

As we have seen, Petrov arrived in Australia not on a general political intelligence mission for the KI but as head of the MGB. MGB agents were concerned with work amongst the Soviet colonies ('SK') and émigré communities ('EM') outside the Soviet Union. Because of the large post-war migration to Australia of communities from the Baltic States, by the early 1950s 'EM' work had assumed here a considerable importance. Before departing Moscow Petrov had received a general briefing in 'EM' operations from Lt.-General Utekhin, the Chief of the First Directorate of the MGB, and from the deputy head of its 'EM' department. Petrov was instructed to penetrate the anti-Soviet Baltic groups which operated in Australia and, if possible, to neutralise their activities by 'disruptive' tactics. Before his arrival here this field of activities was almost entirely undeveloped.

In Moscow Petrov was shown the file of a former Soviet agent, a Latvian named Andrei Fridenbergs (code-named 'Sigma') who now lived in Melbourne. Petrov learned that Fridenbergs, a lawyer, had in 1940-1 supplied the Soviet occupying forces with information about members of the Latvian Government. After the German occupation of his homeland the MVD files recorded that Fridenbergs had supplied information to their High Command but that he had, after his flight at the end of the war to Denmark, renewed his contact with Soviet intelligence through a Second Secretary at the Copenhagen Embassy, one Zilberberg. In 1949, without the knowledge of the MVD, Fridenbergs had moved with his family to Germany and shortly afterwards been selected as an immigrant to Australia. Moscow Centre had discovered his whereabouts only through the interception of a letter he had sent to a sister in Riga. It discovered that 'Sigma' was presently employed at a lady's college in Melbourne — Merton Hall — albeit as a janitor.

Three months after arriving in Australia, Petrov had journeyed to Melbourne and Merton Hall and discovered there Fridenbergs' Collingwood address. Although Petrov was prepared to use the threat of reprisals against his family as a means of reactivating 'Sigma' this proved unnecessary. Petrov claimed that when he had introduced himself, Fridenbergs replied: 'Good, we have found each other'. During Petrov's first two years in Australia the couple met on several occasions. Petrov would send Fridenbergs a postcard signed 'Dombarkas'. They met at 7 p.m., one day after the date which appeared on the postcard, at the foot of the ramp at Collingwood Railway Station and moved to a nearby park. According to Petrov, Fridenbergs had passed him information about the political activities of the Latvian community and had, on request, supplied him with the current addresses of two Latvian émigrés of particular interest to the MVD — a woman, Zosare, who was believed to have displayed 'terrorist tendencies' aimed at Stalin in a displaced persons camp in Germany; and a certain Colonel Krepins, an anti-Soviet military hero of the local community, who had fought the Bolsheviks during the war and was reputed to have stabbed with a paper knife a Soviet agent who had come to a Belgian camp to kidnap him. Petrov had paid Fridenbergs small amounts of money for his assistance. In mid-1953, he had passed 'Sigma' to his 'EM' successor, the Latvian MVD cadre, Plaitkais. In September 1953 an ASIO surveillance officer had actually followed Plaitkais to Collingwood before losing his trail.[57]

Andrei Fridenbergs appeared before the Royal Commission on Espionage in July 1954, strongly protesting his innocence. Several members of his own family had been, he said, deported to concentration camps by the Soviet oppressors of Latvia. The Soviets, he claimed, would rather have given him a bottle of poison than a bottle of brandy! Unfortunately for Fridenbergs both his attempts to provide alibis covering his meetings with the MVD in June and September 1953 collapsed under investigation.[58] Moreover, a member of the Latvian community, one Anton Strazdins, when called before the Commission, testified that Fridenbergs had indeed sought the addresses of Mrs Zosare and Colonel Krepins from him.[59] Finally, when Leo Carter of ASIO drove Petrov to Collingwood, Petrov directed him, without difficulty, to the Collingwood Station, to the park where he claimed they had met and to Fridenbergs' home. He was even able to recollect accurately the position of the furniture in Fridenbergs' front room.[60] There could not be the slightest doubt, as the Royal Commissioners reported, that Fridenbergs had indeed been a minor but useful agent for the MVD on the 'EM' line.

Beyond 'Sigma', however, Soviet 'EM' achievements during the Petrov Residency appeared — if Petrov was to be believed — far from spectacular. According to Petrov, 'Sigma' was his only 'EM' agent. Moscow Centre had cabled him in 1952 with the name of an Estonian woman in Australia, who was said to have been a Soviet agent in the past. Petrov traced this woman, via Fridenbergs, but then heard nothing more from Moscow about this case.[61] Petrov's stories, moreover, suggested that, at best, his successor Plaitkais had been marginally more successful than he. In his fifteen months in Australia Plaitkais had opened potentially fruitful 'EM' contacts with a Ukrainian in Brisbane, whose family had been voluntarily repatriated to the USSR, and with an ethnically Russian ballet teacher in Albury.[62] In addition, in 1953 Plaitkais had begun the cultivation of two fellow countrymen, to whom he had been introduced by a Latvian friend at the Russian Social Club, Alexander Klements. One of these was believed to be a former member of the Komsomol underground in Latvia. His brother, who was personally known to Petrov, had worked for the MVD in Latvia and Sweden and held a high post in the present Latvian Government. Although this cultivation was regarded by both Moscow and Canberra as extremely promising, it had, apparently, not yet — at the time of the Petrovs' defections — proceeded very far.[63] The other cultivation, of Gunars Ritenbergs, had proceeded a little farther. Plaitkais had met with Ritenbergs on a number of occasions, had enthused him with talk about Latvia under Soviet socialism and had persuaded him to deepen his links with the 'Anti-Bolshevik Bloc of Nations' movement in Australia. Unbeknown to Plaitkais, Ritenbergs was a self-styled penetration agent who was reporting his cultivation of Plaitkais to both ASIO and the leader of the anti-Soviet Latvian community in Sydney — Colonel Krepins.*[64]

There is one final story of the Petrov Residency that remains to be told. Late on the evening of June 10 — two months after her husband's defection — Petrova informed her ASIO minders that during the previous year the MVD in Canberra had arranged for the payment to the Communist Party of Australia of $25,000 in US currency. Petrov confirmed his wife's story at once. Inside ASIO the belated account of this substantial Soviet subsidy of the CPA appears to have had an electrifying effect.[65]

According to Petrov during 1952 he had learned of the Party's financial difficulties and had helped arrange for the General Secretary of the CPA, Lance Sharkey, to visit the USSR. Here Sharkey had taken a health cure in the Caucasus and attended the nineteenth Congress of the CPSU.†[66] Some time in the second half of 1953 — after Sharkey's return to Australia — a package containing $25,000 arrived by diplomatic bag. Petrov was instructed to take the money to Sydney and to pass it to Antonov who was, in turn, to pass it to Sharkey in the *Tribune* office. According to Petrov when the money arrived Sharkey was inter-state on Party business. When Sharkey returned to Sydney Antonov telephoned Petrov to inquire of his health. This was the signal for Petrov to come to Sydney with the money. He claims to have travelled by train for reasons of security. According to the evidence of both the

---

* Because of the danger his work might have posed to that part of his family remaining in Latvia, Ritenbergs was permitted to give his evidence at the Royal Commission under the name, Mr 'X'.

† Sharkey informed the delegates that compared with the 'brilliant upsurge' of Soviet agriculture, in Australia capitalism threatened the population with starvation. His speech concluded thus: 'May Comrade Stalin's genius illuminate the path to the victory of world peace and progress! (Loud and prolonged applause growing into an ovation. All rise.)'

Petrovs the first hand-over plan was aborted. On this day Petrov had visited Jean Ferguson on VOKS work. She had passed him a note warning that Antonov should not visit the *Tribune* office as a police raid was anticipated. According to Petrov's first statement on the Sharkey case, one week later Antonov telephoned again. This time Petrov claims to have flown to Sydney, to have proceeded at once to Antonov's flat and to have given him the money. That evening Antonov handed Sharkey the $25,000 in a Party safe house situated either in Manly or Bondi. The following morning, according to Petrov, he returned to Antonov's flat and was presented with the receipt for the transaction Moscow Centre had required from Sharkey.[67]

ASIO soon noticed certain obvious errors of fact in Petrov's first Sharkey statement. Petrov had claimed that the money came in $5 and $25 denominations. In the history of the US Treasury no $25 bill had ever been printed. Moreover the dates in Petrov's statement were vague and muddled. Petrov claimed to have received the money in September and to have spoken to Antonov about it in August. In December 1954 ASIO took Petrov through his Sharkey material for a second time. On this occasion, to sharpen his memory, they presented Petrov with a list of thirty-three dates produced from their surveillance records on Soviet diplomatic couriers and the movements of Petrov, Antonov and Sharkey. These records enabled Petrov to particularise his Sharkey story considerably. It was clear to him now that he had made his first (train) trip to Sydney on October 8 and his second trip by plane on October 16. On the second trip, it now appeared (as Petrova had actually dimly recalled) that Antonov had accompanied him from Canberra to Sydney. Petrov was now certain that the money had been handed over on the evening of October 16 and, according to Petrov's memory of what Antonov had told him, at 8 p.m.[68] Unhappily for ASIO the Sharkey confusion had not even now been fully overcome. ASIO's surveillance records revealed that on the evening of October 16, Lance Sharkey had been in attendance at a Party Central Committee meeting until somewhere between 9 and 10 p.m.[69]

The Sharkey case was heard before the Royal Commission over several days in February 1955. It was Ted Hill's finest hour. Hill was able to exploit with considerable effect his client's cast-iron (ASIO-endorsed) alibi for the mid-evening of October 16; the obvious errors in Petrov's first Sharkey statement; and, above all, the strange initial two month silence of the Petrovs over the $25,000 payment. To substantiate the myth of 'Moscow Gold' had been, he said, 'the age-old dream of the enemies of Communism'. Was not the slander revealed by Petrov's claim to have received his subsidy in non-existent $25 bills? Who could believe that Petrov would adopt security precautions on his first train trip to Sydney but abandon them altogether for his second? Why had the Petrovs held their silence over two months before advising ASIO of the Sharkey payment? Was it not clear that they had invented the whole ridiculous tale in order to justify the £5000 which had been invested in them? Was not ASIO itself implicated in this classic 'frame up', by supplying to

Petrov the evidence on which his case could be built?*[70]

Although there were perfectly good answers to Hill's questions by now the atmosphere surrounding the Commission was such that a significant part of the political nation was uninterested in hearing them. As Mr Justice Owen pointed out, it was in fact hardly surprising that the Petrovs' recall of detail in this matter was less than perfect.

> The questions [put to the Petrovs over the past nine months] have switched from events in Sweden ten years ago to events in the United Kingdom at some other period and events in Russia at some other period and then suddenly back to a payment to Sharkey in 1953, and what was the exact date and so on. It would seem a miracle to me if there were not some discrepancies.[71]

If the Petrovs had concocted their story surely they would have made it less elaborate and would not have introduced a potentially hostile participant — Jean Ferguson — into it? If ASIO had been interested in 'framing' Sharkey surely they would not have presented the evidence in support of his alibi of October 16 to the Commission? There was, finally, a perfectly plausible explanation of the delay in the Petrovs' Sharkey statement. Was it not likely that Party-sponsored accusations that they had stolen from the Embassy had 'goaded' the Petrovs into speaking about a matter they had at first planned to keep to themselves?[72] At least with Owen, Hill's suggestion that the Petrovs had concocted their story as the repayment on ASIO's investment in them weighed not at all. The £5000 'could be justified a hundredfold', he said, 'by the benefit which the free world has got from a great deal of information with which we are not concerned in this Commission'.[73]

The Commissioners were assisted in arriving at their conclusion on the Sharkey matter by evidence presented to them (in an affidavit) from the MVD defector in Tokyo, Yuri Rastvorov. Rastvorov claimed that he had twice been the channel for large subsidies — in the first instance, $30,000 and in the second $150,000 — from Moscow to the Communist Party of Japan.[74] In the end, however, they had to decide whether the Petrovs were concocting their story or Sharkey and the Party lying. No-one who had followed the Royal Commission evidence closely could have arrived at the conclusion either that the Communist Party's leaders felt under the slightest obligation to tell the truth or that Petrov was in the slightest prone to exaggerate the work of his Residency. (Indeed the impenetrable insouciance of Petrov as a witness, and the numberless occasions where he had claimed to have done nothing and not to have acted even upon Moscow Centre's direct instructions, were becoming

---

* On February 15, after this accusation, Richards requested counsel to represent ASIO before the Royal Commission. Tensions between ASIO and Windeyer were now high. 'I . . . informed Windeyer that I felt strongly that it was not made clear at the time that the evidence . . . which supports some of Hill's contentions was in fact supplied by ASIO — the very people against whom he alleges a "frame-up". I feel most strongly about this latest attack, which is quite baseless and was not challenged in the least by anyone.'

notorious in the land.)*[75] Although the Royal Commissioners were never convinced that the time or date that Petrov had settled upon for the Sharkey payment were correct, they concluded that, on the balance of probabilities, the Petrovs' story about the $25,000 payment to the CPA was true.[76]

During their investigations into the Petrov Residency the Royal Commission and ASIO had gained a great deal of valuable information about the methods and ambitions of the MVD. On the other hand, its achievements in Australia after 1951 had come to appear far from impressive. According to Petrov's testimony his Residency had failed in its efforts to penetrate the Department of External Affairs or ASIO, had failed to establish an illegal apparatus in Australia and had failed to derive any really valuable information even from long established supporters like Rex Chiplin or Jack Hughes or, in a different field, Andrei Fridenbergs. Although there existed in Australia contacts of considerable potential value to the MVD — most importantly Mme Ollier in the French Embassy and Fergan O'Sullivan in the Office of the Leader of the Opposition — much work remained to be done by Petrov's successor, Kovalenok, if their potentiality was to be realised. Inevitably the apparent dismal failure of the Petrov Residency raised further questions. Was Petrov a genuine no-hoper? Alternatively, might have concealed from his ASIO debriefers some of the most important details of his work in Australia?

There were certainly grounds for suspecting at least some concealment. As we have seen, two months had elapsed before the Petrovs had decided to tell ASIO about the $25,000 payment to CPA. It appeared, moreover, at least likely that Petrov had misled ASIO about his relationship with Bert Chandler. On several occasions Petrov had denied absolutely making requests to Dr Bialoguski for information of which ASIO had firm evidence.[77] On several others he denied all knowledge of people who ASIO knew he had known. According to Petrov he had never met a certain pro-Soviet immigrant, Jan de Lager. ASIO had evidence that he had stayed overnight at his home.[78] Petrov told ASIO he had never encountered Bruce Yuill.† In fact an inform- ant had told ASIO that in late 1953 he had been introduced to Petrov by Yuill.[79]

---

* Dr Evatt reenacted in the Parliament the following item from a Canberra University College revue.

Counsel: Can you tell us about a man called Ivanawfulkoff?
Petrov: Yes I know Ivanawfulkoff. He was a spy. He was a member of the M.K.V.D. He wrote me a letter from Moscow. He asked me to make contact with Mr Smith.
Counsel: Did you make contact with Mr Smith?
Petrov: No, I was too busy. (Etc.)

† Yuill was a left activist employed by the Department of Immigration in Canberra. In part, ASIO was interested in him because of his close friendship with Fergan O'Sullivan (see below) and, in part, because he had been mentioned in one of the Moscow letters for 1952.

The interrogation of Petrov appeared to the ASIO officers involved in it as a game of great subtlety, whose object was to draw from their subject information which he had never intended to divulge. According to one officer the general view inside ASIO was that Petrov 'purposely withheld information which was of security value. . . . The extraction of information resolved into a tactical battle'. According to the same officer one tactic in this battle was to exploit Petrov's lack of general conversation to lead him into inadvertent disclosures about his intelligence past.[80] Another pointed to the need 'to appeal to the defector's loyalties . . . hopes and fears' and 'to manipulate his weaknesses' in order 'to overcome any reluctance to impart intelligence'. While firmness 'in the face of . . . whims, moods, prevarications, reticence or deception' was necessary, direct accusations of bad faith were counterproductive. 'The art of the interrogator', he concluded, 'must be to make the defector want to tell him'.[81]

One line of explanation offered inside ASIO for Petrov's reticence to divulge intelligence concerned the emotional turmoil he was thought to experience when confronting the fact that he had betrayed the MVD and his former comrades. In addition, ASIO came to believe that, notwithstanding the written guarantee of immunity from prosecution which had been granted him, Petrov feared he would be punished if it was revealed that he had harmed Australia's security. Petrov understood only one political culture deeply. From his Soviet perspective it must have seemed foolhardy in the extreme to gamble his future on a piece of paper. From the moment of his defection Petrov strove to convince his new protectors that 'he had never harmed Australia in any way'.[82] Six weeks after his defection Petrov wrote out the following statement for ASIO.

> I did not desire to be an intelligence operator in other countries. . . . Always I wanted and desired to lead a quiet life. I did not bring any harm upon the Australian Government. I only brought advantage. . . .[83]

Nevertheless — despite his habit of concealment — there are very good grounds for believing that Petrov's incompetence as an intelligence officer was not feigned but genuine. Before arriving in Australia Petrov had spent the overwhelming bulk of his MVD career behind a desk in Moscow. Even in Sweden he had been concerned only with cyphers and surveillance over the Soviet Colony. His promotion in 1952 to the temporary Residency in Australia confronted him with a kind of work — the cultivation and recruitment of foreigners — for which he seemed to have little liking and even less talent. In mid-1952, Moscow Centre had chastised the Canberra Residency harshly. Intelligence work was at a standstill; nothing had been achieved. The predominant tone of the 1952 Moscow letters was irritable schoolmasterliness. The Residency had failed here to utilise its agents effectively; it had failed there to follow proper procedures; its letters home were thoroughly unsatisfactory.[84] When Kislitsyn had arrived in Australia in 1952 he had told Petrov that his reputation at Moscow Centre had fallen very low.[85] By 1953, as Petrov told the Royal Commissioners, he was tired of his work and wanted to be sent home.[86]

In reality, whisky and women appeared to have absorbed the interests and energies of Petrov in Australia far more deeply than did intelligence work. The overwhelming impression he left upon Australians who observed him closely was that of an exceedingly simple man, of peasant stock, who had been promoted — as a consequence of the 'Yezhovshchina' — far above his capabilities. Petrov was well suited to obeying the commands of his superiors in Moscow. He proved to be thoroughly ill-suited to the job he was given in Canberra, which required him to display some initiative and to shoulder some responsibility. After fifteen months of listening to Petrov one ASIO officer admitted to feeling that 'the Soviet intelligence service . . . was not as efficient nor as highly organised as I personally had believed'.[87] His superior, Ron Richards, put the point even more bluntly.

> The Petrov case had demonstrated that since 1950, in Australia at any rate, the skill, efficiency and effectiveness of the MVD as an espionage organization was generally overrated by Security Service officers.[88]

14

THE PETROVS AND WESTERN COUNTER-INTELLIGENCE

When the Petrovs defected there could have been little doubt within the cloistered world of western counter-intelligence that an event of major significance had occurred. Between Gouzenko in 1945 and Rastvorov, the Petrovs and Khokhlov in 1954 there had been no Soviet intelligence defections. Petrov was, moreover, the most senior intelligence officer to defect since 1937 when General Krivitsky — the head of Soviet espionage in Western Europe — came over.[1] Undoubtedly the Petrovs' long and varied service — both had worked inside Soviet intelligence for twenty years — made them of the highest interest to western counter-intelligence. Between them they had experience of cyphers, cryptanalysis, 'SK' and 'EM' work abroad and the 'legal' intelligence apparatuses in Sweden and Australia. From the first moment western counter-intelligence services were most keen to discover what the Petrovs could contribute to their knowledge of the methods, personnel, codes and structure of Soviet foreign intelligence. For ASIO — the counter-intelligence service of a minor power less than five years old — the Petrov defections were a considerable baptismal *coup*.

Concerning the matters of interest to western counter-intelligence ASIO did not debrief the Petrovs alone. From its foundations it had enjoyed a special, perhaps filial, relationship with the service upon which it had been modelled — M15. During the early 1950s an M15 liaison team had been permanently attached to ASIO's headquarters in Melbourne. When Petrov and then his wife defected it appeared the most natural thing in the world to ASIO that M15 should play a key role in the many months of the interrogation that were about to commence. M15 clearly had the linguistic and technical expertise that would be required in some of the most sensitive or complex areas of the interrogations — for example concerning codes and cryptanalysis. Although it was eventually to be cruelly disappointed, at this stage of its history ASIO's trust in the British counter-intelligence services appears to have been near-perfect.[2]

Notwithstanding some later mythology about direct American involvement in the Petrov defections,[3] in reality the relations between ASIO and the counter-intelligence services of the United States — the FBI and the CIA — were considerably less close in 1954 then those between ASIO and the British. Shortly after the Petrov defection, for example, the Secretary of External Affairs, Arthur Tange, sent the following message to his Minister, Richard Casey.

> We are telling governments other than the United Kingdom nothing about the Petrov affair either through diplomatic or security service channels. Spry himself is opposed to giving Americans anything for nothing.[4]

This telegram is an indication of initial attitudes rather than of any settled policy. During the course of the Petrov debriefings the Americans (and many other friendly services) were sent considerable intelligence material which they valued extremely highly. The grand master of American counter-intelligence, James Angleton, was of the opinion that amongst post-war Soviet defections only Anatoli Golitsin (his special favourite) was of greater value to the West that the Petrovs.[5] On the other hand, throughout the interrogations of the Petrovs the Americans posed their questions and received their information indirectly, through British channels.*[6] The extremely close relationship between ASIO and the CIA was established only towards the end of the Petrov Affair. It arose in part as a consequence of ASIO's enhanced reputation because of its recent success and even more as a consequence of the high personal regard in which Brigadier Spry came to be held by the Director of the CIA, Allen Dulles, after the two had met in the United States in mid-1955.†[7]

In the non-Australian aspects of the Petrovs' interrogations the primary burden appears to have fallen on a young linguist of scholarly persuasion from MI5. This man, who must have spent hundreds of hours with the Petrovs, soon won their trust. Within weeks of his arrival in Australia he had begun to convert his conversations with them into intelligence analyses of outstanding quality. His first papers dealt with the professional biographies of both Petrovs appended to which was an extremely valuable chart, 'Guide to

---

* The only Western service, apart from the British, to debrief the Petrovs directly was the Swedish.

† At Sir Charles Spry's retirement the Deputy Director of the CIA sent the following tribute: 'The relationship between the CIA and ASIO started as a very personal one. The real substantive relationship started with Sir Charles' visit in 1955 ... Since Sir Charles' first visit, the relationships with ASIO have continued to become closer and closer until today we have no secrets, regardless of classification or sensitivity, that are not made available to ASIO if it is pertinent to Australia's internal security ... I feel, as does the Director, a type of mutual trust in dealing with ASIO that is exceeded by no other service in the world today.'

Organisational Changes in the Soviet State Security Service', which outlined with great clarity the complex administrative restructurings through which the Soviet service — and the Petrovs — had passed between the formation of the NKVD in 1934 and the KGB in 1954.[8] It was in their descriptions of the latter phase of this administrative experimentation that the Petrovs' substantive contribution to the understanding of western counter-intelligence began.

Between their postings to Stockholm and Canberra the Petrovs had worked in the newly formed 'Komitet Informatsyi' (KI). They were in fact the first reliable witnesses in the West to this particular chapter in the history of Soviet intelligence. Their discussions on the KI formed the basis of a long M15-ASIO paper which was completed in November 1954. As this paper explained, the formation of the KI had represented an attempt — unique in the Soviet intelligence tradition — to separate the domestic security service from the foreign political intelligence branch and to combine in a single service the foreign political with the military intelligence bureaux. The experiment was an almost immediate failure. In mid-1948 the Army restored control over its own intelligence branch when the GRU was allowed to withdraw from the KI. In late 1948 the political branches of the KI concerned with work amongst Soviet colonies abroad ('SK'), with the penetration of emigre communities ('EM') and with intelligence activities in the 'Peoples' Democracies' — were transferred from the KI to the Ministry for State Security (MGB).* Apparently domestic and foreign security work were far too deeply and intimately connected in the Soviet system for the division into separate domestic and foreign compartments to be feasible. In December 1951 the KI experiment was abandoned altogether. Its staff were transferred straight into the First, now the Chief, Directorate of the MGB.

The Petrovs provided their M15-ASIO debriefers with an extremely detailed and fascinating inside account of the structure and function of the KI. They estimated that at its peak some two thousand intelligence cadres had worked for it in the former buildings of the Comintern (in outer Moscow, near the Agricultural Fair) where it had been established. It had been divided into a number of major Directorates and several smaller specialist Departments. The First Directorate was concerned with the 'legal' intelligence gathering networks in the British Empire and North and South America; the Second Directorate with Europe; and the Third with the Near and Far East. The Fourth Directorate, which was itself subdivided into geographic departments, was responsible for the establishment of 'illegal' networks throughout the world; the Fifth with the evaluation of intelligence and its distribution

---

* This particular reorganisation had, as we have seen, personal consequences for the Petrov couple. After returning from Moscow both had worked inside the KI on 'SK' desks. When the 'SK' work was transferred to the MGB Petrov went with his job to the Lubyanka while Petrova transferred to the Scandinavian desk of the KI.

to relevant Party and Ministerial sections. Beyond the Directorates, they outlined the work of specialist departments for wireless communications, cyphers, technical aids and so on. They also revealed the existence of some departments whose work was less well known. One such was the Delegation Department. It was responsible for penetrating foreign delegations visiting the Soviet Union to recruit amongst them, and with placing cadres of its own — as 'talent spotters and agent recruiters' — amongst Soviet delegations travelling abroad. Another was the 'Disinformation' Department, a department which has been of increasing interest in recent years to students of Soviet 'Active Measures'.[9] According to the Petrovs, in the early 1950s the 'Disinformation' Department was headed by Andrey Graur and had a staff of five.

> [It] was responsible (they said) for spreading misleading information abroad: i.e. deception, or else getting published in the Western press items of information embarrassing to the West or profitable to Soviet policy[10]

The Petrovs were, of course, also able to outline on the basis of personal experience (if not success) the *modus operandi* of the 'legal' apparatus of the Soviet intelligence service in western countries. The outcome of the interrogations of the Petrovs in this area was a paper entitled 'Soviet State Security Service: Foreign Intelligence Operational Techniques'. The principal aim of the 'legal' apparatus was, according to them, the gathering of secret material on 'the foreign policies, secret agreements and negotiations of foreign powers'. Their prime target was the Foreign Ministry of the host country, although secondary targets included the security service, other Government departments, political parties, trade unions and scientific establishments. Their prime means for the acquisition of this material was the recruitment of agents in the host country, whose 'degree of access' to the information required was the test of their usefulness. Most desirable as agents were 'executive officers, research workers, typists, archivists and cypher clerks' in target organisations. Before 1947, according to Petrovs, the agents were frequently recruited in association with a specially selected Communist Party member of the host country, usually the Party's 'Secretary, President or Control Commission representative', who would help Soviet intelligence recruit networks of agents. After 1947, however, direct contacts of this kind between the MVD and the Party were discouraged.

According to the Petrovs the MVD's most favoured kind of agent was the one who was recruited through ideological sympathy with the Soviet Union. The second most favoured kind were those whose motives were mercenary. In the process of recruitment weaknesses in the potential agents (who might need to be studied for years) — like fondness for drink or money difficulties — were, whenever possible, to be exploited. However, while blackmail might be used, especially after the recruit had been drawn into the MVD net, the Petrovs made it clear that Moscow regarded blackmail as an unreliable foundation for the cadre-agent relationship. On the other hand the Petrovs were aware that in Moscow in particular the MVD did try and photograph potential recruits in sexually compromising situations.*[11]

The Petrovs provided Western counter-intelligence with a perhaps unparalleled portrait of the working of the 'legal' intelligence apparatus. They described to their debriefers the extremely complex relations that existed within the Soviet Embassies between the State Security and Foreign Ministry arms; the intricate measures adopted to disguise the identity of the security personnel inside the Embassy from their non-security colleagues; and the methods employed in Moscow to recruit intelligence 'collaborators' from the Embassy staff. The Petrovs also outlined a great deal about the actual operational techniques within the Embassy of the MVD Residency — the physical establishment of the secret intelligence quarters beyond the cypher room; the roles of safes, incinerators, radio sets and photographic equipment in their work; the MVD's de-bugging techniques and its attitude to the use of the telephone; their filing and financial systems.[12] The value of all of this was undoubtedly in the fineness of the detail. Petrov, for example, told his debriefers about the patterns on the ties and the stitching on the shoes which were routinely assigned to MVD cadre workers in Moscow.[13]

The Petrovs also gave an extremely detailed account of what one might call the mechanics of the cadre-agent relationship — of the methods adopted by cadres to shake off counter-intelligence surveillance; of the preferred localities for clandestine meetings with agents; of the requirement that all agents should have a 'cover-story' ready if called upon to explain their meetings with a member of the Soviet Embassy. By no means, however, according to the Petrovs, was the cadre-agent relationship a merely mechanical one. Moscow Centre evidently required in the management of relations of its cadre with their agents delicacy and even psychological depth. As Petrova explained any explicit mention of spying was to be avoided, even with a longstanding recruit. 'The realization that he is implicated in Soviet espionage may lead to a revulsion of feeling with disastrous consequences.'

> The ideological agent (they argued) acts from his sense of dedication to a mutual political faith and bares his soul to his Soviet controller. . . . In his meetings with agents, the State Security cadre worker is taught not to limit himself to briefing and de-briefing, but to study the agent with the object of understanding and encouraging his whole personality in the service of the Soviet. The agent-master must be a man who knows life.[14]

In the latter half of their careers the Petrovs had worked extensively within the 'legal' intelligence apparatus. Although neither had direct experience of the 'illegal' apparatus — that is to say that part of the Soviet intelligence

---

* Petrov appears to have been deeply taken with the case of a Japanese diplomat who had been amused rather than mortified when shown a set of such photographs. He drew from this the moral that the MVD must always be sensitive to the vagaries of national culture.

system which operated abroad without diplomatic or quasi-diplomatic cover
— discussions with them led to the production of another useful, if more
general, paper entitled 'Soviet "Illegal" Intelligence Operations'. The
Petrovs made clear that the 'illegal' apparatus was not an alternative to the
'legal' apparatus but a parallel structure. Although the 'legal' Resident might
help initially to establish the 'illegal' structure — by infiltrating intelligence
officers into the target country in the guise of migrants — ideally the 'legal'
and 'illegal' networks should operate quite independently from one another.
Communications between the 'illegal' Resident and Moscow Centre might
be effected through the wireless or by coded correspondence or via couriers
(sailors or businessmen). The 'illegal' networks were regarded as especially
important at time of war, when agents from the 'legal' network could be
transferred to them and when the 'illegal' networks might be the only espionage assets available to the Soviet Union. It was hoped in Moscow that 'illegal' cadres would assimilate deeply into the life of the target country and
become financially independent, by establishing small businesses of their
own. In the Petrovs' last time in Moscow the establishment of the 'illegal'
networks had been (as we have seen) the responsibility of the Fourth Directorate of the KI, which was under the direction of General Korotkov. They
knew that Petrov's successor in Australia — Kovalenok — was a Fourth
Directorate man.[15] Within a few years of the Petrovs' description of the
'illegal' apparatus Western counter-intelligence was to uncover highly significant 'illegal' networks in the United States (under Colonel Abel) and in the
United Kingdom (under the Kroger couple). The circumstances of these cases
followed precisely the general outline of the 'illegal' intelligence system which
the Petrovs had given to their MI5-ASIO debriefers.[16]

   During the course of their debriefings the Petrovs were, of course, asked
for information about some of the most famous and intriguing cases in which
the Soviet intelligence service had been implicated. Neither knew anything
about the case of the Soviet State Security officer in Istanbul — Volkov —
who had somewhat mysteriously been bundled back to Moscow in 1945 after
offering his services to the British,*[17] or of the recent defection of the head
of West German intelligence — Dr Otto John.[18] Nor did they know anything
about the fate of the Swedish diplomat, Raoul Wallenberg, or of the American Communist family, the Fields, who had been arrested by Soviet forces
in Eastern Europe.[19] On the other hand, as we shall see, Petrov had learned
a great deal about the circumstances surrounding the disappearance of the
British diplomats — Burgess and Maclean.

---

* Eventually it was to be discovered that Volkov was betrayed by the MI6 officer who had taken
  over this case, Kim Philby. While I have seen no evidence that the Petrovs were interrogated
  about Philby — who was at the time under great suspicion — it would be remarkable if they
  were not.

Petrov was aware of the work of the Soviet security service's overseas assassination unit, which was under the control of Colonel Serebryansky, and, not surprisingly, obsessed by fear of it. He told his debriefers, in considerable detail, the story of a cypher clerk of his acquaintance — one Bokov — who had been despatched to Teheran in 1941 on a mission to murder the Soviet Ambassador there. Bokov, a brawny fellow, accomplished his task with an iron bar, rolled the Ambassador's body in a carpet and buried it outside the town. For his labours he was decorated with the Red Star.[20] Petrov had also seen with his own eyes the NKVD file on Leon Trotsky. According to him the letters and telegrams in this file showed that NKVD Headquarters had used its New York Residency to fulfil the planned assassination. Within the file there were details of the NKVD agents who had penetrated Trotsky's inmost circle and photographs of his wife, friends and even his dog, taken inside his Mexican 'fortress-villa'. The hero of October, Petrov read, was silenced forever by a blow with the broad and not the pointed end of an ice-axe.[21] Apparently not only Petrov was interested in the fine detail of what the MVD called 'wet affairs'.

Both the Petrovs had spent the better part of their careers working with the Soviet intelligence service's cyphers. In addition, Petrova in the 1930s had worked in the cryptanalytic section of the 'Spets-Otdel', that is to say the section concerned with the breaking of non-Soviet diplomatic and intelligence codes. Between them the Petrov couple had, therefore, accumulated a vast practical knowledge of Soviet cyphers and code-breaking techniques.

Shortly after their defections the Petrovs were shown a series of coded cables (in five figure series) that had passed, via the telegraph office, between Moscow and Canberra, in the hope that they might be able to decipher them. This was over-optimistic. The Petrovs studied these cables carefully but eventually confessed that without their block-notes decipherment was impossible.[22] Short of actual decipherment, however, it is clear that they were able to provide a great deal of very valuable information on Soviet codes and cryptanalytic practices to Western counter-intelligence experts in this field. The released archival material on this aspect of interrogations is, of course, far from complete but what has been released suggests that the Petrovs outlined the basic principles of Soviet intelligence codes, the periods when the code books were changed and the various means by which the coded and non-coded messages were sent between Moscow and its foreign Residences.[23] The released material also indicates that Petrov prepared for Western counter-intelligence a history of the Soviet cypher section,[24] while Petrova outlined for it the methods and success stories of Soviet cryptanalysis in the 1930s. The cryptanalytic debriefings with Petrova were conducted in extreme secrecy, in part because she feared that knowledge in Moscow of what she was divulging here might rebound on her family and in part because 'it would be of distinct intelligence advantage to conceal from the Russians the fact and extent of Mrs Petrov's disclosures to us concerning Soviet cypher and cryptanalytic practices'.[25]

It is outside the knowledge (and technical capacity) of this author to estimate the precise importance of the Petrovs' contributions to Western cryptanalysis. There are however certain facts which suggest it was not insignificant. According to Sir Charles Spry British and American experts in this field were quite satisfied with the cypher information they derived from the Petrovs.[26] Moreover, in his authoritative study of code-breaking, the American expert, David Kahn, draws heavily on the material supplied by the Petrovs in his long chapter on Soviet cryptanalysis.[27]

The second area where the Petrovs inflicted real and immediate damage upon the Soviet State Security service was in the identification of its cadre workers. The contribution of the Petrovs here was probably even more important than in the area of codes. During their interrogations the Petrovs were able to name virtually the entire command structure of the KI and to outline each individual's area of special responsibility within it. The paper on the KI named its operational controllers — Fedotov and Savchenko; the military and naval intelligence chiefs — General Ilichev and Kuznetsov and Admiral Rodionov; and the heads of almost every Directorate and specialist department.[28] They were able to outline the State Security connections of several Soviet Ambassadors who had served in sensitive posts abroad — like Zarubin, who had been Ambassador in London,[29] and Panyushkin, in Washington.[30] On a more humdrum level the Petrovs selected from lists of diplomatic couriers those who had State Security backgrounds.[31] Most importantly of all, from lists of names and photographs of hundreds of Soviet officials who had served abroad, the Petrovs identified those who were members of the MVD. From Britain alone fifteen hundred officials and their dependents were brought to their attention.[32] Whenever possible the Petrovs supplied their debriefers with intelligence biographies of their former colleagues — listing their former postings, their characters and their special talents.[33] By this painstaking method upwards of five hundred Soviet intelligence officers were identified and their names, photographs and intelligence histories circulated within the Western counter-intelligence world.[34] It was in such debriefing sessions and in such unglamorous circumstances that the Petrovs made their most solid contribution to Western security. If the details of their work had not been sent to Moscow Centre by a Soviet double agent working inside British counter-intelligence — in circumstances that we shall presently outline — their contribution would have been even greater.

No one within the world of Western counter-intelligence — neither practitioners like James Angleton nor authorities like Chapman Pincher — appears to doubt that the Petrov defections were a matter of moment in the ongoing war between the Soviet and Western intelligence services. Only in Australia — in part because of the total politicisation of the Petrov Affair and in part, perhaps, because of a native scepticism and a deeply ingrained belief that nothing of international significance could ever happen here — has the genuine importance of the Petrovs been persistently misunderstood.

During the Cold War the British intelligence services (M15 and M16) and the Foreign Office were honeycombed with officers now known to be, or strongly suspected of being, Soviet double agents. In one way or another six of these men were to become implicated in the Petrov Affair. Of these six, two (Burgess and Maclean) had already by 1954 defected to Moscow; one (Philby) was to defect in the future; one (Blake) was to be arrested and then escape to Moscow; and two others (Ellis and Hollis) to come, in the fullness of time, to be regarded by some of their colleagues with the darkest suspicions.

It is the view of the British intelligence authority, Chapman Pincher, that at the time of the Petrov defections the head of the Soviet counter-intelligence section of M15 — Roger Hollis — was a double agent, who was playing in M15 the role that it is now known Philby had played before 1951 in M16. As part of his indictment of Hollis, Pincher in *Too Secret Too Long* suggests that before the Petrov defection someone had sent a message to Moscow Centre warning of its likelihood; that the someone was almost certainly Hollis; and that as a result of this tip-off the Soviet diplomatic couriers — Zharkov and Karpinsky — were rushed to Australia to bring Petrov home. According to Pincher the couriers failed 'only by a few hours' to seize Petrov.[35]

There is actually not one part of Pincher's analysis of the role of Hollis in the Petrov defection that can withstand close scrutiny. As we have seen the Soviet diplomatic couriers who Pincher believes were sent to Australia to seize Petrov actually left Rome airport on April 11, eight days after Petrov had defected and five days after the Soviet Embassy in Canberra had become alarmed about his disappearance.[36] Clearly their mission was to return Petrova and Kislitsyn to Moscow after Petrov's defection. They missed Petrov not by 'a few hours' but by some twelve days. There is, moreover, no credible evidence that Moscow Centre received any tip-off about the imminent defection of Petrov*[37] and, indeed, strong reason to believe that it did not. If Moscow had known of Petrov's plans in advance of his defection it is hardly conceivable that it would have permitted its Ambassador to conduct a security raid on Petrov's consular safe on April 1 and thus to warn him of some coming danger. Moreover, according to Sir Charles Spry, Roger Hollis, as head of M15's Soviet counter-intelligence section, would almost certainly have known about the progress of Operation Cabin 12 through the liaison

---

* As evidence for this proposition Pincher cites a letter from the office of Sir William McMahon and a speech he made to the Australian Parliament on the matter. Unfortunately Pincher does not quote from the letter or indicate the date of the speech. Nor does he explain why he thinks McMahon had special sources of information unavailable, for example, to the Director-General of ASIO at the time.

team in Melbourne during the weeks of planning before Petrov's final defection.[38] If so, Hollis had overwhelmingly reason — if he was indeed a Soviet double agent — to send a warning signal to Moscow about Petrov (what are intelligence double agents for if not to prevent the defections of their opposite numbers?) and ample opportunity to do so without fear of discovery. If Petrov had been bundled back to Moscow ASIO's suspicions would have naturally turned not to M15 but towards Petrov's Australian contacts, beginning no doubt with the garrulous Dr Bialoguski. On balance, if anything, the Petrov defection provides evidence *against* the proposition that Hollis was a Soviet double agent.

Pincher appears to believe that Roger Hollis most likely received his advance notice about Petrov through an enigmatic figure at the centre of the Anglo-Australian intelligence world — Captain C.H. (Dick) Ellis* — a senior figure in M16 who in the early 1950s had been seconded to his native Australia to help establish here the foreign intelligence service modelled upon M16, that is ASIS. According to Pincher, Ellis had learned about the possibility of the Petrov defection in early 1954, many weeks in advance of its actuality, and had returned to Britain suddenly and unexpectedly, presumably in time to pass his information to Hollis. It is, however, Sir Charles Spry's distinct memory that it was in the week *following* the Petrov defection that Ellis arrived in ASIO's office (with the head of ASIS, Alfred Brookes, in tow) with an offer to assume responsibility for the interrogation of Petrov. On the grounds that there was to be an open Royal Commission and that, at the time, ASIS's existence had not even been revealed to the Australian public, Spry politely declined the Ellis-ASIS takeover bid. Only now did Ellis, according to Sir Charles Spry, depart Antipodean shores.[39]

Dick Ellis sailed to Britain via Genoa. Almost at once upon his return — on this point Pincher and Spry concur — Ellis arranged to meet his old colleague from M16, Kim Philby, at Philby's London Club — the Travellers'. At the time Philby was under intense suspicion and surveillance. According to intelligence records to which Pincher has been privy, after his conversation with Ellis, Philby (whose telephone was being tapped) called his current mistress with the news that 'the clouds are parting'.[40] Years later in his autobiography, after his defection to Moscow, Philby wrote thus of the renewal of contact at this time with the Soviet intelligence service.

> I received, through the most ingenious of routes, a message from my Soviet friends, conjuring me to be of good cheer and presaging an early resumption of relations.

---

* Dick Ellis was an Australian who worked for Britain's Secret Intelligence Service (MI6) in Europe in the 1920s and 1930s. Ellis had served in the British Army in the anti-Bolshevik campaigns after 1917 and had married a White Russian who was well connected in anti-Bolshevik circles in inter-war Paris. In the 1940s Ellis worked with William Stephenson ('Intrepid') in a wartime British intelligence outfit in the United States — British Security Co-ordination — before returning to a senior posting in MI6.

It changed drastically the whole complexion of the case. I was no longer alone. It was therefore with refreshed spirit that I watched the next storm gather. It began with the defection of Petrov in Australia and some not very revealing remarks he made about Burgess and Maclean.[41]

The chapter in which these remarks occur is entitled 'The Clouds Part'. It seems likely at least, as Pincher surmises, that Dick Ellis was 'the ingenious route' through which contact between Philby and Moscow Centre had been reestablished and Philby's spirits prepared for the coming storms. When much later Dick Ellis finally fell under the darkest suspicions of his colleagues, who came to believe him to have been first a German* and then later (most likely after blackmail) a Soviet double agent, one of the most telling pieces of evidence against him on the second count were the two false alibis (concerning women he claimed to have intended to marry) he provided in explanation of his hasty return to Britain from Australia following the defection of Petrov.[42]

Three days after his defection Petrov, in the safety of the ASIO interrogation room, spoke to Ron Richards about two quite different Britons involved in Soviet espionage — the 'missing diplomats', Guy Burgess and Donald Maclean.

> They handed copies of documents to London (he told Richards) before they left. For three or four years they were MVD agents. When they were students they were recruited with a special aim to be targetted into the Foreign Office, and they began to take Foreign Office documents for three or four years.... Before they left, the Security people became suspicious and started to put them under investigation, and Burgess and Maclean became alarmed, and it was decided to ask them to go to the Soviet. They went by plane first to Prague, then to the Soviet.[43]

According to Petrov he had learned about this case from his offsider and good friend, Philip Kislitsyn. Kislitsyn, it transpired, had been in London between 1945 and 1948 and had been responsible for translating and despatching to Moscow by cable or diplomatic bag the 'briefcases full' of Foreign Office documents Burgess had passed to his MVD contact for photographing in the Soviet Embassy. While Kislitsyn himself had never met either of the British double agents in London, he had seen Burgess's controller return to the Embassy with muddied clothes after his rendezvous with him. After he had returned to Moscow in 1948 Kislitsyn, according to Petrov, had maintained close contact with this case. He was put in charge of the desk in the KI which was responsible for translating and disseminating their material. He had also

---

* The major evidence of Ellis's betrayal in relation to Nazi Germany concerned the discovery of a leakage of information to Berlin that the telephone line between the German Embassy in London and the Wilhelmstrasse was insecure. When interrogated Ellis denied all knowledge of, or involvement in, this particular operation. However, when Post Office records were checked the name of Captain C.H. Ellis was at the head of the list of those who had been involved in the translation of these telephone intercepts for British intelligence.

been involved — under Colonels Raina and Gorsky — in planning their escape. When Burgess and Maclean arrived in Moscow Kislitsyn had visited them frequently. According to him the pair had settled in Kuibyshev and were acting as advisers to the Soviet Government on 'Anglo-American' policy.[44] There can be no doubt that it was primarily because of Kislitsyn's intimate knowledge of this case — and because he had told Petrov that other Britons besides Burgess and Maclean were also spying for the Soviets — that M15 and ASIO had, as we have seen, decided to tempt Kislitsyn to defect with the offer of a considerable sum (far more than the £5000 given to Petrov) when he passed through Singapore on his return journey to the Soviet Union.[45]

Unfortunately for M15 and ASIO Petrov did not know the identity of the person British newspapers called 'the Third Man' (that is the person inside British counter-intelligence who had warned Burgess and Maclean of the investigation into them) or of the identities of the 'other people in England' who Kislitsyn had told him were 'engaged in the same operations'. Accordingly, from the first moment, Petrov's information about Burgess and Maclean was of far greater significance from the political than the counter-intelligence point of view. Within Britain — in the press, the parliament and most likely also the counter-intelligence services — there were many people who were far from happy with the unwillingness of the Cabinet and Foreign Office to outline to the public the facts of this episode. (So tight-lipped was the Government that it took fully twelve months for the Foreign Office to announce the suspension of Burgess and Maclean from their posts, on the grounds of unexplained absence from duty!)[46] It was clear that if Petrov's information about Burgess and Maclean was ever to become public the British Government's stubborn silence on the matter might at long last be broken.

Petrov's Burgess and Maclean information actually broke in Britain not once but twice. Four weeks after his defection — on April 28 1954 — the London newspapers carried the story that Petrov had information as to the whereabouts of the missing diplomats. Although it cannot be known for certain precisely how this information leaked, it seems most likely that it came from officers inside M15 who were tired of their Government's cover-up. If so, in the short-term at least, their plans misfired. While Petrov himself was at once offered the £1000 ($12,000) reward offered by the *Daily Express* for locating Burgess and Maclean[47] (the ASIO records do not reveal whether he wanted to accept) the Foreign Office stonewalled once more. A statement was released from Whitehall casting doubt upon the authenticity of Petrov's 'hearsay' information. At the same time, behind the closed doors of Australia House, an official of the Foreign Office — Liesching — explained with considerable frankness the deep anxieties of his chiefs on the Petrov/Burgess-Maclean front.

Foreign Office in effort to strangle further speculation on this very sensitive matter (the Australian High Commission informed Canberra) said yesterday that from information so far received it was clear that Petrov had no first hand knowledge of the matter and that any 'hearsay evidence that Petrov may produce must be treated with some reserve'. Liesching mentioned that in the light of this resurrection of the Burgess-Maclean issue the report that the Petrovs might be interviewed by press was likely to worry the United Kingdom authorities. If ... the report is true ... the United Kingdom authorities hope that nothing that could damage United Kingdom interests would be allowed to emerge and especially nothing that could start hares on Maclean and Burgess.[48]

All in vain. On September 18 1955 the Petrov story broke a second time, on this occasion as a sensational lead item in the popular Sunday newspaper, *The People*.[49] This story was a rewrite of the chapter which the Petrovs had included on Burgess and Maclean in their book *Empire of Fear* in the hope of stimulating their sales, particularly in Britain. After *The People* article a storm of press criticism broke, directed at the absurd secrecy of the Government in this affair. Stonewalling was no longer an option. At once the Foreign Office promised and in short order produced a White Paper on their missing diplomats.[50] In its turn this Paper was more or less universally condemned in the London press as, in the famous words of the *Times* editorial of September 24, 'Too Little and Too Late'.[51] The Petrovs had unintentionally triggered the most far-reaching public debate in post-war Britain on Soviet espionage and upper class treason.

The Petrov revelations revived speculation in the press about the 'Third Man' and in particular about Kim Philby. When the House of Commons reassembled for its autumn session on October 25 the Labour member for Brixton, Colonel Marcus Lipton, enquired of the Prime Minister, Anthony Eden, whether he had 'made up his mind to cover up at all costs the dubious third man activities of Mr Harold Philby'.[52] It was clear by now that the revelations about Burgess and Maclean, the White Paper these had provoked and the accusation about Philby which Lipton now raised all pointed towards the need for a full parliamentary debate. In the course of it the Foreign Secretary, Harold Macmillan, sought to justify his Government's first response to the Petrov leak of April 18 1954 on the quite false and, indeed, absurd ground that if the British Government had acceded to the truth of the initial Burgess-Maclean story to appear in London Petrov would have refused to give further evidence before the Australian Royal Commission.*[53] More importantly Macmillan also spoke openly about Colonel Lipton's accusations.

---

* The Labor MP, Richard Crossman, punctured this argument deftly. 'I gather', he said, 'from an extraordinary passage in the Foreign Secretary's speech that Petrov refused to talk if his revelations were published in Britain. Presumably, he wanted to sell his information to a newspaper, because he then would be paid for the articles ...' Crossman added that there was 'reason to believe that we would have had no White Paper if the Petrov case had not forced publication upon the Government'.

While in Government service [Philby] carried out his duties ably and conscientiously. I have no reason to conclude that Mr Philby has at anytime betrayed the interests of this country.[54]

During the course of the debate Marcus Lipton was placed under considerable pressure — especially from a Conservative MP, Dick Brooman-White and the Minister of State at the Foreign Office, Anthony Nutting — either to repeat his accusations concerning Philby outside the House or to withdraw them. In self-defence Lipton pointed out that Philby himself had not issued such a demand.[55] At once Philby hastily improvised a press conference in his mother's living room. There is no better way to conclude this story than with Colonel Philby's own, wonderfully insolent, description.

> Of the first half dozen [questions] shot at me, one mentioned Lipton and I seized on it. 'Ah, Lipton', I said. 'That brings us to the heart of the matter' ... I ... invited Lipton to produce his evidence for the security authorities or repeat his charge outside the House of Commons.... The ball was now in Lipton's court. On the first evening, the BBC reported that he had attended the session of the House but had remained silent. The following evening, he gave in.... In my relief, my first reaction was to congratulate Lipton on a handsome apology. But I decided it was undeservedly fulsome and settled for a more non-committal formula: 'I think that Colonel Lipton has done the right thing. So far as I am concerned, the incident is now closed'.[56]

Within weeks of the Petrov story about Burgess and Maclean, Philby — with a little help from the Eden Government — had managed to win for himself a nine year reprieve from the defector's lot in Moscow and to humiliate his nemesis, the redoubtable Colonel Lipton.

There is a final twist in the tale of the Petrovs and British counter-intelligence. Much of the material that had been produced from the interrogation sessions with them passed in London across the desk of an M16 officer — George Blake — who had recently returned from imprisonment by the Communist side in the Korean War. In 1961, Blake, who had subsequently been posted to Berlin, where he had wrought considerable havoc to Western agents and interests, was arrested, tried *in camera* in conditions of utmost secrecy and sentenced to forty-two years imprisonment. After Blake's sentence the head of M16 sent Brigadier Spry a message of deepest apology. It was now confirmed, he explained, that the material the Petrovs had given to their ASIO-M15 interrogators had been, in turn, sent on to Moscow Centre by George Blake.[57] Five years after his arrest Blake escaped from prison at Wentworth Scrubs and — although he did not quite have their tone — made his way into the expanding colony of British defectors in Moscow. In 1970 he was awarded the Order of Lenin.[58]

ASIO and Western counter-intelligence learnt from their experiences with the Petrovs one last lesson they could quite happily have done without. From

Gouzenko in 1945 to Yurchenko in 1985 — during their transition from the status of privileged cadres of the totalitarian state to the rather unglamorous and frightening future awaiting them in the West — Soviet intelligence defectors have provided many headaches for their counter-intelligence hosts.[59] The Petrovs were no exception. However, like Tolstoy's unhappy families, each defector appears to have been unhappy after his or her own peculiar fashion. In this melancholy history, the story of the Petrovs' first two years in Australia is characteristic if not typical.

ASIO's troubles began from the first moment of the defection. Petrov was a dreadful bundle of nerves, too frightened to be alone even for a few minutes. That it was extremely difficult to get him to work upon the documents was the least of ASIO's problems. For solace he took heavily to the bottle. In the evenings, under its influence, Petrov would dream up heroic schemes 'to storm the Soviet Embassy and rescue his wife'. By the mornings his resolve departed him and he returned, in the words of the sardonic chronicler at the safe house, to 'his usual uncourageous self'. At first, ASIO adopted a liberal regime with him in regard to drink. They knew they had to win Petrov's confidence. Perhaps they hoped his nerves would settle and the problem diminish over time.[60]

These early days must have come to seem halcyon to the safe house team when compared with the complexities that were injected with the arrival of Petrova. The uncynical general public of the mid-1950s was excited by Evdokia's salvation at Darwin not only because they saw in it the triumph of political Good over Evil but also because it represented a romantic vindication of Married Love. The reality was more complex. When Petrov and Petrova were reunited in Sydney there occurred — to the considerable surprise of the ASIO bystanders — a tremendous row.[61] To Petrova's questions — 'Why did you desert me? What have you done to my family?' — Petrov, neither at that time nor subsequently, had satisfactory answers. Petrova had defected, as the safe house chronicler observed, 'because she was repulsed at the probability of being reduced to a penniless human struggling for existence, following a term of imprisonment in a Labour Camp'. Was her life's central struggle — to make something of herself — to be thus rewarded?[62]

Eventually when what she believed she had done to her family sunk in — for she dearly loved her mother and younger sister — Petrova's remorse was pitiful to behold. 'Quite often', the chronicler recorded, 'the ASIO officers heard her long wailing cries echoing through the night, and the following morning noted that her face was drawn and lined'.[63] In his sober moments Petrov accepted philosophically the truth of his wife's accusation, that he had ruined her family. When he was drunk he struck back at her in fury and self-protection. One night the safe house team

was awakened by Petrov bellowing in filthy language at maximum strength. They went upstairs and heard Petrov arguing bitterly with his wife and accusing her of misconduct. When the door was opened Petrov was seen in an almost naked and intoxicated condition and almost screaming. His dog attacked Mrs Petrov.... At one stage he struck his wife a violent blow ... Petrov said that he would have nothing to do with her again and would report her conduct to the Commission. She in turn expressed her hatred of him and wished to die.[64]

Frequently the deep unhappiness of the Petrovs was directed not against each other but against the safe house team in particular or ASIO in general. Despite the fact that ASIO encouraged both to move out of the safe house as much as possible, both complained on many occasions — especially after Windeyer's unfortunate prisoner-of-war allusion in the Commission — about being held in captivity. While in fact Petrova often went in company on shopping expeditions or to the theatre, Petrov — who was far more fearful

Petrova at Artie Shaw concert, August 1954
(courtesy of Herald and Weekly Times)

than his wife about being identified and assassinated — restricted himself to fishing and hunting trips to the country.[65] Apart from drinking he sought his solace in the company of his beloved Alsatian dog from Embassy days and a small assembly of cats he had since acquired and with whom he slept.[66] At the end of 1955 ASIO planned to lift his spirits by purchasing for him, on request, six laying hens.[67]

Petrova was particularly anxious about the couple's uncertain financial future. On one occasion, as Colonel Spry explained to Mr Menzies, she threatened not to testify before the Royal Commission unless this situation was clarified at once.[68] On another she composed a list of claims against the Commonwealth concerning the personal cost to her of leaving the Soviet intelligence service. The claims amounted to £20,000 ($240,000). The couple

Petrov at the Safe House with 'Jack'.

frequently complained to ASIO about providing intelligence debriefings to overseas services without specific financial reward.[69] As we shall see they were also bitterly disappointed with the eventual price their memoir fetched.

On balance, Petrova appears to have been more concerned than Petrov with their financial future, and Petrov more concerned than his wife with the strain of endless appearances before the Royal Commission. Petrov had at first believed that he would be called upon to make 'one big speech' at the Commission in which he would outline Soviet espionage in Australia. As it turned out, he was asked to appear as a witness over the period of nine months and to face there extremely hostile cross-examinations which were designed to destroy his character. Petrov never quite understood how this could be permitted. As he pointed out more than once, in Moscow a defector's stories about Soviet citizens would be accepted and punishment meted out to them without fuss. On many occasions he told his ASIO minders that his experiences at the Commission were driving him into a lunatic asylum; that he would prefer to return to Moscow to stand trial for treason than continue with this torment; and that he intended the next day to denounce to the world his shocking treatment. Fortunately for ASIO, Petrov's evening threats were never converted into action by day. Unlike her husband, Petrova seems to have enjoyed her Commission appearances, dressing for each new day with greatest care and reading press post mortems on her performance with greatest interest. While Petrov was angered and astonished at the tribulation Ted Hill was permitted to subject him to, Petrova actually admired his staunch defence of the Communist cause.[70]

Sexual tensions within the safe house were frequently high. On one occasion Petrov fled it in his underwear in search of women.[71] On another Petrova abused the safe house cook who had touched her husband gently on the arm to console him after an argument over drink. (At this point the cook and her husband left the safe house for good.)[72] Under such conditions, unbeknown to the general public, the safe house team and the Petrovs muddled on together as best they could. As the sensitive and good humoured safe house chronicler concluded 'had not maximum tact and discretion been employed . . . the whole conduct of the Royal Commission on Espionage in Australia, and indeed the future of ASIO, could have been jeopardised'.[73]

PART IV
Resolution

15

THE WAR BETWEEN THE CAMPS

The six months in which the Royal Commission was hearing evidence on Soviet espionage were, as it happened, the months in which a process which led to a realignment of forces within Australian politics commenced. A section of Irish-Australian Catholic supporters of Labor were, first in Victoria and considerably later in other States, severed from their traditional political allegiance. As a consequence, the ALP moved considerably to the left and the post-war balance between Labor and anti-Labor forces in Australian party politics was overturned.

As we have seen the process that led to the split in the ALP began in October 1954, at the height of intra-Labor conflict over Petrov, when Dr Evatt launched his surprise attack on the Movement and, as a direct response, the party's Federal Executive decided to conduct an investigation into its Victorian branch. The hearings in Melbourne began on November 10 and concluded on December 4. Executive decided to order the convening of a special conference of the Victorian branch, where a new state executive was to be elected, and to withdraw official support from the Industrial Groups in that state. At the special conference the two year membership requirement for delegates to conference, written into the party's constitution, was to be waived. On February 11 1955 the old Victorian Executive itself split — largely on sectarian lines — over the question of whether or not to boycott the special conference.[1] The seam along which the Victorian ALP was now torn apart was not the Petrov seam. By opposing the boycott some of the harshest critics of Dr Evatt's Petrovian behaviour and of his assault upon the Movement (for example, Ted Peters of the Federal Parliamentary party or Dinny Lovegrove of the Victorian machine) ultimately found themselves — when it came to the choice — in the camp of Dr Evatt rather than Mr Santamaria.

By the end of February 1955, after the special conference, there existed in reality in Victoria two parties claiming to be the ALP. Both sent delegations to the biennial Federal Conference of the ALP which convened in Hobart in March. The six delegates of the 'old' Victorian executive were refused admission to the conference hall while the six delegates of the 'new' executive were granted permission to vote on the crucial credentialling question. In response there was a fresh boycott. Of the forty-two aspirant delegates to the Hobart Federal Conference only nineteen — six 'new' Victorians, six South Australians, four Tasmanians, two West Australians, one Queenslander and not a single New South Welshman — attended to the end.[2]

From the point of view of public opinion, the Hobart Conference was a disaster for the ALP. Much of the press in Australia concluded that Dr Evatt was finished. Apparently his deputy, Arthur Calwell, had arrived by this time at a similar conclusion. Somewhat unexpectedly he flew to Hobart to address the conference at its concluding session, presumably to launch his long awaited leadership bid. Calwell was reported to have told the delegates that the Labor Party would never be able to return to power while it was led by Dr Evatt. According to the *Age*, he 'traced most of the party's recent troubles back to the moment when Dr Evatt appeared at the [Petrov Royal] Commission, and was highly critical of his conduct once he appeared'. Calwell's speech was greeted by a 'stony silence'. Some non-boycotting delegates told the press that he 'had dwelt too much on the Petrov Commission'.[3] His intervention was, in reality, five months too late. If Calwell had delivered his Hobart address to Caucus on October 13 1954 he may have forced an immediate spill and inherited, then, the leadership of the ALP.

Hobart ended not with a Calwell leadership bid on the issues of Evatt, Petrov and party unity but with the final split in the Victorian branch of the ALP, the threat of similar splits in other state branches and with the consolidation of the anti-Grouper forces under the leadership (at least for the present) of Dr Evatt. A month after Hobart the Cain Labor Government in Victoria fell. To the immense satisfaction of the small Liberal-Country Party under Henry Bolte, two bitterly hostile Labor parties presented themselves in May 1955 to the Victorian electorate.[4] For the next quarter century, until John Cain's son led Labor from the wilderness, Victoria was to be governed by an unbroken succession of conservative Cabinets.

At Canberra, when the Federal Parliament reassembled on April 20 1955, after its long summer recess, the ALP Caucus had lost some of its former number. Seven Victorians who had been expelled from the ALP took their places on the cross-benches. Dr Evatt threw open the party leadership. Tom Burke received 5 votes, Arthur Calwell 22 and Dr Evatt 52. As a result of the prolonged crisis the centre of gravity in the Caucus had shifted noticeably to the left.[5]

In the previous October the Government parties had gagged debate on the interim report of the Royal Commissioners, despite the protest of the ALP left, following the speeches of Mr Menzies and Dr Evatt. With the Victorian elections approaching debate on this matter was unexpectedly resumed. On May 19 1955 Coalition members watched as former Labor colleagues — Bill Bourke and Eddie Ward — tore flesh from each other over Petrov. Bourke informed the House of the horror he had felt during the previous autumn when he had listened in Caucus to Dr Evatt's slanders upon the Royal Commission judges and his 'wild, unsubstantiated and irresponsible attacks' upon the Security Service. His 'Moscow trial' of the Victorian branch was a 'diversionary tactic' to direct attention away from 'his shocking and inexcusable conduct before the royal commission'. Some special anger was reserved by Bourke for Calwell. If those who had aspired to Dr Evatt's office had displayed some 'courage' at the moment of crisis, he told the House, Evatt could have been deposed. Ward replied predictably for the Labor Party. The members on the cross-benches were nothing but treacherous agents of the Security Service. The Labor Party was well rid of them.[6] Following the Victorian split the Petrov Affair had become an extraordinarily bitter and utterly fundamental field of battle in the war that was now being waged between the two political camps of Labor.

As it happened, Arthur Calwell's Hobart attack on Dr Evatt was almost the last significant public criticism of Dr Evatt's Petrov performance to come from the ranks of those within the ALP who did not go with the split. From the autumn of 1955 the leading members of the ALP appear to have divided between those, chiefly on the left, who encouraged Dr Evatt's Petrovian campaigns, and those, in the centre of the Party and on the right, who opted for silence in the hope that his obsession would run its natural course before wreaking further havoc on the fortunes of their party.

Outside the ALP, by 1955, Dr Evatt had become a hero of the left intelligentsia, in part because of his attack on the Movement and in part because of his Petrov crusade. Friendship with his old protégé, Dr John Burton — which had been severed during Dr Evatt's drift to the right before the election of 1954* — was restored.[7] Brian Fitzpatrick of the Australian Council for Civil Liberties — the most talented polemicist for the anti-Petrov cause — showered him with advice and flattery.[8] The artist, Noel Counihan, hoped to paint his portrait for the Archibald Prize.[9] Counihan's party — the Communist Party of Australia — now saw Dr Evatt as a natural leader of the united front with the ALP left they fantasised about building. As the historian of the Communist Party has put it, Dr Evatt 'became a people's hero overnight'.[10] With complete sincerity and endless repetition *Tribune* and the *Guardian* supported every offensive Dr Evatt or Eddie Ward took on the Petrov front. On this issue at least there was complete unanimity between Dr Evatt and the CPA.[11]

With the passage of time Dr Evatt's conviction that the Petrov Affair represented one of the most wicked political conspiracies in world history

---

* In August 1953 Dr Burton had written, thus, on the question of Dr Evatt and the admission of Communist China to the United Nations: 'Dr Evatt and the right-wing now in control of the Labor movement apparently consider a right-wing revolutionary move is legitimate; but a left-wing victory over a corrupt government is to be opposed'.

seems, if anything, to have deepened. By 1955 it was the most solid and dominating feature of his inner political landscape. By this time he had, moreover, bestowed upon his Movement enemies a pivotal position in the affair.

There is in the Evatt Archive at Flinders University in South Australia some rather startling documentary evidence of the atmosphere which was, by 1955, pervading the Evatt camp. Scattered throughout the archive are upward of fifty very strange speculative papers on the Petrov Affair — some very short, others running to three or four closely typed pages — composed for Evatt by a gentleman calling himself 'Phil's Friend'.[12] Clearly 'Phil's Friend' operated as Dr Evatt's private adviser on intelligence matters during 1954 and 1955. As it happens from the evidence of the Evatt Archive the identity of 'Phil's Friend' can be determined with certainty. He was R.F.B. Wake, a former deputy to the first Director-General of ASIO, Mr Justice Reed. Wake had been dismissed from the Organisation, on the grounds of erratic behaviour, when Colonel Spry had taken command in 1950. He bore a deep grudge against both Spry and ASIO.*[13]

The stream of papers Wake delivered to Dr Evatt assumed, without argument, the existence of a vast international and Australian conspiratorial network involved in the Petrov Affair. Wake's purpose was to uncover the chief actors, organisations and interests involved in it. From the broadest perspective Wake regarded the affair as part of some international collaboration between imperialist interests in the United States and the Vatican, whose ambition was to create conditions for a war of aggression against the USSR.

> When was it (he enquired of Dr Evatt) that MENZIES prophesied War in 3 (three) years? In Oct, 51 General Mark Clark a personal friend of Pope Pius XII, Chief of the US Field Forces nominated as first American American Ambassador to the Vatican. Kennan, head of the 'Free Russia Committee' — set up to liberate Russia from Communism — became the new US Ambassador to Moscow. At the same time 4 million copies of an American magazine dedicated to the coming war against the USSR were distributed in the USA. War against the USSR was anticipated in 1952. The point I am making in a cumbersome manner is that Menzies, the Vatican and Washington were all singing the same tune at the same time.

Wake was also certain the Ollier case or what he came to call the 'Ollier-Roche set up' was part of this 'whole worldwide' conspiracy in which ASIO, M. Roche, the French Security Service and the CIA had been involved.

---

* There is in the Evatt Archive a letter written by Wake to Evatt on May 29, 1955, under his own signature, in which he asks for Evatt's assistance in his quest for a transfer from the Department of Works where he was marooned, to the Department of Commerce and Agriculture. In this letter Wake asks of Evatt that he explain to the Secretary of the Department 'that I am an ordinary citizen who has survived severl (sic) campaigns of villification (sic) by Spry and his cohorts'. The handwriting at the foot of this letter is unmistakably that of 'Phil's Friend'.

While the Petrov Affair, then, appeared to Wake to be part of a larger international movement centred upon a Washington-Vatican axis he was also convinced that it had been concocted by a variety of local political organisations to advance their own interests. For Wake the most important of these were ASIO, the Liberal Party, Australian Naval Intelligence, Moral Rearmament, Sir Edmund Herring's 'The Call',[14] General Blamey's 'Association'[15] and, of course, B.A. Santamaria's Movement. The most essential ambition of the intelligence analyses he wrote for Dr Evatt was to reveal the various points at which these apparently disparate organisations were connected, especially at the personal level. In his view all these groups had pulled together to create the Petrov Affair. It was a sinister and nightmarish vision.

For the role of Australian master-conspirator Wake favoured not Mr Menzies or Brigadier Spry or even B.A. Santamaria but a rather kindly Catholic writer from Adelaide, Paul Maguire, who had been from 1953 the Australian Ambassador to Rome. Wake's decision to concoct such a persona for Maguire, while absurd as a matter of fact, is not difficult to fathom. Paul Maguire was one of the very few Australians of the mid-1950s who was genuinely at home in the two social worlds from which Wake believed the Petrov Affair had been conjured — Establishment conservatism and Irish-Australian Catholicism. He had, moreover, genuinely been involved in his public career with several of Wake's 'bêtes noires' — with Australian Naval Intelligence during the Second World War; with Mr Menzies and the 'Wine and Cheese Club'; with Sir Edmund Herring and 'The Call to the Nation'; with B.A. Santamaria and the Movement; with Brigadier Spry and ASIO. As Wake explained to Evatt, during 1951 while Paul Maguire was

> the Chief Jester to Menzies ... he was also wearing a track from Spry's office to Santamaria's office — which was no jest but a very serious activity.... While ... taking his lucheons (sic) with Menzies he was also chief organizer for the 'Call' ...

Wake assured Dr Evatt that Maguire had links with American Catholic interests through Cardinal Spellman. Even his appointment to Rome in 1953 (before the Petrov Affair broke) seemed to Wake sinister, based upon what he described as 'an anxiety to get him out of the country during a vital period'. 'Good God', he exploded to Evatt in May 1955, 'Paul Magguire's (sic) involvement in this business sticks out like bubbles on a washtub'. Throughout 1955 he recommended that Evatt campaign on the slogan of the 'Menzies-Maguire-Santamaria Axis'.

In reality what Wake was feeding Dr Evatt in his Petrov papers was a quite old-fashioned political sectarianism, adapted to present circumstances. Wherever Wake peered he found the mark of the Vatican or 'Catholic Action'. One of his papers was entitled 'Extraneous Catholic Activities (State Within A State)'. It dealt with 'Catholic Action', the 'Knights of St. Columbus' and 'Catholic Guilds'. On one occasion he expressed the view that 'the U.S. and Cath. Action knew ... about Petrov long before ASIO caught up on the deal'; on another that Dr Evatt's wartime typist, Frances Bernie, was a 'Catholic Action' plant on Evatt's staff and the Australian Communist Party. Even the Burgess and Maclean affair had for Wake a Vatican explanation.

> In 1939 over 40 per cent of the British Foreign Office were Roman Catholics. A recent estimate, 1954, suggests that it is now nearer 60%. Is it probable that B & McC got fed up with the RC intrigues in the show and went walkabout?[16]

It is not possible to know what precisely Dr Evatt made of the theories of Wake. It is clear, however, that he did not discourage him from producing his never-ending stream of Petrovian analyses and highly likely that he felt considerable sympathy at least for the general thrust of Wake's analysis of the Petrov Affair. During the 1960s Robert Murray spoke to many participants in the events of the split while memories were still fresh. On the basis of this anecdotal evidence he arrived at the following conclusion.

> By the spring of 1955 Evatt appeared again to be losing control of his complex personality ... He was by now completely obsessive about the Petrov affair, and there are innumerable stories of the lengthy, conspiratorial theories he would expound to often reluctant listeners in private conversations. His obsession with the 'Santamaria Movement' was by now almost as bad. Evatt was morbidly suspicious of people he believed to be 'CA' (Catholic Action) in the Party, the press, the government departments, among employees at Parliament House.... He was wont to believe any story peddled to him, no matter how fantastic or how suspect the source, provided it fitted his conspiratorial vision of the Santamaria-Menzies-Petrov 'plot'.[17]

In his pursuit of the 'truth' about the non-existent Petrov conspiracy Dr Evatt posed an even greater danger to himself than his political enemies. During the latter part of 1954 and early 1955 he embarked upon a series of hostile correspondences. One was with the New South Wales Attorney-General Bill Sheahan, about the supposed leakage in New South Wales of Document 'J'.[18] A second was with the Canberra branch of the Australian Journalists' Association, where he hinted darkly about the Sydney AJA's role in planting Fergan O'Sullivan on his staff.[19] A more protracted correspondence took place in the first half of 1955 with the Solicitor-General, Professor Bailey, where Dr Evatt alleged that ASIO had treated him with 'scandalous deception' by not informing him in 1953 of O'Sullivan's connections with Petrov.*[20] None of this did Dr Evatt much lasting damage. On the other

---

* In response to Evatt's first letter, Brigadier Spry pointed out to Bailey that ASIO itself had not discovered the nature of the relationship between O'Sullivan and the MVD before Petrov's defection in April 1954. He also pointed out that he and Dr Evatt had discussed the Security dimensions of O'Sullivan's appointment in August 1953 and that, as a consequence of this discussion, he had sent Colonel Phillipps to Dr Evatt to give him a detailed briefing on ASIO's concerns about O'Sullivan. In May 1955 ASIO showed Dr Evatt a copy of the briefing paper which had been prepared in August 1953 for his perusal. Dr Evatt denied having ever seen it.

hand, there was one final line of correspondence he embarked upon in early 1955 which was ultimately to inflict upon his reputation immeasurable harm and to prove the decisive event in the politics of the Petrov Affair.

On February 17 1955 Dr Evatt despatched a letter concerning Petrov to the Foreign Minister of the USSR, M. Molotov. Why did he do this? According to one man who ought to know, his Private Secretary Allan Dalziel, Evatt wrote to Molotov because of the profundity of his respect for the rule of law. Dr Evatt was, above all else, according to Dalziel, 'an eminent jurist'.

> The right to enter a defence, to state a case in reply to charges ... was basic to the operation of justice within the framework of the law. He stoutly rejected the idea that, because a person or cause was unpopular or the subject of general disapproval, the right to be heard in one's own defence should be suspended. For him, as a lawyer of unchallengeable integrity, it was vital that the views of the Soviet Government be examined and assessed.

At this critical moment in his career, according to Dalziel, Dr Evatt's finest instinct — his passion for justice — triumphed. While, however, soaring high above the world of petty politics he exposed himself to the scorn and ridicule of the Australian philistines who had long desired to bring him down. Here, encapsulated in Dalziel's account of the Molotov letter, is the Evatt Tragedy or, if you will, the Evatt Myth.[21]

It is actually difficult to imagine an explanation of Dr Evatt's motives in writing to Molotov which could be more misleading than that offered by Dalziel. Within the Evatt Archive there exists a copy of his famous, portentous letter. It reveals not a disappasionate lawyer concerned with even-handed justice but an impassioned political crusader searching even in the most implausible quarter for support and ammunition. In his letter Dr Evatt does not invite Molotov to defend the USSR against the charge of espionage — except as an after-thought.* Rather he implores the Soviet Foreign Minister to lend his assistance in Dr Evatt's struggle to unmask a plot in which the Australian Government and Security Service have been involved. Time is short. The Royal Commission hearings, he reminds Molotov, are drawing to a close. Lest this account should appear exaggerated it is necessary to quote from the Evatt letter at some length.

> I have come to conclusion (Dr Evatt informed Molotov) that few, if any of [the] documents were genuine but that they were deliberately fabricated in 1953 by Petrov and others for the purpose of being subsequently utilised for party political purposes against the Labor Party (of which I am Leader) in the election of May, 1954. ... It is plain that the U.S.S.R. authorities, especially the M.V.D., know whether for certain Petrov has been engaged in a systematic plan to cheat and

---

* Dr Evatt's paragraph suggesting international arbitration of the Petrov Affair was not even included in the near-complete first draft of his letter to Molotov of February 10. He subsequently wrote it in by hand and it was included in the final version of February 17.

defraud the Australian people.... In short, your Government, or its officers are undoubtedly in a position to produce official and absolutely conclusive evidence of the fact (if it be a fact) that the Petrov documents are fabricated and spurious ... In order to expose what I believe to be a crime against humanity, I request an immediate intervention by Your Excellency as the Commission of enquiry seems to be approaching the last stage of their (sic) activities.

Dr Evatt suggested to Molotov that he might then place the matter before an 'international court of jurists' for arbitration.[22]

Evatt's letter to Molotov must rank as one of the strangest ever sent by a responsible western politician to a Soviet leader. To speak of the Petrov Affair, in the language of the Nuremberg trials, as a 'crime against humanity', especially in a letter to one of Stalin's most faithful lieutenants, was grotesque. To place weight upon the words of Molotov in an investigation into Soviet espionage was self-evidently preposterous. Moreover if details of this letter were to leak to the press or Dr Evatt's political enemies in Australia it had the capacity to do him great harm. To appear to prefer the word of Molotov to the findings of an Australian Royal Commission would certainly be offensive to a generation which still had faith in its judicial system. To call in the Soviet Foreign Minister as an ally in his battle with the Menzies Government and ASIO was — especially in the atmosphere of mid-1950s Australia — an act of potential political suicide.

The Soviet Foreign Ministry may have been genuinely puzzled by Dr Evatt's letter. Perhaps they read into it some complex trap. For six weeks there was no reply. When it finally came, despatched on April 9 1955, it must have represented a severe disappointment to Evatt. The letter was signed not by Molotov but by a relatively junior official of the Soviet Foreign Ministry — Ilyichev, Chief of the Press department — who claimed to write on the Foreign Minister's 'instructions'. Its contents were bland and non-commital. Ilyichev expressed the fullest agreement of his Government with Dr Evatt's analysis of the Petrov Affair. It had, indeed, been staged by anti-democratic forces intent upon harming Australian-Soviet relations. The Petrov documents were, he agreed, fabrications. Unhappily, however, Ilyichev offered Dr Evatt neither new evidence on this matter nor even fresh argument. He politely but firmly declined Dr Evatt's suggestion for the arbitration of the affair before an international panel of judges. Such an arbitration, he pointed out, would have no 'subject matter'.[23] Here, at least for the moment, the Evatt-'Molotov' correspondence rested.

In his Petrov crusade Dr Evatt's staunchest ally was the leader of the ALP left in the Parliament, Eddie Ward. During an election rally in May 1954 the name of Ward had been raised with the Prime Minister. 'We must not', he quipped, 'speak ill of the dead'. Menzies' announcement of the political eclipse of his old sparring partner in the parliament was premature. The 'firebrand of East Sydney' had within him still the resolve for one last great campaign. From the first he threw himself into the Petrov Affair with vigour and tenacity.[24]

Before November 1954 Eddie Ward had concentrated upon the Prime Minister as his prime Petrovian target — on his failure to reveal the £5000 payment before the election and on his false statement to the parliament that he had not heard the name of Petrov before April 11 or 12. In November he shifted the focus of his attack. For a considerable time there had been rumours on the left about the Petrov-Bialoguski trade in duty free liquor.* As we have seen, in the spring of 1954 Dr Bialoguski learned that a partner in this trade, George Marue (who blamed him for his dismissal from ASIO) was offering his information about it to the anti-Petrov camp.[25] Either directly or indirectly, by November 1954 Marue's story had reached Ward's ears.[26] He was now convinced that the rumours were reliable. By exposing this unsavoury aspect of the Petrov-Bialoguski relationship Ward hoped, of course, to discredit them both and, through them, to discredit ASIO. Compared with the frontal charges of his leader, Dr Evatt, Eddie Ward's diversionary whisky attack had one great strength. It was based upon the truth.

In early November 1954 Ward raised the matter in the parliament in the form of questions about the amount of liquor the Soviet Embassy had imported before its closure. Mr Menzies replied that this was of no concern and little interest to the Australian Government.[27] During the adjournment debate of November 10 Ward placed his cards on the table. Reliable information had reached him, he told the House, that 'huge quantities' of duty-free liquor had been imported by the Soviet Embassy and later sold for profit in Australia. According to his information the brand of the whisky was 'Bell's Special Scotch'. It had been sold for £1 when it retailed for 47s. It had been obtained by Petrov and distributed by Dr Bialoguski. Ward called upon the Government to investigate this matter.[28] Mr Menzies answered for the Government on the following day.

> I can only treat with contempt, as part of the Communist campaign to discredit the royal commission, attempts that may be made in this House under parliamentary privilege to smear witnesses before the royal commission.[29]

Eddie Ward was, of course, not to be diverted thus from his attack. While parliament was in its long summer recess he conducted a protracted correspondence with the Minister for Trade, Senator O'Sullivan, on the question of the Petrovian trade in whisky. At first Ward was informed that the Department was not in the habit of revealing publicly the private affairs of businesses. Ward pointed out that it was rather odd to treat a foreign legation

---

* For example in a poem circulating in August 1954 entitled 'Not Too Old to Rat'.

'You've heard of Peter and of George
The famous sly grog men'.

as if it were an importing firm. The Minister then changed tack. The full information Ward required could only be extracted from the departmental record with a large expenditure of labour. This was 'impracticable'.

I am bound to say however (he continued) that checks made recently for random periods did not disclose anything unusual or apparently excessive in the importation of spirituous liquors for the Soviet Embassy.

On February 24 Senator O'Sullivan closed the correspondence. Ward's suggestion of an investigation into his allegations had been 'noted'. He called upon him to submit his evidence on the matter. Ward assumed that the Trade and Customs Department would now bury the issue.[30]

In the mean time the anti-Petrov camp had managed at least to raise the question of the whisky trade at the Royal Commission. On January 18 1955 a Sydney solicitor, B.R. Miles, who was representing a certain Norman Russell before the Commission, asked for Petrov to be recalled to give evidence. In the midst of a cross-examination concerning his client Miles suddenly asked Petrov whether he knew Mr Bahrenkamp (sic) of Crawford & Co. the Sydney liquor importers, whether he had obtained from this company large quantities of duty-free Scotch whisky, and whether he had sold such whisky to night clubs in Sydney. Petrov lied. He did not know the gentleman in question or the company. He had most certainly never sold duty-free whisky in Sydney. These accusations were, he exclaimed, 'just a provocation'. The Royal Commissioners permitted Miles to question Petrov on the whisky issue at some length.[31] On the following day, however, they turned down his request to call a representative of Crawford's before the Commission. 'Supposing', Mr Justice Owen explained to Mr Miles, 'you were to get evidence that 500 gallons a week were supplied to the Soviet Embassy: where does that get us?'.[32]

In mid-March Eddie Ward learnt from Miles, no doubt to his surprise, that an investigation into the Petrov-Bialoguski liquor business was in fact being conducted by a member of the Customs Department, Mr Maher.[33] What ASIO thought of this investigation is unclear. What is clear is that it placed it in a rather delicate situation. As we have seen, by late 1953 ASIO had been informed by Bialoguski about the whisky trade.[34] It knew, thus, that Ward's allegations were true and was in a position to provide Maher with information which could clinch his inquiries. It is almost certain, however, that ASIO would not have considered such a course. To have passed on to Customs information received from their agent, Bialoguski, would have represented a great betrayal of trust. Moreover it was certainly in ASIO's interest that the Maher inquiry should prove inconclusive. The less Mr Menzies learned about this matter the easier it would be for him to hold out against Ward in parliament.

When Dr Bialoguski was informed about the Maher inquiry he discussed it at once with his ASIO contact, John Gilmour. Gilmour advised him, unofficially, of his legal rights, which included the right not to answer questions.[35] Bialoguski did not require such advice. In the interview with Maher, which took place on March 23, he admitted that cases of Embassy whisky had on occasions been stored at his flat before being picked up by Soviet drivers, but denied categorically having ever sold any of it. Bialoguski thought the interview went rather well.[36] A transcript of it was prepared by him and passed on personally to both Gilmour and Maher.[37] Maher had advised him not to post it to the Customs Department. He informed Dr Bialoguski that the investigation was being conducted in such secrecy that only one other officer in Customs knew anything about it.[38]

Eddie Ward remained on the offensive. On June 8, with the full support of Caucus,[39] he submitted to the Speaker a motion of public importance urging an investigation into the duty-free whisky dealings of Petrov and Bialoguski. More than half the debate was concerned with whether or not such a matter could properly be debated. Rather strangely, Mr Menzies argued that to canvass issues affecting the credibility of key Royal Commission witnesses might influence the judges who were at the time writing their report. More directly, from the cross-benches, John Mullens argued that parliament ought to 'decline to wallow in the slime'. The Speaker Archie Cameron informed the House that he had been considering the matter for several weeks. He ruled in favour of Ward, who proceeded to outline, in rather general terms, his evidence. Unfortunately for him he was not free to name the source of his information. Menzies replied to Ward. He now revealed, for the first time in public, that there had indeed been an inquiry into this allegation. After a thorough and patient investigation the Crown Law officers had concluded that there had been no breach in the law.* Eddie Ward had been invited more than once to submit his evidence on this matter to the Crown but had failed to do so. 'He preferred to rest, as he always does, on remote gossip . . . and defamatory hearsay.'[40]

Mr Menzies had spoken with considerable skill but had altogether avoided the main issue of fact. On the following day Ward returned to the fray. He framed his question to Menzies very shrewdly. Would the Prime Minister concede that the fact that the opinion of the Crown Law officers had been called upon was itself clear evidence that Customs must have discovered that the Soviet Embassy had indeed imported 'abnormal quantities' of duty-free liquor? Mr Menzies declined to comment. From the political point of view the matter had now been all but disposed of.[41]

Thirty years later the archive on the Petrov Affair was thrown open. Here the results of the Maher inquiry were finally revealed.

> Initial inquiries into the amount of liquor cleared duty free by the Soviet Embassy over a period of some three years disclosed that for the six months ended March,

---

* In the Parliament Ward readily conceded this point but claimed there had been what he called an 'abuse of diplomatic privilege'.

1953, 64 liquid gallons had been cleared. However during the six months ended March, 1954, 650 liquid gallons were cleared from bond by the Embassy. Petrov's signature appeared on a good percentage of the related Customs entries.... Questioned as to why the quantities of liquor cleared by the Embassy rose so sharply during the six months ended April, 1954 Petrov said he knew of no explanation other than that the increased quantities had been ordered by . . . the Social Committee of the Embassy.[42]

Eddie Ward's Petrovian attacks were not, of course, restricted to the whisky front. In December 1954 a Christmas party was held for the Royal Commission staff at which both the Petrovs and the Royal Commission judges had made an appearance. Details of this party leaked at once to the press.[43] Ward, in response, deluged the Prime Minister with telegrams demanding a full explanation of the incident. However, as public interest in this foolish but minor indiscretion quickly passed, Mr Menzies did not oblige.*[44]

The only successes for Ward in his Petrov campaign came as a result of the extremely detailed written parliamentary questions which, between 1954 and 1957, he time and again presented to the Prime Minister. By this means he eventually extracted from the Government itemised expenditure lists of the cost to the Commonwealth of the Royal Commission and the maintenance of the Petrovs, and details of ASIO's role in the writing of *Empire of Fear*. In many of these questions Ward showed himself to be remarkably well-informed.[45] Only when the Ward Archive was deposited in the Australian National Library was it revealed that much of his information came from a mole inside ASIO who was passing it to Dr Evatt's intelligence adviser, R.F.B. Wake (as we have seen, a former senior ASIO officer) who was in turn passing the information to Eddie Ward.†[46]

During the week in which the Parliament debated the whisky question the Australian public was treated to the bizarre spectacle of a newspaper war in which rival accounts of the Petrov Affair were simultaneously serialised — one by Dr Bialoguski, the other by his estranged wife, Patricia. Bialoguski's

---

* The Christmas party incident severely embarrassed the three judges, who claimed not to have been informed about the invitation to the Petrovs. Rather grudgingly, Kenneth Herde — who claimed he had informed Owen about the possible attendance of the Petrovs — agreed to shoulder public responsibility for the matter if that became necessary. It did not.

† Through the Wake channel Ward learned, for example, that *Empire of Fear* had been written by Michael Thwaites; that Thwaites had been recommended to Colonel Spry by Sir Edmund Herring; that passages from *Empire of Fear* had been deleted due to legal advice; that Ron Richards visited Melbourne frequently (after 1956) to see Petrov, who was 'quite a pest' when 'on the grog'; that Petrov had butted a member of the safe house staff with his rifle when under the influence; that the Petrovs had declined an invitation to give evidence before a Congressional committee in the United States; and that Brigadier Spry privately called the Leader of the Opposition 'Herbert "Smear" Evatt'.

articles appeared in newspapers throughout Australia under the title 'I Got Petrov'; his wife's in the Sydney *Daily Telegraph* and the Melbourne *Argus* under the title 'I Married A Secret Agent'. Having read his wife's contribution — which portrayed him, rather convincingly, as a cynical and ruthless egomaniac — Dr Bialoguski proceeded to take out against his abandoned 'Pops' a £50,000 ($600,000) defamation writ.[47]

The fortnight of articles by Michael and Patricia Bialoguski created tremendous excitement on the left. This was in part because between them the Bialoguski couple revealed to the public for the first time some of the seedier aspects of Petrov's Sydney life. Bialoguski wrote, albeit rather euphemistically, of Petrov's interest in women; Patricia, less euphemistically, of his interest in whisky. (One of her articles had Petrov crawling on the floor of her husband's flat in a drunken stupor.) More importantly, the left was delighted to find that in their articles both Dr and Patricia Bialoguski revealed that while he was cultivating Petrov, Dr Bialoguski had travelled to Canberra to see the Prime Minister with complaints about his treatment by ASIO. Both were certain that the man Bialoguski had seen — the Prime Minister's Secretary, Geoffrey Yeend — had brought the matter to the personal attention of Mr Menzies. While this was in fact almost certainly untrue, in the charged political atmosphere of mid-1955 the allegation was sufficient. Was it not now perfectly clear that Mr Menzies had known about Petrov fully six months prior to the defection? Was it thus not plain that Mr Menzies was — as the left had long alleged — a prime Petrov conspirator?[48] Dr Bialoguski's account of his trip to Canberra to see the Prime Minister now joined the *News Weekly* article of January 1953 and the *Sydney Morning Herald*'s political commentary of April 6 1954 (that if Mr Menzies was to win the election he would have to produce one or two rabbits from his hat) — as one of the sacred texts for the Petrov conspiracy theorists.

ASIO was furious with Dr Bialoguski. Although he had shown his contact, Gilmour, some drafts of earlier sections, he had kept the later material — which concerned not only the Canberra trip and Petrov's Sydney night life but also the details of his quarrels with ASIO — to himself.[49] Within ASIO the oldest view of Dr Bialoguski — as a dangerous and unscrupulous mercenary — resurfaced. When in June 1955 ASIO was asked whether it had any objections to allowing Bialoguski to travel overseas, Ron Richards expressed the private opinion that if he stayed away permanently it would be for Australia 'a good riddance'.*[50] Relations between ASIO and Dr Bialoguski once more soured — this time permanently.

---

* Richards was severely embarrassed when his rather naive colleague, Colonel Phillipps, conveyed this view directly to the Prime Minister. Later in the year Dr Bialoguski wrote to Brigadier Spry requesting a written 'release' from him, to enable a character based on Spry to be included in the film of his Petrov book which was being mooted in the United States. Spry replied at once with a resounding and heart-felt rebuff.

After the publication of his articles relations between Bialoguski and the Petrovs also deteriorated. Petrov now spoke of Bialoguski as 'a friend of the Communists'.[51] He was, in particular, severely embarrassed that his old friend had revealed aspects of their night life together in Sydney. In an unpublished catalogue of Bialoguski's 'errors', Petrov protested, 'I do not like visiting night clubs ... I went to night clubs only in the line of duty'. Even more deeply Petrov was offended that his Polish friend had portrayed him as a Russian hick. He had not been astonished to see the swimming pool at the Cliveden Flats; he had not cut a ridiculous figure there.

> I consider that Bialoguski disgraced me in the eyes of the public by describing that I wore a pair of tricky green satin bathing trunks which reached from below my navel to the knees. . . . The trunks I wore were of the standard type which I purchased from David Jones and which were worn by me in the normal way.[52]

The Petrovs were hurt in their pocket as well as their pride by Dr Bialoguski. The value of their book, which was not to appear in advance of the Royal Commission, would certainly be greatly reduced due to Bialoguski's scoop. About this they were, and remained for some time, extremely bitter.

> They feel (an ASIO member of the safe house team reported on September 8 1955) that they were prevented from publishing their book at the opportune time, because they were under the control of ASIO, whereas Dr Bialoguski was not so prevented, and the sale of their book has accordingly suffered such damage that it will no longer provide them with a source of livelihood.[53]

By September 1955 the only moral sentiment uniting the Petrov and anti-Petrov camps was a thorough distrust of Dr Bialoguski — who had managed to discomfit them both. Beyond that it was all-out war. Political wounds had by now opened which a life time would not heal. As the moment approached when the Royal Commission report was to be presented to Parliament the appetites in both the camps for some final vengeance and victory remained keen.

16

CLIMAX

The report of the Royal Commission on Espionage was released to the Australian public on September 14 1955. The Commissioners reported that all the Petrov documents were 'authentic' and that the Petrov couple were 'witnesses of truth'. From its establishment in 1943 to its departure in 1954 the Soviet Embassy in Canberra had been used for conducting espionage activities in Australia. It was certain, they reported, that during this period there had existed two quite separate 'legal' espionage apparatuses in Australia — of the MVD and the GRU — and at least possible that two further parallel 'illegal' apparatuses had also operated during that time.

As the Commissioners reported, the greatest achievement of the Soviet intelligence service in Australia had occurred in the years between 1945 and 1948 when secret documents from the Department of External Affairs — some emanating from Australia's great power allies — had been delivered to the MVD Centre at Moscow. The Royal Commissioners' findings suggested that two former External Affairs officers — Ian Milner and Jim Hill — had been responsible for disclosing documents that eventually had made their way to the Soviet intelligence service. They also found that the chief conduit at this time for information passing between External Affairs at Canberra and the MVD Centre at Moscow was the Communist Party functionary, Walter Clayton. Whether Milner and Hill knew that the information they had passed to Clayton was ultimately destined for Soviet eyes was, according to the Royal Commissioners, uncertain.

The Commissioners found that after 1949, despite considerable effort, the MVD in Australia had achieved nothing which could compare with their External Affairs successes of 1945-8. The Petrov documents certainly revealed MVD interest in the 'study' of some 120 Australian residents of whom 40 had been allotted code-names. However, in the overwhelming majority of these cases, the evidence made clear that even the 'study' of these potential sources of information or recruits had not been pursued either seriously or, indeed, at all. They also reported that it was only amongst Communists (party members or sympathisers) that the MVD could hope to find new agents in Australia. 'Without Communism', they concluded, 'Soviet espionage could have no hope of success in this country'.

Amongst the modest post-1948 successes of the MVD the Commissioners included the authors of Documents 'J' and 'H' — Rupert Lockwood and Fergan O'Sullivan. By composing 'J' inside the Soviet Embassy Lockwood had compromised himself deeply. By composing 'H' O'Sullivan had at least placed himself on a 'small hook'. As O'Sullivan was at the time of the Petrov defection on the personal staff of the Leader of the Opposition — the potential Prime Minister — his vulnerability to Soviet blackmail represented for Australian security a most genuine danger. During Petrov's Residency the MVD had, they argued, an agent inside the Latvian community — Fridenbergs. It had a former Czech agent here — Divisek — whom it hoped to reactivate, but who had actually revealed his intelligence past to the Australian authorities. It had developed a plan to smuggle into Australia an 'illegal' intelligence operative in the guise of a relative of an old Russian migrant (Kasanova). It had, moreover, in Australia a steady group of willing helpers or contacts — Rex Chiplin, Jack Hughes, John Rodgers and Jean Ferguson. In one final case, they concluded, the MVD was playing for very high stakes indeed. The purpose of the protracted cultivation of Mme Ollier was Soviet acquisition of the French diplomatic cypher. As we have seen, the Commissioners concluded that while Mme Ollier had certainly met with Petrov on a number of occasions under clandestine conditions she had never agreed to pass onto him the cypher information he wanted.

The Royal Commissioners reported that after 1949 the MVD had not managed to penetrate either the Department of External Affairs or ASIO or any other Government department. For its lack of success on these fronts Australia's counter-intelligence service — ASIO — received handsome praise. Although, as we have seen, certain ASIO officers privately suspected that Petrov might not have told them the whole truth about his espionage activities in Australia, such doubts were nowhere to be found in the final report of the Royal Commission.[1]

The Commissioners recommended that no prosecutions be launched as a consequence of their inquiry. As they explained, this was in part because of the absence of any Australian law dealing specifically with the subject matter of their investigations — espionage on behalf of a foreign power during peacetime*[2] — and in part because they believed much of the evidence they

---

* The only Australian law of possible relevance to the Royal Commission's inquiries were Sections 70, 78 and 79 of the Crimes Act. Sections 70 and 79 were derived from the British Official Secrets Act of 1911. They were not concerned specifically with espionage but with the unauthorised disclosure by a public servant of information or documents acquired in the course of duties. Section 78 was concerned with espionage, but it was so ambiguously worded as to be regarded by the Royal Commissioners as beyond use. It is not generally known that in September 1952 the Menzies Cabinet had rejected a proposal for a new 'Official Secrets Act' put forward by a committee which had been chaired by the Attorney-General. This proposed legislation dealt with a 'new and specific offense of spying, i.e. acting as a spy for a foreign power or for an enemy'.

had heard during their proceedings would be technically inadmissible in a court of law.[3]

The legal situation can be explained, more concretely, thus. As a result of the Royal Commission findings there were six Australians about whom the question of prosecution at law might conceivably be raised — Rupert Lockwood, Fergan O'Sullivan, Frances Bernie, Walter Clayton, Jim Hill and (if he were to return from Prague) Ian Milner. In composing their own documents and passing them to the MVD neither Lockwood nor O'Sullivan had, however, committed any offense under existing Australian law. While Frances Bernie had certainly broken the law — in passing official documents to Walter Clayton without authorisation — she had only admitted to doing so after having been granted an immunity from prosecution. On the other hand, strangely enough, in *receiving* unauthorised documents from her and others, and in passing them on to the MVD, Walter Clayton had probably not broken the law. Finally, while for their part Milner and Hill had probably committed an offence under existing law, the evidence upon which their cases would rest, even if it were technically admissible, could never be produced in court. As we have seen the leakage of material from Milner and Hill was discovered as a result of the post-war FBI-M15 cryptanalytic breakthrough into MVD codes.[4] The fact that such a breakthrough had occurred was one of the most heavily defended secrets of the Western counter-intelligence services.*[5]

As is the Australian tradition the major findings of the Royal Commission on Espionage were reported in the press extensively and objectively. Moreover, on September 15 most editorial writers praised the report extremely highly, both for the thoroughness of its investigations and the moderation of its tone. Concern at the vaulting ambitions of Soviet espionage in Australia was balanced with relief at the apparent insignificance of its achievements after 1948. ASIO was, in general, commended highly. The editorialists drew from the Royal Commission report two main morals. The Australian law concerning espionage needed to be tightened; the vigilance of the ASIO against the subversive activities of Communists needed to be maintained.[6] Amongst the metropolitan dailies only two dissenters were to be found. In Adelaide one paper thought that the Petrov Commission had proved 'the dampest and dreariest of squibs', of value only to the small minority of Australian McCarthyites; the Melbourne *Argus* (perhaps forgetting that it had once thundered for just such an inquiry) now believed the Royal Commission to have been a colossal waste of taxpayers' money.[7]

Almost before the printer's ink was dry on the Royal Commission report the Petrov and anti-Petrov camps within the labour movement had flown at

---

* So much so that the American public has only discovered in the past few years the most damning evidence of the guilt of the Rosenbergs, which was derived through the cryptanalytic channel.

each other's throats. After a 'quick perusal' of the findings on the day of its release, Dr Evatt expressed his 'surprise at the apparent failure of the Commissioners to expose one of the most transparent political frauds in modern history'. The Petrov Affair, or what he called 'the Petrov-Bialoguski scandal' was 'far worse' than the Zinovieff letter case. McCarthy-like smearings of loyal Australians had been organised by 'anti-Labor groups through agents and informers'.[8] On the following day Dr John Burton — who was now working closely with Dr Evatt — seized his opportunity to initiate his fellow countrymen into his 'gnomes of Melbourne' Petrovian theories. The Petrov Affair had been, he argued in a long press release, conjured by a secret society of revanchist elements within the Defence and Intelligence establishment who had deeply resented the emergence of a genuinely Australian foreign policy under the Evatt-Burton External Affairs regime.

> There are far more sinister forces at work than Communism, aiming to muzzle opinion, to discredit opposition views, to take policy out of the hands of the people in case the people cannot always be persuaded to elect a government which is subject to their control. These forces are at present centred in the Defence and Civilian Intelligence Services, and aided and abetted by the Catholic Action minority in the community which itself had been strongly represented in these Services.[9]

Speaking for these 'sinister forces', Mr Joshua, the leader of the Anti-Communist Labor Party, thought it 'surely impossible' that Dr Evatt could now continue as Leader of the ALP.[10] His deputy, Stan Keon, requested an assurance from the Prime Minister that the Report would soon be debated in Parliament, so that the Australian people could decide for themselves whether the Leader of the Opposition was 'a responsible statesman or a wicked defamer'.[11] Keon's personal views on this matter were far from secret. He soon told a wild Petrov rally held in the Hawthorn Town Hall that Dr Evatt was 'a traitor to Australia'.[12] More soberly *News Weekly* informed its readers that the most serious finding of the Royal Commission concerned the 'substantial infiltration' of External Affairs by Communists and spies while Dr Evatt was the responsible Minister and Dr Burton his departmental head.[13] As traditional and Anti-Communist Labor locked horns once again over Petrov it would have been surprising if the Prime Minister's thoughts had not turned towards the idea of an early election.

The Petrovs' story *Empire of Fear*, which had been ghosted by the ASIO director of counter-espionage, Michael Thwaites, was published and serialised throughout Australia in the same week as the Royal Commission report appeared. Neither as a literary nor as a financial enterprise was it altogether successful. The book modestly assumed its place at the end of a long line of Cold War, Soviet defector, 'I Chose Freedom' books. Unhappily for the Petrovs, by 1955 — in the era of the first post-war East-West détente — this genre had already become somewhat unfashionable. Moreover the rather elegant and Anglo-Saxon style of their ghost sat uneasily with the brutal realities of the story the Petrovs had to tell — of the rise and fall of two Russian peasants within the murderous world of Stalin's security service.

Although ASIO estimated that the Petrovs would eventually gross between £10,000 ($120,000) and £15,000 ($180,000) from *Empire of Fear*, in general they were bitterly disappointed with the financial aspect of its publication. In Britain André Deutsch offered only £1,000 for the book rights; in the United States no publisher could be found at all.[14] Even within Australia interest in their story was waning. The *Sydney Morning Herald's* offer for serialisation rights had been reduced from an original, genuinely fantastic, £25,000 ($300,000) to the far less heady £6,000 ($72,000).[15] In mid-September 1955, the Petrovs felt it advisable to give radio interviews in Australia aimed all too obviously at rekindling some popular interest in their tale.

Mrs Petrov: Volodoya and I have spent a lot of time on this book....
Petrov: As my wife says, it is OUR story and one, I think, that will astonish Australia and the world....
Foster: ... What else can you tell our listeners about your story?
Petrov: It starts in the *Sun-Herald* on Saturday.
Foster: I see. And what ... is the dramatic highlight...?
Petrov: There are plenty of dramatic highlights, and thrills. I'm not far wrong in saying there is a thrill in every instalment.

Towards the end of one of these promotional interviews Petrova had quoted a passage from the concluding words of *Empire of Fear*, which had offered some rather Keatsian 'reflections ... on first hearing the song of an Australian magpie.'

'Perhaps also in our life' (the Thwaites-Petrova passage continued) 'a night of fear is ending and a new morning is beginning.'

Her interviewer, who thought the passage 'lovely', suggested that on another occasion Petrova might like to tell the listeners about her new life in Australia.[16] If Petrova had agreed, and if she had spoken truly, her interviewer and his listeners would have been in for a considerable shock.

By the time of the publication of *Empire of Fear* a profound and genuinely pitiful life crisis had overtaken the Petrovs. Both had become bundles of nerves, fears and resentments. The Petrovs were still obsessed by the idea of finding someone who would write for them the definitive 'refutation' of Dr Bialoguski. When Michael Thwaites refused this commission their anger turned against ASIO. Now that the Royal Commission was over and their book published, neither had the faintest idea what the long-term future held in store for them.*[17] They both wondered why they had not yet been granted

---

* In the short term Brigadier Spry arranged for them to remain salaried servants of the Commonwealth. Interrogations were far from complete. Brigadier Spry recommended that Petrov receive £3000 p.a. ($36,000) and Petrova £1500 ($18,000).

Australian naturalisation. Petrova suspected that her past expressions of fondness for her homeland or concern for her family might have prejudiced Australian authority against her. She had, she told ASIO, lost the 'faith' which had given her the strength to defect; she now considered herself a traitor to the Soviets. For his part, Petrov was, as ever, drinking too much. He felt he was being driven by ill-treatment into a 'mad house'.[18]

Within ASIO it was recognised by mid-September that something had to be done to settle the Petrov's nerves. On September 23 two ASIO cars left Sydney in great secrecy carrying the Petrovs and their retinue to Surfers' Paradise for a month's holiday.[19] Unfortunately, shortly after their arrival, Petrova became gravely ill. She was flown to Sydney at once for an urgent operation, after which she was, apparently, not far from death.[20] Physical collapse now triggered an emotional breakdown. On one evening during her convalescence in hospital she kicked and struck out at her nurses claiming that they were poisoning her.[21] On another occasion she wrote a melodramatic farewell note to her husband.

I insisted for a long time to see you at the hospital but without success. Goodbye, my dear, forever.
I always loved you and always will love you.
I never thought this would happen so soon.[22]

Within the hospital Petrova spoke so openly and bitterly about Australia to the hospital staff that the surgeon attending her wondered aloud to ASIO whether 'it was safe from a security point of view, her staying here and still having criticism of Australia at the back of her mind'.[23]

During his wife's stormy recuperation, Petrov was in an only marginally more robust emotional state than her. On one memorable evening he actually fled the safe house and hitched a ride to Manly with ASIO in pursuit. As he was driven home — under the pretence of collecting broth to take to Petrova's hospital bed — Petrov threatened to leap to freedom from the moving ASIO car and 'waved his arms around to attract the attention of oncoming motorists'.[24] As the Australian Parliament prepared for the debate on the report of the Petrov Royal Commission, one thing at least was clear. The Petrovs' 'new morning' in Australia had not yet dawned.

On the evening of October 19 1955 Dr Evatt initiated the House of Representatives debate on the Petrov Affair. In some ways Evatt had been preparing himself for this moment for the past eighteen months. He informed the House that, if permitted, he could have spoken for 'twelve days'.[25] His deputy had negotiated with the Government leader in the House for 'unlimited time'. In the end he had been allotted the far from miserly two hours.[26] Sensing that this speech might prove of some significance in Australian history someone in ASIO wisely decided to make a recording of Dr Evatt's Petrov address.[27] As it turned out, it was to prove the most important of his political life.

Dr Evatt began, promisingly enough, with a passage suggested to him by his political ally, Brian Fitzpatrick:[28]

> What is the upshot of the Petrov affair? Two foreigners, the Petrovs, and one foreign born Australian spy, Bialoguski, have made a lot of money. The forum in which they appeared cost the taxpayers £140,000 ... The nation has suffered heavy loss in trade, and the breaking of diplomatic relations with a great power. There has been the attempted smearing of many innocent Australians.... but ... no spies have been discovered. Not a single prosecution is recommended.

He moved on, less promisingly, with a passage very much his own. One of the major issues raised by the Petrov Affair, he told the House, was the authenticity of the 'Moscow letters'.

> Determined to ascertain the truth of these grave matters, I took two steps, as follows:- First of all, I communicated with His Excellency, the Foreign Minister of the Soviet Union.... I pointed out that the Soviet Government ... [was] undoubtedly in a position to reveal the truth as to the genuineness of the Petrov documents. I duly received a reply sent on behalf of the Foreign Minister of the Union of Soviet Socialist Republics, Mr Molotov.

There was within the House a momentary pause of unbelief, and then — from that merciless enemy of the absurd — volleys of laughter. The laughter came from both sides of the House. Dr Evatt appeared to be surprised. 'Honourable Members can laugh and clown but they've got to face up to some facts tonight.'[29] The House was now in uproar, but Evatt continued. Mr Molotov had claimed the Petrov documents were fabrications. He attached 'grave importance' to his letter. He suggested the establishment of an international court 'to settle the dispute once and for all'.

With some courage Dr Evatt soldiered on through his written speech. All the old familiar landmarks of the conspiracy theory were there — the *News Weekly* article of January 1953; Dr Bialoguski's tell-tale trip to Canberra to see Mr Menzies; the March 1954 Gallup Poll predicting an ALP victory; the 'Hollywood touch' at the Albert Hall; the undisclosed payment of £5000; the Royal Commission Christmas Party. In addition Dr Evatt had made some discoveries of his own. According to old Dr Monticone the handwriting in one of the 'G' documents was not, as claimed, Sadovnikov's. The use of the term MVD in the translations of the Moscow Letters of 1952 appeared to Evatt a sure sign of forgery. Petrov had in fact in 1952 been employed by the MGB.*[30] Dr Evatt demanded that the Russian originals of the Petrov documents be tabled in the Parliament so that their authenticity could be

---

* This claim of Evatt's was based on the simplest error. As the Royal Commissioners explained they had used the term MVD throughout their report in order to avoid the confusion arising from the endless changes in the name of the Soviet security service between 1943 and 1954.

tested. Once more he rose to the defence of the honour of Mme Ollier who had, he claimed, been 'cleared of the serious imputation of subversion.' (From the cross-benches John Mullens shouted 'She has not'.) Evatt was pleased to see that the Commission had finally lifted the wicked 1952 'nest of traitors' slander from the shoulders of his old departmental head, Dr Burton. Nevertheless there had been such 'jealously and hatred' for the Evatt-Burton foreign policy that two External Affairs officers (whose names he would not mention) were still the victims of a 'degrading' attack. In 1953 ASIO had reopened cases which years before had been closed.

Petrov appeared to Dr Evatt more a drunkard than a spy. 'It is very difficult', he observed, 'to find any case where instructions given to Petrov were carried out'. ASIO had wickedly seduced him from his allegiance to the Soviet Union. The Bialoguski wire recordings were used to blackmail Petrov into complicity in ASIO's plot. His defection had been planned coldly and calculatedly by Australian Security over many months. Its immediate purpose had been a Menzies election victory in 1954; its more long-term and sinister purpose the attack on political non-conformity in Australia. 'The security service was never intended to be a secret police organization.' Strangely enough, in no part of his speech did Dr Evatt mention the *fons et origo* of his conspiracy theory — Document 'J'.[31]

In the printed columns of *Hansard* Dr Evatt's Petrovian address reads like a powerful, if fundamentally wrongheaded, attack upon the Menzies Government and ASIO. However, in the House on October 19 — in the atmosphere created by his reference to Mr Molotov — it was a political disaster. A parliament which has smelt blood is a cruel human assembly. Dr Evatt delivered his speech in a flat, unworldly monotone amidst taunts and jeers. (At one point the Speaker threatened that if he discovered which members were whistling he would have them thrown out of the House.) In his Molotov reference all judgment had deserted him. As he spoke, his isolation from his fellows appeared profound. By the time he had concluded there was, no doubt, gaiety in the hearts of Government members. On the Opposition benches — in a gesture of wonderful eloquence — Dr Evatt's supporters held their heads in their hands.[32]

Inside ASIO Dr Evatt's speech created immediate and profound anger. Brigadier Spry was not a cold man, but a man of passion. His deepest values were those of the soldier. Dr Evatt had impugned not only his own honour and patriotism but also that of his troops. As Director-General of ASIO he could not publicly defend himself or his staff. He relied upon the Prime Minister.

> In view of the virulence and falsity of Dr Evatt's attacks (Spry wrote at once to Mr Menzies' Secretary) I do feel that he has not only jeopardised my own career as a loyal servant of the Crown but also that of my colleagues. This is a shameful situation, which I feel should not be left unanswered . . . ASIO has behaved under

my direction with the utmost impartiality and scrupulousness. As to being a party to forgery and fabrication, this strikes directly at the integrity of myself and my colleagues.[33]

On the morning following Dr Evatt's Petrov speech the resources of the Government were fully mobilised in preparation for Mr Menzies' reply which was due in six days' time. The people best positioned to answer the many specific allegations about forgery and fraud were those who had been daily involved in the proceedings of the Royal Commission. Three critical demolitions of Dr Evatt's case had been forwarded to the Prime Minister's department from the Commission Secretary, Kenneth Herde; from one of the counsel assisting, George Pape; and from Brigadier Spry.[34] By the use of this material Mr Menzies could have refuted each of Dr Evatt's conspiracy allegations, detail by detail. He received however quite different and extremely shrewd advice from an anonymous member of his department.

> For any charge of conspiracy to succeed, in the light of the Royal Commission findings, there would have to be a fundamental psychological adjustment in the community.... A multiplicity of detailed points laboured on for four hours could create the impression that there is something in the charge after all. The object of the exercise would be achieved if each point raised were meticulously disposed of by the Prime Minister. The Prime Minister will want to avoid this.[35]

While consideration was being given to Mr Menzies' response to Dr Evatt, a fresh source of anxiety arose, unexpectedly, for the Government. From Paris, it was reported on October 20 that Mme Ollier had been acquitted by the French military court. Although the Menzies Government might know that this judgment did not reveal the Petrovs' evidence about her to be false, it was not so clear that the Australian public would see things this way. There were some signs of panic. Brigadier Spry decided now to summarise for Mr Menzies' use the evidence in the supposedly secret Ramier report.[36] Moreover, at once a series of urgent telegrams were despatched from Canberra to Paris requesting detailed information about the evidence which had been presented at her trial.* As usual, the French displayed little concern for the

---

* Canberra telegrammed Paris thus on October 21 1955:

'Radio reports in considerable detail acquitted of Madame Ollier ... Please advise by telegram whether Ollier admitted:
 (i)   receipt of watch
 (ii) meeting with Petrov at Cooma
 (iii) meetings with Sadovnikov
 (iv) truth of Ramier Report ...
Please telegraph all relevant sections of the judgment bearing in mind that:
 (a) Leader of Opposition has said publicly that acquittal justifies his belief that whole Petrov case was fabrication;
 (b) Prime Minister will shortly speak in parliamentary debate on Royal Commission Report.'

domestic needs of the Menzies Government.[37] If Dr Evatt had not so comprehensively shot himself in the foot over Molotov he would have been excellently placed to inflict some real damage on the Prime Minister on the eve of his Petrovian address in reply.

Mr Menzies spoke in the House on the evening of October 25. The speech he delivered — which was, like Evatt's, recorded by ASIO for posterity — revealed him at the top of his form. It is justly regarded as one of the greatest moments of his parliamentary career. Wisely, he had accepted the advice of his department. A painstaking refutation of Dr Evatt, no matter how successful and intellectually satisfying, would have been politically self-defeating. Mr Menzies' ground was not that of the advocate but the conservative elder, whose duty it was to protect tradition, institution and character from what he called Dr Evatt's 'reckless and villainous charges'.

The Royal Commission on Espionage had been established, Mr Menzies reminded the House, with the unanimous support of Parliament. It had listened patiently to evidence over ten months. Dr Evatt's suggestion that the Parliament could now set itself up as a court of appeal over the Commission was ridiculous, 'frivolous and offensive'. The judges who had sat upon it, whose findings were disputed by Dr Evatt and so damaging to him, were outstanding lawyers of unquestioned integrity. Two had been chosen to serve the Curtin-Chifley Governments in different capacities. They had done so with distinction. All three had rallied to the nation's flag in the First World War. Mr Windeyer had been in the Second War a highly decorated soldier. The very name Windeyer represented 'all that is best in the New South Wales legal tradition'. And as for Brigadier Spry — the central target of Dr Evatt's 'venomous' attacks, for whom Evatt had said 'peace' was a 'dirty word — had he not been wounded on the Kokoda trail in the service of his country? (Eventually this catalogue of military virtue proved too much for one Labor backbencher who asked Menzies to outline his own military record. Menzies suggested he rather ask 'Bert and Eddie' about theirs.)

Mr Menzies dealt in detail only with the charges that had been brought by Dr Evatt against himself, 'the chief of which', he suggested impishly, 'is that I am Prime Minister'. He had not, he told the House, heard the name of Petrov before April 1954, although he had been told in mid-February of the possibility of a Soviet defection. A certain Dr Bialoguski had travelled to Canberra in October 1953 to see him but his secretary, Geoffrey Yeend, had wisely handled the matter without reference to the Prime Minister. He had not heard of the £5000 payment to Petrov until a meeting with Windeyer and Spry on May 9. Given the importance of the defection of Petrov for the security of Australia and her allies this amount was amply justifed. And as for Dr Evatt's central accusation — that he had manipulated the affair for electoral advantage — Menzies reminded the House that if had permitted the names of O'Sullivan or Grundeman to be revealed to the public before the election, Dr Evatt would not now be seated on the Opposition benches. All members on the Government benches could attest that he had issued the firmest instructions at the beginning of the campaign that the matter of the Petrov defections was not to be raised on the hustings.

Dr Evatt's motives throughout this affair had been thoroughly contemptible. He preferred the word of Molotov to that of distinguished Australian judges. His mind was 'unbalanced', filled with 'fantasies', 'delusions' and 'obsessions'. He posed as a defender of justice; he was in reality interested only in himself.

> If there is a charge to be made (he concluded) it is this: the Leader of the Opposition has, from first to last in this matter, for his own purposes, in his own interests and with the enthusiastic support of every Communist in Australia, sought to discredit the judiciary, to subvert the authority of the security organization, to cry down decent and patriotic Australians and to build up a Communist fifth column. I am, therefore, compelled to say that in the name of all these good and honorable men, in the name of public decency, in the name of the safety of Australia, the man on trial in this debate is the right honorable gentleman himself.

It was a cruel and devastating and decisive speech.[38]

Tempers were exceedingly short in the House after Menzies had spoken. A furious argument erupted over what precisely had transpired in discussions between Sir Eric Harrison and Arthur Calwell over the time to be allotted to Stan Keon in the debate that evening.[39] When Keon finally spoke he delivered a melancholy historical address on the relation between the Petrov Affair and the Split. 'We are in this corner', he began, 'because of the attempts of ... [Dr Evatt] to prevent us from expressing our views in the caucus of the Australian Labor Party' on his behaviour at the Royal Commission. Dr Evatt had defiled the good name of the Party by his defence of Communists and traitors. The Anti-Communists were its only faithful defenders. The split was tragic and needless. It had driven from the Party men 'born and bred' in the Labor tradition. One day the Party would rediscover its soul. This speech was the parliamentary swansong of a man once regarded as a future Prime Minister.[40]

On the afternoon following his Petrov address Mr Menzies announced in Parliament what had been confidently predicted for the past week — there would be an early election on December 10 for both Houses.[41] Menzies' justification was the good sense of realigning the elections for the Senate and the Representatives. His reason was the split in Labor and the quality over the past months of Dr Evatt's leadership. If any doubts existed in his mind about this course, Evatt's injection of the name of Molotov into the Petrov Affair had surely resolved them. There were now, once again, rumours of moves to replace Dr Evatt.[42] The independent leftist, Allan Fraser, had, once again, broken ranks in order to tell the truth. Dr Evatt's reference to Molotov had 'astounded' his Caucus colleagues.[43] After the Menzies' announcement of the early election, Dr Evatt threw at him a premonitory text from Corinthians: 'Let him that thinketh he standeth take heed lest he fall'. A political journalist on the *Sun-Herald* thought a more appropriate text for present circumstances was to be found in the Book of Samuel. 'The Lord had delivered thee today into mine hand.'[44] A landslide victory, in the lower House at least, seemed inevitable.*[45]

The overwhelming issue of the 1954 election was the cost of Dr Evatt. If there was any issue which dominated the 1955 election it was his character. As one Coalition advertisement put it: 'Evatt has wrecked the Labor Party. Don't let him wreck Australia.'[46] No doubt in deference to his colleagues' wishes and fears Dr Evatt did not so much as refer to the Petrov Affair in his opening campaign address. This was a telling omission.[47] Everyone (except *Tribune*) now knew that the Petrov Affair had become for the ALP an electoral liability. Whenever Dr Evatt himself raised the issue later in the campaign it was in self-defence.[48] The cry of 'Molotov' pursued him from one election rally to the next.[49] In May 1954 Sir Arthur Fadden had posed to Dr Evatt 'thirteen questions' about Communism. In November 1955 he asked him to answer a more modest nine about Molotov.[50]

All this was probably in the end of little account. The arithmetic of Australian politics after the Split was all too clear. While Anti-Communist Labor could take a substantial vote from traditional Labor and pass its preferences to the Coalition the prospects for the ALP were bleak. At the polls the Coalition received 47.6% of the vote for the House of Representatives, traditional Labor 44.6% and Anti-Communist Labor 5.2%. While the combined Labor vote (by now a metaphysical concept) was almost identical to that of May 1954, the preferences of Anti-Communist Labor (at least in Victoria where they won 15.8% of the vote) proved critical.[51] In the new House of Representatives the Government had 75 seats, the Opposition 47. This was not a mere electoral victory; the Menzies era had arrived.

---

* At no time since September 1954 had Gallup discovered a level of support for the ALP in excess of 48%. In one poll (July 1955) it measured ALP support at 42%. In the election of May 1954 the ALP had not won government despite a vote of more than 50%. The Gallup Polls for most of 1955 did not allow voters to express a preference for Anti-Communist Labor.

NOTES

Abbreviations:

AA CRS   Australian Archives, Commonwealth Record Services (Canberra)
ANL   Australian National Library, Manuscript Room (Canberra)
F.U.   Flinders University Library (Adelaide)
H. of R.   Commonwealth of Australia, *Parliamentary Debates*,
             House of Representatives, Canberra.
RCE   Royal Commission on Espionage.

Note:
Details of books are given in full in the initial citation, thereafter in shortened form.

1: AN NKVD COUPLE

1. AA CRS A6119/XR1/7, ff. 3-5, Memoranda, Principal Section Officer, B2, February 6 1951.
2. For the first ASIO intelligence biographies of the Petrovs, see AA CRS A6283/80, ff. 123-151, 'Report on the Background History of Vladimir Mikhailovich Petrov', June 28 1954; AA CRS A6283/XR1/14, ff. 130-141, 'Personal History of Evdokia Alexeyevna Petrova', undated.
3. Vladimir and Evdokia Petrov, *Empire of Fear*, André Deutsch, London, 1956, chs. I-IV.
4. *Ibid.*, p. 105.
5. *Ibid.*, chs. IX-XI.
6. AA CRS A6283/XR1/14, ff. 37-41, 'Mrs Petrov's statement concerning her past intelligence history', May 15 1954; AA CRS A6283/XR1/14, f. 59, E. Petrova, Explanatory Note, undated.
7. V. and E. Petrov, *Empire of Fear*, chs. V-VIII. For a general account of this period of NKVD history see Robert Conquest, *The Great Terror: Stalin's Purge of the Thirties*, Penguin, London, 1971.
8. RCE, Transcript of Proceedings, Evidence of E.A. Petrova, September 2 1954, p. 707.
9. V. and E. Petrov, *Empire of Fear*, chs. XII-XIII.
10. *Ibid.*, ch. XIV.
11. *Ibid.*, ch. XV; AA CRS A6283/80, ff. 123-51, 'Report . . .' etc., June 28 1954, pp. 1 and 5-6.
12. V. and E. Petrov, *Empire of Fear*, ch. XVII.
13. *Ibid.*, ch. XVI.
14. The clearest description of the post-Swedish career paths of the Petrovs are in AA CRS A6283/80, ff. 123-51, 'Report . . .', etc., June 28 1954, pp. 7-11, and AA CRS A6283/XR1/14, ff. 130-141, 'Personal History . . .', etc., undated, pp. 6-7. For an account of the rise and fall of the KI see, AA CRS A6283/XR1/7, ff. 26-50, 'The Committee of Information ('K.I.'), 1947-1951', November 17 1954.

15. RCE, Transcript of Proceedings, Evidence of E.A. Petrova, July 6 1954, p. 155; AA CRS A6283/XR1/18, ff. 206-7, Statement, E.A. Petrova re: Ia Mikhailovna Griazanova, September 14 1954.
16. AA CRS A6283/80, ff. 123-151, 'Report . . .', etc., June 28 1954, pp. 11-17; AA CRS A6283/XR1/14, ff. 130-141, 'Personal History . . .', etc., undated, pp. 7-9.

2: DIABOLO

1. AA CRS A6119/XR/8, f. 29, Report of 'J. Baker', July 9 1951.
2. AA CRS A6119/XR1/7, f. 41, Letter, NSW Branch ASIO, October 31 1951.
3. AA CRS A6283/XR1/6, ff. 94-5, 'EM Operations of the State Security Service'.
4. AA CRS A6119/XR/8, f. 28, Report of 'J. Baker', July 9 1951.
5. V. and E. Petrov, *Empire of Fear*, pp. 279-80.
6. Michael Bialoguski, *The Petrov Story*, William Heinemann, Melbourne, chs. 4-6.
7. AA CRS A6119/XR1/1, 'Application for employment, Michael Bialoguski', August 29 1949.
8. A contact of Dr Evatt's informed him that a Macquarie Street doctor, Blacket, had told him that Dr Bialoguski was a 'notorious abortionist . . . [another doctor] recently had to handle one of Bialoguski's patients. A young girl, about eighteen, and the unfortunate girl died. She was in a bloody mess'. F.U., Evatt Papers, Petrov Affair files, correspondence — relating to case, Frank Clancy to Dr Evatt, October 13 1955. On July 4 1955 Lydia Mokras told ASIO about Dr Bialoguski's abortion practice, which 'incensed' her. AA CRS A6119/XR1/192, f. 80, Interview with Lydia Mokras, July 5 1955.
9. The unpublished manuscript of books concerning Dr Bialoguski written by Patricia Bialoguski and Lydia Mokras are preserved amongst the Evatt papers. F.U., Evatt Papers, Petrov Affair files, Miscellaneous (Lydia Mokras); Mrs Bialoguski, autobiography (a) and (b).
10. M. Bialoguski, *The Petrov Story*, *passim*.; AA CRS A6119/XR1/1, f. 125, Report on ASIO career of M. Bialoguski.
11. M. Bialoguski, *The Petrov Story*, p. 64; AA CRS A6119/XR1/192, ff. 50-61, Statement of Lydia Mokras, June 10 1954; AA CRS A6283/XR/85, ff. 216-9, Statement by V.M. Petrov regarding Lydia Mokras, March 7 1955; AA CRS A6119/XR1/192, ff. 68-78, Interview with Lydia Mokras, April 14 1955; AA CRS A6119/XR1/192, ff. 80-6, July 5 1955; AA CRS A6119/XR1/192, ff. 87-9, Interview with Lydia Mokras, July 8 1955. The manuscript of *Cloak and Beggar* is in F.U., Evatt Papers, Petrov Affair files, Miscellaneous.
12. AA CRS A6119/XR1/7, ff. 34 and 50.
13. *Ibid.*, f. 34, Report by M. Bialoguski, July 31 1951 and *ibid.*, f. 38, Report by M. Bialoguski, August 8 1951.
14. M. Bialoguski, *The Petrov Story*, p. 78; AA CRS A6283/XR1/85, ff. 216-9, Statement by V.M. Petrov regarding Lydia Mokras, March 7 1955.
15. Michael Thwaites, *Truth Will Out: ASIO and the Petrovs*, Collins, Sydney, 1980, pp. 77-8.
16. AA CRS A6283/XR1/6, ff. 216-38, 'Defection of Vladimir Mikhailovich Petrov alias Proletarski and Evdokia Alexeyevna Petrova alias Kartseva', undated, p. 3.
17. AA CRS A6119/XR1/7, ff. 151 and 147, Bialoguski report, July 14 1952.
18. AA CRS A6119/XR1/8, f. 100, Bialoguski report, March 3 1953.
19. M. Bialoguski, *The Petrov Story*, p. 112.
20. AA CRS A6119/XR1/7, f. 133, Bialoguski report, May 6 1952.
21. AA CRS A6119/XR1/8, f. 67, Bialoguski report, February 5 1953; M. Bialoguski, *The Petrov Story*, pp. 145-6.
22. AA CRS A6119/XR1/8, f. 70, Bialoguski report, February 5 1953.
23. *Ibid.*, f. 254, Bialoguski report, May 19 1953.
24. M. Bialoguski, *The Petrov Story*, pp. 113-4.
25. Richard Pipes, *Russia under the Old Regime*, Penguin, Middlesex, 1979, p. 156.

26. AA CRS A6119/XR1/7, f. 81, Bialoguski report, March 1952.
27. *Ibid.*, f. 154, Bialoguski report, July 1952.
28. M. Bialoguski, *The Petrov Story*, pp. 71-2 and p. 94.
29. AA CRS A6283/XR1/6, ff. 216-38, 'Defection . . .' etc., (undated), p. 4.
30. AA CRS A6119/XR1/7, f. 84, Bialoguski report, February 22 1952.
31. *Ibid.*, f. 93, Bialoguski report, March 10 1952.
32. AA CRS A6119/XR1/8, f. 99, Bialoguski report, February 26 1953.
33. AA CRS A6283/XR1/6, ff. 216-38, 'Defection . . .' etc., (undated), p. 1; RCE, Transcript of Proceedings, Evidence of G.R. Richards, September 7 1954, p. 735; Interviews, Sir Charles Spry, May 3 and 7 1985.
34. AA CRS A6119/XR1/7, f. 73, Minute, February 14 1952.
35. AA CRS A6283/XR1/6, ff. 216-38, 'Defection . . .' etc., (undated), p. 4.
36. AA CRS A6119/XR1/7, f. 96, Report on Petrov, April 1952.
37. AA CRS A6119/XR1/8, f. 44, Report, December 1952.
38. AA CRS A6119/XR1/1, ff. 125-8, Report on payments to Dr Bialoguski, undated.
39. AA CRS A6283/XR1/6, ff. 216-38, 'Defection . . .' etc., (undated) esp. pp. 5-6.
40. AA CRS A462/211/1/8, S.J. Maruszewski to Mr R.G. Menzies, Prime Minister, September 26 1951.
41. *Ibid.*, Col. Spry, Director-General, ASIO to Mr R.G. Menzies, Prime Minister, March 6 1952.
42. Sydney *Sun*, July 4 1956.
43. AA CRS A462/211/1/8, Brig. Spry, Director-General, ASIO to Mr R.G. Menzies, Prime Minister, February 27 1956.
44. F.U., Evatt Papers, Petrov Affair files, 'Keep Your Mouth Shut — Or Else!!!' by George Marue, pp. 10-14.
45. M. Bialoguski, *The Petrov Story*, p. 116.
46. AA CRS A6119/XR/8,f. 191, Bialoguski report, April 21 1953.
47. *Ibid.*, f. 222, Bialoguski report, April 30 1953; M. Bialoguski, *The Petrov Story*, p. 117.
48. Quoted in RCE, Transcript of Proceedings, September 9 1954, p. 787.
49. AA CRS A6119/XR/8, f. 191, Bialoguski report, April 21 1953.
50. *Ibid.*, f. 221, Telephone message from Director B2, April 29 1953.
51. *Ibid.*, f. 190, Bialoguski report, April 21 1953.
52. *Ibid.*, ff. 224-8, Bialoguski report, May 5 1953.
53. M. Bialoguski, *The Petrov Story*, p. 107.
54. AA CRS A6283/XR1/6, ff. 216-38, 'Defection . . .' etc., (undated), p. 5.
55. Dr Bialoguski's letter is reprinted in M. Bialoguski, *The Petrov Story*, pp. 119-21.
56. Sydney *Sun*, July 4 1956.
57. M Bialoguski, *The Petrov Story*, p. 121.
58. *Ibid.*, pp. 122-4.
59. AA CRS A6119/XR1/2, ff. 53-4, Director-General, ASIO to R.W. Whitrod, Director, Commonwealth Investigation Service, June 24 1955; AA CRS A6119/XR1/2, ff. 95-8, R.W. Whitrod to Director-General, ASIO, July 26 1955.
60. AA CRS A6119/XR/8, f. 254, Bialoguski report, May 18-19 1953.
61. *Ibid.*, f. 255, Bialoguski report, May 19 1953.
62. *Ibid.*, f. 259, Bialoguski report, May 21 1953.
63. M. Bialoguski, *The Petrov Story*, p. 127.
64. AA CRS A6119/9, ff. 7a-7d, Bialoguski report, June 1 1953.
65. *Ibid.*, ff. 16-22, Bialoguski report, June 18 1953.
66. AA CRS A6283/XR1/6, ff. 216-38, 'Defection . . .' etc., (undated), p. 6.
67. RCE, Transcript of Proceedings, Evidence of G.R. Richards, September 7 1954, p. 737.
68. AA CRS A6283/XR1/6, ff. 216-38, 'Defection . . .' etc., (undated), p. 6.
69. *Ibid.*, p. 7.
70. AA CRS A6119/9, f. 104, Telephone message, Regional Director, NSW, to Director, B2, 4.30 p.m., July 23 1953.

71. RCE, Transcript of Proceedings, Evidence of H.C. Beckett, September 8 1954, p. 764.
72. *Ibid.*, Evidence of M. Bialoguski, September 10 1954, p. 792.
73. AA CRS A6119/9, f. 72, Telephone message, Regional Director, NSW, to Director, B2, 3.15 p.m., 24 July 1953.
74. AA CRS A6283/XR1/71, ff. 244-6, Memorandum for Principal Section Officer, B2, 24 August 1954.
75. M. Bialoguski, *The Petrov Story*, p. 134.
76. *Ibid.*, p. 135.
77. RCE, Transcript of Proceedings, Evidence of G.R. Richards, September 7 1954, p. 737.
78. AA CRS A6119/9, f. 140c, Bialoguski report, August 22 1953.
79. AA CRS A6283/XR1/6, ff. 216-38, 'Defection ...' etc., (undated), pp. 7-8.
80. AA CRS A6119/9, f. 140(e), Bialoguski report, August 22 1953.
81. AA CRS A6283/XR1/6, ff. 216-38, 'Defection ...' etc., (undated), p. 8; RCE, Transcript of Proceedings, Evidence of H.C. Beckett, September 8 1954, p. 764.
82. AA CRS A6119/XR1/1, ff. 125-8, Report on Payments to Dr Bialoguski, undated.
83. M. Bialoguski, *The Petrov Story*, pp. 136-9.
84. AA CRS A6213/RCE/G/7, Note by Mr Geoffrey Yeend, June 6 1955, ff. 111-2 and Memorandum, Geoffrey Yeend, June 17 1955, ff. 116-7.
85. M. Bialoguski, *The Petrov Story*, ch. 20; AA CRS A6119/XR1/2, ff. 23-31, ASIO commentary on Bialoguski's article of June 10 1955 in Sydney *Sun*.

3: TERROR AUSTRALIS

1. Commonwealth of Australia, *Report of the Royal Commission on Espionage, August 22 1955*, Government Printer, New South Wales, Sydney, 1955, Appendix no. 1, p. 331.
2. AA CRS A6283/XR1/6, f. 4, Statement by V.M. Petrov, September 12 1954.
3. AA CRS A6119/XR1/1, ff. 123-7, 'The Year 1953', Statement by V.M. Petrov, May 12 1954.
4. According to Petrova Antonov was timid and completely lacking in initiative while Kislitsyn was useless on the illegal line and 'did nothing'. Petrov admitted that he got 'no results' out of Kharkovetz and thought that he was not suited to intelligence work. He also thought Kovaliev 'a bad man, stupid ... always scared'. For Petrova's opinion of Antonov see, for example, A6215/4, Statement of E.A. Petrova regarding Fergan O'Sullivan, September 12 1954. For her opinion of Kislitsyn, RCE, Transcript of Proceedings, Evidence of E.A. Petrova, July 7 1954, p. 163. For Petrov's view of Kharkovetz, RCE, Transcript of Proceedings, Evidence of V.M. Petrov, July 6 1954, p. 150. For his view of Kovaliev, AA CRS A6283/XR/2, f. 101, Interview with Petrov at Safe House, commencing April 6 1954.
5. For accounts of these events see Wolfgang Leonhard, *The Kremlin Since Stalin*, (trans. E. Wiskemann and M. Jackson), Oxford University Press, London, 1962, ch. III; G.D. Embree, *The Soviet Union between the 19th and 20th Party Congresses, 1952-1956*, Martinus Nijhoff, The Hague, 1959. I would like to thank Dr Ferenc Feher who discussed this period of Soviet politics with me.
6. AA CRS A6119/9, f. 100, Report from McKillop's travel agency, July 20 1953; AA CRS A6119/9, f. 126, Col. Phillipps, Regional Director, ACT to Director, B2, August 11 1953.
7. AA CRS A6119/XR1/1, f. 143, 'Petrov's first draft on some pages of his statement about Moscow directives received in 1953/4'.
8. RCE, Transcript of Proceedings, Evidence of E.A. Petrova, July 9 1954, p. 201.
9. RCE, Report, Appendix no. 1, p. 335.
10. AA CRS A6215/4, Royal Commission on Espionage, Exhibit no. 61a.
11. See, for example, RCE, Transcript of Proceedings, Evidence of V.M. Petrov, July 5 1954, p. 135. 'She is a woman who likes the truth, and when the truth is not spoken she reacts'.

12. V. and E. Petrov, *Empire of Fear*, pp. 246-7; M. Thwaites, *Truth Will Out*, p. 84. Thwaites writes, 'Her meticulous attitude, she recounts, brought her into collision with Ambassador Lifanov, who was annoyed when she refused to bend regulations to his convenience'.
13. V. and E. Petrov, *Empire of Fear*, p. 247.
14. AA CRS A6119/9, f. 78, Report of Bialoguski, June 3 1953.
15. AA CRS A6122/XR1/13, f. 238, Memorandum by G.R. Richards, April 28 1954.
16. AA CRS A6119/9, f. 22a, Report of Bialoguski, June 21 1953.
17. V. and E. Petrov, *Empire of Fear*, pp. 248-9.
18. AA CRS A6119/XR/8, f. 44, ASIO report, December 1952.
19. AA CRS A6119/XR1/1, ff. 144-7, Minute for Regional Director, ACT, January 5 1954.
20. AA CRS A6119/XR/10, f. 211, Report for Regional Director, ACT, March 17 1954.
21. RCE, Transcript of Proceedings, Evidence of Jean A. Ferguson, February 15 1955, p.2257.
22. *Ibid.*, Evidence of E.A. Petrova, July 9 1954, p. 200.
23. *Ibid.*, Evidence of V.M. Petrov, July 5 1954, p. 133.
24. *Ibid.*, Evidence of E.A. Petrova, July 12 1954, p. 218.
25. *Ibid.*, Evidence of V.M. Petrov, July 5 1954, p. 133.
26. *Ibid.*, Evidence of V.M. Petrov, July 5 1954, p. 133 and Evidence of E.A. Petrova, July 9 1954, p. 200. See also AA CRS A6119/XR1/1, f. 143.
27. *Ibid.*, Evidence of E.A. Petrova, July 9 1954, p. 200.
28. AA CRS A6122/XR1/13, f. 130, V. Petrov to E.A. Petrova, April 16 1954.
29. RCE, Transcript of Proceedings, Evidence of V.M. Petrov, July 5 1954, p. 133.
30. *Ibid.*, Evidence of E.A. Petrova, August 31 1954, pp. 640-1.
31. V. and E. Petrov, *Empire of Fear*, pp. 252-3.
32. AA CRS A6119/9, f. 103, Report of Bialoguski, July 23 1953.
33. *Ibid.*, f. 170, Report of Bialoguski, September 23 1953.
34. *Ibid.*, f. 167, Report of Bialoguski, September 23 1953.
35. RCE, Transcript of Proceedings, Evidence of M. Bialoguski, September 10 1954, p. 792.
36. *Ibid.*, Address by V. Windeyer, May 17 1954, p. 7.
37. AA CRS A6119/9, f. 102, Report of Bialoguski, July 23 1953.
38. *Ibid.*, f. 165, Report of Bialoguski, September 18 1953.
39. *Ibid.*, f. 171, Report of Bialoguski, September 18 1953.
40. *Ibid.*, f. 102, Report of Bialoguski, July 23 1953.
41. *National Times* 'Magazine', September 3-8 1973, p. 14.
42. AA CRS A6119/9, f. 240e, Report of Bialoguski, August 21 1953.
43. F.U., Evatt papers, Petrov Affair files, 'Keep Your Mouth Shut — Or Else!!!' by George Marue, pp. 12-13.
44. RCE, Transcript of Proceedings, Evidence of V.M. Petrov, September 21 1954, p.1012.
45. AA CRS A6283/XR/2, f. 95, Interview with Petrov at Safe House, commencing April 6 1954.
46. AA CRS A6119/9, f. 165, Report of Bialoguski, September 18 1953.
47. *Ibid.*, f. 140e, Report of Bialoguski, August 26 1953.

4: OPERATION CABIN 12

1. M. Bialoguski, *The Petrov Story*, p. 144.
2. RCE, Transcript of Proceedings, Evidence of V.M. Petrov, July 5 1954, p. 134.
3. *Ibid.*, Evidence of E.A. Petrova, August 3 1954, p. 659.
4. M. Bialoguski, *The Petrov Story*, pp. 151-4; RCE, Transcript of Proceedings, Evidence of M. Bialoguski, September 17 1954, p. 966.
5. RCE, Transcript of Proceedings, Evidence of M. Bialoguski, pp. 995-8.
6. M. Thwaites, *Truth Will Out*, p. 86.
7. M. Bialoguski, *The Petrov Story*, p. 154.

8. AA CRS A6122/XR1/18, f. 22, Petrov Diary, November 23 1953.

9. *Ibid.*

10. Interview, Sir Charles Spry, May 3 1985.

11. AA CRS A6122/XR1/18, f. 21, Draft Memorandum 'Mr and Mrs Petrov', November 25 1953.

12. *Ibid.*, ff. 19-20, Memorandum, November 26 1953.

13. M. Bialoguski, *The Petrov Story*, p. 155.

14. AA CRS A6283/XR1/6, ff. 216-38, 'Defection . . .' etc., (undated), p. 8.

15. AA CRS A6122/XR1/18, f. 23, Memorandum, G.R. Richards, December 8 1953. In certain ASIO papers there is also reference to 'Operation Cabin II'. By early February 1954, however, the code-name was stabilised to 'Operation Cabin 12'.

16. AA CRS A6122/XR1/18, f. 22, Re Petrov — Diary, November 30 1953.

17. AA CRS A6119/XR/10, f. 59, Report of Senior Field Officer, E.O. Redford, December 11 1953.

18. M. Bialoguski, *The Petrov Story*, pp. 160-2.

19. RCE, Transcript of Proceedings, Evidence of H.C. Beckett, September 8 1954, p. 765.

20. M. Bialoguski, *The Petrov Story*, pp. 165-8; AA CRS A6119/XR1/1, f. 69, 'Notes re events leading to the defection of Petrov', September 8 1954.

21. RCE, Transcript of Proceedings, Evidence of H.C. Beckett, September 8 1954, p. 765.

22. M. Bialoguski, *The Petrov Story*, pp. 168-9.

23. AA CRS A6119/XR1/1, f. 147, Minute for Regional Director, ACT, January 5 1954; AA CRS A6283/83, f. 70, Memorandum for Counsel, Police report on accident to Petrov's car on December 24 1953.

24. M. Bialoguski, *The Petrov Story*, pp. 169-170.

25. AA CRS A6119/XR/10, f. 109, Memorandum, January 25 1954.

26. The translation of the wire recording can be found in AA CRS A6283/94, ff. 170-2, January 11 1954.

27. *Ibid.*

28. He told Gordon Hawkins that he would be returning to Moscow permanently in 'two or three months time'. AA CRS A6119/XR/10, f. 109, Memorandum, January 25 1954.

29. V. and E. Petrov, *Empire of Fear*, p. 287; M. Thwaites, *Truth Will Out*, p. 85; AA CRS A6283/XR1/6, ff. 216-38, 'Defections . . .' etc., p. 10.

30. RCE, Transcript of Proceedings, Evidence of H.C. Beckett, September 8 1954, p. 765.

31. *Ibid.*, Evidence of M. Bialoguski, September 10 1954, p. 795.

32. *Ibid.*, Evidence of G.R. Richards, September 7 1954, p. 739.

33. AA CRS A6122/XR1/18, ff. 24-5, G.R. Richards to Col. Spry, January 25 1954.

34. *Ibid.*, f. 40. The letter from Spry to Richards was not sent. Instead Spry spoke to Richards about the matter.

35. M. Bialoguski, *The Petrov Story*, ch. 25.

36. AA CRS A6122/XR1/18, ff. 45-6, 'Considerations concerning a possible Soviet defector'.

37. *Ibid.*, ff. 43-4, Record of Interview between Col. Spry and Professor Bailey, February 10 1954.

38. *Ibid.*, f. 44, Comments, Alan Watt.

39. *Ibid.*, ff. 47-8, Record of Interview between Col. Spry and Mr Tange, February 10 1954.

40. *Ibid.*, f. 47, Record of Interview between Col. Spry and Mr R.G. Menzies, February 10 1954.

41. Sir R.G. Menzies, *The Measure of the Years*, Cassell Australia, Melbourne, 1970, p. 156.

42. AA CRS A6122/XR1/18, ff. 64-78, 'Operation Cabin 12: Necessary Action in Preparation for Possible Defection', February 17 1954.

5: END GAME

1. M. Bialoguski, *The Petrov Story*, p. 188.

2. AA CRS A6283/94, Minifon recording transcription, February 19 1954, f. 167.

3. AA CRS A6283/94, Minifon recording transcription, February 19 1954, ff. 158-168.
4. RCE, Transcript of Proceedings, Evidence of M. Bialoguski, September 10 1954, p. 799.
5. *Ibid.*, Evidence of G.R. Richards, September 7 1954, p. 739.
6. AA CRS A6283/94, Minifon recording transcription, February 20 1954, ff. 154-6.
7. RCE, Transcript of Proceedings, Evidence of V.M. Petrov, July 5 1954, p. 125.
8. AA CRS A6283/94, Minifon recording transcription, February 27 1954, ff. 48-58.
9. Nicholas Whitlam and John Stubbs, *Nest of Traitors: The Petrov Affair*, Jacaranda Press, Brisbane, 1974, pp. 143-4.
10. AA CRS A6283/94, Minifon recording transcription, February 27 1954, ff. 18-43. See also RCE, Transcript of Proceedings, Evidence of G.R. Richards, September 7 1954, p. 740.
11. RCE, Transcript of Proceedings, Evidence of G.R. Richards, September 8 and 17 1954, pp. 746-7 and 961-2; *ibid.*, Evidence of M. Bialoguski, September 10 1954, pp. 801-2.
12. AA CRS A6283/94, ff. 1-11, Memorandum, G.R. Richards, for Director-General, March 22 1954.
13. *Ibid.*
14. AA CRS A6283/XR1/77, f. 81, Memorandum, J.M. Gilmour, of conversation with Mrs Petrov, July 8 1955.
15. AA CRS A6281/P15B and P16F, Minifon recording (on cassette), March 25 1954.
16. AA CRS A6119/XR/10, f. 135, Memorandum re Petrov, March 4 1954.
17. AA CRS A6281/P16B and P17F, Minifon recording (on cassette), March 26 1954.
18. AA CRS A6283/94, Minifon recording transcription, March 30 1954, ff. 96-9.
19. *Ibid.*, Minifon recording transcription, March 31 1954, ff. 100-4.
20. *Ibid.*, Minifon recording transcription, April 1 1954, ff. 105-11.
21. RCE, Transcript of Proceedings, Evidence of G.R. Richards, September 8 1954, pp. 752-3.
22. *Ibid.*, Evidence of G.R. Richards, September 8 1954, pp. 754-5.
23. AA CRS A6281/P20B, Minifon recording (on cassette), April 2 1954.
24. V. and E. Petrov, *Empire of Fear*, pp. 295-7; RCE, Transcript of Proceedings, Evidence of G.R. Richards, September 8 and 16 1954, pp. 755-8 and 934; Evidence of M. Bialoguski, September 10 1954, pp. 804-5.

6: THE ANNOUNCEMENT

1. AA CRS A6215/4, RCE Exhibit 61a, V. Petrov to Rufina Vasilievna Vislykha, April 3 1954.
2. Interview, Sir Charles Spry, May 3 1985.
3. AA CRS A6213/RCE/N/6, ff. 29-42, Statement of V.M. Petrov, April 3 1954.
4. Richards subsequently told the Royal Commission that 'it had a lot of names which I recognised as being of interest to me . . . I was particularly interested in "G" '. RCE, Transcript of Proceedings, Evidence of G.R. Richards, September 16 1954, p. 922.
5. AA CRS A6202, Exhibits, single letter series, 1954; Exhibit 'H'.
6. *Ibid.*, Exhibits, single letter series, 1954; Exhibit 'J'.
7. AA CRS A6213/RCE/N/6, ff. 29-42, Statement of V.M. Petrov, April 3 1954, p. 12.
8. *Ibid.*, p. 8.
9. See below, ch. 15.
10. RCE, Transcript of Proceedings, Evidence of G.R. Richards, September 9 1954, p. 778.
11. See S.R. Graubard, *British Labour and the Russian Revolution*, Harvard University Press, Harvard, 1956, pp. 283-8. The impact of the Zinoviev letter on the election of 1924 was less serious than customarily supposed.
12. Interview, Sir Charles Spry, May 3 1985.
13. AA CRS A6213/RCE/G/7, f. 138, Brig. Spry to Mr A. Brown, Prime Minister's Department, October 11 1955; RCE, Transcript of Proceedings, Evidence of G.R. Richards, September 8 1954, pp. 760-1.

14. H. of R., October 25 1955, p. 1867.
15. AA CRS A6213/RCE/G/7, f. 138, Brig. Spry to Mr A. Brown, Prime Minister's Department, October 11 1955.
16. Interview, Sir Charles Spry, May 7 1985.
17. AA CRS A6213/RCE/G/7, f. 138, Brig. Spry to Mr A. Brown, Prime Minister's Department, October 11 1955.
18. H. of R., August 11 1954, p. 157.
19. AA CRS A6283/XR/2, f. 69, Interview with Petrov at Safe House commencing April 6 1954.
20. *Ibid.*, ff. 68-105, *passim*; AA CRS A6283/XR/70, f. 76, Col. Spry to Professor Bailey, April 9 1954.
21. AA CRS A6283/XR/2, ff. 70-1, Interview with Petrov at Safe House, commencing April 6 1954. (April 10)
22. V. and E. Petrov, *Empire of Fear*, ch. XXV.
23. AA CRS A6122/XR1/13, f. 10, Record of conversation between Bialoguski and Richards, April 8 1954.
24. *Ibid.*, ff. 45-7, Notes by Bialoguski, April 10 1954.
25. *Ibid.*, f. 87, Note by ASIO Travel Officer, C Section, April 15 1954.
26. *Ibid.*, f. 18, Telephone message for F. Stuart from A. Tange, April 8 1954.
27. AA CRS A6213/RCE/H/21, f. 3, Department of External Affairs, Canberra, to Australian Embassy, Moscow, April 13 1954.
28. AA CRS A4907, Fifth Menzies Ministry, Cabinet decision no. 992, April 13 1954.
29. AA CRS A6122/XR1/13, f. 65, Secrecy call, Col. W. Phillipps to Headquarters, April 12 1954, 4.15 p.m.
30. AA CRS A6213/RCE/H/21, f. 3, Department of External Affairs, Canberra, to Australian Embassy, Moscow, April 13 1954, 11.30 a.m.
31. Alan Reid, 'Labour Claims Evatt "Framed" on Petrov Statement', *Sun-Herald*, April 25 1954. According to Whitlam and Stubbs, Reid told them that as a consequence of this article Mr Menzies wrote to the management of the *Sydney Morning Herald* hoping to have him dismissed. N. Whitlam and J. Stubbs, *Nest of Traitors*, pp. 79-80.
32. J.B. Paul, 'Labor's Petrov Legend: A Suitable Case for Interment', pp. 119-20 in Robert Manne (ed.), *The New Conservatism in Australia*, Oxford University Press, Melbourne, 1982.
33. Sir Percy Joske, *Sir Robert Menzies 1894-1978: A New Informal Memoir*, Angus and Robertson, Sydney, 1978, p. 248.
34. H. of R., April 13 1954, pp. 325-6.
35. AA CRS A6122/XR1/13, ff. 74-6, Instructions from G.R. Richards to L. Carter and J. Gilmour, April 14 1954.
36. *Ibid.*, ff. 77-9, L. Carter and J. Gilmour to G.R. Richards, April 14 1954.
37. *Sydney Morning Herald*, *Age*, April 14 1954.
38. AA CRS A6122/XR1/13, f. 92, ASIO Field Officer to Regional Director, NSW (Richards), April 15 1954.
39. H. of R., April 14 1954, pp. 372-3.
40. Interview, Sir Charles Spry, May 3 1985.
41. F.U., Evatt Papers, Petrov Affair files, Statements by Dr Evatt, Press release, April 16 1954.
42. AA CRS A6213/RCE/R/3, Mr R.G. Menzies Press release, April 17 1954.

7: EVDOKIA

1. AA CRS A6227, Prime Minister's press conference, transcript, April 15 1954.
2. AA CRS A6122/XR1/13, ff. 103-5, Notes for Director-General, April 15 and 16 1954; A. Tange to Mr R.G. Menzies, April 16 1954.
3. *Ibid.*, f. 80, Memorandum, G.R. Richards, April 15 1954.

4. AA CRS A6213/RCE/H/8, Department of External Affairs, Canberra, to Australian Embassy, Moscow, April 16 1954.
5. AA CRS A6122/XR1/13, ff. 109-10, Senior Section Officer to Principal Section Officer, B2, April 16 1954.
6. RCE, Transcript of Proceedings, Evidence of E.A. Petrova, July 7 1954, p. 168.
7. AA CRS A6122/XR1/13, f. 86, Travel Officer, C Section, to Principal Section Officer, B2, April 15 1954.
8. *Ibid.*, ff. 115-7, Leo Carter and John Gilmour to G.R. Richards, April 17 1954.
9. *Ibid.*, f. 114, V. Petrov to P. Kislitsyn, April 17 1954.
10. AA CRS A6122/XR1/8, ff. 33-4, Col. Spry to Mr R.G. Menzies, April 26 1954.
11. AA CRS A6122/XR1/13, ff. 160-1, Col. Spry to Regional Director, Northern Territory, April 17 1954.
12. AA CRS A6122/XR1/9, Draft Instructions, Kingsford Smith airport, April 19 1954.
13. *Sydney Morning Herald*, April 19 1954.
14. AA CRS A6122/XR1/13, ff. 148-51, Telephone messages from and for W.C. Wentworth, April 19 1954.
15. RCE, Transcript of Proceedings, Evidence of G.R. Richards, September 9 1954, p. 775.
16. M. Thwaites, *Truth Will Out*, p. 95.
17. AA CRS A6122/XR1/13, f. 173, undated.
18. V. and E. Petrov, *Empire of Fear*, ch. XXV; AA CRS A6122/XR1/13, ff. 238-40, Notes by G.R. Richards of interview with Evdokia Petrova on morning of April 21, April 28 1954.
19. V. and E. Petrov, *Empire of Fear*, ch. XXVI; AA CRS A6122/XR1/13, ff. 238-40, Notes by G.R. Richards of interview with Evdokia Petrova on morning of April 21, April 28 1954; AA CRS A 6283/XR1/14, ff. 55-6, Mrs Petrov Statement re her departure, May 7 1954; RCE, Transcript of Proceedings, Evidence of E.A. Petrova, July 7 and 8 1954, pp. 166-8 and 185-6.
20. V. and E. Petrov, *Empire of Fear*, ch. XXVI; AA CRS A6283/XR1/14, RCE Exhibits 12, 14 and 15, Statements of E.A. Petrova, April 22 and May 7 1954; AA CRS A6122/XR1/13, f. 268, G.R. Richards to Col. Spry, April 20 1954; RCE, Transcript of Proceedings, Evidence of E.A. Petrova, July 8, July 12 and August 31 1954, pp. 185-8, 220-2, 654-6, and 658; Evidence of G.R. Richards, September 9 1954, pp. 774-5. Newspapers consulted for the events at Mascot, *Age*, *Sydney Morning Herald*, *Argus*, Sydney *Sun*, *Daily Telegraph*, *Daily Mirror*, Melbourne *Herald*. Interview with W.C. Wentworth, November 3 1985.
21. *Age, Sydney Morning Herald*, April 20 1954.
22. Sydney *Sun*, April 20 1954.
23. Interview, W.C. Wentworth, November 3 1985.
24. *Ibid.*
25. AA CRS A6122/XR1/8, ff. 27-34, 'Report upon request for political asylum of Mrs Evdokija Alekseevna Petrov', Col. Spry to Mr R.G. Menzies, April 26 1954, p. 3.
26. The press release, which was written by Col. Spry was printed in the *Sydney Morning Herald*, April 20 1954.
27. AA CRS A6122/XR1/8, ff. 27-34, 'Report . . .', etc., Col. Spry to Mr R.G. Menzies, April 26 1954, p. 4.
28. V. and E. Petrov, *Empire of Fear*, ch. XXVI; RCE, Transcript of Proceedings, Evidence of E.A. Petrova, July 8 and 12, August 31 and September 2 1954, pp. 185-8, 220-2, 639, 645-6, 658 and 715.
29. AA CRS A6122/XR1/8, ff. 27-34, 'Report . . .', etc., Col. Spry to Mr R.G. Menzies, April 26 1954, pp. 4-5.
30. *Ibid.*, p. 4; AA CRS A6122/XR1/11, Statement by the Government Secretary, Mr R.S. Leydin concerning Mrs Petrov, undated, p. 1.
31. AA CRS A6122/XR1/8, ff. 27-34, 'Report . . .', etc., Col. Spry to Mr R.G. Menzies, pp. 4-6; AA CRS A6122/XR1/11, Statement by . . . Mr R.S. Leydin, pp. 1-2.
32. AA CRS A6122/XR1/11, Statement by . . . Mr R.S. Leydin, p. 2-3; *ibid.*, ff. 27-32, 'Statement of Keith Stacey Edmunds, Acting Crown Law Officer, Darwin', undated, p. 1; *ibid.* ff. 56-61,

Memorandum, Regional Director, Northern Territory (Barrington), April 27 1954, p. 1-2.

33. *Ibid.*, ff. 27-32, 'Statement of Keith Stacey Edmunds . . .', pp. 1-2; *ibid.*, ff. 14-15, Report of Constable E.T. Davis, Removal of Pistol from Mr Karpinsky, April 20 1954; *ibid.*, Statement by . . . Mr R.S. Leydin re Flight-Lieut. McCluskey, p. 8.
34. *Ibid.*, Statement by . . . Mr R.S. Leydin, pp. 3-4.
35. *Ibid.*, ff. 27-32, 'Statement of Keith Stacey Edmunds . . .', p. 3.
36. *Ibid.*, ff. 56-61 Memorandum, Regional Director, Northern Territory (Barrington) p. 2; AA CRS A6122/XR1/8, ff. 27-34, 'Report . . .', etc., Col. Spry to Mr R.G. Menzies, p. 7.
37. AA CRS A6122/XR1/8, ff. 27-34, 'Report . . .', etc., Col. Spry to Mr R.G. Menzies, p. 7.
38. AA CRS A6122/XR1/13, Leo Carter to G.R. Richards, April 20 1954.
39. AA CRS A6122/XR1/8, ff. 27-34, 'Report . . .', etc., Col. Spry to Mr R.G. Menzies, pp. 7-8; AA CRS A6122/XR1/11, Statement by . . . Mr R.S. Leydin, pp. 5-7; *ibid.*, ff. 56-61, Memorandum . . . (Barrington) pp. 2-3; *ibid.*, ff. 27-32, 'Statement of Keith Stacey Edmunds', pp. 3-5.
40. AA CRS A6122/XR1/11, ff. 27-32, 'Statement of Keith Stacey Edmunds', pp. 5-6; *ibid.*, ff. 2-5, Statement, Frank Walter Angell, Qantas Manager, Darwin, April 21 1954, pp. 3-4.
41. Melbourne *Herald*, April 20 1954.
42. Sydney *Sun*, April 21 1954.
43. Melbourne *Herald*, April 21 1954.
44. Interviews with Sir Charles Spry, May 3 and 7·1985.
45. *Daily Mirror*, April 21 1954.
46. *Argus*, April 21 1954.
47. *Daily Telegraph*, April 21 1954.
48. *Sydney Morning Herald*, April 21 1954.
49. AA CRS A462/211/2/24, f. 53, M. Woll to Mr R.G. Menzies, April 22 1954.
50. *Age*, April 21 1954.
51. *Sydney Morning Herald*, April 21 1954.
52. AA CRS A6213/RCE/H/21, f. 36, B. Hill (Moscow) to A. Tange (Canberra), April 23 1954.
53. *Ibid.*, ff. 45-7, B. Hill (Moscow) to A. Tange (Canberra) via London, April 24 1954.
54. *Ibid.*, ff. 50-1.
55. *Ibid.*, f. 53, A. Tange (Canberra) to B. Hill (Moscow) via London, April 25 1954.
56. *Ibid.*, f. 40, R. Casey (Paris) to Sir P. McBride and A. Tange (Canberra), April 24 1954.
57. *Ibid.*, f. 74, R. Casey (Geneva) to A. Tange (Canberra), April 27 1954.
58. *Ibid.*, f. 65, A. Tange (Canberra) to B. Hill (Moscow), April 26 1954.
59. *Ibid.*, f. 71, Minute, J. Backen, Prime Minister's Department, April 27 1954.
60. *Ibid.*, f. 78, A. Tange (Canberra) to R. Casey (Geneva), April 28 1954.
61. *Ibid.*, f. 80, L. McIntyre (London) to K. Waller (Canberra), April 28 1954.

8: THE ELECTION

1. Dean Jaensch and Max Teichmann, *The Macmillan Dictionary of Australian Politics*, Macmillan, Melbourne, 1979, p. 176.
2. F.U., Evatt Papers, Petrov Affair files, unpublished typescript.
3. D. Jaensch and M. Teichmann, *The Macmillan Dictionary of Australian Politics*, p. 176.
4. F.U., Evatt papers, Petrov Affair files, unpublished typescript. My emphasis.
5. Russel Ward, *A Nation For A Continent, A History of Australia: 1901-1975*, Heinemann, Melbourne, 1979, p. 310.
6. N. Whitlam and J. Stubbs, *Nest of Traitors*, pp. 94 and 105.
7. See above, ch. 2.
8. The Gallup Poll results were published regularly in the Melbourne *Herald* and Sydney *Sun-*

Herald. In the polls of June 1953 and September 1953 Coalition support stood at 45% and ALP support at 54%.

9. See above, ch. 2.
10. AA CRS A6122/XR1/18, f. 23, Memorandum, G.R. Richards, December 8 1953.
11. See above, ch. 4.
12. See above, ch. 5.
13. See above, ch. 2.
14. AA CRS A6122/XR1/18, f. 47, Record of Interview between Col. Spry and Mr R.G. Menzies, February 10 1954.
15. AA CRS A4909/XM1/8, Cabinet Minute, Decision no. 932, February 12 1954.
16. *Sydney Morning Herald*, February 10 1954.
17. Melbourne *Sun*, April 14 1954.
18. *Argus*, February 2 1954.
19. *Sydney Morning Herald*, April 15 1954.
20. *Sun-Herald*, April 18 1954.
21. N. Whitlam and J. Stubbs, *Nest of Traitors*, p. 82.
22. Melbourne *Sun* and *Herald*, April 22 1954; F.U., Evatt Papers, Petrov Affair files, unpublished typescript.
23. RCE, Transcript of Proceedings, Address by V. Windeyer, May 18 1954, pp. 29-30.
24. H. of R., October 25 1955, p. 1867.
25. See, for example, *Sunday Telegraph*, April 18 1954; *Sydney Morning Herald*, April 19 1954; Melbourne *Sun*, April 20 1954.
26. *Age*, May 5 1954.
27. *Sydney Morning Herald*, May 6 1954.
28. *Age*, May 6 1954.
29. *Sydney Morning Herald*, May 6 1954; Melbourne *Herald*, May 6 1954.
30. Melbourne *Herald*, May 4 1954.
31. *Ibid.*, April 30 1954.
32. H. of R., October 25, p. 1867.
33. *Age*, May 8 1954.
34. *Daily Telegraph*, May 8 1954.
35. F.U., Evatt Paper, Elections: 1954 files, 'Miscellaneous Notes on Possible Political Points'. For a discussion of R.F.B. Wake see below ch. XV.
36. *Sun-Herald*, May 2 1954.
37. *Age*, May 17 1954.
38. *Argus*, May 11 1954.
39. *Daily Telegraph*, May 25 1954.
40. *Age*, May 12 1954.
41. *Ibid.*, May 26, 1954.
42. Melbourne *Herald*, May 26 1954.
43. *Age*, May 10 1954.
44. *Ibid.*, May 11 and 13 1954.
45. *Ibid.*, May 19 and 26 1954.
46. Melbourne *Herald*, May 19 1954; *Age*, May 26 1954.
47. *Age*, May 29 1954.
48. Melbourne *Herald*, April 20 1954.
49. *Ibid.*, April 23 1954.
50. *Age*, April 21, 22 and 27, 1954. See also *Brisbane Courier-Mail*, April 19 1954 and *Daily Telegraph*, April 22 1954.
51. *Argus*, April 23 1954.
52. *Ibid.*, May 18 1954.
53. Dr Evatt's campaign speech is found in F.U., Evatt Papers, Election 1954 files. See also, *Age*, *Sydney Morning Herald*, May 7 1954.

54. Bill Bourke's attack on the abolition of the means test is in *Age*, March 15 1954. He reaffirmed his position after Dr Evatt's campaign opening. *Age*, May 11 1954. For Kennelly's 1953 views, *Sydney Morning Herald*, April 27 1954.
55. Sydney *Sun*, May 7 and 11 1954.
56. Melbourne *Herald*, May 24 1954.
57. *Age*, May 21 1954.
58. *Ibid.*, May 8 1954.
59. *Ibid.*, May 11 1954.
60. *Ibid.*, May 11 1954; Sydney *Sun*, May 14 1954; *Age*, May 27 1954.
61. *Age*, May 22 1954.
62. *Ibid.*, May 19 1954.
63. *Daily Telegraph*, May 25 1954.
64. *Sydney Morning Herald*, May 18 1954.
65. *Sunday Telegraph*, May 23 1954.
66. *Age*, May 24 1954.
67. Colin A. Hughes and B.D. Graham, *Voting for the Australian House of Representatives, 1901-1964*, Australian National University Press, Canberra, 1974, pp. 308-24.
68. Colin A. Hughes and B.D. Graham, *A Handbook of Australian Government and Politics, 1890-1964*, Australian National University Press, Canberra, 1968, pp. 385-97.
69. N. Whitlam and J. Stubbs, *Nest of Traitors*, pp.93-4.
70. *Sun-Herald*, April 11 1954.
71. *Ibid.*, May 23 1954.
72. Henry Mayer and Joan Rydon, *The Gwydir By-Election, 1953*, Australian National University Press, Canberra, 1954, p. 156.
73. *Argus*, May 28 1954.

9: THE ROYAL COMMISSION

1. Don Watson, *Brian Fitzpatrick: A Radical Life*, Hale & Iremonger, Sydney, 1979, ch. 10, 'McCarthyist Australia'.
2. Lynne Strahan, *Just City and the Mirrors: Meanjin Quarterly and the Intellectual Front, 1940-1965*, Oxford University Press, Melbourne, 1984, p. 161.
3. R. Ward, *A Nation for a Continent*, p. 310.
4. D. Jaensch and M. Teichmann, *The Macmillan Dictionary of Australian Politics*, p. 176.
5. *The Guardian*, April 14 1954.
6. Thomas C. Reeves, *The Life and Times of Joe McCarthy*, Stein and Day, New York, 1982, chs. 21 and 22. The Army-McCarthy hearings, which eventually destroyed McCarthy's reputation, took place in the months of greatest public excitement in Australia about the Petrov defections, April-May 1954. The hearings were widely reported in the Australian press.
7. See above, ch. 6.
8. F.U., Evatt Papers, Petrov Affair files, Annotated material (b), 'Act Relating to the Royal Commission on Espionage', Section 23, August 11 1954.
9. F.U., Evatt Papers, Petrov Affair files, Commission — terms of reference, undated typescript.
10. *Ibid.*, Commission — terms of reference, Senator McKenna to Senator Spicer, Attorney-General, April 29 1954.
11. Interview with Sir Charles Spry, May 7 1985. In Parliament on August 12 1954 Mr Menzies hinted at his approach to Sir Owen Dixon. 'When it was decided to appoint a royal commission, I first of all had discussions with the Chief Justice of the High Court of Australia'. According to Mr Menzies it was made clear to him in discussion why the High Court traditionally refused to allow its members to serve on Royal Commissions. 'Very well', he concluded, 'I accepted that situation'. H. of R., August 12 1954, p. 247.

12. Sir Owen Dixon spoke thus on the question of requests made to the High Court for its members to serve on Royal Commissions. 'I have been a judge of the High Court a very long time, and during that period there have been a number of requests made. Looking back in restrospect I feel we were right. Events as they have gone on, have shown that embarrassments would have occurred at a later date if a judge had participated in the Royal Commission'. *The Australian Law Journal*, vol. 29, August 19 1955, p. 272.

13. H. of R., August 12 1954, p. 247.

14. Melbourne *Herald*, April 28 1954. The attitude of the Victorian Supreme Court on the question of Royal Commissions is discussed by J.D. Holmes in 'Royal Commissions', *The Australian Law Journal*, vol. 29, August 19 1955, pp. 256-7.

15. N. Whitlam and J. Stubbs, *Nest of Traitors*, pp. 96-7. The Irvine letter is published in the J.D. Holmes article. The letter established the tradition in Victoria upon which Sir Edmund Herring drew.

16. H. of R., August 12 1954, pp. 247-9.

17. D. Jaensch and M. Teichmann, *The Macmillan Dictionary of Australian Politics*, p. 176.

18. Interview, Sir Charles Spry, May 7 1985.

19. AA CRS A6283/XR1/124, f. 1, Col. Phillipps to Director, B1, May 4 1954.

20. AA CRS A6213/RCE/G/7, ff. 28-30, Mr V. Windeyer to Mr R.G. Menzies, September 10 1955. On the career of Arthur Birse see AA CRS A6283/XR/70, ff. 262-6, Statement by Birse, undated.

21. F.U., Evatt Papers, Petrov Affair files, unpublished typescript.

22. AA CRS A6213/RCE/G/7, ff. 28-30, Mr V. Windeyer to Mr R.G. Menzies, September 10 1955.

23. AA CRS A6213/RCE/R/1, Col. Spry to Col. Phillipps (for Mr A. Brown), May 10 1954.

24. AA CRS A6213/RCE/G/7, ff. 28-30, Mr V. Windeyer to Mr R.G. Menzies, September 10 1955.

25. RCE, Transcript of Proceedings, Evidence of G.R. Richards, May 18 1954, pp. 33-9.

26. AA CRS A6213/RCE/G/7, ff. 28-30, Mr V. Windeyer to Mr R.G. Menzies, September 10 1955.

27. AA CRS A6213/RCE/L/1, Australian High Commissioner, Ottawa, to Department of External Affairs, Canberra, May 6 1954 and A. Tange to K. Herde, May 11 1954.

28. AA CRS A6213/RCE/G/7, ff. 28-30, Mr V. Windeyer to Mr R.G. Menzies, September 10 1954.

29. H. of R., August 12, 1954, p. 224 (Dr Evatt) and p. 229 (E. James Harrison). Harrison, incidentally, argued that every person named in the Petrov documents must be called before the Royal Commission and required, in public, to 'declare his attitude'. The 'ordinary rules' of Royal Commissions were, in his view, insufficient to deal with questions of espionage.

30. AA CRS A6213/RCE/X/1, Mr Justice Owen to Mr R.M. Taylor, Department of Works, May 24 1954.

31. *Ibid.*, Mr K. Herde to Mr R.H.C. Loot, Parliament House, May 24 1954.

32. *Ibid.*, Mr J. Allsopp to Mr K. Herde, May 21 1954.

33. RCE, Transcript of Proceedings, Address by V. Windeyer, May 17-19 1954, pp. 2-43.

34. Rupert Lockwood, *What Is In Document J?*, June 19 1954. (A copy of this pamphlet is in the Evatt Papers.)

35. RCE, Transcript of Proceedings, Evidence of F. O'Sullivan, July 16 1954, p. 304.

36. F.U., Evatt Papers, Petrov Affair files, correspondence — miscellaneous, Dr Evatt to F. O'Sullivan, June 4 1954.

37. Allan Dalziel, *Evatt the Engima*, Lansdowne Press, Melbourne, 1967, pp. 17-18.

38. *Argus*, May 28 1954.

39. Robert Murray, *The Split: Australian Labor in the Fifties*, Hale & Iremonger, Sydney, 1984, p. 155.

40. John Douglas Pringle, *Have Pen: Will Travel*, Chatto and Windus, London, 1973, pp. 119-120. I owe my knowledge of this account to J.B. Paul, whose excellent essay on the Petrov Affair

kindled my interest in the subject. R. Manne (ed.), *The New Conservatism in Australia*, ch. 6.

41. RCE, Transcript of Proceedings, June 11 1954, pp. 47-58.
42. ANL, Menzies Papers, MS 4936, Series 1, Mr R.G. Menzies to Editors, Melbourne *Sun* and *Argus*, June 29 1954.
43. *Brisbane Telegraph*, July 1 1954.
44. *Argus*, July 1 1954.
45. RCE, Transcript of Proceedings, Evidence of V. Petrov, June 30, July 1-2, July 5-6, 1954.
46. *Ibid.*, Evidence of V. Petrov, July 5 1954, p. 136.
47. AA CRS A6283/XR/3, ff. 23-6, Statement by V. Petrov, July 5 1954.
48. RCE, Transcript of Proceedings, Evidence of V. Petrov, July 6 1954, p. 141.
49. *Ibid.*, p. 145.
50. *Ibid.*, p. 145.
51. Ronald McKie, 'The Petrov Inquiry', *AM*, July 13 1954.
52. RCE, Transcript of Proceedings, Evidence of E.A. Petrova, July 8 1954, pp. 185-7. At one point Windeyer interrupted her narrative with a question. 'May I', Petrova inquired, 'continue?'.
53. The first Communist Party pamphlet on the Petrov Affair was entitled *Menzies Concocted Spy Plot*. A copy can be found in AA CRS A6213/RCE/G/7, ff. 163-4.
54. *Tribune*, April 28 1954; *Queensland Guardian*, June 16 1954.
55. *Tribune*, April 28 1954.
56. *The Petrov Conspiracy Unmasked*, Melbourne, 1973, (first published 1956), 'Mrs Petrov — and the Mascot Act', pp. 105-10.
57. *Guardian*, April 14 1954; AA CRS A6283/XR1/128, ff. 87-87A, 'The Petrov Commission', A Fortnightly Bulletin, August 5 1954, 'The Witch Hunt'.
58. AA CRS A6283/111, ff. 14-18, 'Operation Cabin 12', Operational Progress Report, B2 to Regional Director, Victoria, May 20 1954.
59. AA CRS A6283/94, Minifon recording transcription, conversation between Dr Bialoguski and J. Rodgers, June 13 1954, ff. 130-53.
60. RCE, Transcript of Proceedings, Address by E. Hill, June 30 1954, pp. 93-6.
61. *Ibid.*, Address by E. Hill, July 7 and 8 1954, pp. 169-71 and 175-84.
62. On these legal matters see AA CRS A6213/RCE/R/3, Mr R.G. Menzies press release, July 12 1954. Copies of Rupert Lockwood's High Court writ can be found in AA CRS A6213/RCE/L/4.
63. RCE, Transcript of Proceedings, Evidence of R. Lockwood, July 9 and 12 1954, pp. 210 and 213.
64. *Ibid.*, July 8, 9, 12, 13 and 14, 1954, *passim*.
65. *Ibid.*, Address by E. Hill, July 14 1954, p. 262.
66. *Ibid.*, Evidence of R. Lockwood, July 12 1954, p. 213.
67. *Ibid.*, Evidence of E.A. Petrova, July 9 1954, pp. 200-1.
68. *Ibid.*, Evidence of V. Petrov, July 13 and 14 1954, pp. 237-9 and 253-65.
69. *Ibid.*, Evidence of F. O'Sullivan, July 14 1954, pp. 267-8.
70. *Ibid.*, Evidence of F. O'Sullivan, July 15 1954, pp. 284-98.
71. *Ibid.*, pp. 296-8.
72. *Ibid.*, p. 298.

10: CONSPIRACY MOST FOUL

1. RCE, Transcript of Proceedings, Address by V. Windeyer, August 16 1954, p. 382.
2. F.U., Evatt Papers, Petrov Affair files, Dalziel, Grundeman, O'Sullivan, Dr Evatt to Mr R.G. Menzies (telegram), July 16 1954.

3. RCE, Transcript of Proceedings, July 16 1954, p. 309.

4. *Ibid.*, Address by Owen J., July 16 1954, p. 309.

5. F.U., Evatt Papers, Petrov Affair files, Statements by Evatt, press release, July 16 1954.

6. A. Dalziel, *Evatt the Enigma*, pp. 92-3.

7. F.U., Evatt Papers, Petrov Affair files, Barkell & Peacock to K. Herde, July 21 1954.

8. 'A Bill for an Act Relating to the Royal Commission on Espionage', August 11 1954. A copy of this draft bill is in the Evatt Papers.

9. ANL, Calwell Papers, MS4738, Box 50, Minutes of Federal Parliamentary Labor Party, August 11 1954, 11 a.m. and 7 p.m.; R. Murray, *The Split*, p. 163; *The Age*, *Sydney Morning Herald*, *Sydney Sun*; *Daily Telegraph*, August 12 1954.

10. H. of R., August 12 1954, pp. 216-49.

11. F.U., Evatt Papers, Petrov Affair files, Statements by Evatt, press release, August 12 1954.

12. H. of R., August 12 1954, pp. 282-4.

13. *Ibid.*, pp. 284-6.

14. *Sydney Morning Herald*, August 17 1954.

15. *Age*, August 16 1954.

16. *Sydney Morning Herald*, August 13 1954.

17. *Ibid.*, August 14 1954.

18. *Ibid.*, August 13 and 14 1954; Melbourne *Sun*, August 13 and 14 1954.

19. F.U., Evatt Papers, Petrov Affair files, Dalziel, Grundeman, O'Sullivan, List of Caucus and text of telegram, August 16 1954.

20. *Sydney Morning Herald*, August 17 1954.

21. RCE, Transcript of Proceedings, August 16 1954, pp. 379-86.

22. *Ibid.*, Ligertwood J., p. 381.

23. Dr Evatt expressed this view privately to Ted Hill, see Michael G.L. Dunn, 'The Royal Commission on Espionage, 1954-1955', unpublished Ph.D., University of Adelaide, 1980, p. 137.

24. RCE, Transcript of Proceedings, Ligertwood J. and Dr Evatt, August 16 1954, p. 382.

25. *Ibid.*, August 16 1954, pp. 396-404.

26. *Ibid.*, August 16 1954, p. 403.

27. *Ibid.*, August 16 1954, pp. 406-7.

28. *Ibid.*, August 17 1954, p. 411.

29. *Ibid.*, August 17 1954, p. 417.

30. *Ibid.*, August 17 1954, p. 411.

31. *Ibid.*, August 17 1954, pp. 415-6.

32. *Ibid.*, August 17 1954, p. 413.

33. *Ibid.*, August 18 and August 19 1954, pp. 449 and 477.

34. *Ibid.*, August 18 1954, pp. 428-9.

35. *Ibid.*, Evidence of A. Grundeman, August 18 1954, pp. 431-49.

36. *Ibid.*, Evidence of F. O'Sullivan, August 18 1954, pp. 450-5.

37. *Ibid.*, Evidence of R. Lockwood, August 20 1954, p. 496.

38. *Ibid.*, Evidence of R. Lockwood, August 24 1954, p. 525.

39. *Ibid.*, Evidence of R. Lockwood, August 19 1954, p. 475.

40. *Ibid.*, Evidence of R. Lockwood, August 24 1954, p. 525.

41. *Ibid.*, Evidence of R. Lockwood, August 24 1954, pp. 530-1.

42. *Ibid.*, Evidence of R. Lockwood, August 19 1954, p. 476.

43. *Ibid.*, Evidence of R. Lockwood, August 20 1954, p. 496.

44. *Ibid.*, Evidence of R. Lockwood, August 19 1954, pp. 476-8.

45. *Ibid.*, Evidence of R. Lockwood, August 19 1954, pp. 500-1.

46. *Ibid.*, Dr Evatt, August 24 1954, pp. 509 and 535.

47. *Ibid.*, Dr Evatt, August 27 1954, p. 602.

48. *Ibid.*, Evidence of R. Lockwood, August 24 1954, pp. 533-5.

49. *Ibid.*, Dr Evatt, August 24 and August 25 1954, pp. 535 and 541-5.

50. *Ibid.*, Evidence of Inspector Rogers, August 25 and August 27 1954, pp. 554-64 and 579-85.

51. *Ibid.*, Evidence of G.R. Richards, August 26 1954, pp. 567-75.
52. *Ibid.*, Evidence of Inspector Rogers, August 27 1954, pp. 588-90.
53. *Ibid.*, August 27 1954, pp. 591-4.
54. *Ibid.*, Evidence of Inspector Rogers, August 30 1954, pp. 609-12.
55. ANL, Calwell Papers, MS4738, Box 50, Minutes of Federal Parliamentary Labor Party, August 25 1954; *Sydney Morning Herald*, August 26 1954; Alan Reid 'Tomahawks flash at Labor Pow-wow', Sydney *Sun*, August 31 1954.
56. AA CRS A6227, Prime Ministerial files on Royal Commission on Espionage, draft letter, undated.
57. RCE, Transcript of Proceedings, Evidence of E.A. Petrova, August 31 and September 1 1954, pp. 637-61 and 665-70.
58. *Ibid.*, September 1 1954, p. 672.
59. *Ibid.*, September 1 1954, pp. 681-5.
60. *Ibid.*, E. Hill, August 24 and September 1 1954, pp. 513 and 686-7.
61. *Ibid.*, J. Meagher, September 1 1954, p. 686.
62. *Ibid.*, V. Windeyer, September 1 1954, p. 687.
63. Interview, Sir Charles Spry, May 7 1985.
64. AA CRS A6283/XR1/71, ff. 244-6, Report, J. Gilmour, of conversation with Dr Bialoguski, August 24 1954; *ibid.*, ff. 353-5, Report, J. Gilmour, of conversation with Dr Bialoguski, September 2 1954.
65. RCE, Transcript of Proceedings, Dr Evatt, August 30 and September 2 1954, pp. 632-3 and 717-8.
66. *Ibid.*, Owen J., September 3 1954, pp. 721-4.
67. Sydney *Sun*, September 3 1954.
68. AA CRS A6213/RCE/R/6, ff. 18-20, Memorandum, K. Herde, September 6 1954.
69. *Sun-Herald*, September 5 1954.
70. RCE, Transcript of Proceedings, September 7 1954, pp. 727-32.

11: THINGS FALL APART

1. *Sydney Morning Herald*; *Age*; *Argus*; Sydney *Sun*, September 9 1954; R. Murray, *The Split*, pp. 169-70.
2. *Sydney Morning Herald*, September 9 1954.
3. Sydney *Sun*, September 10 1954.
4. *Age*; *Daily Telegraph*; Sydney *Sun*; Melbourne *Sun*, September 10 1954; *Age*, September 13 1954.
5. *Sydney Morning Herald*, September 11 1954.
6. Sydney *Sun*, September 10 1954.
7. For 'Doctors of Honour Not Common Informers', see AA CRS A6215/5, RCE, Exhibit no. 279. Hollway's comments are found in ANL, Ward Papers, MS 2396/7/1881. Hollway said on September 29 1954, 'Not much has been derived from the Royal Commission on espionage ... except a revelation of the deplorable condition of the medical profession in New South Wales'. For the recriminations against Dr Beckett and his wife, see AA CRS A6283/XR1/128, Report, Royal Commission Section, ASIO, on interview with Dr Beckett, September 20 1954.
8. RCE, Transcript of Proceedings, Evidence of G.R. Richards, September 7, 8 and 9 1954.
9. *Ibid.*, Evidence of G.R. Richards, September 8 1954, p. 760.
10. On September 19 Fitzpatrick wrote to Dr Evatt, thus: 'Is something to be done, in the House or the commission, about the glaring discrepancies between the account by Richards on September 8 in the commission, and by the Prime Minister on August 11 and 12 in the House, of the PM's knowledge of the Petrov documents ...'. F.U., Evatt Papers, Brian Fitzpatrick

files, B. Fitzpatrick to Dr Evatt, September 19 1954. On September 28, Eddie Ward raised this discrepancy in a parliamentary question. H. of R., September 28 1954, p. 1625. On September 30 Fitzpatrick wrote to Ward congratulating him on his work and enclosing the manuscript of his new Petrov pamphlet, *Civil Liberties*, F.U., Evatt Papers, Brian Fitzpatrick files, B. Fitzpatrick to E. Ward, September 30 1954.

11. RCE, Transcript of Proceedings, Evidence of G.R. Richards, September 8 1954, pp. 746-51.
12. See above, ch. 5, note 17.
13. RCE, Transcript of Proceedings, Evidence of G.R. Richards, September 8 1954, p. 756.
14. The incomplete transcription of the conversation of March 26 1954 can be found in AA CRS A6283/94, Minifon recording transcription, March 26 1954, ff. 59-67.
15. RCE, Transcript of Proceedings, Dr Evatt, August 30 1954, p. 609.
16. *Ibid.*, Evidence of G.R. Richards, September 7 1954, p. 735.
17. AA CRS A6283/XR1/71, ff. 353-5, Report by J. Gilmour of conversation with Dr Bialoguski, September 2 1954.
18. *Ibid.*
19. *Ibid.*, ff. 313-4, Report by J. Gilmour of conversation with Dr Bialoguski, August 31 1954.
20. AA CRS A6283/XR/70, f. 643, Report, Senior Section Officer 'S', June 15 1954.
21. AA CRS A6283/XR1/71, f. 440, Report by J. Gilmour of conversation with Dr Bialoguski, September 21 1954.
22. Interview, Sir Charles Spry, May 7 1985.
23. RCE, Transcript of Proceedings, Evidence of M. Bialoguski, September 9 and 10 1954, pp. 781-7 and 791-810.
24. Quoted in *ibid.*, September 9 1954, p. 780.
25. RCE, Transcript of Proceedings, Evidence of A. Dalziel, September 13 1954, pp. 815-37.
26. *Sydney Morning Herald*, October 8 and 9 1954; *Sydney Morning Herald*, editorial, October 23 1954.
27. *Argus*, September 14 1954 put this point in a headline 'Evatt's Secretary Clears O'Sullivan as Author of "J"'.
28. A. Dalziel, *Evatt the Enigma*, p. 110.
29. These questions are taken from interviews with Barkell and Haylen conducted for a television documentary entitled 'Like A Summer Storm'. My thanks to Peter Crocker for making this videotape available to me.
30. RCE, Transcript of Proceedings, Evidence of R. Lockwood, September 13, 14 and 15, 1954, pp. 838-45, 851-66, 869-78 and 883-95.
31. *Ibid.*, Owen J., September 20 1954, p. 1004.
32. *Ibid.*, Owen J., September 15 1954, p. 887.
33. *Ibid.*, September 14 1954, pp. 866-8.
34. *Ibid.*, September 15 1954, pp. 881-3.
35. *Age*, September 16 1954.
36. ANL, Calwell Papers, MS4738, Box 50, Minutes of Federal Parliamentary Labor Party, September 15 1954. Emphasis in original.
37. *Age*, September 16 1954.
38. *Sydney Morning Herald*, September 23 1954; *The Age*, September 23 1954.
39. RCE, Transcript of Proceedings, G. Sullivan, September 15 1954, p. 902.
40. *Age*, September 16 1954.
41. RCE, Transcript of Proceedings, Address by Dr Evatt, September 16 1954, pp. 915-20. For accounts of the atmosphere inside and outside the courtroom, *Sydney Morning Herald* and *Age*, September 17 1954.
42. RCE, Transcript of Proceedings, Ligertwood J., September 16 1954, p. 918.
43. *Ibid.*, Address by E. Hill, September 16, 17, 20 and 21, pp. 930-44, 949-61, 977-99, 1026-33.
44. *Ibid.*, V. Windeyer, September 17 1954, pp. 963-4. As we shall see these words of Windeyer's made more impression on the Petrovs than the Party.
45. *Ibid.*, Evidence of G.R. Richards, September 16 1954, p. 928.

282 The Petrov Affair

46. AA CRS A6283/XR1/71, f. 427, Telephone message to Col. Phillipps, Regional Director, ACT, Minute, September 17 1954.
47. RCE, Transcript of Proceedings, Evidence of M. Bialoguski, September 20 1954, pp. 995-8.
48. *Ibid.*, Evidence of V. Petrov, September 21 1954, p. 1013.
49. AA CRS A6283/XR1/71, ff. 508-11, Report by J. Gilmour of conversation with Dr Bialoguski, October 2 1954.
50. RCE, Transcript of Proceedings, September 21 1954, pp. 1033-5.
51. AA CRS A6119/XR1/1, f. 153, Memorandum for Headquarters, February 5 1953.
52. AA CRS A6283/XR1/71, f. 472, Minute for Acting Regional Director, Victoria, September 23 1954.
53. ANL, Calwell Papers, MS4738, Box 50, Minutes of Federal Parliamentary Labor Party, September 22 1954; *Sydney Morning Herald*, September 23 1954; *Age*, September 23 1954; R. Murray, *The Split*, pp. 173-4.
54. RCE, Transcript of Proceedings, Philp J., September 27 1954, p. 1053.
55. *Ibid.*, J. Meagher, September 27 1954, p. 1055.
56. *Ibid.*, Owen J., September 27 1954, p. 1058.
57. *Ibid.*, September 27 1954, pp. 1059-65.
58. *Ibid.*, Owen J., September 27 1954, p. 1065.
59. *Ibid.*, P. Evatt, September 28 1954, p. 1071.
60. *Ibid.*, Owen J., September 27 1954, p. 1066.
61. *Ibid.*, Address by E. Hill, September 28, 29 and 30 1954, *passim*.
62. *Ibid.*, Owen J., September 28 1954, p. 1092.
63. A copy can be found in AA CRS A6283/XR1/130, ff. 169 ff., E.F. Hill, *The Petrov Conspiracy*.
64. *Ibid.*, J. Meagher, October 1 1954, p. 1176.
65. *Ibid.*, J. Meagher, September 27 1954, p. 1067.
66. *Ibid.*, J. Meagher, October 1 1954, p. 1176. F.U., Evatt Papers, Petrov Affair files, press release, October 1 1954.
67. *Ibid.*, Address by Sir G. Barwick and V. Windeyer, October 6, 7 and 8 1954, *passim*. (For the quotations from Ted Hill see p. 1183.)
68. For Dr Evatt's relations with Mr Santamaria, see B.A. Santamaria, *Against the Tide*, Oxford University Press, Melbourne, 1981, pp. 140-3. For Dr Evatt's comment on the Groups in August 1953, J.D. Playford, 'Doctrinal and Strategic Problems of the Communist Party of Australia', unpublished Ph.D., Australian National University, 1962, pp. 218-9.
69. *Age*, September 30 1954; *Sydney Morning Herald*, September 30 1954.
70. Sydney *Sun*, September 21 and 28 1954.
71. B.A. Santamaria 'The Movement of Ideas in Australia'. The Evatt Papers at Flinders University have Dr Evatt's annotated copy of this paper and J.P. Ormonde's note to him about it. F.U., Evatt Papers, Catholic Action and Santamaria file. See also R. Murray, *The Split*, p. 177. F.U., Evatt Papers, Petrov Affair files, Statements by Evatt (b), Dr Evatt's Statement to the Federal Executive, October 27 1954.
72. *Sydney Morning Herald*, October 6 1954; R. Murray, *The Split*, pp. 179-81.
73. R. Murray, *The Split*, Part One.
74. *Sydney Morning Herald*, October 7 1954.
75. F.U., Evatt Papers, Petrov Affair files, correspondence — relating to case, Telegram, A. Dalziel and A. Grundeman to D. Lovegrove, October 7 1954.
76. F.U., Evatt Papers, Petrov Affairs files, Statements by Evatt, press statement regarding L. Short and D. Lovegrove, October 7 1954.
77. *Age*; October 11 1954.
78. *Age*; *Argus, Sydney Morning Herald*, Ocober 14 1954.
79. *Age*; October 18 1954; *Sydney Morning Herald*, October 19 and 20 1954.
80. *Age*; *Sydney Morning Herald*, October 21 1954. R. Murray, *The Split*, pp. 191-3.
81. *Age*; *Sydney Morning Herald*, October 29 1954.

82. F.U., Evatt Papers, Petrov Affair files, Statements by Evatt (b), Dr Evatt's Statement to the Federal Executive, October 27 1954.
83. RCE, Report, August 22 1955, Appendix no. 2, Interim Report of the Commissioners, October 21 1954, pp. 418-29.
84. *Argus*, October 29 1954.
85. H. of R., October 28 1954, pp. 2467-81.

12: THE CASE

1. There is a vast library on this subject. Amongst the most important general works on Soviet espionage are David J. Dallin, *Soviet Espionage*, Yale University Press, New Haven, 1955; and Chapman Pincher, *Too Secret Too Long*, Sidgwick & Jackson, London, 1984. Rebecca West, *The New Meaning of Treason*, Viking Press, New York, 1964, is an outstanding reflective essay.
2. AA CRS A6283/80, ff. 148-9, 'Guide to Organisational Changes in the Soviet State Security Service'.
3. F.W. Deakin and G.R. Storry, *The Case of Richard Sorge*, Chatto and Windus, London, 1966.
4. This is probably the most thoroughly discussed episode in the history of Soviet espionage. The best accounts are Andrew Boyle, *The Climate of Treason: Five Who Spied for Russia*, Hutchinson, London, 1979; Patrick Seale and Maureen McConville, *Philby: The Long Road to Moscow*, Penguin, London, 1978; Robert Cecil, 'The Cambridge Comintern', in Christopher Andrews and David Dilks (editors), *The Missing Dimension*, Macmillan, London, 1984; and C. Pincher, *Too Secret Too Long*. There are, in addition, two accounts from the inside: Kim Philby, *My Silent War*, Panther, London, 1969; and Michael Straight, *After Long Silence*, W.W. Norton, New York, 1983.
5. A. Boyle, *The Climate of Treason*, pp. 199, 201; C. Pincher, *Too Secret Too Long*, p. 51.
6. *The Report of the Royal Commission*, (Gouzenko), June 27 1946, Edmond Clothier, Ottawa, 1946, pp. 69-83.
7. This was certainly the case with Philby, Burgess and Maclean.
8. For the espionage career of Whittaker Chambers see the outstanding, Allen Weinstein, *Perjury: The Hiss Chambers Case*, Hutchinson, London, 1978, esp. pp. 99-131; for details of the espionage roles of Fred Rose and Sam Carr see *The Report of the Royal Commission* (Gouzenko), Section 1, chs. 1-2.
9. D. Dallin, *Soviet Espionage*, esp. ch. 6; C. Pincher, *Too Secret Too Long*, *passim*.
10. David C. Martin, *Wilderness of Mirrors*, Harper & Row, New York, 1980, esp. chs. 3-4; C. Pincher, *Too Secret Too Long*, *passim*; Robert J. Lamphere and Tom Schachtman, *The FBI-KGB War: A Special Agent's Story*, Random House, New York, 1986.
11. Alexander Foote, *Handbook for Spies*, Museum Press, London, 1964; Whittaker Chambers, *Witness*, André Deutsch, London, 1953. See also A. Weinstein, *Perjury*.
12. For the contribution of Krivitsky see C. Pincher, *Too Secret Too Long*, *passim*. There is a good popular account of the contribution of Gouzenko, H. Montgomery Hyde, *The Atom Bomb Spies*, Atheneum, New York, 1980. The best account is still, however, *The Report of the Royal Commission*, (Gouzenko).
13. AA CRS A6213/RCE/H/3 and A6213/RCE/L/1.
14. AA CRS A6283/XR/70, ff. 561-3, Col. Spry to V. Windeyer, June 2 1954.
15. Interviews, Sir Charles Spry, May 3 and 7 1985.
16. For example, AA CRS A6283/XR/72, f. 407, Files shown to the Royal Commissioners on 'The Case', March 11 1955.
17. C. Pincher, *Too Secret Too Long*, pp. 135-6; RCE, Transcript of Proceedings, Evidence of Dr J. Burton (in camera), November 2 1954. (Burton's testimony was not released until 1984.)

18. RCE, Transcript of Proceedings, Evidence of Dr J. Burton (in camera), November 2 1954, p. 18.
19. *Ibid.*, p. 4.
20. Chapman Pincher, *Their Trade is Treachery*, Sidgwick & Jackson, London, 1981, pp. 47-50; D. Martin, *Wilderness of Mirrors*, ch. 2; C. Pincher, *Too Secret Too Long, passim*; R.J. Lamphere and T. Schachtman, *The FBI-KGB War, passim*.
21. C. Pincher, *Too Secret Too Long*, pp. 135-6.
22. RCE, Transcript of Proceedings, Evidence of Dr J. Burton (in camera), November 2 1954, pp. 18-19.
23. AA CRS A6213/RCE/H/9, Paper on Ian Frank George Milner, ff. 1-2.
24. Public Records Office (Kew Gardens, London), Cab 81/46, PHP (45)6(0), War Cabinet, Post-Hostilities Planning Staff, May 1945, 'Security in the Western Mediterranean and the Eastern Atlantic'.
25. RCE, Transcript of Proceedings, Evidence of Brig. Chilton (in camera), November 1 1954. (This testimony was not released until 1984.)
26. AA CRS A6213/RCE/H/9, Paper on Ian Frank George Milner, ff. 1-2.
27. Public Records Office (Kew Gardens, London), Cab 81/46, PHP (45)15(0), War Cabinet, Post-Hostilities Planning Staff, May 1945, 'Security of India and the Indian Ocean'.
28. AA CRS A6213/RCE/H/9, Paper on Ian Frank George Milner, ff. 1-2.
29. Lloyd Churchward, 'Archival Memories', *Melbourne Journal of Politics*, no. 4, 1971, p. 69.
30. Interview, Ken Gott, June 28 1986.
31. AA CRS A6119/18, f. 11, Minute, Deputy Director-Generals (Ops), July 1954.
32. AA CRS A6119/XR1/17, *passim*. (ASIO Personal File, Ian Milner.)
33. *Ibid.*, f. 31, Report by P.L. Griffiths, Deputy Director of Security, Tasmania, June 17 1943.
34. See AA CRS A6122/1A, *passim*.
35. AA CRS A6213/RCE/H/9, ff. 16-17.
36. Paul Hasluck, *Diplomatic Witness, Australian Foreign Affairs, 1941-1947*, Melbourne University Press, Melbourne, 1980, chs. 13 and 16.
37. AA CRS A1066/H/1010/3/1/5, Memorandum, I. Milner to G. Legge, September 24 1945.
38. *Ibid.*, I. Milner to G. Legge, November 6 1945.
39. *Ibid.*, G. Legge to I. Milner, November 15 1945.
40. AA CRS A6283/XR/72, ff. 423-4, ASIO Royal Commission Section to Deputy Director-General (Ops), March 14 1955.
41. AA CRS A6119/18, ff. 33-4, Minutes, Brig. Spry, 3 and 4 November 1954.
42. RCE, Transcript of Proceedings, Evidence of Dr J. Burton (in camera), November 2 1954, pp. 20-1.
43. AA CRS A6213/RCE/H/9, f.17, Paper on Ian Frank George Milner.
44. *Ibid.*, ff. 1-2.
45. H. of R., May 27 1952, pp. 808-9 and 870-4. The Royal Commission's investigation of this issue occurred in February and March of 1955. Their report on Burton is found in RCE, Report, August 22 1955, p. 137. Petrov's comments on Burton in AA CRS A6283/83, f. 38, Statement by V. Petrov, October 1 1954.
46. Interviews, Sir Charles Spry, May 3 and 7 1985; the *National Times* information is quoted in Richard Hall, *The Secret State, Australia's Spy Industry*, Cassell Australia, 1978, p. 41.
47. Interviews, Sir Charles Spry, May 3 and 7 1985.
48. RCE, Transcript of Proceedings, Summary by V. Windeyer of evidence given by Brig. Chilton (in camera), November 1 1954, p. 16.
49. AA CRS A6119/18, Memorandum for Deputy Director-General (Ops), November 4 1954; AA CRS A6119/XR1/17, f. 83, Brig. Chilton to Mr Justice Reed, Director-General, ASIO, November 10 1949.
50. RCE, Transcript of Proceedings, Evidence of Dr J. Burton, November 2 1954, *passim*.
51. AA CRS A6119/92, ff. 86-95, Case summary, J.F. Hill. (ASIO Personal File, Jim Hill.)

52. Douglas Brass, 'Former Australian Diplomat Puzzles Friends', *Adelaide Advertiser*, November 22 1951; AA CRS A6213/RCE/K/9, Ian Milner, Personal Statement, Prague, March 1 1956.
53. AA CRS A6213/RCE/N/6, ff. 29-42, Statement by V. Petrov, April 3 1954, pp. 9-10.
54. RCE, *Report*, August 22 1955, Appendix no. 1, 'G2' and 'G3', pp. 402-3.
55. AA CRS A6119/XR1/1, f. 114, Memorandum, June 1 1954.
56. RCE, Transcript of Proceedings, Evidence of J. Hill, February 4 1955, pp. 2055-61; RCE, *Report*, August 22 1955, pp. 130-1.
57. AA CRS A6119/18, ff. 2-3, Interview with V. Petrov at Safe House, commencing April 6 1954, Extract regarding Ian Milner, April 9 1954.
58. *Ibid.*, ff. 4-5, Statement by V. Petrov regarding Ian Milner, May 21 1954.
59. RCE, Transcript of Proceedings, Evidence of R. Chiplin, February 23 and 24 1955, pp. 2392-3 and 2398-9; RCE, *Report*, August 22 1955, pp. 144-5.
60. AA CRS A6119/18, f. 17, Memorandum, E. Redford, Royal Commission Section, August 14 1954; AA CRS A6283/XR1/6, ff. 15-19, Statement by E.A. Petrova, September 14 1954.
61. AA CRS A6283/XR1/7, f. 97, Statement by V. Petrov, November 23 1954.
62. AA CRS A6119/18, ff. 84-5, Memorandum, E. Redford for Deputy Director-General (Ops), November 23 1954.
63. AA CRS A6122/XR1/96, f. 76, 'Conduct and Problems of a Safe House', undated.
64. RCE, Transcript of Proceedings, Evidence of Dr J. Burton (in camera), November 2 1954, p. 3.
65. *Ibid.*, Evidence of Brig. Chilton (in camera), November 1 1954, *passim*.
66. AA CRS A6283/XR/72, f. 407, Files shown to the Royal Commissioners on 'The Case', March 11 1955.
67. RCE, *Report*, August 22 1955, pp. 143-6.
68. AA CRS A6213/RCE/N/6, ff. 29-42, Statement by V. Petrov, April 3 1954, p. 10.
69. Ric Throssell, *Wild Weeds and Wind Flowers*, Angus & Robertson, Sydney, 1975, esp. ch. 22.
70. AA CRS A6213/RCE/H/9, ff. 12-13, Paper on Ric Prichard Throssell.
71. RCE, Transcript of Proceedings, Evidence of V. Petrov, February 1 1955, pp. 1979-81.
72. AA CRS A6215/4, RCE Exhibit no. 380, Statement by V. Petrov, May 21 1954; AA CRS A6283/XR1/14, Statement by E.A. Petrova, May 28 1954; AA CRS A6283/XR1/6, Statement by V. Petrov, September 12 1954; RCE, Transcript of Proceedings, Evidence of E.A. Petrova, February 2 1955, p. 2001.
73. RCE, Transcript of Proceedings, Evidence of R. Throssell, February 2 and 3 1955, pp. 2015-23 and 2027-37.
74. RCE, *Report*, August 22 1955, pp. 139-43.
75. *Ibid.*, Appendix no. 1, 'G1', 'G2' and 'G3', pp. 401-3.
76. RCE, Transcript of Proceedings, Evidence of Dr J. Burton (in camera), November 2 1954, p. 2.
77. AA CRS A6215/5, RCE Exhibit no. 232, Statement by Frances Bernie, September 8 1954.
78. RCE, Transcript of Proceedings, Evidence of F. Bernie, October 22 1954, pp. 1327-44.
79. RCE, *Report*, August 22 1955, Appendix no. 1, 'G4', p. 404.
80. AA CRS A6283/XR1/76, ff. 56-9, Brief for Interrogation of C.R. Tennant, May 27 1954.
81. RCE, Transcript of Proceedings, Evidence of L. Tennant, November 4 1954, pp. 1525-31.
82. RCE, *Report*, August 22 1955, Appendix no. 1, p. 407.
83. RCE, Transcript of Proceedings, Evidence of J. Legge, October 29 1954, pp. 1488-1503.
84. AA CRS A6119/XR1/19, Col. Spry to Mr R.G. Menzies, July 31, August 17 and September 9 1953, ff. 49-50, 55-6 and 107-9.
85. AA CRS A6283/XR1/79, ff. 102-3, Statement by V. Petrov regarding G. Legge, May 22 1954.
86. AA CRS A6119/XR1/19, f. 146, A. Tange to Col. Spry, May 13 1954.
87. RCE, Transcript of Proceedings, Evidence of G. Legge, October 26 1954, pp. 1392-1403.
88. RCE, *Report*, August 22 1955, Appendix no. 1, 'G2', p. 402.
89. AA CRS A6215/5, RCE Exhibit no. 237, Statement by June Barnett, June 25 1954. Concerning this question the Royal Commission report was in error in suggesting she had only spoken

frankly to ASIO after the Petrov defection. RCE, *Report*, August 22 1955, p. 132.

90. RCE, Transcript of Proceedings, Evidence of J. Barnett, October 25 1954 and March 18 1955, pp. 1352-67 and 2543-4.
91. Interview, Sir Charles Spry, May 3 1985.
92. RCE, Transcript of Proceedings, Evidence of W. Clayton, March 15, 16, 17 and 18 1955, *passim*.
93. RCE, *Report*, August 22 1955, ch. 10, esp. pp. 146-51.

13: THE PETROV RESIDENCY

1. See ch. 12, note 72.
2. RCE, *Report*, August 22 1955, Appendix no. 1, Moscow letters, pp. 312-4, 387.
3. AA CRS A6283/XR/2, ff. 68-105, Interview with Petrov at Safe House commencing April 6 1954, p. 20, (April 7 1954).
4. RCE, Transcript of Proceedings, Evidence of V. Petrov, March 22 1955, pp. 2587-9.
5. *Ibid.*, Evidence of A. Body and E.A. Petrova, November 8 1954, pp. 1552-5 and 1564-6. RCE, *Report*, Appendix no. 1, Moscow letters, pp. 335, 356 and 372.
6. RCE, *Report*, August 22 1955, pp. 161-3.
7. AA CRS A6119/XR1/1, ff. 74-5, Statement by V. Petrov regarding G. Legge, May 22 1954; AA CRS A6119/XR1/19, ff. 133-4, G.W. Legge to Mr R.G. Menzies, April 22 1954.
8. AA CRS A6122/XR1/65, ff. 10-11, Interview with V. Petrov, April 3 1954; AA CRS A6283/XR1/84, ff. 171-3, Statement by V. Petrov regarding Rex Chiplin, December 8 1954; RCE, Transcript of Proceedings, Evidence of V. Petrov, February 14 1955, p. 2236.
9. RCE, *Report*, August 22 1955, Appendix no. 1, p. 387.
10. AA CRS A6119/XR1/77, ff. 109-16, Statements by E.O. Redford (December 1 1954) and L.E. Watson (December 3 1954), regarding the raid on H.B. Chandler's home. Interview, Sir Charles Spry, May 29 1985.
11. AA CRS A6201/RCE Exhibits nos. 302 and 303.
12. AA CRS A6119/XR1/19, ff. 49-50, Col. Spry to Mr R.G. Menzies, July 31 1953.
13. AA CRS A6122/XR1/18, f. 67, 'Operation Cabin 12: Necessary Action in Preparation for Possible Defection', February 17 1954.
14. AA CRS A6283/XR/18, ff. 19 and 22, Extracts of Interview with Petrov at the Safe House commencing April 6 1954.
15. RCE, Transcript of Proceedings, Evidence of H.B. Chandler, December 3 1954, p. 2853.
16. AA CRS A6119/XR1/76, f. 103, Overseas travel notification, May 4 1954.
17. *Ibid.*, ff. 104-5, Memorandum, Regional Director, ACT, May 7 1954.
18. AA CRS A6119/XR1/77, ff. 56-7, Principal Section Officer, B2, May 7 1954.
19. AA CRS A6213/RCE/R/5, f. 9, Australian Government Trade Commissioner's Office, Hong Kong, to Department of External Affairs, Canberra, May 9 1954.
20. AA CRS A6283/XR1/127, Memorandum for Regional Director, Victoria, June 21 1954.
21. AA CRS A6119/XR1/77, f. 70, Memorandum, E. Redford and J. Gilmour, July 30 1954.
22. AA CRS A6283/XR1/6, ff. 191-2, Memorandum, Royal Commission Section, October 20 1954.
23. RCE, Transcript of Proceedings, Evidence of E. Redford and L. Watson, December 6 1954, pp. 2867-76 and 2876-81.
24. *Ibid.*, Evidence of G.R. Richards (in camera), December 8 1954, pp. 6425-33. (Richards' testimony on this occasion was not released until 1984.)
25. *Ibid.*, Evidence of H.B. Chandler, December 3 1954, p. 2853.
26. *Ibid.*, E. Hill, December 6 1954, p. 2881.

27. AA CRS A6213/RCE/N/6, f. 58, Royal Commission Section, Questionnaire for V. Petrov, December 14 1954.
28. AA CRS A6283/XR1/82, ff. 68-71, Statement by V. Petrov regarding G. Anderson, September 16 1954; RCE, *Report*, August 22 1955, Appendix no. 1, Moscow letters, pp. 312, 341 and 371; RCE, Transcript of Proceedings, Evidence of G. Anderson, January 25 and 26 1955, pp. 1935-47 and 1952-66. M. Bialoguski, *The Petrov Story*, ch. 12.
29. AA CRS A6283/XR1/14, ff. 188-91, Statement by V. Petrov regarding leakage of information from ASIO, August 23 1954.
30. AA CRS A6283/XR1/9, ff. 114-8, Interview with V. Petrov, April 18 1955; AA CRS A6283/XR1/77, f. 93, Memorandum, J. Gilmour, August 5 1955.
31. RCE, *Report*, August 22 1955, Appendix no. 1, Moscow letters, pp. 308-11.
32. *Ibid.*, pp. 337-9.
33. AA CRS A6283/80, f. 76-7, Statement by E.A. Petrova, June 26 1954.
34. AA CRS A6283/XR1/82, ff. 50-1, Further Statement by V. Petrov regarding Mme Ollier, September 13 1954.
35. RCE, Transcript of Proceedings, Evidence of V. Petrov and E.A. Petrova (in camera), July 20 1954.
36. AA CRS A6283/XR/70, f. 444, Note, Keith Waller re Madame Ollier, May 19 1954.
37. *Ibid.*, and Mme R.M. Ollier 'Note rappelant sous forme d'éphémérides les circonstances de l'affaire PETROV' in F.U., Evatt Papers, Petrov Affair files, Madame Ollier, December 1954.
38. AA CRS A6283/XR/70, f. 627, Memorandum, Regional Director, ACT, June 10 1954.
39. F.U., Evatt Papers, Petrov Affair files, Madame Ollier, 'Note ...' etc., December 1954.
40. AA CRS A6215/6, Report by Col. Ramier, Personal Data re Mme Ollier, 22 pages, undated.
41. AA CRS A6213/RCE/R/8, ff. 13 and 15-7, Extracts from *Le Monde* and *Le Figaro*.
42. AA CRS A6213/RCE/M/13, ff. 28-34. Col. Ramier had sought this information from the Australian authorities.
43. This was a complex case involving alleged defence leaks to the PCF. *See* D. Dallin, *Soviet Espionage*, pp. 321-2.
44. AA CRS A6213/RCE/M/13, Australian Embassy, Paris, to Department of External Affairs, Canberra, July 30 1955.
45. Details of Dr Evatt's friendship with Mme Ollier and of her wartime sojourn in the Lebanon can be found in AA CRS A6215/6, Report by Col. Ramier, Personal Data re Mme Ollier, 22 pages, undated.
46. AA CRS A6213/RCE/K/10, Evatt press release, September 4 1954.
47. F.U., Evatt Papers, Petrov Affair files, Madame Ollier, Evatt Press release, October 1 1954; AA CRS A6283/83, ff. 6-9, Statement by V. Petrov regarding Mme Ollier, October 5 1954; AA CRS A6215/6, Report by Col. Ramier, Personal Data re Mme Ollier, 22 pages, undated.
48. AA CRS A6213/RCE/M/13, ff. 37-8, Department of External Affairs, Canberra, to Australian Embassy, Paris, February 18 1955.
49. *Ibid.*, f. 47, Australian Embassy, Paris, to Department of External Affairs, Canberra, June 14 1955.
50. RCE, *Report*, August 22 1955, pp. 167-79.
51. *Ibid.*, Appendix no. 1, Moscow letters, pp. 331-5.
52. AA CRS A6201/199, Memoranda, Commonwealth Investigation Service, June 23 and October 14 1949; AA CRS A6213/RCE/N/3, ff. 1-7, Note on intelligence aspects of Divisek's case, undated; RCE, Transcript of Proceedings, Evidence of V. Divisek, October 18, 19 and 20 1954, pp. 1253-60, 1263-83, 1293-6.
53. RCE, Report, August 22 1955, Appendix no. 1, 'G11' and 'G12', pp. 411-2.
54. AA CRS A6215/4, RCE Exhibit no. 193, Statement by E.A. Petrova regarding V. Divisek, October 13 1954; AA CRS A6215/4, RCE Exhibit no. 192, Statement by V. Petrov regarding V. Divisek, October 18 1954; AA CRS A6283/83, Statement by E.A. Petrova regarding V. Divisek, October 19 1954.

55. Regarding Kasanova, see AA CRS A6283/XR1/143, ff. 114-7, Statement by V. Petrov regarding Kasanova, July 23 1954; RCE, Transcript of Proceedings, Evidence of M. Bialoguski, September 9 1954, pp. 783-5. For summaries of the Daghian and Sandy matters see RCE, *Report*, August 22 1955, pp. 264-6 and pp.81-3, 266-7 and 417.
56. RCE, Transcript of Proceedings, Evidence of E.A. Petrova, October 19 1954, pp. 1286-7.
57. AA CRS A6119/XR1/1, ff. 103-12, Statement by V. Petrov regarding A. Fridenbergs, May 30 1954; AA CRS A6283/XR/3, ff. 39-40, Statement by V. Petrov regarding A. Fridenbergs, July 22 1954; AA CRS A6283/XR/82, Statement by V. Petrov regarding A. Fridenbergs, September 13 1954.
58. RCE, Transcript of Proceedings, Evidence of A. Fridenbergs, July 21, 22, 23 1954, pp. 325-34, 341-7 and 372-5. The alibis collapsed during *ibid.*, Address by G. Pape and Evidence of A.W.G. Hayes, October 20 1954, pp. 1301-9.
59. *Ibid.*, Evidence of A. Strazdins and A. Fridenbergs, October 20 1954, pp. 1311-23.
60. AA CRS A6283/XR1/81, ff. 117-19, Memorandum, Leo Carter, undated; AA CRS A6283/XR/3, Statement by V. Petrov regarding A. Fridenbergs, July 22 1954.
61. AA CRS A6283/XR1/143, f. 112, Statement by V. Petrov, July 7 1954.
62. AA CRS A6283/XR1/82, Memorandum regarding F., September 29 1954 and AA CRS A6283/80, f. 91, Statement by V. Petrov regarding R., undated.
63. AA CRS A6283/81, ff. 59-60, Statement by V. Petrov regarding B , July 10 1954; *ibid.*, ff. 104-6, Statement by E. Petrova regarding B, August 18 1954; *ibid.*, ff. 108-9, Statement by V. Petrov regarding B , August 18 1954.
64. AA CRS A6215/5, RCE Exhibit no. 282, Statement by G. Ritenbergs; AA CRS A6215/4, Statements by V. Petrov regarding G. Ritenbergs, June 22 and September 30 1954.
65. AA CRS A6283/XR/85, ff. 108-9, Memorandum, E. Redford and L. Carter for Deputy Director-General (Ops), February 13 1955.
66. Quoted in RCE, Transcript of Proceedings, February 10 1955, pp. 2175-6.
67. AA CRS A6215/4, RCE Exhibit no. 396, Statement by V. Petrov regarding payment to L. Sharkey, August 24 1954.
68. AA CRS A6215/4, RCE Exhibit no. 397, Statement by V. Petrov regarding payment to L. Sharkey, December 10 1954.
69. AA CRS A6283/XR/72, ff. 315-27, Re L.L. Sharkey, Chronological Schedule of Events, September 27 to October 20 1953.
70. RCE, Transcript of Proceedings, February 8-23, *passim*. The quotations from Ted Hill in this paragraph are to be found on pages 2275 and 2239. For Richards' memorandum, AA CRS A6283/XR/72, f. 309, Memorandum, G.R. Richards, February 15 1955.
71. RCE, Transcript of Proceedings, Owen J., February 16 1955, p. 2288.
72. *Ibid.*, Owen J., February 17 1955, p. 2294.
73. *Ibid.*, Owen J., February 17 1955, p. 2305.
74. AA CRS A6201/513, Affidavit by Y.A. Rastvorov, March 2 1955.
75. H. of R., October 19 1955, p. 1715.
76. RCE, *Report*, August 22 1955, pp. 102-10.
77. AA CRS A6283/XR1/9, f. 168, Memorandum for Deputy Director-General (Ops), June 15 1955.
78. AA CRS A6119/XR/10, f. 135, Report on V. Petrov, March 4 1954.
79. *Ibid.*, f. 226, Memorandum, Regional Director, ACT, April 22 1954; AA CRS A6283/XR1/7, f. 176, Statement by V. Petrov regarding B. Yuill, December 13 1954.
80. AA CRS A6122/XR1/96, ff. 72-3, 'Conduct and Problems of a Safe House', undated.
81. *Ibid.*, f. 60, 'Control of Defectors for Interrogation', August 4 1955.
82. *Ibid.*, f. 80, 'Conduct and Problems of a Safe House', undated.
83. AA CRS A6119/XR1/1, ff. 79-81, Petrov's written statement, May 15 1954.
84. RCE, *Report*, August 22 1955, Appendix no. 1, Moscow letters, *passim*.
85. See above, ch. 3, note 2.

86. RCE, Transcript of Proceedings, Evidence of V. Petrov (in camera), March 9 1955, p. 9537. (This testimony was not released until 1984.)

87. AA CRS A6122/XR1/96, f. 5, 'Report on the Defection of Vladimir Petrov', May 15 1955.

88. *Ibid.*, f. 7, G.R. Richards, 'Some Aspects of the Petrov defections which should be kept in mind in future defection operations', May 18 1955.

14: THE PETROVS AND WESTERN COUNTER-INTELLIGENCE

1. AA CRS A6213/RCE/W/7, f. 17, Brig. Spry to Mr R.G. Menzies, October 22 1956.

2. This view is based on discussions with Sir Charles Spry, May 3, 7 and 29 1985.

3. For example, A. Dalziel, *Evatt The Enigma*, ch. 10.

4. AA CRS A6213/RCE/R/5, f. 1, A. Tange (Canberra) to R. Casey (Singapore), April 16 1954.

5. Angleton's views are quoted in R. Hall, *The Secret State*, p. 52. For Angleton's relations with Golitsin see the remarkable book D.C. Martin, *Wilderness of Mirrors*.

6. Interview, Sir Charles Spry, May 7 1985.

7. This message is in the personal possession of Sir Charles Spry.

8. Information concerning this MI5 officer comes from Interview, Sir Charles Spry, May 7 1985. For two of his early papers, AA CRS A6283/80, ff. 125-51, 'Report on the Background History of Vladimir Mikhailovich Petrov', June 28 1954 and AA CRS A6283/XR1/14, ff. 130-40, 'Personal History of Evdokia Alexeyevna Petrova', undated.

9. Richard H. Shultz and Roy Godson, *Dezinformatsia: Active Measures in Soviet Strategy*, Pergamon-Brassey's, Washington, 1984.

10. AA CRS A6283/XR1/7, ff. 26-50, 'The Committee of Information ('KI')', November 17 1954.

11. AA CRS A6283/XR1/9, ff. 129-48, 'Soviet State Security Service. Foreign Intelligence Operational Techniques ("Legal" Residency System)'.

12. *Ibid.*, and AA CRS A6283/17, ff. 4-23, 'Internal Organization and Functions of a Soviet Embassy'.

13. AA CRS A6283/XR1/81, ff. 252-3, V. Petrov, 'Dress of Soviet Intelligence Personnel'.

14. AA CRS A6283/XR1/9, ff. 129-48, 'Soviet State Security Service. Foreign Intelligence Operational Techniques ("Legal" Residency System)', esp. Sections IV-XV.

15. AA CRS A6283/149, ff. 1-18, 'Soviet "Illegal" Intelligence Operations'.

16. For interesting accounts of the Abel and Kroger cases see R. West, *The New Meaning of Treason*.

17. AA CRS A6283/XR1/8, f. 83, 'Miscellaneous Soviet Intelligence Personalities'. See also K. Philby, *My Silent War*, pp. 112-21 and C. Pincher, *Too Secret Too Long, passim.*

18. AA CRS A6283/XR1/82.

19. AA CRS A6283/80, f. 122, June 5 1954.

20. AA CRS A6283/XR1/8, f. 84, 'Miscellaneous Soviet Intelligence Personalities'.

21. AA CRS A6283/XR1/9, f. 128, V.M. Petrov, 'Intelligence Report: Assassination of Trotsky'.

22. AA CRS A6122/XR1/55, ff. 7-21, Various papers.

23. AA CRS A6283/XR1/79, f. 139, 'MVD Cables'; AA CRS A6283/XR1/84, 'USSR-Embassy officials — Mail', January 4 1955; AA 6283/XR1/9, ff. 108-11, 'Soviet Diplomatic Couriers'; AA CRS A6283/XR1/79, ff. 54-5, Memorandum, May 11 1954.

24. AA CRS A6283/87, E. Redford and J. Gilmour to Deputy Director-General (Ops), June 3 1954.

25. AA CRS A6283/XR1/14, f. 59, Explanatory Note.

26. Interview, Sir Charles Spry, May 29 1985.

27. David Kahn, *The Codebreakers*, Weidenfeld and Nicolson, London, 1966, ch. 18.

28. AA CRS A6283/XR1/7, ff. 26-50, 'The Committee of Information ('KI')', November 17 1954.

29. AA CRS A6283/XR1/81, f. 41, Statement by V. Petrov regarding Zarubin.

30. AA CRS A6283/XR/2, f. 210, 'MVD Personnel Abroad'.
31. AA CRS A6283/XR1/82, ff. 54-61.
32. AA CRS A6283/XR1/6, ff. 139-53, 'Identification of Soviet Personnel'.
33. *Ibid.*, ff. 139-53, ff. 183-9; AA CRS A6283/XR1/7, ff. 185-93.
34. AA CRS A6213/RCE/W/7, f. 17, Brig. Spry to Mr R.G. Menzies, October 22 1956.
35. C. Pincher, *Too Secret Too Long*, pp. 214-5 and 447-9.
36. See above, ch. 6, note 25.
37. Interviews, Sir Charles Spry, May 3 1985 and January 27 1986.
38. Interview, Sir Charles Spry, January 27 1986.
39. *Ibid.*
40. C. Pincher, *Too Secret Too Long*, p. 448.
41. K. Philby, *My Secret War*, pp. 171-2.
42. For the Ellis case see C. Pincher, *Too Secret Too Long*, ch. 45. Apart from the question of the timing of Dick Ellis' return to London Sir Charles Spry has confirmed to the author the central details contained in Pincher's account. Interview, Sir Charles Spry, January 27 1986. There is an impassioned but somewhat unconvincing defence of Dick Ellis in William Stevenson, *Intrepid's Last Case*, Michael Joseph, London, 1983.
43. AA CRS A6283/XR/2, f. 94, Interview with V. Petrov at Safe House, commencing April 6 1954.
44. V. and E. Petrov, *Empire of Fear*, ch. XXIII; AA CRS A1209/60/76, ff. 56-8, V. Petrov, Statutory Declaration regarding Burgess and Maclean, March 29 1956. This declaration was prepared in lieu of an American visit by the Petrovs to give evidence before a Congressional Committee.
45. Interview, Sir Charles Spry, May 29 1985.
46. Quoted by Col. Lipton in the House of Commons, *Parl. Deb.*, H. of C., November 7 1955, col. 1575.
47. AA CRS A6122/69, f. 26, Telephone message to Director-General, April 29 1954.
48. AA CRS A6213/RCE/X/7, f. 1, L. McIntyre (Australian High Commission, London) to A. Tange (Department of External Affairs, Canberra), April 29 1954.
49. *The People*, September 18 1955.
50. 'Report Concerning the Disappearance of Two Former Foreign office Officials', September 23 1955, *Cmnd 9577*.
51. The *Times*, September 24 1955.
52. *Parl. Deb.*, H. of C., October 25 1955, col. 29.
53. For Macmillan's comments *ibid.*, November 7 1955, col. 1497; for Crossman's reply, *ibid.*, November 7 1955, cols. 1530-1.
54. *Ibid.*, November 7 1955, col. 1497.
55. *Ibid.*, November 7 1955, cols. 1574-88.
56. K. Philby, *My Secret War*, p. 176.
57. Interview, Sir Charles Spry, January 27 1986.
58. C. Pincher, *Too Secret Too Long*, pp. 258-63.
59. Shortly after the Petrov defection Douglas Copland, of the Australian mission to the United Nations telegrammed Canberra about the present reputation of Gouzenko. He said he was regarded as a 'problem child' and a 'prima donna' with an 'insatiable desire for publicity and remuneration' who was ready 'to exploit present hysteria among the new administration in the United States'. AA CRS A6213/RCE/L/1, Copland (New York) to Department of External Affairs (Canberra), April 14 1954. W. Stevenson, *Intrepid's Last Case*, defends the reputation of Gouzenko from such charges. Concerning Konstantin Yurchenko, the KGB defector who re-defected to the USSR in the same year, 1985, see United States Information Service, 'Active Measures' no. 2, November 25 1985 and K. Simes, 'Yurchenko: Probably a KGB Plant', *Christian Science Monitor*, November 22 1985.
60. AA CRS A6122/XR1/96, ff. 75-6, 'Conduct and Problems of a Safe House', undated, Senior Field Officer, South Australia.

61. Interview, Sir Charles Spry, May 3 1985.
62. AA CRS A6122/XR1/96, ff. 79-80, 'Conduct . . .' etc.
63. *Ibid.*, f. 75.
64. *Ibid.*, f. 70.
65. *Ibid.*, ff. 71-2.
66. *Ibid.*, f. 69 and AA CRS A6283/XR/73, ff. 333-4, 'Trouble at the Safe House with Mr V.M. Petrov', J. Gilmour, October 13 1955.
67. AA CRS A6283/XR/73, f. 408, Memorandum, J. Gilmour, December 6 1955.
68. AA CRS A1209/77/0818, f. 1, Col. Spry to Mr R.G. Menzies, July 15 1954.
69. AA CRS A6122/XR1/96, f. 71, 'Conduct . . .' etc.
70. *Ibid.*, ff. 73-4.
71. *Ibid.*, f. 70.
72. AA CRS A6283/XR/73, f. 244, 'Domestic Trouble at Safe House', September 20 1955.
73. AA CRS A6122/XR1/96, f. 80, 'Conduct . . .' etc.

15: THE WAR BETWEEN THE CAMPS

1. R. Murray, *The Split*, chs. 13 and 14. For a somewhat different view which argues that the realignment of Irish-Australian Catholic voters began in 1949, not 1954-5, see John Warhurst, 'Catholics, Communism and the Australian party system: a study of the Menzies years', *Politics*, XIV (2), November 1979, pp. 222-42.
2. R. Murray, *The Split*, ch. 15, esp. pp. 224-8.
3. *Age*, March 19 1955; *Sydney Morning Herald*, March 19 1955.
4. R. Murray, *The Split*, ch. 16.
5. *Ibid.*, ch. 17.
6. H. of R., May 19 1955, pp. 895-903.
7. Burton spoke of the resumption of relations in a television interview for 'Like A Summer Storm'. His major paper written for the Royal Commission was passed on to Dr Evatt. For his August 1953 attack see F.U., Evatt Papers, Dr John Burton file.
8. F.U., Evatt Papers, Brian Fitzpatrick file. Fitzpatrick wrote to Evatt on the Petrov Affair on August 13, August 16, September 15 and September 19 1954 and on October 10 and 14 1955. He also sent him a copy of his Petrov poem 'Laudate' and copies of his pamphlets 'On Royal Commissions: Some Facts and Opinions', 'The Royal Commission on Espionage' and 'Saddled Cats and Royal Commissions'.
9. ANL, MS 4965/2/336, Brian Fitzpatrick Papers, Noel Counihan to Brian Fitzpatrick, June 28 1955.
10. J.D. Playford, 'Doctrinal and Strategic Problems of the Communist Party of Australia', ch. 7. As late as February 1954 Ted Hill had accused Evatt of being 'concerned with two things, his anxiety to serve big business and his overpowering personal ambition', p. 262.
11. There is a useful collection of the Communist Party press on the Petrov Affair in AA CRS A6122/3-6.
12. F.U., Evatt Papers, Petrov Affair files, 'Phil's Friend'; F.U., Evatt Papers, ALP-Industrial Groups 'The Movement and the Split' (c); F.U., Evatt Papers, Catholic Action and Santamaria; F.U., Evatt Papers, 'Phil's Friend' files.
13. F.U., Evatt Papers, Correspondence: Miscellaneous (a), R.F.B. Wake to Dr Evatt, May 29 1955; on Wake's downfall in ASIO, Interview, Sir Charles Spry, May 3 1985.
14. Sir Edmund Herring's 'Call to the Nation' was published in Australian newspapers on Remembrance Day 1951. It called upon Australians to stand firm by the old virtues and was, in the main, signed by religious leaders. In rather Aesopian language its line was conservative anti-Communism.

15. For an interesting account of 'The Association', see John Hetherington, *Blamey, Controversial Soldier*, Australian War Memorial and Australian Government Publishing Service, Canberra, 1973, pp. 89-92.

16. F.U., Evatt Papers, Petrov Affair files, 'Phil's Friend'; Catholic Action and Santamaria file; 'Phil's Friend' file, *passim*. Most of these papers are undated and untitled. They are written in crayon or in ink or typed. Some are signed 'Phil's Friend', some are unsigned.

17. R. Murray, *The Split*, p. 272.

18. F.U., Evatt Papers, Petrov Affair files, Correspondence: Miscellaneous, F.W. Sheahan, Attorney-General, New South Wales to Dr Evatt, November 22 1954; Dr Evatt to F.W. Sheahan, November 23 1954; F.W. Sheahan to Dr Evatt, November 5 1954.

19. F.U., Evatt Papers, Petrov Affair files, Dalziel, Grundeman, O'Sullivan, R.L. Hume, Australian Journalists' Association (ACT) to Dr Evatt, September 15 1954; Dr Evatt to R.L. Hume, undated.

20. This issue can be traced in the following correspondence, AA CRS A1209/77/0642, Dr Evatt to Professor Bailey, January 27, 1955; Professor Bailey to Dr Evatt, February 2 1955; Brig. Spry to Professor Bailey, February 9 1955; Senator Spicer to Dr Evatt, February 23 1955. F.U., Evatt Papers, Petrov Affair files, Correspondence: Prof. Bailey and Sen. Spicer, Dr Evatt to Senator Spicer, March 2 1955; Senator Spicer to Dr Evatt, April 19 1955. After being shown the O'Sullivan paper by Col. Phillipps Dr Evatt wrote a draft letter to Senator Spicer, denying he had even been shown it.

21. A. Dalziel, *Evatt the Enigma*, ch. 14.

22. F.U., Evatt Papers, Petrov Affair files, Molotoff letter, Dr Evatt to His Excellency, V.M. Molotov Esq., Foreign Minister of the USSR, February 17 1955.

23. *Ibid.*, L. Ilyichev, Member of the Collegium, Chief of the Press Department of the Foreign Ministry of the USSR, to Dr Evatt, April 9 1955. (Translation and original.)

24. Elwyn Spratt, *Eddie Ward, Firebrand of East Sydney*, Rigby, Adelaide, 1965, chs. 11-14.

25. See above, ch. 11, note 49.

26. The references to this source of information in the Ward Papers in the Australian National Library do not make clear how precisely Ward received his information. ANL, MS 2396/7/1799, Note handed to Ward by Gordon Anderson, MHR. 'Bahrenkamp, Representative of Crawford Co. Distributors of Bell's Whisky. Sold to Petrov . . .'.

27. H. of R., November 9 1954, pp. 2712-3.

28. H. of R., November 10 1954, pp. 2844-5.

29. H. of R., November 11 1954, pp. 2864.

30. The Ward correspondence with the Minister and Acting Minister for Trade and Customs can be followed in ANL, Ward Papers, MS 2396/7/1802-1816.

31. RCE, Transcript of Proceedings, Evidence of V. Petrov, January 18 1955, pp. 1796-7.

32. *Ibid.*, Owen J., January 19 1955, p. 1814.

33. ANL, Ward Papers, MS 2396/7/1795, March 24 1955.

34. See above, ch. 3, note 40.

35. AA CRS A6283/XR/72, ff. 434-7, Report by J. Gilmour of conversation with Dr Bialoguski, March 21 1955.

36. *Ibid.*, f. 446, Report by J. Gilmour of conversation with Dr Bialoguski, March 23 1955.

37. *Ibid.*, ff. 458-61, Transcript of Interview between Maher and Bialoguski, March 23 1955.

38. *Ibid.*, ff. 462-3, Report by J. Gilmour of conversation with Dr Bialoguski, March 24 1955.

39. ANL, Calwell Papers, MS 4738, Box 50, Minutes of the Federal Parliamentary Labor Party, June 8 1955.

40. H. of R., June 8 1955, pp. 1508-20.

41. H. of R., June 9 1955, p. 1570.

42. AA CRS A6213/RCE/G/7, ff. 106-10, F.A. Meere, Comptroller-General, Department of Trade and Customs, to A.S. Brown, Prime Minister's Department, October 4 1955.

43. The Christmas Party affair was widely reported. Some articles are collected in AA CRS A6213/RCE/X/11. On December 20 1954 the Sydney *Sun* had an editorial on the matter,

'The Strange Affair of Mr Herde's Party'.

44. For Mr Justice Owen's and Kenneth Herde's embarrassment see AA CRS A6213/RCE/X/11, ff. 14-15, W.F.C. Owen to Mr R.G. Menzies, December 20 1954 and *ibid.*, ff. 24-6, Report by Kenneth Herde on Christmas Party, December 21 1954. Ward's spate of telegrams to Mr R.G. Menzies are collected in the Prime Minister's file on the Petrov Affair, AA CRS A6227.

45. Ward's questions and the correspondence they produced are contained in AA CRS A6213/RCE/G/3.

46. ANL, Ward Papers, MS 2396/7/1883-2151. These typewritten notes are undated and, except for one signed 'Bob', anonymous. However the overlap of material with that signed by 'Phil's Friend' and delivered to Dr Evatt make it clear that Ward's informant was R.F.B. (Bob) Wake.

47. *Sydney Morning Herald*, June 4 1955.

48. The *Guardian's* headline tells the tale. 'Mrs Bialoguski bares Petrov plot'. *Guardian*, June 9 1955.

49. AA CRS A6283/XR/72, ff. 310-3, Report by J. Gilmour of conversation with Dr Bialoguski, February 15 1955.

50. For Richards' views and discomfort see AA CRS A6119/XR1/2, f. 48, Memorandum, Professor Bailey, June 18 1955; *ibid.*, f. 52, Memorandum, G.R. Richards, June 24 1955; and *ibid.*, Memorandum, Col. Phillipps, June 28 1955. For Brig. Spry's rebuff, AA CRS A6119/XR1/2, f. 177, Brig. Spry to K. Herde, December 23 1955.

51. AA CRS A6283/XR/73, f. 174, 'Attitude of Mr and Mrs Petrov at Safe House', September 8 1955.

52. AA CRS A6119/XR1/2, ff. 148-57, 'Discrepancies appearing in the newspaper articles of Dr Michael Bialoguski under the heading "I Got Petrov" ', August 11 1955.

53. AA CRS A6283/XR/73, f. 175, 'Attitude of Mr and Mrs Petrov at Safe House', September 8 1955.

16: CLIMAX

1. RCE, *Report*, August 22 1955, *passim*, esp. ch. 21.

2. For the proposed anti-espionage legislation see AA CRS A4905/XMI/13, Submission to Cabinet no. 343, Attorney-General's Department, Official Secrets. For the Cabinet decision on this matter, AA CRS A4909/XMI/5, Cabinet Minute, Decision no. 530, September 9 1952.

3. RCE, *Report*, August 22 1955, ch. 20.

4. See above, ch. 12.

5. R.J. Lamphere and T. Schachtman, *The FBI-KGB War*.

6. *Sydney Morning Herald*, 'The Communist Enemy in Our Midst', September 15 1955; *Age*, 'Petrov Report Reassuring', September 15 1955; The (Melbourne) *Herald*, 'The Petrov Report', September 15 1955; *The West Australian*, 'Proof of Russian Spying in Petrov Report', September 15 1955; the Launceston *Examiner*, 'Australian Traitors', September 15 1955; the Hobart *Mercury*, 'Willing — And Unwitting', September 15 1955; the Adelaide *Advertiser*, 'Report on Petrov Enquiry', September 15 1955.

7. Adelaide *News*, 'A damp squib brings a yawn', September 15 1955; *Argus*, 'Where did it get us?', September 15 1955.

8. F.U., Evatt Papers, Petrov Affair files, Annotated material (c), press release, September 15 1955.

9. F.U., Evatt Papers, Petrov Affair files, Dr J. Burton, 'The Petrov Affair: Dr Burton gives his view: Warns against Intelligence Organizations', September 15 1955.

10. *Age*, September 15 1955.

11. *Ibid.*, September 16 1955.

12. *Ibid.*, September 20 1955.

13. 'Commission Indicts Communist Party' and 'Nest of traitors in Evatt's department', *News Weekly*, September 21 1955.

14. AA CRS A6283/XR/73, ff. 160-3, Memorandum, Deputy Controller, Royal Commission Section, 'Attitude of Mr. and Mrs. Petrov at Safe House', September 7 1955. *Ibid.*, f. 180, Letter V. and E. Petrov to S.A.F. Pond c/- Whiting & Byrne, September 8 1955.

15. AA CRS A6122/69, f. 42, General Manager, John Fairfax & Sons to V. Petrov c/o Col. Spry, May 4 1954; AA CRS A6122/XR1/76, f. 4, Statement, Michael Rayner Thwaites, undated.

16. AA CRS A6283/XR/73, ff. 205 and 217, Transcripts of radio interviews, September 1955.

17. AA CRS A6213/RCE/G/7, Draft notes, undated, 'Future of Mr. and Mrs. Petrov'. Seen by Prime Minister, October 18 1955.

18. AA 6283/XR/73, ff. 160-3, 172-6 and 244-6, 'Attitude of Mr and Mrs Petrov at the Safe House', September 7 and 8 1955 and 'Domestic Trouble at Safe House', September 20 1955. All these papers were prepared for the Deputy Controller, Royal Commission Section.

19. AA CRS A6283/XR/73, ff. 233-4, 'Proposed Visit of the Petrovs to Brisbane', September 19 1955.

20. *Ibid.*, ff. 272-3, 'Operation on Mrs Petrov', September 30 1955; *ibid.*, f. 279, 'Illness of Mrs Petrov', October 4 1955.

21. *Ibid.*, ff. 289-90, Report on Mrs Petrov, October 10 1955.

22. *Ibid.*, f. 351, Translations of letters from E. Petrova to Petrov and Richards, undated.

23. *Ibid.*, ff. 336-7. 'Illness of Mrs Petrov', including a report of interview between J. Gilmour and Dr W., October 14 1955.

24. *Ibid.*, ff. 333-4, 'Trouble at the Safe House with Mr V.M. Petrov', report by J. Gilmour, October 13 1955.

25. H. of R., October 19 1955, p. 1718.

26. H. of R., October 25 1955, p. 1882.

27. AA CRS A6281/P1-10, (on cassette).

28. F.U., Evatt Papers, Brian Fitzpatrick file, B. Fitzpatrick to Dr Evatt, October 10 1955. Fitzpatrick's biographer has noticed this passage in Dr Evatt's speech. D. Watson, *Brian Fitzpatrick*, pp. 239-40.

29. Hansard records this comment inaccurately as 'Honourable members may laugh . . .' H. of R., October 19 1955, p. 1695.

30. RCE, *Report*, August 22 1955, pp. 16-17.

31. H. of R., October 19 1955, pp. 1694-1718.

32. Kylie Tennant, *Evatt: Politics and Justice*, Angus and Robertson, Sydney, 1970, p. 334.

33. AA CRS A6213/RCE/G/7, ff. 169-70, Brig. Spry to Mr A.S. Brown, Prime Minister's Department, October 21 1955.

34. *Ibid.*, ff. 159-67 (Brig. Spry); ff. 12-18 (Herde); and ff. 19-27 (Pape).

35. *Ibid.*, ff. 37-9, 'Suggested Plan for Prime Minister's Speech'.

36. *Ibid.*, f. 169, Brig. Spry to Mr A.S. Brown, Prime Minister's Department, October 21 1955.

37. AA CRS A6213/RCE/M/13 — Tange (Canberra) to Stirling (Paris), October 21 1955; Stirling (Paris) to Tange (Canberra), October 21 1955; Tange (Canberra) to Stirling (Paris), October 22 1955; Stirling (Paris) to Tange (Canberra), October 22 1955. *Ibid.*, pp. 86-7, 'Translation from the French Permanent Court of the Armed Forces at Paris', October 20 1955, C.R. Alpen (Prime Minister's Department) for the Prime Minister, October 25 1955.

38. H. of R., October 25 1955, pp. 1858-75.

39. *Ibid.*, pp. 1879-83.

40. *Ibid.*, pp. 1883-90.

41. 'Menzies-Fadden Election Talks', *Sydney Morning Herald*, October 19 1955; 'Polls Hints Seen in P.M.'s Replies', *Sydney Morning Herald*, October 20 1955; 'Dr Evatt Clinches the Case for an Election', *Sydney Morning Herald*, October 24 1955, (editorial). Mr R.G. Menzies' announcement was made on October 26 1955. H. of R., October 26 1955, pp. 1895-6.

42. 'Bid to Oust Evatt from Party Leadership Likely', *Sydney Morning Herald*, October 21 1955.

43. *Sydney Morning Herald*, October 24 1955.

44. 'Onlooker' in *Sun-Herald*, October 30 1955.
45. *Sun-Herald*, November 6 1955.
46. Quoted in R. Murray, *The Split*, p. 277.
47. Sir R.G. Menzies, *The Measure of the Years*, p. 197.
48. For example in Brisbane on November 11 1955, in reply to Mr Joshua, *Sydney Morning Herald*, November 12 1955.
49. K. Tennant, *Evatt: Politics and Justice*, ch. 23.
50. *Sydney Morning Herald*, November 25 1955.
51. C.A. Hughes and B.D. Graham, *A Handbook of Australian Government and Politics, 1890-1964*, pp. 397-403; C.A. Hughes and B.D. Graham, *Voting for the Australian House of Representatives, 1901-1964*, pp. 325-48. The ALP had 10 fewer seats in the House of Representatives of 1955 and the Coalition 11 more. (There had been a redistribution.) The ALP lost five seats in Victoria — Ballaarat, Bruce, Fawkner, Maribyrnong and Wannon. In Wannon the Coalition candidate (Malcolm Fraser) received 48.85% of the primary vote; in Bruce 47.65%; in Fawkner 46.16%; in Ballaarat 38.25%; and in Maribyrnong 37.44%.

INDEX

receives translations of three 'Moscow letters', 70; decides to ask Cabinet to create Royal Commission, 70; at Cabinet, April 13, 72-3; motive for self-denying ordinance discussed, 73; failure to inform Dr Evatt of impending defection announcement discussed, 73-4; announces defection in Parliament, 74; instructs Spry to pass requests for information to him, 76; first public clash with Dr Evatt over Petrov, 76; and Soviet kidnapping allegation, 77; letter from Spry to, 79; failed telephone call from Wentworth, 80; response to Mascot demonstration, 82-3; friendship with Spry sealed, 87-8; praised for success at Darwin, 90; supposed role in Petrov conspiracy, 93-4; actual role in Petrov defection summarised, 95-6; and election timetable, 96-7; treatment of Dr Evatt during 1954 election campaign, 98-101; places Coalition ban on mention of Petrov during 1954 election campaign, 101-3; motives for pre-election Royal Commission hearings, 105-6; attacks Dr Evatt's Welfare State proposals, 107-8; impact of Government's economic success on victory in 1954 election, 110-1; and establishment of Royal Commission terms of reference, 113-4, 116; role in appointment of Royal Commissioners, 114-5; at meeting, May 9, 116-8; recipient of Dr Evatt telegram, 133; refutes Dr Evatt conspiracy allegations, 137-8; invited to character trial before Presbyterian elders, 138n.; concerned about Dr Evatt's appearance before Royal Commission, 146-8; not named by Dr Evatt as conspirator, 149; Richards' evidence at Royal Commission contradicts, 155; Dr Evatt plans to cross-examine, 159; debates Dr Evatt on interim report, 172.

  Vice-President 'Sheepskins for Russia', 182; receives letter from Spry concerning G.W. Legge, 192; and Chandler, 198; letter from Spry concerning Petrovs, 235; in Wake's theories, 242-3; and Eddie Ward, 246-9; and Bialoguski's account of Canberra trip, 251; reply to Evatt in debate on Royal Commission report, 261-3; announces early election, 263-4
Menzies Government, Possibility of Soviet defection raised with, 46-9; decision to create Royal Commission on espionage, 72-3; decisions

concerning approaches to Petrova, 77-82 *passim*; and breach in relations with Soviet Union, 90-2; supposed role in, and beneficiary of, Petrov defections, 93-4; possible advantages of the Petrov defections for, 98; and references to Petrovs during the 1954 election campaign, 101-3; Evatt attacked by on Communist issue during 1954 election campaign, 103-4; attacked for weakness of its anti-Communism, 104-5; Evatt's Welfare State proposals attacked, 107-8; electoral support for, 108-11; final decisions concerning establishment of Royal Commission, 116-8; Lockwood apologises to victims of, 121; Dr Evatt suspects involved in conspiracy, 124, 139; CPA view of involvement in election stunt, 126; submits revised Royal Commission Act to Parliament, 135-6; backbenchers taunt Dr Evatt, 137-8; predicted fall, 153; linked by Dr Evatt to the Movement, 168; withdrawal of Chandler's passport, 199; request to France for release of Ramier report material, 207-8; Evatt's hopes for Molotov as ally against, 246; and the election of December 1955, 263-4
Mertsova, Lidia, 189
MGB — Ministry of State Security, (see also MVD), 7-8, 9, 10, 14, 22, 63, 67, 67n., 175n., 176n., 211, 221, 259
MI5, 78-9, 178-80 *passim*, 183-5 *passim*, 189, 219-221 *passim*, 224, 227-8, 230, 255
MI6, 224n., 227-8, 232
Miles, B.R., 248
Milner, Ian, (MVD code-name 'Bur'), 181-8, 193, 194, 197, 253, 255
Minifon Recordings, 43-4, 52-3, 54, 58n., 59-61 *passim*, 96, 128, 149, 154, 156n.
'Miss Edgar', (Petrov's Sydney friend), 36, 41
Mokras, Lydia, 10-13 *passim*, 50
Mokras, Victor, 11n.
Money Payment (to Petrov), 50, 54-63 *passim*, 106, 117, 126, 130, 137, 139, 145n., 149, 155-6, 161, 171-2, 196, 214-5, 247, 259, 262
Molotov, V.M., 245-6, 259-64 *passim*
Monticone, Dr Charles, 150, 162, 165, 259
Moral Rearmament, 22, 243
Morrison, William, 91
Morton-Clarke, Alan and Joan, 22
'Moscow Centre' — Headquarters of KI-MGB-MVD, 12, 27, 28, 67, 131, 176, 177, 179, 180, 181, 184, 186, 189, 190,